Source Book of Uganda's Land Law

John Tamukedde Mugambwa

Fountain Publishers

Fountain Publishers Ltd
P.O. Box 488
Kampala
E-mail:fountain@starcom.co.ug
Website:www.fountainpublishers.com

Distributed in Europe, North America and Australia by African Books Collective (ABC), The Jam Factory, 27 Park End St., Oxford OX1 HU, United Kingdom. Tel: 44 (0) 1865-726686, Fax:1865-793298

First published 2002

ISBN 9970 02 288 1

1 2 3 4 5 05 04 03 02

Cataloguing-in-Publication Data

Mugambwa, John Tamukedde,
Source book of Uganda's land law/ John Tamukedde Mugambwa – Kampala: Fountain Publishers, 2002
___ p. ___ cm
Includes index ISBN 9970-02-288-1
1. Land laws – Uganda 2. Property laws – Uganda I. Title
343.02'096761 – Dc 21

Contents

Preface

In 1995, while on vacation in Uganda, a friend of mine sought my legal opinion over certain land matters. Having been away from the country for a long time, I did not feel confident enough to express an opinion without researching the subject matter. There was no textbook on Ugandan land law that I could refer to. Finding the current Ugandan case law on the subject proved to be most frustrating. I discovered, to my horror, that apart from the *High Court Bulletin ('HCB')*, which is a publication of the Law Development Centre, there were no law reports of Ugandan cases in the last twenty years. The *HCB*, though a useful source of cases, is not a law report; it is a digest of select judgements. To find the original judgements was extremely difficult. I spent several hours, with the assistance of the LDC Library staff, going through dozens of files trying to find the original judgements. For some cases, there were no copies of the judgements in the LDC Library (which has by far the better collection of cases than the Makerere University Library). I obtained copies of some of the judgements from the High Court Library, Makerere lecturers and practitioners. Getting access to the reported cases was also cumbersome and frustrating.

After my ordeal, I could not imagine what law students had to go through to "find" the law applicable. I recalled that when I was student at Makerere, each student had two bound volumes of East African cases and other materials on land law. It was in this frame of mind that I promised to myself to collect cases on Ugandan land law with a view, one day, to publishing them as a case book for student use. With the funding of the British Government Department For International Development Eastern Africa ("DEIDEA"), I was able to collect more materials on Ugandan land tenure law. This source book is a partial fulfillment of my promise.

The main aim of this book is to provide materials for teaching Ugandan land law. The target audience is law students and generally members of the legal fraternity. However, non-lawyers will also find several chapters of the book a useful source of information of Uganda's land tenure law. The book incorporates extracts of discussion papers, reports and debates leading to the enactment of the *Land Act*, 1998. These materials are essential reading for the understanding of the Act and its underlying policy.

The book is divided into thirteen chapters. Chapters 1-7, deal mainly with land tenure law and policy in Uganda both historically and currently. The materials in particular focus on the debates leading to the enactment of *Land Act*, 1998, and the post enactment discussion of the problems surrounding its implementation. The rest of the chapters contain extracts of mainly Ugandan cases dealing with general principles of land law. All chapters have notes and questions for discussion. Readers of this book will find more useful if read with my textbook: *Principles of Land Law in Uganda*, also published by Fountain Publishers. The two books complement each other.

As usual, work of this kind is impossible without the assistance of several people. Apart from the individuals and institutions whose contribution I formally acknowledge elsewhere, I wish, in particular, to thank the following. My thanks to Flavia Nabakooza, Rashida Batanulwa and Joseph Isanga (Makerere University law students), for their excellent research and editing skills, and for their valuable suggestions, from a student perspective, for improvement of the content of the materials. Likewise, I wish to express my gratitude to Elvis Onyoru (law student, Murdoch University) and Sanyu Mugambwa (law student, University of Technology Sydney) for organising and sorting the materials. My thanks go to David Markovich, Darrel Chia, Elouise Dellit (former law students at Murdoch University) and my colleague, Andrew McRobert, whose mastery of the computer saved me anxious moments. I wish to express my deep appreciation to Beatrice Kavuma-Kiwanuka and Harriet Byenkya for typing the bulk of the materials with speed and accuracy. I should also acknowledge the assistance and support of the Honourable Mr Benjamin Odoki, Chief Justice of Uganda, Elijah Wante, Director of the Law Development Centre, and Joanne Bosworth, DFIDEA Uganda Land Act Implementation Project. For institutions, I am especially indebted to the DFIDEA, for its funding of the original project, the Law Development Centre for allowing me unlimited use of its library, and the School of Law, Murdoch University, for its financial and moral support of my project. I should also express my thanks to Justus Mugaju, Associate Editor, Fountain Publishers, for his patience and understanding of my viewpoint on a number of problems that arose in the course of publication. Finally, my deepest gratitude is to Juliet, Sanyu and Paul for their unending support and love.

John T. Mugambwa J P
School of Law
Murdoch University
Perth, Western Australia
2002

Acknowledgement

I gratefully acknowledge permission to reproduce materials from the following persons and institutions. The Law Development Centre for permission to reproduce extracts from the *High Court Bulletins* and the *Uganda Law Reports*. The Makerere Institute of Social Research (MISR), for permission to reproduce extracts of the MISR and the Land Tenure Centre of the University of Wisconsin, *'Land Tenure and Agricultural Development in Uganda Report"* and the discussion papers, which followed the report. For permission to reproduce excerpts from public documents: the Parliamentary Clerk, the Ministry of Justice and Constitutional Affairs, and the Ministry of Water, Lands and Environment. For permission to reproduce extracts of reports and discussion papers of the Uganda Land Act Implementation Project: DFIDEA. For permission to reproduce extracts of a paper 'Experiences in the Implementation of the Land Act': the Honourable Benjamin Odoki, Chief Justice of Uganda. For permission to reproduce excerpts of a paper 'Land disputes in Uganda: An overview of the types of land disputes and the dispute settlement *fora'*: John Kigula. For permission to reproduce extracts from the Eastern Africa Law Reports and the all England Law Reports: Butterworths Division of Reed Elsevier (UK) Limited. For permission to reproduce extracts from the English Law Reports and the Weekly Law reports: Incorporated Council for Law Reporting for England and Wales.

Specific acknowledgements follow and appropriate citations appear throughout the book. While every care has been taken to trace and acknowledge copyright, I tender my apologies for any accidental infringement where copyright has proven unascertainable.

J.T.M.
2002

Table of Cases

Table of Statutes

Uganda

1
Background to Uganda's Land Tenure Law

INTRODUCTION

The *Land Act*, 1998, is arguably the most important law affecting land tenure law in Uganda, though, of course, it does not operate in isolation. There are other written and unwritten laws, which, together with the *Land Act* constitute Uganda's land law and land tenure system. To understand the current land tenure system one needs to be familiar with the history of Uganda's land law and land tenure policy. For present purposes Uganda's land tenure history can conveniently be divided into three phases:

1. Land tenure system prior to colonial rule
2. Land tenure system in colonial and post colonial Uganda
3. The *Land Reform Decree* 1975

The materials below describe the land tenure systems during the three phases.

PRE-COLONIAL LAND TENURE SYSTEM

Justice Benjamin Odoki (Chairperson), *The Report of the Uganda Constitutional Commission: Analysis and Recommendations* (Entebbe: Uganda Government Printer, 1992)

Buganda

It is difficult to identify a single land tenure pattern for Uganda as a whole for this period. The situation may be partially indicated by reference to the customary land tenure system in Buganda as contrasted with other parts of Uganda. In Buganda, one would say that land was by and large held by the Kabaka on behalf of and in trust for the people. By about 1840, the Kabaka had effectively undermined the power of the clan heads largely by means of the power to appoint chiefs of various grades who had both administrative and military duties. In return, chiefs also got the right to use the land and produce of the peasants under them (beer, food etc). There were at least four categories of rights of control over land: These included:

Obutaka (rights of clans over land)

These rights accrued to heads of clans and sub-clans who were known as "*bataka*". The particular land involved was viewed as clan or ancestry land, the traditional seat of the head of the clan or sub-clan who determined a right to reside on such land. Other members of the clan or sub-clan had no right to reside there but had a right after their death to be buried on such lands. *Butaka* land was spread over Buganda and as of 1911, there were 522 *butaka* estates. The *butaka* estates were held by individual heads of clans and sub-clans rather than collectively. While *butaka* tenure was not strictly collective tenure, it was also not private ownership. A *mutaka* might allocate the right to use land and receive profits from it but consent of the clan was always necessary for a *mutaka* to give away *butaka* land or any part thereof. *Butaka* land was not divided among the children of a *mutaka* when he died, rather it passed to his successor in the role of *mutaka*. The Kabaka had power to remove a *mutaka* and evict him from *butaka* land for good cause. *Butaka* land was under all circumstances not alienable to strangers.

Obutongole (rights of the Kabaka and the chiefs)

The Kabaka held paramount title in all the land in Buganda. He granted land to his great chiefs (*bakungu*) who were few in number and to his lesser and more numerous chiefs called *batongole*. These rights in land are collectively described as *obutongole*. The grantees had right of use in the estates attached to their chiefly offices. These rights were good during the continuance in office of the particular chief. The *batongole* exercised the same rights towards the peasants on their lands as those exercised by *bataka* with regard to the tenants on *butaka* land.

Obwesengeze (individual hereditary rights)

These were individual rights over land stemming from long and undisputed occupation and/or original grant by the Kabaka. They could be acquired by a chief or an individual tenant. This type of tenure carried no political rights or duties like *butongole* tenure, and unlike *butongole* tenure, if the holder died, the land passed on to his heir. The holders were not subject to labour obligations like peasants.

Ebibanja (peasant rights of occupation)

The peasants formed the majority of the population. The peasants were free to choose a chief under whom to live. A peasant got a piece of land for his undisturbed occupation under a chief of his choice who would organise for his security and general welfare while the peasant was to respect his chief, render him some tribute and occasionally work for him. It should be noted that notwithstanding the fact that the peasant performed various customary services, he was still subject to being evicted from his *kibanja* (plot) by the chief at any time. His right of tenure, therefore, depended on his maintaining the correct social and political behaviour. Upon his death, a peasant successor had a right to remain in occupation.

Rest of Uganda

Aspects of the foregoing semi-feudal structure of land rights were replicated in other kingdom areas of pre-colonial Uganda, namely, Ankole, Bunyoro and Toro. The rest of pre-colonial Uganda was basically egalitarian. It would, therefore, be unrealistic to generalise about the patterns of land tenure that obtained in those parts then because conditions varied from place to place. However, some studies of the system of customary tenure have indicated certain regularities [sic] which definitely occurred elsewhere in Uganda – Acholi, Lango, Kigezi and Sebei. Generally speaking, customary tenure did recognise various rights of the individual to possess and use land subject to the superintendence of his family, clan and/or community. Land was regarded as a common heritage. In essence, the following rules applied:

(a) The individual land holder had his right under customary tenure to utilise his holding as he thought best, to rest or lend his piece of land for temporary purposes; to pledge crops on his land but not land itself; sell land subject to the approval of the family, dispose of the land according to the customary laws of inheritance and prohibit grazing near his homestead. He could also fence his homestead.

(b) The clan or family had the rights to settle land disputes within the area of control; exercise the right to buy any land offered for sale by its members; prohibit sale of clan land to undesirable persons and declare void any land transaction which had not received its approval.

(c) The general community had the following rights over land:
   (i) the right to graze communally over the whole areas but damage to crops had to be made good;
   (ii) the right of free access to salt licks; watering of cattle at running or open waters and access to water from springs and other common rights.

LAND TENURE IN COLONIAL UGANDA

Morris and Read, *Uganda the Development of its Laws and Constitution*, London: Stevens & Sons, 1966, pp: 44-45

It was not until after 1920 that any clear consistent policy regarding land tenure was adopted by the Protectorate Government and the early years of the Protectorate present an interesting, if somewhat bewildering, picture of conflict in the authorities' outlook on the form of land tenure which would be in the best interest of the country. In the first place, there was the fundamental question of what the Crown's powers to dispose of land in a Protectorate were, then there was the question of whether European settlement was to be encouraged and, thirdly, there was the problem of whether individual title should be given to Africans holding their land under customary title and, if so, whether such title should be granted to the chiefs who claimed to control the occupancy of the land or to the cultivators.

In the early days of the Protectorate, grants of land for government purposes would be obtained from the Kabaka. The acquisition of land in East Africa was, however, becoming a serious problem with the construction of the railway from the coast and in 1899 the question whether the Crown could acquire land rights, irrespective of grants by treaty, was resolved by the Law Officers of the Crown, who gave the opinion that in Protectorates where the Crown exercised authority under the treaties which did not confer the right to deal with waste or uncultivated land such right accrued to the Crown by virtue of its right to the Protectorate. (See H B Thomas and A E Spencer, *A History of Uganda Land and Surveys* (Entebbe, 1938, chap 12). The opinion further distinguished between states with a settled form of government in which land was apportioned either to the sovereign or to individuals and those "occupied by savage tribes," adding that in the latter case the establishment of a Protectorate involved assumption of control over all lands unappropriated which might be declared to be Crown lands and grants of title to which might be made. The Uganda Order in Council, 1902, defines Crown lands as "all public lands which are subject to control of His Majesty by virtue of any treaty convention or agreement of His Majesty's Protectorate and all lands which have been acquired by His Majesty for the public service or otherwise whatsoever," and presumably the words "by virtue of ... His Majesty's Protectorate" were intended to be interpreted in relation to the Law Officers' opinion of 1899.

[T]he Buganda Agreement 1900 provided for a detailed land settlement whereby the waste and uncultivated land was vested in the Crown and the remainder divided into private and official estates. Here there was no question of the Crown exercising any rights over the land other than those which the Agreement granted. In Ankole and Toro the position was different. Here the Agreements merely granted estates to a limited number of chiefs and vested in the Crown all land at the time waste and uncultivated. No mention was made in the Agreements of land which was cultivated but was not included in the freehold estates. The estates allocated were treated, unlike *mailo* estates in Buganda, as grants from the Crown under the Crown Lands Ordinance of 1903.

The Crown Lands Ordinance, 1903, provided for the manner in which Crown land might be allocated by the Governor, but it does not take the definition of Crown land any further than does the Order in Council. It was not until the Crown Lands (Declaration) Ordinance was passed in 1922 that the Crown's rights over land, other than unoccupied land, land acquired for public purposes and that covered by the Agreements, was clarified. The Ordinance stated that "all land and any rights therein in the Protectorate shall be presumed to be the property of the Crown unless they have been or are thereafter recognised by the Government by document to be the property of a person or until the contrary thereof be proved." Persons claiming rights against the Crown were given a year in which to lodge their claims and, in fact, no such claims were lodged. Thereafter, until the termination of the Protectorate, the legal position was that, outside Buganda, all land not held under title, and very little was held, was deemed to be Crown land theoretically at the absolute disposal of the Governor but in practice held by him in trust for the African occupiers. ...

... Although no clear decision had been made by the early nineteen-thirties as to the details of how the occupation of Crown land outside Buganda was to be controlled, certain principles had, however, by then been established. There would be no alienation of land in freehold to non-Africans and even the grant of leaseholds would be on a comparatively small scale. ... Crown land, other than forests and land in townships, would continue to be available for occupation by Africans according to native custom, such occupiers paying no rent to the Crown and, after the introduction in the nineteen-twenties of salaries for chiefs, no tribute for their occupancy to the chiefs... [A]lthough a small area in Ankole was granted to chiefs in fulfilment of past promises, no further freehold estates would be granted to African notables.

Justice Benjamin Odoki (chairperson), *The Report of the Uganda Constitutional Commission: Analysis and Recommendations* (Entebbe: Uganda Government Printer, 1992)

The colonial state in Uganda was built on the official philosophy of protectorate and indirect rule rather than colony, territory or direct rule. The colonial state did not introduce radical changes in the system of customary tenure in Uganda. Elsewhere on the African continent there had been resistance from Africans to borrowed policies of change introduced by the colonialists. The dominant economic structure chosen for Uganda by the colonial masters was one of small peasant agriculture under the prevailing customary tenure. It was considered dangerous to modify customs as arbitrary imposition of change would cause a total failure of efforts to administer the local indigenous population.

However, in order to appease the local chiefs and get local political allies in the effective administration of the country, the colonial administration introduced other land policies which could accommodate customary tenure. Thus, besides the preservation of customary tenure, mailo land tenure, freehold and leasehold tenures were introduced.

Mutyaba MP (chairperson), *Report of the Sessional Committee on Lands Water and Environment,* Parliament of Uganda Parliamentary Debates (Hansard), 20 June 1998, pp: 4046-4047

Mr Bennedict Mutyaba: Mr Speaker, as stated by the Minister in his background paper to the Land Bill, prior to 1975, there were four major land tenure systems;

(a) the mailo tenure,
(b) the freehold tenure
(c) the leasehold tenure and;
(d) customary land tenure.

I will describe them briefly.

Mailo tenure

The mailo tenure is a system of landholding which was introduced by the 1900 Buganda Agreement and improved upon by the land law of 1908. The term 'Mailo' is merely Luganda for the allocation of land which under the 1900 Buganda Agreement was expressed in multiples or fractions of a square mile. The term came to donate a form of absolute ownership and is applied to land held irrespective of area and method of acquisition. Henry West in his book *Land Policy in Uganda* gives a vivid description of this type of tenure and I quote.

> The title is vested in the mailo interest holder. He is free to sell his interest or give it away or pass it to his heirs on death, only he may grant or refuse a tenancy, but once the tenancy has been granted, the owner's power to eviction is severely circumscribed and his own right to resume the land for his own use is similarly limited.

> The tenant has the right to remain on that land so long as he cultivates it properly. The rent he pays is controlled by statute at a very low level and is his protection from arbitrary eviction. He holds only user rights which may not be transferred or sublet, but it is inheritable and this gives him virtual permanence of occupation.

The *Busuulu and Envujjo* Law of 1928 further entrenched the rights of the tenant by providing in Clause 11, that no peasant could be evicted by the mailo owner from his *kibanja*, save for public purposes or for other good and sufficient causes and unless the order of eviction was made by court having the jurisdiction. The peasant could, however, lose his *kibanja* if he left it unattended for more than six months without other occupants or without obtaining the consent of the mailo owner. The mailo owner was required to first report the matter to the sub-county chief and obtain his consent to the eviction. In addition to paying ground rent, the tenant was also subject to paying some amount of money for every acre of land that had cash crops.

Freehold

Freeholds were first allocated in Toro in 1900 under the 1900 Toro Agreement where 255 square miles were allocated to private individuals and 122 square miles were given out as official estates to the Omukama and his chiefs. The same process was followed in Ankole, by the 1901 Ankole Agreement. Later, however, the Colonial Government granted selective freeholds on Crown Land for agricultural and industrial development.

The leasehold tenure

This is a system under which a tenant holds an estate less than a freehold, for example, for a period of 99 years. A viable rent is nearly always payable and the owner has the power to determine the lease if the tenant does not fulfil the conditions of the grant. In Uganda most of the leases have been granted on former public land, basically because the Public Lands Act 1969 had vested the land in the state. Mailo owners and freeholders were also entitled to lease out part or all their land if they so wished.

Customary tenure

Mr Speaker, Hon. Members, most of the land held under the Public Lands Act 1969, which had not been delineated either as freehold or leasehold, is held under Customary Law.
Customary tenure refers to a system of land holding governed and regulated by customary principles and in the majority of cases sanctioned by customary authorities Council of Elders, Village Chiefs, Village Headmen, etc. Under this, the owner has user rights. The owner may be an individual or a community, in the latter case, the land is then said to be held on a communal basis.

With the exception of Buganda and a few areas in Ankole, Toro and Bunyoro, where titling took place, most of the land in Uganda is held under customary tenure.

(Makerere Institute of Social Research and the Land Tenure Center of the University of Wisconsin, Madison, USA, *Land Tenure and Agricultural Development in Uganda Report*, 1989)

Freeholds: Freeholds were originally established for limited, specific purposes such as churches and similar special uses, including specific commercial ventures. The Crown Lands Ordinance of 1903 gave the Crown the authority to grant land in freehold, but very little area was ever converted under this ordinance. Freeholds in Ankole and Toro were based on the 1900 Agreements, modified by the Landlord and Tenant Law in 1937 and the Crown Lands Ordinance, some of the provisions of which were incorporated into the Public Lands Act of 1969. In 1958 special rules were adopted for adjudicated freeholds. The adjudicated freehold provisions were used extensively in certain areas, such as in Ankole, Kigezi and Bugisu, providing registration and title to those previously using the lands.

Justice Benjamin Odoki (chairperson), *The Report of the Uganda Constitutional Commission: Analysis and Recommendations* (Entebbe: Uganda Government Printer, 1992)

Freehold Tenure: Freehold means absolute ownership of land. Outside Buganda, there were three types of freehold which were introduced:

(a) First, there were freeholds created under the Crown Lands Ordinance of 1903 from Crown lands to individuals by the Colonial Government. The Crown Lands Ordinance gave the Crown power to alienate land in freehold. Very few freeholds were given under this Ordinance. The Ordinance attached development conditions which were carried forward by the Public Lands Act, 1969. The State however, reserved the right to enter and inspect the adjudicated freeholds.

(b) Second, there were freeholds converted from customary tenure pilot schemes in the districts of Kigezi, Bugisu and the Kingdom of Ankole. In these schemes there was surveying and actual registration of existing customary holdings. In some areas, consolidation of fragmented plots was also carried out. Adjudication was carried out by local committees whose co-operation and local knowledge were crucial to the success of the project. The schemes turned out to be more time consuming and expensive than had been originally anticipated.

(c) Third, the Colonial Government also set up native freeholds which were grants of land under the Toro and Ankole agreements of 1900 and 1901, respectively. It was agreed that chiefs would be allocated such land under a special distribution scheme. These freeholds were similar to mailo land in Buganda. In Ankole, the result of the 1901 agreement was the demarcation of 50 square miles for private freehold and 26 square miles for official estates. In Toro, 255 square miles became private freehold and 122 square miles official estates. These freeholds were highly restricted freeholds. The allodial title was vested in the colonial power. The land could be transferred only to a native of the Kingdom. The terms of the tenure between the native freehold and any tenant were not freely negotiable but were fixed by the Ankole Landlord and Tenant Law, 1947 and by Toro Landlord and Tenant Law, 1937. The effect of these two laws was effectively to curtail the powers and rights of the freeholder vis-à-vis the customary tenant on the land.

Leasehold Tenure: A leasehold estate is an estate created in land as a result of an agreement between a lessor and a lessee to the effect that the latter will enjoy exclusive possession of the land subject to a specified and certain duration in consideration of a cash payment called rent moving from the lessee to the lessor. In Uganda, there are two types of leases, the private lease and the public or statutory leases. A private lease is granted by an individual landowner to an individual or an organisation. The statutory leases are given by a public authority.

[P]ublic statutory leases [were] provided for under the Public Lands Act, 1969. The leasehold system represented a major feature of the land tenure system in Uganda until the enactment of the Land Reform Decree 1975. …

Customary Tenure: Under the Public Lands Act, 1969, any person is authorised to hold land by customary tenure without any grant, lease or licence from any controlling authority provided the land is not in urban area and has not been alienated.

Note

For detailed discussion of the land adjudication scheme in Kigezi and Ankole, see Okec S, 'Pilot Schemes for the Registration of Land Titles in Uganda' in Obol-Ochola (ed.), *Land Law and Reform in East Africa*, Kampala, Milton Obote Foundation, 1969, pp: 255-64.

THE LAND REFORM DECREE 1975

The *Land Reform Decree*, 1975, enacted during Amin's military regime, was the first major post-colonial legislation aimed at reforming Uganda's land tenure system. The Decree was enacted without any public debate or even prior warning. Most people heard of the Decree for the first time when it was read over the radio. The reforms that the Decree attempted to introduce are explained in the following excerpts. As will be seen in these materials (see also excerpts in Chapter Two), the Decree generated confusion and apprehension throughout the country. In the end, most of its provisions were never implemented until the *Land Act* 1998 formally repealed it

Mutyaba MP (chairperson) *Report of the Sessional Committee on Lands Water and Environment,* Parliament of Uganda Parliamentary Debates (Hansard), 20 June 1998, pp: 4047-4048

Mr Speaker, the aforesaid system of land tenure was disrupted by the Land Reform Decree of 1975. Again, I will quote from section 1 of the Decree which provides that

> With effect from the commencement of this Decree all land in Uganda shall be public land to be administered by the Land Commission in accordance with the Public Lands Act 1969, subject to such modifications as may be necessary to bring that Act into conformity with this Decree.

The Decree abolished freehold and mailo tenure and converted these into leases of 99 years for individuals, and leases of 199 years for public bodies, religious organisations and other charitable organisations.

Although the Decree saved customary tenure, it reduced it to a tenancy by sufferance and gave the Land Commission powers to lease such land to any person. Occupants on mailo and freehold land were also converted into customary tenants and excused from payment of *Busuulu* and *Envujjo*. Their tenure was, however, held at sufferance.

The Decree was intended to strengthen the Central Government's control over land. In this quest it failed miserably and it remained a law in the books, as the Minister has already said, with the exception [sic] of creating unnecessary suffering to the customary tenants on public land who, because of lack of security of tenure, did not feel the enthusiasm to fully develop their land in the economic sense.

... Although it failed in its intentions, the Decree sought to address a need which had been recognised in the early fifties; the need to enact a comprehensive law which would enable and empower the State to require good agricultural practices, to compel development to lower [sic] the sale of undeveloped land. Referring to the mailo tenure, one author said: "The mailo owner has ownership without inducement to invest and the tenant is in occupation without the power to progress."

It was also argued that the freehold system was not well suited for Africa and that the state should hold the reversionary interest in trust for the people.

The distortions created by the Decree helped in re-energizing people's interest in land. In the Odoki Commission Report on the Constitution, land was greatly highlighted. The interests of the people were, however, contradictory. The former freehold and mailo tenure holders wanted the system to be re-instated. The customary tenants wanted more secure occupation.

Justice Benjamin Odoki (chairperson), *The Report of the Uganda Constitutional Commission: Analysis and Recommendations* (Entebbe: Uganda Government Printer, 1992)

The Land Reform Decree substantially changed the legal basis of land tenure in Uganda. All land was declared public land to be administered by the Uganda Land Commission. The Decree abolishes freehold interests in land other than where such interests are vested in the Commission, in consequence whereof all freeholds and individual mailos were transformed into leases of 99 years for individuals, and 199 years for public/religious and other charitable bodies.

The legal protection which a customary tenant had under the Public Lands Act, 1969 whereby, no dealings including transfer or removal from land could be effected without his consent, was removed by the Decree. The customary tenant then became a tenant at sufferance, and could be thrown out on notice at any time. However, the Decree provides that customary tenants on public land may not be evicted except under terms and conditions imposed by the Commission and approved by the minister. The Decree further provides that the system of holding land by customary tenure may continue, but acquisition of new customary holdings is prohibited unless permission has been obtained. Any person who occupies land without such consent commits an offence and is liable on conviction, to a fine or imprisonment.

A customary tenant on public land does not have transferable interest in land. He may, however, transfer his improvements on the land after giving not less than three months notice to the prescribed authority. It is an offence to enter into an agreement to transfer any interest in any public land occupied by customary tenure without permission of the prescribed authority. Under the Decree, no person may occupy public land by customary tenure except with the written permission of the prescribed authority.

Under the Decree, the *Busuulu and Envujo Law*, the Ankole Landlord and Tenant Law and the Toro Landlord and Tenant Law were repealed. The Decree further extends the scope of public control of land transactions. Before the Decree, land used to change hands freely among Ugandan Africans. Only land transactions between Africans and non-Africans were required by the Land Transfer Act to be effected with the consent of the minister. In addition, written consent of the Commission is now necessary before the lessee can transfer the whole of his lease for value. Under the Land Reform Decree, practically all land transactions in Uganda now need the consent of the controlling authority.

The hitherto special position of customary tenant on public land has become precarious in that he is now a tenant at sufferance. The implementation of the Decree has met considerable opposition. For example, section 2(1), which purports to abolish mailo and freehold estates has not been implemented and by and large land transactions are being conducted as if the Decree is not in place. The great majority of views received by the Commission are demanding for a repeal of the Decree. It does not, therefore, enjoy support among the people of Uganda.

Questions

1. What are the possible reasons for the non-implementation of the *Land Reform Decree*?
2. What were the main policy objectives of the *Land Reform Decree*? Compare and contrast these objectives with those of the *Land Act*, 1998 (see extracts in the following chapter).

******

2

Proposal For Land Tenure Reform

INTRODUCTION

In 1983, the Government established an agriculture policy committee for the purpose of co-ordinating, directing and reviewing key policies and programmes in the agricultural sector. This was to be carried out in conjunction with the Agricultural Secretariat, Bank of Uganda. A working group carried out some studies in consequence of which it recommended, inter alia, re-examination of the *Land Reform Decree*, the formulation of sound national land tenure conducive to agricultural development and a reform of the land registry.

The Makerere Institute of Social Research (MISR) was asked to carry out detailed studies on land tenure and agricultural development in conjunction with the Land Tenure Centre, University of Wisconsin. The team carried out studies and field surveys in some districts such as Luwero, Masaka, Mbale, Mbarara, Bushenyi, Kampala, Tororo, Iganga and Mukono. The studies focused on mailo tenure and customary tenure. To a large extent the *Land Act*, 1998, is based on the recommendations of the team's report and that of the Odoki Constitutional Commission,[1] which followed it. Below are excerpts of both reports.

Makerere Institute of Social Research and the Land Tenure Centre of the University of Wisconsin, Madison, USA, *Land Tenure and Agricultural Development in Uganda Report*, 1989

POLICY ALTERNATIVES

Reform of land tenure means changing the rules by which individuals relate to one another with respect to land. The rules of land tenure define each individual's rights and duties with respect to other people concerning the use and transfer of land. (The term "individual" also includes groups such as a co-operative society, farmer's grazing association, corporation or other entity).

In some situations, changing land tenure rules by changing the law may involve fundamental change in how individuals interact with respect to land. In other cases, individuals may alter the way in which they interact regarding land, and the law simply changes to recognise and legitimise this new reality.

Most African countries have viewed land tenure reform as a means to increase agricultural productivity. Many African countries are also concerned that their land tenure laws protect the most vulnerable members of the society from loss of their access to land for subsistence production. Most African nations have multiple goals for land tenure policy, hoping to stimulate agricultural development while protecting the uniquely African concept that all individuals should have access to enough land for subsistence production. The fact that most African land tenure systems provided easy access to land for all individuals has been one factor in preventing the development of a large landless class such as exists in many countries of Asia and Latin America. At the same time, it is important that the land tenure system make a positive contribution to the economic development of agriculture.

The most successful land tenure reforms in Africa have been those which: (1) recognise how traditional land tenure has evolved over time; and (2) attempt to guide future evolution by encouraging those changes that are beneficial and preventing those changes that would be harmful. Land tenure reform must begin with an understanding of current law and practice, the elements

[1] Justice Benjamin Odoki (Chairperson), *The Report of the Uganda Constitutional Commission: Analysis and Recommendation*, supra.

of the existing system that stimulate agricultural development and the policy alternatives for constructive change.

Goals for Land Tenure Reform in Uganda

Alternative land tenure policies must be analysed according to some set of goals. The most appropriate goals for land tenure reform in Uganda are that land tenure law and practice should contribute to the economic and social development of agriculture, protect the land rights of farmers who have no alternative source of income, and contribute to the evolution of a single, uniform efficient and equitable tenure system for the nation.

Goal 1

The land tenure system should contribute to economic development of agriculture and the nation.

Land tenure policy must contribute to economic development. But the economic development of agriculture is dependent on more than simply a good land tenure system.

Fundamentally, agriculture must be profitable. Otherwise the farmer has no incentive to increase productivity and output.

The profitability of agriculture is determined by the price farmers received for the product, credit availability and cost, input costs and supplies, and many other factors including the land tenure system which determines who has access to what land.

The most progressive farmers will respond to the new opportunities in agriculture if it is profitable and will lead the entire agriculture sector to higher levels of productivity and output. But if progressive farmers cannot get access to land to expand their operations to respond to new opportunities, agricultural development will be constrained. Therefore, a land tenure system must be flexible enough to allow progressive farmers to respond to opportunities in order to contribute to agricultural development.

The land tenure system is also tied to industrial development. Industrial development will increase the demand for agricultural products, which will increase the profitability of agriculture and lead to an increased demand for agricultural land. The land tenure system must be flexible enough to allow progressive farmers to obtain access to land to respond to this new demand for agricultural products.

Industrial development is also important for the economic development of agriculture. An expanding industrial and non-farm economy will create jobs for people from rural areas. Those farmers with few resources or little land who have low farm income will be drawn off the land and will find employment in the expanding industrial/urban economy. The land tenure system must not hinder their movement out of agriculture and must be flexible enough to allow progressive farmers to obtain the use of the land vacated by those who move to the urban area or to non-farm jobs in rural areas.

While the industrial and non-farm economy is growing, the land tenure system has a second important function: providing economic opportunity for individuals who have no real earning possibilities elsewhere. In the early stages of development there will not be enough demand for industrial labour to absorb all those in rural areas who might otherwise wish to leave agriculture. It is important that the land tenure system provide these individuals with an opportunity to be productively employed.

If the land tenure system forces people from the land prematurely, before there are jobs created in the non-farm economy, the nation suffers in at least three ways:

1. The process of national economic development is slowed because a segment of the population is not productively employed in any activity;
2. Social problems are created, such as crime, and a large unemployed urban population can create political instability;

3. Those displaced from agriculture suffer from lack of any means of earning income. Thus, a goal of a land tenure system is to avoid forcing people from the land prematurely, before there are any employment opportunities elsewhere in the economy.

Thus, the most basic goal of a land tenure system is that it contributes to the process of the economic development of agriculture. In meeting this basic goal, two other goals for a land tenure system are created: the system must be flexible enough to allow progressive farmers to gain access to land to respond to economic opportunities in agriculture, yet the land tenure system must avoid forcing people off the land before there are sufficient employment opportunities elsewhere in the economy.

Goal 2

The tenure system should provide flexibility in transfer of land so that progressive farmers who can make the best use of land are able to obtain land for their farm operations.

This is an important goal for land tenure policy in Uganda. The surveys in Luwero and Masaka also showed clearly that progressive farmers are able to obtain land through a land market. The land tenure system allows for an active land market, and the land market is absolutely critical for the economic development of agriculture. As these progressive farmers obtain a gradually increasing share of the nation's land through the land market, productivity in agriculture will increase and national economic development will be enhanced. Any change in land tenure law should ensure that the system is flexible enough to allow the most productive land users to gain access to land to use.

Goal 3

The land tenure system should protect the access to land for people who have no income earning possibilities outside the agricultural sector of the economy.

This is a common goal of land tenure reform in Africa, to avoid creating a landless class of people who have no way to earn their living. In Uganda this is an important goal because the Luwero and Masaka surveys showed clearly that there is a group of small farmers with very low income who are nevertheless able to exist because they have access to land to grow their own food.

At this point in time there are no significant opportunities for substantial numbers of these people in the urban areas. These people should not be evicted or pushed off their land. As the urban and industrial economy grows, many of these people may choose to leave farming because they will perceive better opportunity in the urban and industrial sector. This has occurred in the past, and will occur again in the future. However, until there are other income earning opportunities for people in the non-farm economy, protecting the access of small holders to land is an important goal of land tenure policy.

Goal 4

Land tenure law should facilitate the development of land tenure toward a single, uniform, and efficient land tenure system for the entire nation.

As much as possible, land tenure law should encourage the development of a single land tenure system for all land in the nation. Although this goal might not be practical to implement immediately, any land tenure reform should facilitate the development of a single tenure system for the entire nation rather than separate complex systems for different areas that increase administrative costs and lead to confusion among land users about the rights in land under different complex systems.

Options for land tenure change

In this chapter, the policy alternatives for land tenure reform will be considered, and the implications of the various alternatives will be discussed. The intent is to analyse a wide range of options so that the reader will understand the advantages and disadvantages of all the options and be able to select the option that seems the most reasonable for Uganda at this particular point in its history. The recommendations of the study team are contained in the last section of this chapter.

In considering land tenure reform, changes in land tenure law and practice, several questions must be addressed:

1. Should the Land Reform Decree of 1975 be enforced or abolished?
2. Should land tenure law revert to its pre-1975 status?
3. Should land be held by leasehold or freehold?
4. What should be the status of mailo tenure?
5. What should be the status of customary tenancy ?
6. Should development conditions be imposed on freehold or leasehold?
7. Should a land tax be adopted?
8. Should the land registry be rehabilitated, and if so, how?

This chapter will address each of these questions, providing the policy alternatives and the implications of each alternative.

Question 1: Should the Land Reform Decree be implemented or abolished?

The policy options have two extremes', either implement the Decree or abolish it; in the middle ground are an almost limitless number of possible amendments. Minor amendments will not be discussed because much of the discussion of particular specific amendments is contained in the discussion of other policy alternatives and implications. Most of these other alternatives could be integrated into the basic form of the Land Reform Decree as amendments to various sections.

Option 1: Implement the Land Reform Decree of 1975

Implications of Option 1

1. Over time the Decree will result in a single uniform system of land tenure for the nation. All land will be owned by the state and all individuals and groups will be leaseholders.
2. Vesting title to all land in the state is consistent with the tradition of collective ownership of land in traditional indigenous cultures. In effect, the national government takes the place of the community (village, chiefdom, clan, or other communal group) in ownership of land and the responsibility for allocating land to individuals who need it.
3. Government could easily develop agricultural land use planning programs and implement them through zoning and development conditions in the leases granted to individuals. Government could impose strong controls and determine which crops could be grown in various areas. Or, government could zone land for livestock or crop use (this could also be accomplished within other tenure arrangements).
4. Government could allocate land to those in most need of it. Other systems that rely on the land market result in land being owned by those able to pay for it, while government could allocate land to those most in need.
5. Vesting ownership of all land in the state lowers the amount of compensation that government must pay if it takes land for a public project such as a road.
6. Implementation of the decree will make mailo tenants and customary tenants subject to eviction by the landowner or lease holder. This violates one of the goals of the land tenure system, to provide access to productive economic activity for those with no economic opportunities outside of their farm.

It is clear that the rate of eviction of small farmers would increase if the Decree were implemented. Under the Decree tenants would be subject to eviction at any time, with only the question of compensation hindering full-scale evictions of tenants by owners. To date there have been few evictions on mailo land, but the trend will undoubtedly increase as mailo owners and tenants begin to understand more clearly what the law actually provides, and as pressure on the land increases from both population growth and increased economic opportunity in agriculture. The Decree has not had extremely negative effects, to date, simply because it has not been widely implemented.

Many observers note that many mailo owners and householders have not evicted tenants because of strong cultural ties they share with the tenants. However, as land changes hands through the market or even through inheritance, many of the new owners will not share same cultural background and values as the former and the tenants. New owners may be much less constrained by social ties to tenants. Thus, the potential for eviction may increase over time.

Customary tenants on public land would be in a similar vulnerable position. Land users, particularly small holders in all parts of the country would be vulnerable to eviction by those who have more political power and are able to convince the land commission that they should be given leases with minimal compensation to sitting tenants.

Also, evictions may be low because the Land Reform Decree is generally misunderstood by both mailo owners and mailo tenants, both of whom think that the law protects tenants against owners; the opposite is the case. The survey in Luwero and Masaka areas and the discussions with farmers and officials show this clearly.

7. Implementation of the Decree will hinder agricultural development. This violates one of the fundamental goals of a land tenure system.

   The survey in both Luwero and Masaka showed clearly that the land market is very important for agricultural development because the progressive farmers who will invest and increase agricultural productivity obtain their land through the land market.

   The Decree would substitute an allocation process based on ability to understand the terms of the Decree and the political or economic power to obtain a lease. There is no guarantee that those who would obtain these leases would increase productivity. In fact, the evidence suggests that, on average, individuals obtaining land through the political process would decrease overall productivity. The land market allocates land to those with the best ability to use it. The political allocation process would allocate land to those with the most political power. Productivity of the nation's agriculture would suffer from such a change.

8. Implementation will require an increase in administrative expenditure. The Decree requires leases which must be renewed at 99-year intervals. To date this provision has not been enforced and relatively few leases have been formerly grated. If the Decree is not abolished the government must continue to not enforce its terms, or incur great expense in constructing leases for all properties in the nation. On the other hand, implementing the Decree will avoid the expenditure of energy and time necessary to develop new land tenure for the country.

Question 2: Should land law revert to pre-1975 status?

A return to the land law in effect prior to 1975 would mean that the Public Land Act of 1969 would be in effect for land held under customary tenure, adjudicated freehold land would be governed by the provisions of various laws enacted between 1900 and 1969, including certain provisions of the Crown Lands Ordinance and the Public Lands Acts of 1969, and mailo land would be governed by the Envujjo Laws of 1927 and various modification thereafter. Other special provisions would apply to ordinary freehold.

Implications

1. This option would be most easily understood by farmers and others because a familiar system would be re-instituted. This option would involve the least of cost and problems in developing new administrative procedures and communicating the meaning of the new law to people.
2. The agricultural development of Uganda was proceeding at a fairly rapid pace under this old set of laws. The experience was very positive, so returning to the old -would involve minimal risk of seriously interfering with the process of agricultural development. The pre -1975 laws meet the goal that a land tenure system should promote agricultural development.
3. The pre-1975 set of laws offered protection from eviction for all mailo tenants under the *envujjo* and *busuulu* laws and prevented much serious abuse of the leasehold provisions on public lands by limiting the size of leases that could be granted and requiring approval for leases of large acreages. Thus, the pre-1975 laws meet a critical goal of a land tenure system.
4. A single, uniform tenure system would not be created by this option. Rather, a series of complex tenure rules would apply to various lands in different parts of the country. This would violate one of the basic goals of a land tenure system.
5. Instead of assisting in the evolution of a land tenure system to facilitate economic development, land tenure law would hinder an evolution of re-instituting a set of laws that in many areas were widely ignored and simply unenforceable. For example, many transactions in the land market involving parcels of public land technically violated the Public Lands Act of 1969. Many of the provisions of leasehold tenures were widely ignored.
6. Returning to the pre-1975 laws will re-institute the deadlock between mailo owners and mailo tenants. Prior to 1975 it was widely believed that the mailo system was flawed in that tenants were discouraged from fully developing their parcels while owners were prevented from using their land. The Land Reform Decree of 1975 broke this deadlock, in theory, although it was never fully implemented and would result in many evictions if it were implemented. Returning to the pre-1975 laws would simply re-create the negative aspects of the mailo system that were well-recognised as early as 1950 (see Mukwaya, 1953)
7. A return to the past would re-create all of the problems of the previous system, would destroy the opportunity to begin to create a uniform land tenure system for the entire nation and would re-institute laws that were at odds with land tenure practice and agricultural development needs even before 1975.

Question 3: Should land holding be by freehold or leasehold?

The two basic options for landholding are freehold or leasehold. Land under customary tenure can be integrated with either a freehold or leasehold system.

A first question might be: should land tenure be individualised? In some African countries this is an important question of land tenure policy. In many areas of Uganda the question is moot: land tenure is already individualised. In districts as far removed as Kabale, Mbale and Luwero, significant changes in traditional land tenure systems have occurred and land tenure is highly individualised in many, though not all areas of the country. In many parts of the country these individual rights have existed for half a century or more. In other areas individualisation is occurring rapidly under pressure of population growth and economic opportunity. Abolishing the concept of individual rights in land is not a viable option.

Option 1: Freehold tenure

How freehold might operate

Individual rights in land might be granted in freehold. In mailo areas this would mean that mailo owners would have freehold rights instead of lease rights under the Land Reform Decree or mailo rights as under the Envujjo and Busuulu Laws and the Public Lands Act 1969. The question of the rights of mailo tenants could be received in favour of either tenants or owners (see question 4). Development conditions could be imposed, or not imposed (see question 6). Government could reserve the right to take land for public purposes, such as for roads, subject to full and prompt compensation to the landholder. Existing leaseholds could be converted to freehold, with the possible exception that leases on government-sponsored ranches or other large leaseholds of over 500 acres could be reviewed. Customary tenants on public land could apply for freehold tenure, subject to verification of their rights by elders in the community and government committee. A detailed and costly survey need not occur if the property boundaries are marked and verified by the chiefs and RC officials at parish level. The mailo registry would be maintained and rehabilitated, except that the registry would legitimise freehold rather than other districts, integrating any existing land records.

Government could require that all purchases of the land be registered as freehold, as well as allowing anyone who wishes to obtain freehold title to apply. This would offer tenure security to those most in need (progressive framers who purchase land) and allow others to register as they see the need. Gradually, over several decades, all tenure in the country would be converted to freehold.

Advantages of freehold

1. Individuals are offered maximum protection for their rights in property.

Freehold tenure gives individuals maximum protection from arbitrary and unwarranted interference by government. If government has the ability to take people's property then government can destroy an individual's source of livelihood. The potential for abuse of power by government is great if people do not have the right to their property. A leasehold system simply invites meddling by some future government in the basic rights of property.

The Luwero and Masaka surveys illustrate the importance of ensuring individual rights in property. In both areas the progressive farmers were quite uncertain about their ability to hold onto their property (customary tenants in Luwero and mailo owners in Masaka). Yet these progressive farmers are most in need of security to give them an additional incentive to invest. If progressive farmers are not secure in their ownership of property, the government risks destroying the incentive to invest among the group of people most likely to invest. The productivity of the agricultural sector will be damaged.

2. Freehold tenure would recognise the reality of the land tenure system that has existed in the mailo areas for many decades, and in other regions of the country that have adjudicated freehold.

The fact is that freehold tenure has existed, in effect, for several decades for mailo owners who farm their own land or do not have tenants, for mailo tenants on their *bibanja*, and for holders of adjudicated and ordinary freehold. This system has worked very well for the development of agriculture because individuals have shown a great willingness and ability to respond to profitable opportunities in farming. In fact similar observations were made in the study assessing the impact of the Rujumbura Pilot Land Registration Scheme – Kigezi, (MISR and LTC 1988).

3. The demands on government are less from freehold than leasehold.

Under a leasehold system government must prepare leases, renew the leases periodically, maintain a register of leases and make decisions on granting leases. Under freehold the government must only maintain a registry. Freehold tenure will free government resources and manpower to use in other tasks that contribute to the social and economic development of the nation.

4. Freehold gives individuals maximum ability to transfer land through a land market.
Under leasehold government is a party to land transitions, particularly if the lease contains lease conditions that restrict the use of land. Under freehold transactions are strictly between the buyer and seller.

The Luwero and Masaka research illustrated the importance of the land market in the economic development of agriculture. Any government policy that interferes with the ability of progressive farmers to gain access to land through the land market will hinder the economic development of agriculture.

5. Freehold tenure will give farmers the greatest degree of security in their land.
The Luwero and Masaka surveys, and the RRA discussions in Mbale and elsewhere revealed that farmers under all types of tenure are investing in their land. The differences in the degree of security offered by different land tenure systems is less important than the ability of the land tenure system to allow an active land market to function so that progressive farmers can gain access to land.

However, it is also true that farmers in Luwero, Masaka, Mbale, Bushenyi and elsewhere are applying for leases on public land or attempting to obtain mailo title by buying out the mailo owners. Obviously these farmers believe that the increased security of a lease or mailo freehold is worth the considerable expense of obtaining title or purchasing their *bibanja*.

6. Freehold tenure is most likely to result in increased credit for agriculture.
Banks have shown reluctance to give credit to those without clear title to land. In Mbale there are numerous applications for leasehold because of the pressure on land and the uncertainty surrounding traditional tenure rules as they apply to land that has been purchased. Farmers in Mbale area indicate that they believe that clear title will lead to increased access to credit. Many farmers in both Luwero (37 percent) and Masaka (85 percent) indicated that one constraint to making more investments in agriculture was "lack of funds", suggesting that increased credit for agriculture might stimulate more investment. (However, of the four farmers in Luwero who were successful in using land as collateral for a loan, three used the funds for non-agricultural purposes.)

It is not likely that changing tenure to either freehold or leasehold will cause farmers to invest significantly more in their parcels. The survey data from Luwero and Masaka and the RRA results from Mbale, Bushenyi and elsewhere indicate that progressive farmers are already investing in agriculture.

However, it is possible that freehold tenure will increase the willingness of banks to loan to farmers who want to invest, paving the way for even more investment in agriculture. (A thorough investigation of private credit for agriculture would be an important project for government.)

Option 2: Leasehold tenure

How leasehold might operate
Leasehold might operate in essentially the same manner as freehold except that additional government resources would be required to make decisions on issuance of leases, develop and implement procedures for monitoring leases and provide for lease renewal. The status of mailo tenants could be resolved in favour of owners or tenants (See Question 4). Lease conditions might or might not be applied (see question 6). Government could reserve the right to take land, with compensation, for public projects such as a road. Registries should be developed in the same manner as for freehold tenure. Customary tenants on public land could be granted leases instead of freehold. Purchases of public land could be registered as leases, as well as offering registration to anyone who feels the need for more clear tenure rights. Transactions and

registration could be verified by elders of the community and by government committees, just as with freehold tenure. In sum, leasehold and freehold could operate in a similar manner, except for the requirement of additional government resources to manage the leasehold system.

Advantages of leasehold

1. Leasehold is closest to the existing situation for individuals holding public land who have applied for leases. A leasehold system would have the least variation from the system under the Public Lands Act of 1969, or for that matter the formal system under the Land Reform Decree of 1975 (except that any leasehold system must give more protection to individual rights than the Decree).
2. To the extent that the lease system is well administered, and to the extent that future governments do not interfere by changing the terms or conditions of leases, a leasehold system could have many of the same economic effects as freehold.

   A well-administered leasehold system means that government must adopt a reasonable lease instrument and, perhaps most important, government must monitor the term of each lease. Government must develop administrative procedures and manpower to inform the leaseholder that the lease is due to expire and government should arrange a system for the individual to renew the lease. In addition, this conversion of an old lease to a new lease must be done well in advance of the expiration date of the lease. For example, for a 99-year lease, the renewal might come in year 60, so that the individual leaseholder has certainty of tenure at least several decades into the future. This is particularly important in agriculture where many investments may be fixed on the land and the farmer may not realize the full return for 10 or even 20 years.

   The alternative of placing the burden of renewal on the lessee is not likely to work well because evidence with mailo land shows that individuals are not aware of the importance of keeping titles up-to-date. But the investment behaviour of a farmer will not be affected by an about-to-expire lease if the farmer is unaware of lease provisions.

   If the leasehold system is well administered, many of its economic effects would be identical to freehold – individuals would have certainty of rights to use land, lending institutions would have the same incentives to use land as collateral, the land market function in the manner as with freehold.
3. Government maintains some control over land and ownership could be exercised at the time of lease renewal. (Development conditions could be applied to either freehold or leasehold and are discussed in a later section.) Freehold offers government no opportunity to adjust the pattern of land ownership or land use that results from the land market and the pattern of inheritance.
4. Leasehold offers the possibility of changing any development conditions that might be attached to the granting of a lease. Freehold means that the conditions of ownership could be imposed only at the time of granting freehold and could not be changed. At the time of renewing a lease (say every 49 or 99 years), government could change the development conditions of the lease to reflect changes in basic economic conditions or technological advances. If land is held in freehold government could impose conditions only at the point in time, at the issuance of freehold title, and would have no opportunity to adjust any development conditions at a later time.
5. Concept of leasehold in which the state owns the land and administrates it in trust for the people is closer to traditional indigenous concepts of land and its control than is freehold tenure.
6. Government would not be required to offer as much compensation for taking property for public purposes for land under leasehold compared to land under freehold.

Question 4: What should be the status of current mailo tenants?

Given that tenure is converted to either freehold or leasehold, what should be the status of those who are currently mailo tenants?

There are two feasible options:

i) recognize or legitimise, and confirm all tenants in their occupation of the land by making them freehold or leasehold owners ;

ii) Confirm occupation of tenants for only those parcels where the owner and tenants agree to make tenants freehold or leasehold owners. Either option could include compensation to mailo owners.

The option of making mailo owners holders in freehold or leasehold is not discussed here because, depending on the specific details of mailo owner rights to evict tenants, this option is either a variation on the option of reinstating the 1975 Land Reform Decree, or reinstating the pre-1975 land laws. Both of these options have been discussed previously.

Option 1. Distribution of freehold or leasehold rights in land to sitting tenants

Implications of Option 1

1. Giving tenants freehold or leasehold rights in the land they farm would simply be confirming a situation that has existed, in effect, since the Envujjo and Busuulu Laws were adopted in 1927. Tenants have not been subject to easy eviction (except under the terms of the 1975 Land Reform Decree) *bibanja* are inheritable, and many tenant families have been on the land for several generations.

2. Giving tenants clear rights in their property would resolve the mailo owner/tenant deadlocks and will lead to increased investment in mailo tenancy land. This meets an important goal of a land tenure system.

   In both Luwero and Masaka, the level of investment on mailo tenant land fell midway between the investment levels on public land and mailo land operated by owners. It is possible that changes in law confirming tenants in their occupation would increase investment but such an effect is likely to be small at least in the short run. However it is clear that many mailo tenants are attempting to purchase their parcels from the mailo owners, just as has occurred for many decades. The higher level of security is obviously valuable to these farmers.

   In addition, it is likely that investment in mailo tenancy land will increase in the long run if mailo tenants are confirmed in their occupation of land. The results in Luwero and Masaka indicate that the land market will allow the more progressive farmers to gradually increase their farm operations and this will increase investment and output in the agricultural sector.

3. Confirming tenants in their occupation increases the overall economic security of small holders. This meets an important goal of a land tenure system. Until the industrial sector provides enough jobs to draw labour from the agricultural sector, it is important that individuals with no alternative sources of income not be displaced from their agricultural land. Giving tenants freehold or leasehold ownership in their land would provide the economic security that is important in the process of economic development.

4. Converting mailo tenancy land to freehold or leasehold will bring tenure in former mailo areas under the same laws that apply in other parts of the country. This would meet an important goal of a land tenure system.

   Confirming tenants in their occupation by granting freehold or leasehold would convert the system of mailo tenure to the same tenure system that exists in other areas of the country. This step is extremely critical in encouraging the evolution of land tenure to a single, uniform system for the entire country.

5. Mailo owners who are also progressive farmers could gain access to mailo tenancy land through the land market. Currently a mailo owner who wishes to expand his farm operation

on his tenant's land must either induce the tenant to sell the *kibanja* voluntarily or must attempt to evict the tenant and go through the difficult process of determining compensation, and face the social pressures that will arise from his attempt at eviction. Very few evictions have occurred in the mailo areas as a result. If tenants were given ownership the mailo owners would simply buy out the tenant, just as individual mailo owners requiring more land to farm for many years have bought out tenants. (Likewise, the progressive tenants have been buying out the mailo owner's interests in their *bibanja* for many years, a practice that would continue under this alternative.)

6. Some mailo owners may argue that converting mailo tenancy to freehold or leasehold and confirming tenants in their occupation will deprive them of property and compensation must be provided.

   The compensation issue is complex, both from a legal perspective and simply in determining what is a fair policy to pursue. Resolving the issue involves deciding: (1) what compensation is required by constitution law or concepts of fairness; (2) if compensation is to be provided, who should pay and how should it be done.

What compensation is required?

As a matter of national policy it is extremely important that individual rights in property be recognised and respected by government. Property is the basis for protection of individual freedom, so careful attention to the protection of individual rights in property is an important duty of government. The protection of individual rights in property is so fundamental to the integrity of the state that property rights should not be neglected for the momentary convenience of policy, even those policies such as land tenure law that facilitate economic development.

Two fundamental issues arise in considering the compensation that might be required: (1) what property is taken by converting mailo tenancy land to tenant freehold or leasehold ownership? (2) What are the constitutional limits on taking of property and compensation?

The value of the mailo owner's interest in mailo land occupied by tenants is difficult to determine. On the one hand, some mailo tenants are buying out the owner's interests, often at considerable expense. This implies an economic value of the owner's interests. On the other hand, most owners receive no economic return from mailo land occupied by tenants, especially since 1975 when most tenants stopped paying any *envujjo* or *busuulu*. The owner has no rights of occupancy, except as provided under the Land Reform Decree, but most people incorrectly believe that the Decree deprived mailo owners of their rights in land occupied by tenants. The mailo owners lost much of the value of their lands under the 1927 *Envujjo and Busuulu* Laws which restricted eviction and set fixed rents that became almost worthless with inflation. Thus, it is possible to argue that the mailo owners have very little value in their land, other than the value of the prestige that might come from being a landowner.

The constitutional questions are also complex. The first question is whether there is a public purpose in the conversion of mailo tenancy to freehold or leasehold and confirmation of the tenants' occupation of the land. Clearly there is a public purpose served in the rationalization of tenure systems and breaking the deadlock between owners and tenants to stimulate economic development.

The second constitutional question is what property has been taken. Government has not physically occupied the land. The occupation of the land does not change. Future rights to the use of the land do not change. The income of the mailo owner is not affected. The owner may feel his prestige has declined, but is one's perception of prestige deemed property subject to compensation? Thus, it could be argued that nothing changes but the words used to describe the rights of the tenant in the land. If any property has been taken, the taking occurred in either 1975 or in 1927. On the other hand, the fact remains that some tenants are buying out the mailo owner's interest in their *bibanja*. But does the owner have rights in that *bibanja* that require compensation, or are the tenants buying their way out of the threat of eviction that arises out of the 1975 Land Reform Decree?

These legal and constitutional questions could ultimately be resolved through the legal process. But the decision of the political system about what is fair compensation may be as important as the decision of the legal system about what compensation is required.

Who should provide compensation?

If compensation is required, it should be paid from several sources.

(a) Tenants pay part of all of the compensation. This alternative would be difficult to implement but it is reasonable to expect those who benefit from a program to pay at least a part of the cost. Tenants could be required to pay a certain percentage of whatever compensation is paid to the landowner. Government or international donor agencies could provide a loan scheme so those tenants could compensate owners at once and repay their loan over several years. Negotiating compensation amounts must involve a check by government or an independent authority. Otherwise tenants and owners are given an incentive to collude to produce a high payment from the non-local authority. Tenants must be offered an incentive to apply for these loans if freehold or leasehold status is automatically granted to all mailo land; otherwise tenants have no reason to apply because all of the gain would accrue to the landowner.

(b) International donors pay part or all of the compensation. International donor organisations have provided part of the funds needed to compensate freehold landowners displaced by land redistribution programs in a few other countries. Donor agencies might be approached for funds to finance a compensation program for mailo owners.

(c) Government pays part of all of the compensation. This payment from government could be in cash, in kind or in the form of bonds maturing at some future date. A government role in paying compensation would require a government role in determining the value of the mailo owner's interests that are changed by the confirmation of the occupation of tenants on mailo land.

How to provide compensation?

There are several different ways to provide compensation to landowners. Some are quite simple, such as direct cash payment, while others are much more complex and would require careful consideration.

(a) Provide compensation in cash. This is the simplest option. Cash payments could be spread over several years. Owners would be given lump-sum payments and the funds available for private investment in the economy would increase.

(b) Compensation through provision of agricultural credit. The government could provide credit in kind in the form of implements, planting material, or other agricultural inputs. This option would directly relate compensation payments to agricultural productivity but would require a different scheme for compensation of mailo owners who do not farm any of their land or where land is fully occupied by tenants. A slightly different alternative would be to provide credit tied to investment in any productive activity, including non-agricultural enterprises.

(c) Compensation in bonds redeemable at some future date, carrying coupons for annual interest. This option would reduce the annual payment required from government and would allow the compensation to be amortised over time. Owners who wish immediate compensation could sell the bonds on the private market. This alternative is feasible only if government strictly honours the payment schedule stipulated in the bond. Otherwise the value of the compensation is greatly reduced or eliminated.

(d) Compensation in stocks in enterprises. Mailo owners could be given ownership shares in economic enterprises. These enterprises could be government-owned such as a utility or a basic industry, or could be new industrial or commercial enterprises financed by government or financed by international donor agencies. Mailo owners would have a strong incentive to insure that these enterprises were successful because the amount of their compensation would depend on the success of the enterprise. A similar program was extremely successful in stimulating the economic development of Taiwan.

In any compensation scheme it will be necessary to certify that those applying for compensation be the actual owners of the land. If government were to assume this burden it might involve very great expense. An alternative is to provide compensation only to owners whose parcels have up-to-date registration. This would update the mailo registry for many parcels and registration fees could be set at a level to ensure that all costs of the registration process, including the costs of staff salaries and new equipment, are recovered from those who have benefited from the registration system in the past and are about to receive compensation for loss of future rights in the property.

Option 2. Purchase of mailo owners' rights on a voluntary basis

The rights of mailo owners would be purchased only if the tenants requested such a purchase and the mailo owner agreed to the purchase. A mechanism would be established for valuing the rights of the owner that are relinquished in the buy-out program. A strong role of government will be required if there are any public funds used. The compensation could be provided in the same manner as discussed under Option 1.

Implications of Option 2

1. Most of the consequences of option 1 also apply to the alternative, for those lands where owners and tenants choose to convert to freehold or leasehold: increased security for current mailo tenants, resolution of owner/tenant deadlock, stimulation of investment, and facilitation of the land market. For those lands where owners and tenants decide not to convert these benefits of conversion would not occur.
2. If government decides that compensation is required, then providing compensation under a voluntary conversion program would be less costly than providing compensation under a program that affects all mailo land. Under the voluntary system only a few tenants and owners would request conversion in any given year, thereby reducing the cost of any compensation that might be provided in any given year. If payments are provided over time, and if eventually most mailo owners and tenants apply for conversion the costs of compensation would be about equal under the two options.
3. Not all tenants and owners would apply for conversion to freehold or leasehold for the land occupied by the tenants. Therefore, the legal status of the mailo land and mailo tenancy must be defined in the new land tenure law. Government must tolerate a dual system of land tenure for those mailo lands occupied by tenants – some land would be converted to freehold or leasehold while other land would remain in some undefined legal status that should be clarified in any new land tenure law.

   The evolution of land tenure and practice to a single system for the country would be delayed. If, after several decades, most owners and tenants have chosen to convert to freehold or leasehold, the remaining land might be converted without the agreement of all concerned.

Question 5: What should be the status of customary tenure?

If tenure is converted to either freehold or leasehold, what should be the status of tenure rules that continue to exist and be enforced under customary indigenous law in parts of the country?

Option 1: Convert all customary tenure to either freehold or leasehold immediately.

Implications

1. The same laws would cover all land in the nation immediately.
2. The process of evolution of tenure systems toward more individual rights in land would be speeded. Many owners in some areas under population pressure, such as Mbale, are already applying for leases on public land to protect their individual rights. Immediate conversion would enhance the tenure security of individuals in areas where tenure is rapidly evolving.

Option 2: Allow indigenous customary tenure to continue to operate, but allow individuals to apply for freehold or leasehold on their property, or require conversion if parcel of land is sold to a new buyer.

Implications

1. Traditional indigenous customary tenure law works very well in many parts of the nation. Since the system of customary law is functioning well there is no reason to spend government resources and risk creating additional problems by forcing conversion of land tenure to leasehold or freehold in these areas.
2. Individuals in areas where customary law works well would not be subjected to a new land tenure system that would prematurely convert customary tenure to a more individualised system.
3. Allowing customary tenure to continue to operate would avoid the disturbances to the local agricultural economy that would occur with a premature conversion of tenure to freehold or leasehold.
4. Government would avoid the costs of registering a large number of freeholds or leasehold titles in areas of the country where customary tenure provides individuals with all tenure security they feel is needed.

Question 6: Should development conditions apply to freehold or leasehold?

If a goal of land tenure policy is to stimulate or facilitate economic development, a logical question is whether conditions should be tied to freehold or leasehold ownership of land, to permit government to impose conditions on land ownership that would encourage economic development. There are advantages and disadvantages to this policy alternative.

Option 1. Apply development conditions to all grants of freehold or leasehold land

Implications of Option 1

1. To the extent that government can develop reasonable leasehold conditions and administer them effectively, the government may maintain some influence over land use decisions of individuals.
2. If government were able to develop reasonable lease conditions, the threat of government re-possession of the land might be sufficient to motivate some landowners to use the property. Lease conditions that are not realistic and practical will not likely influence behaviour. A realistic lease or freehold condition might be simply that the land be used for some agricultural purpose, including grazing. Land unused for some specified period of time, say five consecutive years, might be subject to revocation of title and reallocation as freehold or leasehold to some other individual.
3. Development conditions requiring use of land held in freehold or leasehold is consistent with traditional concepts of access to as much land as can be cultivated, but not more land than can reasonably be used by the landholding unit. A simple lease condition that the land

be used for agricultural or some other productive purpose would be consistent with traditional concepts of land tenure.

4. Reasonable, practical and effective development conditions will be difficult to identify.

   Using land in its highest and best economic use will stimulate the economic development of agriculture and the nation. But the best use of land is difficult to identify on a national, district, county, sub-county or even village level.

   The best use of land depends first on its physical characteristics. Yet physical characteristics can vary greatly even over a distance of a few metres. Soil structure, soil moisture levels, slope, drainage, and other characteristics typically vary even within a single parcel, and may vary greatly. ... Second, the best economic use of land also depends on prices of agricultural products, costs of production under local conditions, and the alternative enterprises available to the farmer. The local marketing conditions also influence profitability. Identifying the most profitable agricultural activity is not possible at any level above the village or perhaps the sub-county. When combined with the fact that the most profitable use also depends on the physical characteristics of the parcel, identifying the best use of land is possible only at the parcel level.

   Therefore, development conditions such as those specifying that a certain crop be produced will be inappropriate when applied to specific parcels. On the other hand, very general development conditions, such as use of the land for agriculture, are so general as to have very little usefulness in stimulating economic activity.

5. Government will incur high administrative costs in an attempt to identify appropriate development conditions, change development conditions as the economy changes or new technology makes possible new uses of land, monitor the use of land to ensure that development conditions are met, and enforce the development conditions when they are ignored by landowners.

   Identifying appropriate development will involve much manpower in the attempt to identify the physical characteristics of parcels and the most profitable economic activities.

   The most economic use of land will change as technology and market conditions change, so any development conditions must be periodically revised in order to remain realistic and practical.

   High administrative costs will be involved in monitoring parcels to ensure that development conditions are met. Development conditions are meaningless if there is no mechanism to enforce the conditions in cases when landowners do not comply. If there is no monitoring then any landowner activity is voluntary and the conditions have no effect on behaviour.

   Development conditions must be enforced or will become meaningless. Enforcement will bring administrative costs of bringing court actions and taking possession of land after court judgements.

6. Development conditions are not likely to be effective in influencing land use in Uganda.

   If agriculture is profitable, Ugandan farmers have responded to new economic opportunity. If agriculture is not profitable, government will not be able to force farmers to produce products that involve more cost than benefit for farmers. If activity is profitable, farmers will do it; if an activity is not profitable for farmers, government will not be able to force people to do it. The evidence from Luwero and Masaka suggests that development conditions would have little effect on agriculture activity.

In Luwero some agricultural land is not used. Some parcels, particularly larger parcels, are owned by individuals who want to develop but claim they lack access to credit. For example, specific owners who wanted to begin dairy operations were stymied by their inability to receive consideration for loan applications. Owners of smaller parcels in Luwero who are not using all of their land lack labour that is required to begin cultivation. Lease conditions requiring development will not induce either large or small holders to begin production because in fact they already wish to use the land but are constrained by lack of labour or capital.

In Masaka there is very little land that is not used. What land is unused is often on steep slopes best suited for grazing or on less productive parcels. Lease conditions are not likely to have any effect because it is not profitable to develop most of these parcels at current levels of prices and yields.

7. From the experience of the Land Tenure Centre, other African countries have had negative experiences with development conditions in leases.

   Several countries include conditions in leases. In Somalia, leases on irrigated land include conditions that the land must be used for agriculture. Lease conditions restrict the number of parcels an individual may hold and restrict the individual's right to sell, rent or subdivide the parcel. These conditions are widely ignored. In Zambia, leasehold conditions stipulate that transfer of leases must be based only on the value of improvements, not on the value of the land. Thus, land has little cost to the leaseholder and some argue that this has produced an inefficient pattern of extensive use of land compared to other inputs. In Sudan, lease conditions on rained mechanized farming schemes have not been enforced, which has led to encroachment of tractor farming into pastoral areas and increased soil erosion. In irrigation schemes in Sudan, leasehold conditions that control production decisions of farmers are blamed for decreases in yields. In Nigeria, lease conditions on irrigation schemes are not well defined and, in the combination with corruption and favouritism have caused many small farmers to avoid taking leases on land. In Zaire, cash crops can be grown only on land under some type of concession from government. Lease conditions specify the mix of crops to be grown on the land. Small farmers are then restricted in what they can plant and are exposed to exactions from police and party officials charged with enforcing the lease conditions. The lease conditions pose a serious disincentive to the production of cash crops.

8. Other policy alternatives are more effective in ensuring productive use of agricultural land.

   The most effective way to ensure productive use of land is to make agriculture profitable to the farmer. Experience in Uganda shows that farmers respond to economic incentives and profitable activities.

   Second, farmers can be induced to use land by making it very expensive not to use the land. The most important way to increase the cost of non-use is to make agriculture profitable. In addition, a tax on land serves as an incentive to use the land, because the tax must be paid regardless of use, and therefore increases the cost to the farmer of leaving land idle. A land tax could even be graduated, with a higher tax applying to unused land than land that is cultivated or grazed.

Option 2: Use development conditions only on specific development projects and only impose very general conditions.

Implications of Option 2

1. In government-sponsored projects, government officials will likely know a great deal about the specific physical conditions on each parcel. In addition, analysis of the economics of production is presumably a part of the decision to undertake the project, so government is assured that some type of production on the land is profitable. Thus, government can develop lease conditions, especially very general conditions with less chance of imposing unrealistic or counter-productive conditions than attempting to impose conditions widely.
2. Government investment in a project creates value in the land, so individuals who receive the benefit of that value should agree to lease conditions that are realistic and allow profitable use of the land.
3. Lease conditions on specific development projects would be easier and less expensive to monitor and enforce than lease conditions imposed broadly on all agricultural land.

4. Ugandan experience with development conditions in leases has been negative. Development conditions have not been effective in stimulating development of leasehold ranches in the grassland areas, although part of the failure is undoubtedly due to the unsettled conditions in the area in the past. Also, it is possible that lease conditions may yet prove effective in evicting leaseholders who have not developed their parcels. In general ranches were not developed because of looting, disease resurgence and lack of development funds. Lease conditions requiring development were meaningless in this situation. However, it is possible that, given profitable opportunities in livestock sector, most leaseholders would develop their ranches and lease conditions can be used to evict those who acquired the land through improper procedures and who hold only for speculation.

Question 7: Should a land tax be adopted?

In many countries a tax on land, or on land and improvements, is a major source of government revenue. In Uganda, a land tax would have both advantages and disadvantages, some depending on what type of tax might be adopted and how the tax is administered. Several basic questions must be answered in establishing a land tax. There are alternative answers for each question.

Tax Base: First, what will be the tax base? Will the tax apply to all land, or only certain types of land such as land used for agriculture? For purposes of discussion, assume that the tax is a tax on agricultural land. Application of the tax to other types of land should be considered by government, but the options and their effects on non-agricultural land are not appropriate to analyse in detail in this report. If the tax applies to agricultural land only, it is an incentive to invest in sectors other than agriculture. However, the magnitude of this incentive is likely to be very slight, assuming that the tax is in the range of one percent of the value of the land, a typical rate in many developed countries. Application of the tax to grazing land would involve special problems where grazing land is held in common by the community. As a result, grazing land could be subject to the tax only when the land is registered in the name of an individual or organisation such as a farmers' grazing association. The most administratively simple alternative is to limit the tax to land under cultivation, although this would provide a slight incentive to keep land in grazing use rather than cultivation.

The tax could also be based on district local improvements on the land. For example, a house might be included in the tax base, or certain improvements such as a well, tree crops or fences. This alternative would be difficult to administer, except for improvements such as a house, because determining the extent of value of the improvements would be very difficult. The tax should not be levied on improvements that are easy to conceal because the result might be a tax on those honest enough to reveal the existence of the improvement. Taxing improvements would create a disincentive to invest in agriculture and would be counter to the goal of using the land tenure system and related policies as an instrument of economic development.

A related question is whether to apply the tax to all land, or exempt land held by certain types of individuals or organisations. For example, many countries exempt government organisations or religious bodies from the tax on property. Such exemptions are usually employed to encourage activities deemed "worthy" by government. Providing a tax exemption will indeed provide an incentive for these activities but will also shrink the tax base and open government to appeals from many groups or individuals who consider their causes equally worthy of tax exemption.

Tax Rate: Second, how will land be taxed? Most countries that tax real property do so on the basis of the property's value, usually the value as reflected in market exchanges. This requires the tax administration system to place a value on each property, in theory each year in which a tax is levied. To reduce the administrative costs of a tax, in the early years a flat tax per acre might be imposed.

Alternatively, land might be classified into two or three categories depending on its suitability for agricultural production, location and other factors and the per acre tax rate might vary according to the quality of the land. This level of land valuation could be carried out by anyone with a good knowledge of the agriculture in an area. For example, land could be classified as above average, average, or below average in quality. As the tax administration authorities gain experience with the valuation system, more complexity could be gradually added to the system so that the tax would evolve into one based on valuation determined by a sophisticated valuation process.

Tax Collection and use: Third, what level of government will collect the tax and what level of government will use the revenue? Two basic alternatives can be considered:

(a) Tax collected by central government and used by central government.

(b) Tax collected by local administration of (RC 3) and used at the sub-county level.

Variations might involve the district local administrations (RC 5) in either the collection or spending of the tax revenue.

Alternatively, tax could be collected by one level of government and used by another. The two basic alternatives represent extreme positions on the continuum and will be discussed in detail. Combinations or use of the district level of government will entail a combination of the effects noted for the polar extremes.

Central government administration of a land tax would ensure more uniform administration than if hundreds of local officials are involved. The effect of the tax on economic development depends in part on how the tax is used. For example, the tax might be used to replace revenue generated by the tax on coffee, thereby raising the price received by the farmer, providing a powerful incentive for increased production and increasing income in rural areas. Alternatively, the tax could be used for public infrastructure and numerous other important projects. The magnitude of the tax revenue available depends totally on the tax rate that is applied and what land is included in the tax base. A centrally administered and expended tax might generate more opposition than a tax that is raised and spent on a district or sub-county basis.

Sub-county administration of a land tax would mean less uniform administration nationwide. Yet local administration would be less expensive than a centrally administered tax. Also, local tax collection would result in more revenue generated per unit of time spent in collection because informal social pressure will operate at the local level and local administrators will more easily contact landowners that owe their tax. Local administration would also allow government to consider the option of basing the tax on a simplified system of estimating land productivity classes for agricultural land.

Public resistance to a land tax might be minimized if the tax were to be collected locally and used locally to support some public service, such as schools, that virtually all local people consider important. The sub-county Chiefs and Resistance committees could gain valuable experience in operating essential public services and could be guided by central government institutions such as the Ministry of Education in the early years of increased local funding of schools. Funds for education from the central government could remain at current levels or could be gradually reduced over time. However, if decreases in central government support exactly offset revenue collected from the land tax, any local support for the tax might evaporate quickly.

It is clear that the effects of a tax on land will depend on what type of tax is adopted and how the tax is adopted and how the tax is administered and used. However, it is possible to make several generalisations about the effects of a land tax:

1. The land tax offers a potentially large source of government revenue. The magnitude of the revenue depends on the level of the tax but even a very low tax will generate much revenue when applied to the entire land area of the country.
2. The land tax may provide a strong incentive for landowners to use their land. The tax must be paid regardless of land use, so the owner has an incentive to use the land. Further, the tax does not increase as more productive use is made of the land, so the tax does not provide a disincentive to increasing agricultural productivity.
3. The tax on land approximates a tax on wealth in the rural areas, since larger landowners tend to be wealthier than small holders. However, the land tax is a tax only on wealth held in the form of land, not wealth represented by ownership of cattle, automobiles or non- farm businesses.

4. The tax may be difficult to administer unless local authorities, e.g. sub-county leaders, are closely involved in its administration. However, the more localised the administration the less uniform the administration nationwide.
5. The tax may be difficult for rural people to accept. However, if the tax is administered locally and funds are used locally for programs most local people want, such as schools, popular support might be significant.
6. Local administration of the tax and expenditure of revenue for a much-desired local service will build the capacity of local government and local people to administer their own public affairs and provide needed public services locally.

Arguments against the land tax may be as follows:

1. A land tax will increase the tax burden on the agricultural sector of the economy relative to other sectors and may therefore provide a disincentive to invest in agriculture. Thus leading to a de-capitalisation of the agricultural sector and actual retardation of agricultural development. Already the farmer is being taxed directly on the farm through graduated tax and indirectly through the relatively lower prices of cash crops like coffee, cotton, tea and tobacco.
2. The land tax will not take account of the differences among individuals in the ability to pay the tax out of current income, except to the extent that current income is correlated with the amount of the land owned. There is therefore the broad issue of social equity which must be articulated before any tax is contemplated. The poor holders will most likely pay a higher proportion of their income in land tax than the rich ones.
3. Does the farmer get just return for his labour? Is the farmer reasonably rewarded for his coffee, cotton, maize, and tobacco? They already pay an indirect tax on these.
4. What is the rate of return to the rural population in terms of goods and services delivered to them by government? Do the rural people have access to good roads, reasonably priced education and medical care etc? Would it be fair to impose a land tax on top of existing taxes before any of these services reach the rural poor? Even if one were to have the land tax collected and used at lower levels of administration, one cannot be certain that the principal beneficiaries will not be local bureaucrats.
5. One cannot seriously commit oneself to a land tax without some insight into the general structure of the entire tax system. One needs to have a general tax profile of the country. How does the tax structure affect non-farm activity? What strata of the population are taxed more than others? What alternative taxable items, other than land, could be tapped on to broaden the tax base? What would generally be the long-term agricultural effect of a land tax?
6. The abstraction of land as a taxable item from the overall profile of taxable items is misleading as it leads to misplaced concreteness. Thus a policy-oriented study into the general structure of the entire tax system is necessary before a final decision on a land tax is made.

Question 8: Should the land registry be rehabilitated?

The relevant issue is not whether to rehabilitate the land registry, but how the registry should be rehabilitated. The register must be rehabilitated if the Land Reform Decree is implemented, if the pre-1975 mailo tenure is re-instituted, and if either freehold or leasehold ownership of land is adopted as the basic form of land tenure. The policy issue is how to rehabilitate the registry system. The two options are a rapid or a gradual rehabilitation.

Option 1. Rapid rehabilitation of the mailo land registry and introduction of detailed land registries for other areas of the country

Implications of Option 1

1. Rapid rehabilitation will be extremely costly. The land registry is in very poor condition and the land offices are understaffed, under-equipped, staff are underpaid and demoralised. The registry records are in such disrepair that it is difficult to estimate the cost of rehabilitation because the extent of damage and inaccurate records cannot be estimated. It is clear, however, that the expense involved will be quite large.

2. The registry would be brought up-to date relatively quickly, compared to a more gradual approach.

Implications of Option 2

1. Registering only land sales will provide almost the same level of benefit as a complete rehabilitation, at a small fraction of the cost.

   First, relatively few parcels change hands each year through sales. If a parcel does not transfer during the year, an up-to-date land record has no use and therefore is of little value.

   Second, many transfers of land take place through succession, where sons, daughters and relatives inherit the land of a deceased person. The rules for succession are well established in customary law and practice and disputes are usually handled through the family so that there is little use for a land register in determining who has rights in the land. Registering successions is important in keeping an up-to-date registry but is not generally critical in providing security of tenure or resolving disputes.

   Third, land transactions are important to register because they are most likely to result in disputes, the new owner is most in need of registration to provide security of tenure, and the land market is critical in enabling progressive farmers to obtain land which in turn is a key step in the process of agricultural development.
2. Over a long period of time most parcels will be registered. At some future date any remaining unregistered parcels can be added to the registry to provide a complete registry for all land in the country.
3. The gradual registration process could be applied uniformly throughout the country.

   In former mailo areas the boundaries of many parcels are already established. In areas of customary tenure on public land, the boundaries of parcels involved in land sales would be established by the elders of the community and certified by a government authority. The parcel could then be surveyed and added to the official registry.
4. This gradual process of registering only parcels involved in sales and parcels of owners voluntarily requesting registration will mean that the country will not have a complete and up-to-date land registry system for many years into the future.

DECENTRALISATION OF REGISTRATION

Regardless of the option chosen, government should consider a process of decentralizing the registration process. The survey of the district land offices clearly suggested benefits to both landowners and government from a more decentralized system. If more of the registration processes were carried out at the district level, local knowledge of land ownership rights could be drawn upon and perhaps the high costs of surveys could be avoided in ascertaining boundaries of holdings and ownership. The elders' resistance council officials and chiefs could certify that ownership and boundaries are clearly and permanently marked and records professionally kept at county level for local uses with a copy to the district land offices.

In considering decentralisation reference is made to the operations of the land Adjudication Committees during the Pilot Land Registration Schemes in the then districts of Kigezi, Ankole and Bugisu (Uganda Government 1955) MISR/LTC (1988).

The colonial government in Uganda issued Land Tenure Proposals (Uganda Government, 1955) in which it accepted the recommendations of the East African Royal Commission 1955 to the effect that thenceforth land tenure be based on individualised freehold titles.

The Land Tenure Proposals 1955 provided that the adjudication of land rights prior to registration of titles would be provided on district basis and in accordance with existing customary tenure. To this end, government issued the Crown Land (Adjudication) Rules 1958. These later came to be known as the Public Lands Adjudication Rules. In general these rules were used to grant freehold titles to Ugandan Africans who had been holding land outside Buganda under customary tenure. These rules initiated what later came to be known as Pilot Schemes in the then districts of Ankole, Bugisu, and Kigezi.

The rules gave the Minister power to apply them to a district which he would designate as an Adjudication District. The rules provided for the setting up of Land Adjudication Committees.

An Adjudication Committee was to consist of 10-20 tax payers chosen by a meeting of all the adult members of a parish. The parish chief was the Chairman of the Adjudication Committee. Once the Rules were applied to a district, any occupier of land under customary tenure who wished to be registered as the owner/proprietor of a freehold estate in respect of the same became eligible to apply so that he might be adjudged owner of the land under customary tenure. A customary owner completed two forms and paid a deposit of shs. 110/= (then about US $ 18) if the application involved open land, or of shs. 137/= (then about US $ 23) if the land to be adjudicated was bushy. The completed application forms would then be returned to the District Land Office. The District Commissioner (who was also the Chairman of the District Land Committees) had to satisfy himself that there were enough applications to warrant a survey. He would then declare the relevant parish to be an Adjudication area. The declaration by the District Commissioner of an Adjudication area was a condition precedent for the formation of the Adjudication committees. The District Commissioner now in his capacity as Chairman of the District Land Committee, would issue a public notice naming the applicants and indicating that their applications would be considered by the Adjudication Committee after the expiration of 30 days from the date of the notice. The sub-county chief got involved in the process by being entitled to receive 25 copies of the notice issued by the District Commissioner displaying one on his notice board and sending the rest to the members of the Adjudication Committee. After the statutory 30 days, the Adjudication Committee would then hear the application of the occupier in public. The committee would then hear the objections, if any, to the occupier's application. If the committee concluded that the applicant/occupier was the true owner, the committee physically went to the land with a surveyor who marked out the applicant/occupier's boundaries with concrete marks. After this, the committee then reported its conclusions to the chairman of the District Land Committee through the District Land Office where the conclusions were first cross-checked. The decisions of the Adjudication Committee was appealable to a Magistrate Grade II within 30 days. Where no appeal to the Magistrate Grade II or further appeal to the High Court was lodged, the surveyor went back and carried out a proper survey according to plan. All survey plans had to be submitted to the Land Office in Entebbe for approval. A final notice was issued declaring the applicant/occupier as the owner by native custom. After all this, the applicant/occupier was entitled to be registered as the proprietor of an estate in freehold. The applicant/occupier also became entitled to be issued with a certificate of title on payment of the prescribed fee.

The first attempt to implement the Land Tenure Proposals 1955 was the system of land adjudication and registration introduced in Rujumbira, Kigezi, Western Uganda, in the late 1950s pursuant to the Crown Lands (Adjudication) Rules 1958. This system came to be known as the Pilot Registration Scheme.

The government sought to have the adjudication and registration exercise to be voluntary and not an imposition upon the people. Though the system was not without weakness, a similar improved procedure could be adopted.

Arising from this experience the following steps could be taken to decentralise the registration procedure.

1. Adjudication committees could be formed at the parish level consisting of some LC officials, chiefs and supported by the technical staff from Sub-county level particularly Assistant

Husbandry Officers, Assistant Agricultural Officers, Assistant Co-operative Officers etc and supervised by LC III officials. The functions of these committees will include the establishment of boundaries and ascertainment of ownership of the various parcels. They will also be responsible for the assessment of the land tax according to a given formula.

With the help of the committees, a surveyor will mark out the boundaries and a rough estimate of the area. The committee will then report its conclusions to the county level through their sub-county authorities.

Using parish level adjudication committees will mean that the district land committees (LDC) will not need to visit the parcels in order to ascertain ownership and boundaries. The office of the District Executive Secretary will remain with overall supervisory powers over the Land Adjudication Committees and records will be kept at county level with copies at the district.

2. The field offices of the lands and surveys should be expanded to allow for some technical supervision of land records at the county level. This will mean (to begin with) making a Surveyor or an Assistant Land Officer responsible for a county just like many ministries with field offices e.g. Agriculture, Animal Resources, Co-operatives, etc. Consideration could later be given to posting a staff surveyor or land officer at this level, as the staffing position in the ministry improves.

   As mentioned above, these officers will assist the Parish Adjudication Committees in the county in ascertaining boundaries and issuing county level record certificates.
3. Two types of certificates should be issued namely, the Record certificate at county level and Registration Title at national level. The staff at county level will forward the conclusion of the committee. Also the county level record certificate shall be surrendered before obtaining the national title. It is, however, hoped that even credit institutions will eventually accept the county record certificate as a collateral for small to medium development loans.
4. For those with mailo, freehold or leasehold titles adjudication will not be necessary except where there is a transfer - purchase or inheritance.
5. In the long run, the surveying should be privatised so that after obtaining a county level certificate, it will be up to the holder to get a surveyor for the parcel. It is envisaged that it will be in the interest of these private surveyors to see to it that their clients obtain the titles. This could be similar to the architects who after designing and drawing a plan for a building follow through and obtain its approval. One of the reasons for the many steps in obtaining a title is because one needs to apply to the Uganda Land Commission for the land. With the proposal of converting adjudicated parcels to freeholds, the services of the Uganda Land Commission and its subsidiaries may be gradually phased out.

Recommendations

The study clearly recognizes that any policy choice has both advantages and disadvantages. This is the reason for providing a discussion of alternatives and implications so that each person can make his own judgement of which alternatives are best, based on the weight of the evidence. However, the study team has had the benefit of many weeks of study, conversation with local and national leaders, conversations with public officials in land administration, and extensive conversations and surveys of farmers who use the land. As a result of these experiences the team has developed some notions of the best policy for the nation, and those ideas will be shared in this section.

Change in the land tenure system in Uganda should be based on several goals:

1. A land tenure system should support agricultural development. This is best accomplished by ensuring that the land tenure system is flexible enough to enable progressive farmers to gain access to land. In particular, in many parts of Uganda this means that land tenure policy should support the development and smooth functioning of a land market.

2. A land tenure system should not force people off the land, particularly those who have no other way to earn a reasonable living or to survive. This means that the land tenure system should protect people's rights in land, so that they are not forced off the land before there are jobs available in the non-agricultural sector of the economy.
3. A land tenure system should provide for a uniform system of laws throughout the country. This uniformity need not be imposed immediately, but land tenure law should assist the evolution of land tenure systems toward uniformity nationwide.

The most appropriate form for land tenure in Uganda involves a series of changes that will encourage the evolution of land tenure practice toward a system that meets all of the goals stated above. The specific recommendations are:

1. The Land Reform Decree of 1975 should be repealed.
   The law violates goal number three in this report which states that a land tenure system should protect people from eviction if there are no other income-earning alternatives available in the non-farm sector of the economy. The Decree also hinders agricultural development because it interferes with the land market that allows progressive farmers access to land.
2. All mailo land should be converted to freehold. Mailo tenants would become freehold owners of their land. Mailo owners would have freehold title to the mailo land they own that is not occupied by tenants.
   The reality in mailo areas is that tenants have had virtual freehold for many years. Mailo owners have had effective freehold on their parcels for many years. It is necessary to break the deadlock that existed prior to 1975 between mailo owners and tenants. Freehold is preferable to leasehold because it interferes less with private property rights and involves much less cost to government.
3. Mailo owners should receive compensation for the interest in land that they lose from conversion of tenancy land to freehold. This compensation should be provided over a period of years and tenants should share in part the cost.
   The mailo owner should be compensated for the loss of his interest in land. Compensation can be provided partly by the tenant, partly by government perhaps financed partially by international donor agencies. Government should sponsor a study to determine the value of the mailo owner's interest in mailo land occupied by tenants.
4. Tenants on customary tenure on public land should apply for freehold titles upon certification of their rights in land by community leaders and technically supervised.
5. Existing leases on public land should be converted to freehold automatically, except that leases on government-sponsored schemes such as ranches and other leases of over 500 acres should be reviewed on a case-by-case basis. In accordance with the Public Lands Act, 1969, a lease of 500 hundred acres and above requires the minister's consent. Conversion to freehold should not be allowed for those properties acquired illegally.
6. No development conditions should be imposed on any freehold, except for land on government-sponsored development schemes.
   Development conditions have not been effective in causing development of property in several African countries. If an activity is profitable farmers will undertake it; if the activity is not profitable it is impossible for government to force farmers to undertake it.
7. A land tax could be adopted as an alternative to development conditions appropriate to leasehold. If adopted the tax should be administered at the sub-county level and the revenue should be used at that level for programs, such as schools, that are desired by local people. The tax should be based on the productive capacity of the land, with different levels of tax for good, average and poor land. The tax on unused land should be double that on land that is used. A guideline of a tax structure similar to that of the graduated tax should be worked out and forwarded to the local administrations to familiarise themselves before it is administered. A tax on land will provide an incentive to use land by making it expensive to leave land idle.

The tax could also provide a source of revenue for the sub-county authorities and will relieve some fiscal pressure on the national treasury.

8. The land registry should be updated gradually by registering all transfers of land and other parcels at the application of the owner. A feasibility study on the computerisation of the land registry system should be undertaken. Meanwhile an internal gradual process of up-dating the data to be entered into the computer should be intensified. The land registry system should be decentralized and a simpler and clearly understandable registration process should be adopted that reduces the costs for both landowners and government. Local Lands and Survey Offices should be empowered to carry out many of the steps independently at the district level and land adjudication committees be introduced at parish level within the RC system. A demarcation and record process by the local community, technically supervised, should be adopted as a first step towards registration. Fees should be set at realistic levels and reassessed periodically to reflect costs. Provisions of adequate facilities, sufficient supplies and equipment together with reasonable wages and allowances are necessary pre-conditions to the implementation of any project to rehabilitate and update systematically the mailo land records.

The study team is convinced that Uganda faces a unique opportunity to institute changes in its land tenure law that will provide for the evolution of land tenure practice and ensure that the land tenure system will stimulate agricultural development, protect people's rights in land and lead to a uniform system of land tenure nationwide.

Note

The Report prepared by the Makerere Institute of Social Research and the Land Tenure Centre of the University of Wisconsin (see extracts of the report above) was discussed at several forums. Below is an extract of some of that discussion.

COMMENTS ON THE REPORT

***Agricultural Policy Committee Proceedings and Recommendations of the Workshop on Land Tenure Resources Management and Conservation Studies* Jinja, 18-19 May 1989, prepared by the Ministry of Planning and Economic Development**

(The comments of the discussants were summarised by the workshop rapporteur).

1. *Mr Okello-Okello, the Acting Commissioner for Lands and Surveys*, ... made the following observations:

The title of the study is "Land Tenure and Agricultural Development in Uganda." In his view the study should have attempted to analyse the historical and field data to investigate the relationship between land tenure systems and agricultural production in Uganda, but the report did not contain any statistical analysis of this relationship. The study also did not answer questions such as: Whether agricultural production is affected by land tenure? Is the present decline in agricultural production or productivity due to present land tenure systems: in other words, whether the present land tenure systems constrain increases in agricultural production? Mr Okello-Okello argued that comprehensive statistical data should have been collected and analysed to determine the functional relationship between land tenure and agricultural production in Uganda.

The study aims at providing free and easy access to land to the progressive farmers. Who this privileged progressive farmer is has not been defined in the study. If a progressive farmer is one who is already successfully farming on land then why should he require free access to land? Mr Okello-Okello asked, if he is a beginner, how is he a progressive farmer? By providing free access to land, are we not opening opportunities in the land market for potential land grabbers and speculators? Examining in detail the provisions of the 1975 Land Reform Decree, Mr Okello-

Okello pointed out that the main intention of the Decree was … to make land available to the majority of Ugandans, by converting all lands to leaseholds, on payment of ground rent and fulfilment of minimal development conditions. The ground rent and development conditions were instruments used to stop speculators to acquire land, make it expensive to hold large tracts of unused land and redistribute land equitably to the users. Because the Land Reform Decree was not implemented, to condemn it outright was not justified; rather it was unfair. Conditions that prevailed during the last 15 years made it virtually impossible to implement the Decree just as many other programmes suffered.

The study team did not make a strong case for repeal of the 1975 Land Reform Decree and for recommending the freehold option in place of the leasehold option. Mr Okello-Okello pointed out that the leasehold option as reflected in the 1975 Land Reform Decree had the following merits, which were ignored completely and deliberately by the study team.

(a) Land is the free gift of God and a vital natural resource for the country. Government has responsibility to plan its use for present development and conserve it for posterity.

(b) The 1975 Land Reform Decree effectively removed the negative effects of concentration of land in the hands of absentee landowners.

As against this, the freehold option recommended by the study team would pose the following problems.

(a) Converting customary tenants into freehold and issuing titles to farmers throughout the country would be impracticable and expensive in terms of resources, manpower and logistics.

(b) Converting mailo tenants into owners would lead to fragmentation which would result in the decline of production.

(c) Completely free access to land could lead to concentration of landholding with a few powerful rich speculators, with consequent emergence of a landless class in the countryside, which could have serious socio-political and economic implications.

The proposal to impose a land tax on all freehold land would unduly penalise small farmers who were already heavily taxed. It could in the long run discourage them from producing and encourage them to sell off their lands to the so-called progressive farmers and become landless.

At this point, the Prime Minister [Professor Nsibambi] intervened to clarify who is considered to be a progressive farmer. … He argued that unless the farmer proved himself as qualified to do commercial farming as any other professionals, he could not be regarded as a progressive farmer. It was only progressive farmers who would commercialise our agriculture. The country cannot rely on peasant farmers to become commercial farmers and develop agriculture.

2. *Comments on Land Tenure and Agricultural Development by the Discussant: Prof. J. Bibangambah, Uganda Co-operative Alliance.*

Prof. J. Bibangambah pointed out that the land tenure problem was a component of a much broader problem viz. the land policy problem. For a social scientist, the land policy problem is much more than the rules, regulations and laws that govern land ownership rights. In the case of Uganda, the land policy problem is much more than the 1975 Land Reform Decree. The existence of the Public Lands Act of 1969 was clear evidence that a land policy problem was in existence long before the introduction of the 1975 Land Reform Decree. Indeed, we ought to ask what prompted the 1975 Decree.

For the research, the land policy problem, or even at a narrower level the land tenure problem, was perceived by the consultants as a legal ownership problem as a product of law of the 1975 Land Reform Decree. To emphasise that this was how the problem was perceived, the authors of the Report stressed on page 24 of the Report that the terms of reference were translated directly into research objectives of the project and that the general objective for the research project came from the Terms of Reference No. 4 which states as follows:

> Make recommendations as to whether Government should embrace the policy of the 1975 Land Reform Decree or not and what changes are required in the land tenure policy of the 1975 Land Reform Decree considering the socio-economic development objectives.

The land tenure problem in Uganda was therefore both a development problem and a policy problem. It was a development problem because it involved trends that have emerged over time and it was a policy problem because it involved conflicts among land users or uses. The land tenure system in Uganda was also a product of cultures, customs, history as well as the law. The 1975 Land Reform Decree was not the origin of the conflicts over land. It simply compounded the problem by declaring that all land in Uganda was state owned and that no person other than the state could hold an interest in land greater than leasehold. Lawyers can therefore restrict their interest to the 1975 Land Reform Decree and its consequences but development and policy analysts go beyond the 1975 Decree both in history and in future development. Accordingly, the report rightly points out on page 25 'that an analysis of the effects of land tenure on agricultural development cannot easily proceed without some discussion of whether the process of transferring land from the generation to the next functions properly.' The problem of use and transferability or non-transferability of land existed under customary land tenure systems and mailo landlord/ tenure systems long before the 1975 Decree. What the 1975 Decree did was to transfer ownership of all land to the state leaving all the other claimants with a claim or ownership only to the developments on the land. It is true that the Decree has changed land tenure rules but it is also true that the Decree itself was prompted by a search for a better tenure system. It was therefore for us to judge whether the resultant arrangement was a better system or not.

From the perspective of land policy, the land problem in Uganda consists of the following:

(a) Competition or conflict between crops and animals and between man and wildlife for land especially in areas most suitable for agricultural production. Evidence of this conflict is the human settlements in forest reserves, game reserves and national parks in Uganda.

(b) An ever increasingly landless class of rural dwellers, not necessarily because of scarcity of land, but because of lack of enforcement of laws and rules that govern land ownership rights or lack of rules and procedures that protect the powerless especially the poor. People are easily evicted from land in spite of existence of land laws.

(c) A trend of excessive sub-divisions, and fragmentation of the land under population pressure and inheritance laws.

(d) An opposite trend of a tendency of land concentration into the hands of a few financial and political magnates resulting in a landless class of rural dwellers. In a way this may be a "second generation problem" of the 1975 Land Reform Decree as it has unfairly and unjustly favoured the rich, big and powerful who have the contacts, knowledge, power and money to exploit corruption and nepotism to secure land leases.

(e) Existence of large tracts of land, acquired through inheritance, purchase, grabbing or any other means, which are not being utilised for the good of the nation.

These issues and trends are within the framework of "the individual's rights and duties with respect to other people concerning the use and transfer of land." The first element was covered in a separate study and report on settlements in forest reserves, game reserves and national parks. The second element was covered by recommendation No. 2. The third, fourth and fifth elements were however not covered by any of the recommendations. Prof. Bibangambah enquired as to where the issue of sanctions and incentives would arise if it were not on the matter of large tracts of land that were not being utilised and had not been utilised since 1900?

The purpose of the research was to show or demonstrate or determine how land tenure could affect and had affected agricultural development in Uganda. The extent to which the study was able to determine this was limited by failure to define measurements of agricultural development. Possibly they were assumed to be obvious since the study was mainly for those who ought to know. But how about the rest of interested readers? One hoped to find in the study analysis of:

(a) Land tenure and agricultural productivity
(b) Land tenure and agricultural investments
(c) Land tenure and adoption of agricultural innovations (or technology)
(d) Land tenure and levels of management.

The study analysed only land tenure and investment in the use of modern farm inputs viz. item (c) above under "the effect of land tenure on investment and productivity in agriculture."

In Uganda, the word "progressive farmer" has become a political expression for reasons of seeking an advantage or a favoured position. It was good that the study was mindful of the need to restore scientific meaning to this description. However, even after constructing what was termed "progressively index," the study did not provide a clear or concrete definition or description of who was a "progressive farmer." A progressive farmer in the view of Prof. Bibangambah is a farmer practising "a science based agriculture." He could be distinguished from the rest whose agriculture is based on resources provided by nature.

There were other serious questions that were not the subject of this study but which ought to be a subject of study by those concerned with agricultural development policy. These were:

(a) Where were the progressive farmers located or how were they spread?
(b) How many were they as a proportion of the total farming population?
(c) What percentage of farm output originates from their farms and what percentage is purchased?
(d) What percentage of total agricultural output originates from the farms of "progressive farmers?"
(e) What amount in aggregate of purchased inputs do they utilise in a year?
(f) Can one really say that Uganda has a "progressive agriculture? If not, why and what has prevented its development? It is land tenure.

3. *The discussions by participants on Land Tenure and Agricultural Development mainly centred on the following critical issues:*

(a) Freehold versus leasehold land tenure system and repeal of the 1975 Land Reform Decree.
(b) Mailo tenancy and compensation
(c) Development conditions and land use planning
(d) Land tax

Freehold versus leasehold

Prof. Nsibambi leading the discussion on the 1975 Land Reform Decree, informed the participants that at present no statistical data were available on land ownership, land distribution and landlessness in Uganda. In the absence of reliable data, unscrupulous people have tended to manufacture their data to state their own cases. There was also a total paralysis in the enforcement of land laws. The Land Transfer Act did not allow transfer of land to non-African Ugandans. Did this not hinder agricultural development? ... Section 7 of the Land Reform Decree allows one to evict tenants, but the Ministry of Lands and Surveys says No! Prof. Nsibambi said that there was no clear land policy in the country. Although he was in favour of a freehold land tenure policy as recommended by the study team, he was however not convinced of the basis and timeframe for the recommendation of the study team. The study was mainly Buganda centred and other areas were not covered. Masaka and Luwero districts also could not be said to represent Buganda region, let alone other regions. The study team had not given serious thought on how its recommendations could be implemented and what was the timeframe. He also expressed doubts on government's capacity to implement the recommendations effectively and efficiently.

There was a detailed and interesting discussion on the freehold versus leasehold tenure systems and their merits and demerits. Whilst the 1975 Land Reform Decree represented a leasehold system, in considering a future policy option the questions posed were whether government should retain and implement the 1975 Land Reform Decree, with leasehold arrangements throughout the country, or replace it with a freehold system nationwide. [Some discussants] ... strongly argued in favour of the leasehold land tenure system and effective implementation of the 1975 Land Reform Decree with appropriate amendments. They maintained that there was a need for government to maintain overall control on allocation and use of land resources, which form the basis of life in Uganda and cannot be handed over to individuals to own and use as they like in perpetuity. Leasehold ensures trusteeship of government on land. The Permanent Secretary,

Ministry of Lands and Surveys also did not support uncontrolled freehold land tenure system in Uganda and argued that there was need for government intervention to protect the rights of small peasant farmers who are the majority. State supervision of land use planning and development was also essential.

The opponents of the leasehold system ... on the other hand advocated strongly for freehold land tenure arrangements throughout the country as recommended by the study team. They argued that:

(a) The role of government should be restricted to only administrating the issuing of titles to land and registration. Ownership of land should not be vested in the state.

(b) Like any other property, ownership rights on land should rest absolutely with individuals who own the incentives to invest and develop the land on a commercial basis. It would also facilitate obtaining credit from the bank against land as security.

They also argued that a freehold system does not aim at completely abolishing government roles in land use policy and taxation. Government is free to acquire any land for public use on payment of compensation. ... [T]he right of government in this regard was guaranteed by the "Law of Eminent Domain". All freeholders of land must abide by all the laws of the state including land laws. Prof. Bruce (Wisconsin) at this juncture pointed out that the world over experience indicated that whenever government involved itself in the ultimate ownership and allocation of land through leaseholds, rampant corruption and nepotism in allocation of land to the rich and powerful became the rule rather than the exception. The recent experience in Uganda merely corroborated this.

The Permanent Secretary, Ministry of Agriculture, suggested that the most appropriate land tenure system for Uganda should be one which takes into consideration the merits of both freehold and leasehold land tenure systems. Owners of land should be free to use land but at the same time, government has a duty to guide and supervise to ensure that land is put to proper use. This would avoid speculation and abuse of land. The enforcement of policy instruments and laws should be made effective to avoid concentration of land holding with a few.

After detailed discussions, which brought out several divergent views, a general consensus (on balance) emerged in the workshop which favoured a freehold rather than a leasehold system. There was also a general consensus that the 1975 Land Reform Decree should be repealed and a new land legislation embodying freehold system be drafted.

Mailo tenancy and compensation

Once the freehold land tenure system was accepted, the workshop concentrated on the issue of what should be the status of the mailo tenants who at present cultivate parcels of mailo land. The study team recommended that mailo tenants should become freehold owners of lands they occupy and cultivate, and mailo owners would receive compensation for the land they so lose. The compensation should be paid over a period of time and the tenants should share part of the cost.

Contributing on this subject, Prof. Nsibambi informed the meeting that section 7 of the Land Reform Decree allows the mailo owners to evict the tenants without compensation. The proposal to make mailo tenants freeholders would pose practical problems of determining mailo tenancy holdings and also generate conflict between mailo owners and mailo tenants. If a small owner wanted to re-possess his land for cultivation, was it a right policy to deprive him of his ownership right to the land because it was presently occupied by a tenant? He also expressed his doubts on the practicability and availability of the compensation proposal. Mr Okello-Okello argued that since mailo tenancy holdings were scattered, the proposal would result in fragmentation of mailo land. He also argued that the compensation to the mailo owners would create a precedent for sub-tenants in customary tenancy holdings to demand compensation. There would also be a question of the status of sub-tenants in the mailo land. This proposal would thus open the Pandora box of social conflicts.

There was, however, a general agreement on the proposal of allowing mailo tenants have been on the land for several generations and could not be evicted without causing social and political problems. This would also provide incentives to the tenant cultivators to invest in the land. It was also agreed that where a small mailo owner wishes to re-possess his land from the tenant for his personal cultivation, he could do so through negotiations and payment of compensation to the tenant for getting freehold interest on his land.

On the issue of compensation, there were many different views and the workshop could not come to a general agreement. Three questions were raised on this issue:

(i) What was "fair" compensation and who could determine it?

(ii) Who should pay and what would be the source of funds and mode of payment?

(iii) Why tenants should not bear full costs of compensation since they become owners of land and why Government should bear part of it as suggested by the study team? There was also a question as to the mechanism of the compensation scheme and who could implement it. After detailed discussion on these questions, it was decided that:

(a) Government should set up a Technical Committee to study the problem, establish the claims, determine the compensation formula and prepare a compensation scheme.

(b) The cost of compensation should be borne by the tenant beneficiary. Wherever the tenants could negotiate with mailo owners for agreed compensation and were able to pay the compensation to acquire the freehold rights, they should be allowed to do so.

(c) In the case of mailo tenants who are small cultivators and poor and cannot be in a position to pay compensation in lump-sum, government should work out a scheme for a compensation fund to provide financial assistance through the banks by way of credit to enable the tenants to acquire freehold rights by paying compensation to the mailo owners.

Agricultural development conditions

The 1975 Land Reform Decree imposed development conditions requiring that land leased should be developed within a period of 5 years from the date of acquiring leasehold rights or else land reverts to government for reallocation to other applicants who are capable of developing it. The study team recommended that no development conditions should be imposed on any freehold except for land on government sponsored development projects. They argued that the development conditions have not been effective in achieving agricultural development in several African countries. If the farming enterprises were profitable and adequately contributed to the farmer's livelihood, he would not abandon the land; rather, he would develop it and undertake farming.

The representatives of Ministry of Lands and Surveys (Okello-Okello, Tibasasa) argued in favour of stipulating development conditions. If the proper planning and land use was to be guaranteed, the development conditions in allocation of land resources were essential. Government cannot and should not allocate land to those who would not develop and use it within the overall planning framework of government. Dr Batungi argued that the physical planning requirements make it necessary to impose development conditions on use of land for present and future. Otherwise there will be abuse of both urban and rural land. Hence, the need for some state supervision or control to ensure orderly planning and development cannot be questioned. Dr Kabera also supported the imposition of development conditions on the ground that the land belongs to everyone and government has a duty to direct its use.

Others ... argued against stipulation of any development conditions on freehold land as it was difficult to monitor and implement, and ... also costly in terms of resources and manpower. Any development conditions should be consistent with the overall land use planning strategy which required detailed region-wide technical land use capability and development studies. Hence, land use patterns, and development problems of land should be tackled separately and should not be tied to land rights. It also violates the freehold rights. Since the owner of land has maximum interest in his land, he should be the sole decision maker on how best to use the land within the overall government planning framework.

At this juncture the Chairman clarified that government had already decided to undertake land use planning studies in Kabale district, which would be extended to other areas in future. He also informed the workshop that the objective of the development conditions can be achieved more effectively by government by using other policy instruments such as land tax, price incentives etc.

After deliberating on the Chairman's contribution on the subject, the workshop agreed that there was no need to stipulate development conditions when issuing freehold titles for land.

Land tax

The study team had recommended that a land tax could be adopted as an alternative to development conditions. The land tax would be based on the production capacity of the land; with different levels for good, average and poor land. The tax rate on unused land should be double that on used land. It was also proposed that the land tax should be administered at the sub-county level as a source of revenue for local administration and local development programmes.

The land tax proposal provoked opposition from some workshop participants. They argued that:

(a) Farmers in Uganda were already over-taxed and there was no justification for further taxation on their land.

(b) Tax on land would be a disincentive to production as the bulk of our farmers were small farmers who could not afford to pay tax.

(c) It was unjust and unrealistic to impose tax on the basic factor of production.

(d) The proposal was not feasible as government did not have an effective revenue collection machinery. To collect tax from a very large number of small peasant farmers was not an easy task and would be a costly affair.

[Others] supported the members of the study team in defending the land tax proposal. The Chairman argued that a tax on land would provide an incentive to use land by making it more expensive to leave it idle. The tax would also provide a source of revenue for local government to undertake development programmes such as schools. It would also relieve fiscal pressure on national government revenue for regional development. Dr Batungi supported land tax since all over the world land was taxed. He only expressed his doubts about how effectively it could be implemented. The study team had not looked into this carefully. Dr Bruce argued that land has a rent. Government was therefore justified to levy land tax as rent for allocation of scarce national production resources to the individuals. There was also an argument on equity considerations. The land tax would curb concentration of land and minimise abuse of land. Small farmers should either be exempted or taxed only marginally whereas larger owners of land should be taxed heavily on a progressive basis.

Recommendations

The Workshop noted the contribution of various participants on the subject of "Land Tenure and Agricultural Development" and agreed by general consensus to recommend for government consideration the following:

1. To repeal the 1975 Land Reform Decree and replace it with a new legislation incorporating freehold land tenure system throughout country without any development conditions. This will involve:

(a) Mailo tenants to become freeholders and mailo owners who lose their land to be compensated through a government sponsored compensation fund or bank credit scheme.

(b) Customary tenants to become freeholders upon certification of their rights in land by an Adjudication Committee.

(c) Existing leases on public land to become automatically freehold except those leases on government sponsored ranching schemes and others exceeding 500 acres which should be reviewed on merit on a case by case basis.

2. To consider the proposal for a graduated tax based on the income generating potential of land. Tax on unused land should be higher than that on used land so as to provide incentives to use land.

ODOKI COMMISSION REPORT

What sort of land tenure system do the grassroots people of Uganda desire for their country? The Uganda Constitutional Commission, chaired by Justice Benjamin Odoki (hence the 'Odoki Commission'), was appointed in accordance with the Constitutional Commission Statute (No 5 of 1988) to review the Constitution and make proposals for a new Constitution. In order to carry out its powers the Commission was required to 'seek the views of the general public through the holding of public meetings and debates, seminars, workshops and any other form of collecting public views'. Below are excerpts from its report of the people's views with reference to land tenure.

Views of the grassroots

Justice Benjamin Odoki (Chairperson), *The Report of the Uganda Constitutional Commission: Analysis and Recommendations,* Entebbe, Uganda Government Printer, 1992

25.1 The people of Uganda regard land as perhaps the most important resource of the people and the country as a whole. This is not surprising in view of the fact that Uganda is a predominantly agricultural country, and is likely to remain so for many years to come. Because of the importance they attach to land, it has been one of the issues on which many people from all parts of the country have submitted views. [Section one] ... deals with the underlying principles and concerns that have emerged from the views of the people.

Section one: Importance, concepts and principles

Importance of the Issue

25.2 Land is a major factor of production alongside labour and capital. The agricultural and industrial development of Uganda will depend on, among other things, the land use and management policies adopted. It can be argued that some land tenure systems promote socio-economic development better than others. Further, sound land tenure and proper land utilisation will have a bearing on environmental issues.

25.3 Land is viewed by the people as a vital natural resource and common heritage which cannot be matched by any other natural resource. Ownership of land by the individual, family or community confers real or potential wealth, social prestige and a sense of economic security. Population growth continues to put a great deal of pressure on land, and hence the need to look at the land issue very carefully.

Concerns of the people

25.4 Land is one of the issues on which the people have expressed a great diversity of views. It is unlikely that a consensus will emerge on the matter in the near future. This is because Uganda is a country of diversity in terms of cultural, social and economic experience and orientation. Different communities in Uganda are used to different kinds of land tenure and policy. Each community tends to extol the virtues of the policy and land management to which it is used in relation to the other systems.

25.5 Despite the diversity of views, some common concerns and principles have emerged from the submissions made by the people. The Commission has attached a great deal of importance to the views expressed by the people in evaluating the various options they offered. The main concerns on land shared by all the people of Uganda include those discussed below.

Land grabbing by the rich and the powerful

25.6 There is fear that the rich, powerful and well-connected people are using their wealth and influence to grab land from poor peasants, many of them being rendered landless in the process. This is of real concern as many of the people dispossessed of land depends on it as their source of livelihood.

Fear of foreigners taking over land

25.7 There is concern that foreigners coming to Uganda may take over land from citizens and yet Ugandans cannot do the same in other countries.

Too much centralisation of land administration

25.8 The people were very unhappy about too much centralisation, as well as the costly and complicated process of acquiring title to land. This has discouraged many people from taking steps to acquire titles to their land.

Corruption in land office

25.9 People complain that the process of acquiring land titles in riddled with corruption at every stage. This has increased the cost of acquiring titles and led to fraudulent issuance titles. Many people say that they have simply given up trying to obtain titles to their 1and because of corruption in the land office.

Principles emphasised by the people

25.10 According to the views, there is a general consensus regarding what would constitute a good land tenure policy. We discuss some of the principles under this sub-heading.

Fair and equitable allocation of land

25.11 People want a land tenure system and policy that would ensure a fair and equitable allocation of land among the citizens, while at the same time preserving its capacity to satisfy present and future generations.

Right to land

25.12 There is agreement that every citizen should be guaranteed access to land. People regard this as very important because most of the people are engaged in agriculture or pastoral activities which depend on availability of land.

Balance between development and protection of peasants

25.13 The people recognise that all categories of farmers and other developers should have easy access to land, but at the same time they want the peasants and others whose livelihood solely depend on the land to be protected from eviction.

Agriculture and other forms of socio-economic development

25.14 People want land tenure and policy which can lead to a balance in development by opening up opportunities for agricultural and other forms of socio-economic development in the rural areas instead of concentrating development opportunities in the urban areas.

Guaranteeing use of land to investors

25.15 It is recognised that farmers and other developers should be guaranteed continued use of land until they have made reasonable returns on their investments. In this way, they will be encouraged to make long term investments in the land.

Discouraging holding of land for prestige or speculative purposes

25.16 People are totally opposed to the practice of holding large tracks of land for prestige or speculative purposes by some people, while serious developers or landless people are without land.

Phased introduction of changes

25.17 It will take sometime before consensus can emerge on a uniform land tenure system acceptable to all the people of Uganda. However, in light of the views expressed by the people, we think it is time we laid the foundation upon which future generations can build, and hence the recommendations contained in this chapter - advocating for phased introduction of freehold system for rural areas and leasehold system for urban areas throughout the country.

Analysis of views and recommendations

25.49 The principal issues addressed by the people include ultimate ownership, forms of tenure, size of land holdings, institutional administrative framework, the introduction of land tax and acquisition of land by foreigners.

Ownership

25.50 A number of people expressed the view that land should be vested in the State, which should in turn hold it in trust for all the people of Uganda. The underlying consideration for this proposal is that land is a gift from God, a common national heritage and asset, to which everyone is entitled by reason of birth and citizenship. The State has the duty to work out a clear policy that would ensure that land is fairly and equitably distributed and put to the most profitable and economical use by those to whom it is granted. Those who advance this view propose that the State should be given the power to grant the land - either in freehold or leasehold - to applicants on the basis of approved plans. As ultimate owner of the land on behalf of all the people of Uganda, the State should also have the power to repossess the land if it is not being used according to the development conditions attached to the grant. In addition, the State should compulsorily acquire any land that is required for public purpose.

25.51 Submission from some sections of the people addressed the issue of compensation in the event of compulsory acquisition. Many people felt that payment of compensation to the persons affected is often inadequate and delayed. In many cases, they are not offered comparable alternative places to settle. People want the situation to be rectified. A few people have advocated that ultimate ownership of land should belong to individuals. In this case, even the regulating role of the State would be severely restricted. Advocates of this view argue that if individuals are left free to develop, acquire or dispose of their land according to the dictates of the market forces, there would be rapid and sustained economic development. The role of the State is viewed by such people as restrictive.

25.52 In our view, land is the common heritage of all the people of Uganda. As such every citizen of Uganda is entitled to a share in this vital and strategic resource. The State is the collective embodiment of the wishes, hopes and aspirations of the people. It should also be the guarantor of the national interest. The State should hold land in trust for the people who are the ultimate owners. This is particularly important in view of the fact that land is a limited resource on which there will be increasing pressure as the population of Uganda expands. The State's role becomes important in ensuring that every citizen has a fair deal. We also agree that the right of the State to own land for public purposes should continue to be protected.

Recommendation

(a) *The State should hold land in Uganda in trust and for the benefit and well-being of all the people of Uganda, including future generations.*
(b) *Water and mineral resources within the territorial boundary of Uganda should belong to the State.*
(c) *The government should have the right to own land for public purposes.*

Land tenure

General policy considerations

25.54 It is necessary to adopt a land tenure and policy that can try to accommodate the wishes of Ugandans, and suits our circumstances. Any ill-planned, hastily conceived land policy resulting in massive displacement of people and the creation of a big class of landless citizens would sow the seed for future political and socio-economic unrest and upheavals. We should therefore put in place a mechanism for careful monitoring and evaluation of land distribution or allocation with a view to ensuring that the right of every citizen to land is not compromised. Secondly, we need to guard against the tendency of subjecting land management policy to methods which result in land degradation. The ideal land tenure and policy we adopt should address the concerns of the people and the considerations mentioned above. The recommendations contained in this chapter aim at achieving that.

25.55 Views differ on whether or not Uganda should have a uniform system of land tenure. A number of people across the country support the introduction of a uniform system of land tenure. They argue that a unified land tenure system would, among other things, consolidate national unity and make the administration of land simpler and easily understood by the ordinary person. However, when it comes to the type of land tenure to be adopted for the whole country if we opt for a uniform land tenure system, the preferences differ considerably. There is considerable support in favour of each of the existing land tenure systems, namely, mailo/freehold, customary, and leasehold tenures.

Mailo/freehold tenure

25.56 In the central region, with the exception of Rakai and Luwero districts, there is overwhelming support for the mailo system. However, mailo is not only to be found in Buganda, but also in some areas in Eastern and Western Uganda, where support for it is mixed. There is also considerable support for freehold tenure in other areas outside Buganda.

25.57 Those who support mailo/freehold tenure contend that:

(a) the system enhances the economic value of land as it can be offered as security for loan facilities;
(b) the sense of security enjoyed by owners of mailo/freehold land encourages them to make long term investment in the land and to take proper care of the land in which they have permanent interest; and
(c) under the mailo system it is argued that even the tenants had assured security of tenure because they could not be easily evicted from the land as long as they paid their dues. It is because the mailo tenure was seen to be offering security to both the landowners and tenants that the system enjoys such strong support in Buganda. Supporters of the system go so far as to assert that the relatively more advanced socio-economic development of the central region in comparison with the rest of Uganda is because of the existence of mailo tenure.

25.58 Those who oppose mailo/freehold tenure point out a number of problems associated with the system:

(a) In some areas, people have complained bitterly about absentee landlords. The situation in Kibale district, which is made up of the former 'lost counties which were returned to Bunyoro from Buganda' is an extreme illustration of this problem. The counties were returned to the then Bunyoro kingdom, but the owners of mailo land in the area who are mainly Baganda retained ownership of their land. The people of Kibale contend that this is a matter which must be solved by the Constitution because both the 1962 and 1967 Constitutions guarantee mailo rights.

(b) The owner of mailo land is not compelled to put the land to the best economic use. Large tracts of land lie unused and government cannot allocate it to landless people because it lacks the power to do so.

(c) It is contended by opponents of mailo/freehold tenure that the system is unfair in that those who originally got the land did nothing to deserve it. The apparent security offered to the tenant is no guarantee that the tenant may not be evicted from the land.

Customary tenure

25.59 Many people from the areas where it is still practised want customary tenure to be continued. In these areas land is regarded as a common heritage to be used for the benefit of all the members of the society. To many people in these areas, mainly in the North and North East, the idea of individual titles to land is considered alien.

25.60 It is important, nevertheless, to point out that except for areas set aside for grazing animals and other communal activity, individuals and families in these areas do in reality own land which they can pass on to their successors or even dispose of in accordance with agreed customary or modern practices. Quite a number of people dispose of their land for monetary considerations.

25.61 The real concern of the people in areas where communal land ownership is dominant is caused by the fear that rich and powerful individuals or organisations may grab large chunks of prime land through leasing. There is a feeling of insecurity caused by the unknown. It should be remembered that many people in these areas are not well informed on the procedures and process of leasing land. Otherwise, in practice, many individuals and families holding land under customary tenure have something akin to freehold tenure. The only difference is that they have no formal land titles. The exception to this practice is to be found in areas where the pastoral way of life is still dominant and where most of the land is held and used communally.

25.62 The great disadvantage of the customary tenure is that it tends to emphasise cultural values more than the economic and financial gains from the land. This retards development. Land users are not encouraged to make long-term investments in the land; nor can they take as good care of the land as they would have done if they had clear titles to it. Land held under such customary tenure especially for communal use tends to suffer from neglect and consequent degradation.

25.63 Notwithstanding the disadvantages associated with customary tenure, any abrupt change in the system would cause hardships and economic and social upheavals. That is why many people have suggested that the system should be gradually changed to avoid economic, social and cultural hardships and shocks. Particular care should be taken not to render large numbers of people landless. At the same time, however, changes need to be made to encourage developers to invest in the land and bring about socio- economic development in these areas.

Leasehold tenure

25.64 Support for leasehold tenure is spread throughout the country, except in the central region. It is, however, the least preferred land tenure system. Those who support leasehold tenure contend that it accords with the interests of all the people as:

(a) on the one hand it guarantees the regulatory role of the State in land transactions;

(b) on the other hand it guarantees everyone the right to apply for and be granted land in accordance with one's development needs;

(c) the State, acting on behalf of the people, should have the right to impose development conditions for the benefit and general well-being of the people as a whole. This would ensure that land is granted to those with the ability to develop it. The State would retain the right to take-away land from those who lack ability to develop it and replace them with serious developers; and

(d) under leasehold tenure the right of reversion is entrenched, thus guaranteeing the ultimate ownership and controlling authority of the State on behalf of the people of Uganda as a whole.

25.65 Those who oppose leasehold tenure are mainly concerned that it gives too much power to the State in land transactions. In their view, the State intervention distorts the land market and leads to corruption. For them, land transactions should be left to market forces, which would guarantee that only those with the ability to develop the land will have access to them. They argue that this can best be achieved in a freehold system. It is also clear that the majority of Ugandans feel that leasehold tenure does not guarantee them adequate security to the land.

25.66 There is need for a system of land tenure that can guarantee security of tenure, promote sustainable development and advance the cause of national unity. There is also need to consider the interest of the population as a whole. The system which the people prefer is that which gives them undisturbed tenure to the land. Freehold tenure would be accepted in most parts of Uganda.

25.67 In the short run, it is not possible to have a uniform land tenure system for the whole country without disrupting the lives of the people, whatever system is adopted. In the long run, however, we consider that land should be granted in freehold in the rural areas and in leasehold in the urban areas. It would not be difficult to convert the leasehold tenures into freehold tenure. It has already been pointed out in this chapter that many customary land holdings, particularly where people practise settled agriculture, are akin to freeholds. However, customary owners of land would need to be educated over time on the need to get titles to their land. Great care should be taken to see that people are not rendered landless in the process. Special consideration should be given to land used for gazing and other communal purposes.

25.68 All land held under mailo system should, in our view, be converted into freehold. The conversion of mailo to freehold does not involve any substantive change because mailo is already a freehold tenure. The objective of our recommendation is to free mailo from the encumbrance of the *bibanja* while at the same time giving the *kibanja* owner an opportunity to convert his holding to freehold so as to have the benefits of that tenure. *Kibanja* holders should be granted freehold titles to the land occupied by them, but the former mailo owner of such land should be compensated by the *kibanja* holders for loss of the land. The amount of compensation to be paid by the *kibanja* holder should be determined by an independent lands tribunal. To ensure proper planning and development, urban land should continue to be granted in leaseholds. This is a view which is widely held by a cross-section of Ugandans.

25.69 Recommendation

(a) In regulating and managing the utilisation of land, the following factors should be taken into consideration:

(i) *all people who are legally occupying land should be guaranteed security of tenure and enabled to register their interests and obtain certificates of titles;*

(ii) *there should be maximum utilisation, of land, while at the same time ensuring that land is equitably distributed among the people;*

(iii) *division of land into uneconomic units should be avoided.*

(b) In the long run land should be granted:

(i) *in freehold in rural areas, and*

(ii) *in leasehold in urban areas.*

(c) All land held under the mailo and leasehold tenure in the rural areas should in the long run be converted into freehold tenure.

(d) Bibanja holders should be granted freehold titles to the land occupied by them but

(i) *government should make arrangements for compensation to the mailo owners; and*

(ii) *the amount of compensation payable to the mailo owner should be determined by a Lands Tribunal.*

(e) *The system of holding land under customary tenure should continue but the customary tenant should be encouraged to acquire title land.*
(f) *Parliament should have powers to make laws to give effect to the above recommendations and better management of land.*

Size of land holding

25.70 There was overwhelming support for the idea of imposing restrictions on the size of land that can be granted to an individual or organisation. The main consideration is that if no restrictions are imposed, the rich and powerful who constitute a small minority of the population would grab land from the people using their political and economic power. Such a situation would in turn lead to serious economic, social and political upheavals. Some people point out that there are already such problems in some parts of the country, including Kibale district where large tracts of land are owned by absentee landlords.

25.71 A very small minority of views did not favour imposition of restriction on the size of land holdings. They argue that the overriding consideration should be the ability to develop the land. This view does not enjoy widespread support and it ignores the social and political implications of unrestricted size of landholding.

25.72 Recommendation

(a) The size of landholding should be subject to control and limitation.
(b) In determining the size of land an individual or organisation can acquire, due regard should be paid to the following considerations:
    (i) *the purpose for which the land applied for is required;*
    (ii) *the ability of the applicant to put the land to proper use;*
    (iii) *the size of land available to prospective developers in the area concerned; and*
    (iv) *the interest of other people who may be affected by the grant.*
(c) Parliament should make laws for regulating the size of the land to be granted to any person or authority by the Uganda Land Commission and the conditions under which land may be held.

Institutional administrative framework

25.73 The people want the system of land administration to be substantially restructured in order to meet the needs and expectations of the people. There is general agreement that the Uganda Land Commission and District Land Committees as presently constituted have failed to deliver services to the people in accordance with their wishes and aspirations.

25.74 The people have suggested that the restructuring of the existing structure should include;
(a) Greater decentralisation and increasing the powers of the District Land Committees. This would mean that most of the powers vested in the Uganda Land Commission would be exercised by District Land Committees in the name of the Commission. The people want District Land Committees to have power to issue land titles without having to refer the matter to Kampala or Entebbe. This would bring services nearer to the people and expedite the process of obtaining title. People believe that decentralisation and devolution of powers would eliminate the massive corruption which has characterised land administration at all levels.
(b) People favour further decentralisation to lower levels in matters relating to the processing of applications for land title and forwarding such applications to the District Land Committee. This would reduce the costs and inconvenience which applicants have to undergo in dealing with the District Land Committee. Most of the people have suggested the establishment of Sub-county Land Committees to process applications for land titles.

25.75 There is need for the Uganda Land Commission and the District Land Committees to work independently of any political pressure or influence as the allocation of land and administration of land generally are very sensitive matters. It is, therefore, important that members of Parliament or District Councils should not sit on the Uganda Land Commission or District Land Committees, so that they can be seen to be politically neutral.

25.76 It is not the responsibility of the Uganda Land commission to make policies, which is the responsibility of the government. However, once the policy has been made, the Commission should have a free-hand in carrying out its functions. The independence of the Uganda Land Commission can be strengthened by, among other things, guaranteeing tenure of office for the members and making it a self-accounting body.

25.77 Recommendation

(a) *The Uganda Land Commission should be retained in the Constitution.*
(b) *The Uganda Land Commission should consist of a Chairman and not less than four members all of whom should be appointed by the President with the approval of the National Council of State.*
(c) *Members of the Uganda Land Commission should be appointed for a period of five years, which should be renewable.*
(d) *A member of the Uganda Land Commission should be removed from office by the President with the approval of the National Council of State only for inability to perform his or her functions due to physical or mental incapacity or for gross misbehaviour or misconduct.*
(e) *A person should not be appointed a member of the Uganda Land Commission if he is a Member of Parliament or District Council.*
(f) *The Uganda Land Commission should not be subject to direction or control by any authority or person in performing its functions. It should, however, take into account government policy on land when performing its functions.*
(g) *The Uganda Land Commission should be self-accounting and the salaries and allowances of its members should be charged on the Consolidated Fund.*

25.78 The functions of the Uganda Land Commission should not only be to allocate land, but also to advise government on land tenure system, utilisation of land, the system of registering land, and the planned and co-ordinated development of designated areas. This expanded role is necessary as the tenure system and administration of land in Uganda needs to be evolved over a period of time to meet economic and social changes in the country.

25.79 Recommendation

The Uganda Land Commission should have the following functions:

(i) *to allocate land which is not occupied or owned by any person or authority;*
(ii) *to regulate the use of land in Uganda as provided for in the Constitution and other laws;*
(iii) *to make recommendations to government on the land tenure system, utilisation of land and the system of registering land;*
(iv) *to give advice to the Central Government, District Governments and lower level authorities on the planned and co-ordinated development of designated areas; and*
(v) *to carry out other functions as may be vested in the Commission by Parliament.*

25.80 There was consensus in the views of the people on the need to enhance the powers of the District and lower level Land Committees in the belief that this would reduce on the time and cost of obtaining land titles. In addition, the people believe that decentralisation would reduce corruption as the officials in charge of land administration would be nearer to the people who are affected by their actions. A District Land Committee would perform the functions of the Uganda Land Commission in the district. There is, however, need for the Uganda Land Commission to co-ordinate the activities of the District Land Committees to ensure that they are performing their functions in accordance with the Constitution and other laws of the land.

25.81Recommendation

(a) *Each district should have a District Land Committee which should perform the functions of the Uganda Land Commission in the district.*
(b) *The Uganda Land Commission should co-ordinate the activities of the District Land Committees.*
(c) *The Composition and mode of appointments of the members of the District Land Committees should be determined by Parliament.*

25.82 The people want the procedure for acquiring land titles to be made simpler and cheaper. They believe that this can be achieved in part by decentralisation to levels below the district. Decentralisation below the district level is seen as necessary to avoid transferring red tape and corruption from the centre to the district headquarters, which in many districts are far from remote parts. There is overwhelming support in favour of effective Sub-county Land Committees made up of people who are knowledgeable on land matters. Since most people are not well informed on the procedure for acquiring land titles, the Sub-county Land Committees should take on the responsibility of educating the people on the procedure, in addition to processing applications for land titles before passing them on to the District Land Committees.

25.83 Recommendation

(a) *There should be at every sub-county a Sub-County Land Committee which should be responsible for processing applications for land titles and forwarding such applications to the District Land Committee. The Committee should also be responsible for educating the people on the procedure for acquiring land titles.*
(b) *The composition, mode of appointment and rules of procedure of the Sub-county Land Committees should be determined by Parliament. They should, however, adopt simple methods of work which can be easily understood by ordinary people.*

25.84 There is need to have mechanisms for settling land disputes which shall inevitably arise. People are dissatisfied with the way that the ordinary courts settle land disputes. The courts are seen as being far removed from the people, and their procedures are said to be complex, costly and time consuming. There is a demand from the people to adopt simpler, cheaper and speedier procedures than those of the ordinary courts in settling land disputes. The aim should be to settle land disputes, especially at the lower levels, speedily and at the least possible cost to the litigants. This can be achieved by establishing land tribunals at various levels to deal with land disputes. There should, however, be a right of appeal to the courts of law by any person who is aggrieved by the decision of a tribunal.

25.85 Recommendation

(a) (i) *Parliament should be authorised to make laws establishing Land Tribunals.*
(ii) *The functions of a Land Tribunal should be to decide on disputes in respect of any land registered or intended to be registered under the Registration of Titles Act or any dispute regarding compensation in the event of compulsory acquisition of land. The tribunal should aim at settling disputes speedily and at affordable cost to the litigants.*
(iii) *The powers and privileges of the Lands Tribunal should be determined by an Act of Parliament.*

(b) (i) *The Chairman of a Land Tribunal should be appointed on the advice of the Chief Justice.*
(ii) *A member of a Land Tribunal should hold office on such terms and conditions as may be prescribed by Parliament.*
(iii) *The procedure of a Land Tribunal should be determined by an Act of Parliament. It should provide for a right of appeal from the decision of a Land Tribunal to a court of law.*

Land tax

25.86 There is some support in favour of introducing land tax. It has been suggested that the least developed the land, the greater should be the tax that such landholder should pay. It is argued that if such a tax policy on land is introduced, it would compel the holder of undeveloped land to put the land to productive use in order to avoid heavy taxation or sell part of it. Some people, while not opposed to the policy of taxing land altogether, are of the view that land tax should only be imposed at the time of transfer or its acquisition. Some people are totally opposed to any idea of land tax. They maintain that land should not be a taxable item.
25.87 There is need for utilising every piece of land economically and according to approved plans and conditions. At the moment, there is plenty of land lying idle, and there is no urge on the part of holders of such land to develop it because they are not compelled to do so. At the same time, there are many people who do not have enough land, even though they may have the ability to invest in its development.
25.88 A land tax computed on a development basis is likely to compel landowners to think of all means of developing the land to avoid taxes, or to sell off the extra land, which they cannot develop. It would also be an additional source of income to the government. Great care should be taken not to levy taxes on those who preserve part of their land for the purpose of protecting and conserving the environment.

25.89 Recommendation
(a) In principle land should be taxed.
(b) Idle and undeveloped land should attract higher taxes.
(c) Parliament should make laws for the imposition of taxes on land.

Ownership of land by foreigners or foreign organisations

25.90 There is near unanimous opposition among the people to the idea of giving foreigners unconditional and unrestricted access to land in Uganda. There is concern that giving foreigners or foreign organisations unrestricted access to our land would impinge on our sovereignty and deprive our own citizens of this vital resource. All over the world, land is jealously guarded by nationals as it is limited in supply. It is even more vital for us to do so in an agriculturally dominant country like Uganda.
25.91 Some people agree that deserving non-citizens and foreign organisations should be granted land, but on certain conditions. Among the conditions mentioned, the following are the most common:
(a) A foreigner or foreign organisation should only be granted land in leasehold.
(b) The foreigner or foreign organisation must show clear evidence of ability to make serious and substantial investment, preference being given to those who apply for industrial rather than agricultural land.

25.92 We need to attract foreign investors into the country, but at the same time there is need to exercise control on the size of land that can be allocated to foreigners or foreign organisations. They should follow certain clearly laid down procedures, in addition to fulfilling the conditions outlined above.

25.93 Recommendation

(a) Any foreign investor should be eligible to apply for land in Uganda.

(b) The application for grant of land by a foreign investor must satisfy the following conditions:

(i) The applicant must have immediate plans for putting the land to proper and productive use.

(ii) The applicant must show that if granted land he or she will develop it in accordance with an approved plan.

(iii) The application must be supported by three prominent and respectable nationals of Uganda.

(c) Parliament may make laws for the control, possession and transfer of land by non-citizens.

******

3

The Land Bill

INTRODUCTION

The Land Bill, which became the Land Act, 1998, was debated for over five years before it was finally passed by Parliament. The debate generated so much controversy, both within and outside Parliament that the government feared it could spark off civil unrest.[2] The excerpts in this chapter are from the Parliament of Uganda Parliamentary Debates (Hansard) 3rd Session, Issue No 18, during the second reading of the bill. The excerpts contain the outline of the bill and its underlying policy objectives. Several provisions of the *Land Act* are quite complicated and, in some cases, the policy objective is not apparent. The Parliamentary debates and pre-Parliamentary materials relating to the Act (such as the MISR and the Odoki reports)[3] are part of the context of the Act and facilitate its understanding.

From a legal perspective, although the courts when interpreting a statutory provision to determine the legislative intention are not bound by statements made during parliamentary debate of the bill, they may consider them where the meaning of a provision is ambiguous, obscure or leads to an absurdity.[4]

In the English case of *Pepper v Hart,*[5] the House of Lords held that it was no longer the law that Parliamentary debates reported in the Hansard could not be cited in order to ascertain the meaning of an Act of Parliament. Lord Griffiths said:[6]

> My Lords, I have long thought that the time had come to change the self-imposed judicial rule that forbade any reference to the legislative history of an enactment as an aid to its interpretation. The ever-changing volume of legislation must inevitably result in ambiguities of statutory language which are not perceived at the time the legislation is enacted. The object of the court in interpreting legislation is to give effect so far as the language permits to the intention of the legislature. If the language proves to be ambiguous I can see no sound reason not to consult Hansard to see if there is a clear statement of the meaning that the words were intended to carry. The days have long passed when the courts adopted a strict constructionist view of interpretation which required them to adopt the literal meaning of the language. The courts now adopt a purposive approach which seeks to give effect to the true purpose of legislation and are prepared to look at much extraneous material that bears on the background against which the legislation was enacted. Why then cut ourselves off from the one source in which may be found an authoritative statement of the intention with which the legislation is placed before Parliament.

It is submitted that there is no reason why the courts in Uganda should not, where appropriate, refer to the legislative history of the Act as aid to its interpretation.

---

[2] President Museveni, New Vision, 19 May 1998.

[3] See Chapter two.

[4] Cross, *Statutory Interpretation* (3rd ed, London: Butterworths, 1995), p. 154.

[5] [1993] 1 All ER 42.

[6] Ibid, at 49-50.

OBJECTIVES OF THE LAND BILL

Ministerial perspective

***Parliament of Uganda Parliamentary Debates (Hansard)*, 20 June 1998, pp: 4041-4043**
The Minister, Office of the President (Mr Ayume Francis): Thank you, Mr Speaker. I beg to move that the Bill entitled the Land Bill, 1998 be read a Second Time. Mr Speaker and Hon. Members, the object of the Land Bill is to provide for the tenure, ownership, management of land, to amend and consolidate the law relating to tenure, ownership and management of land and to provide for related or incidental methods. The basic principle underlining the Bill is that a good land tenure system should support agricultural development, and overall economic development through the functioning of a land market which permits those who have rights in land to voluntarily sell their land and for producers and investors to gain access to land.

The Bill has been formulated bearing in mind that a good land policy should not force people off the land and that a good land tenure system should protect individual's rights on land and ensure social justice as enshrined in the Constitution. Furthermore, a good land tenure should ensure sustainable utilisation of land as a resource and the protection of the environment. Mr Speaker, the Land Bill therefore, is intended to do the following:

One, to operationalise all the Constitutional reforms and provisions relating to land.

Two, to provide security of tenure to all land users.

Three, to resolve the land use impasse between the registered owners, that is to say: mailo, freehold, and leasehold owners of land on the one hand and the lawful or bona fide occupants of that land on the other. In this connection, Mr Speaker, the Constitution has mandated Parliament to make a law regulating the relationship between the registered owners and the lawful or bona fide occupants.

Four, to provide institutional framework which determines how the interests of all the stakeholders including the individuals, the State and Local Governments, are to be taken into account in terms of land ownership, use and management, under a decentralised system which is provided in the Constitution.

Five, to amend and consolidate the law relating to tenure and management of land in order to conform to the Constitutional provisions, taking into account changes that have taken place in the areas of Economic Policy, Economic Liberalisation, Privatization, Divestiture, Civil Service Reforms, Institutional Reforms and Decentralisation of Government functions among other things.

Six, to make it possible for Government or a Local Government to acquire land compulsorily in the public interest and for public use, in the interest of defence, public safety, public order, public morality or public health in terms of Article 26, Clause 2, paragraph (a) and Article 237, Clause 2, paragraph (a) of the Constitution.

Seven, to ensure proper planning and well co-ordinated development of urban areas. Mr Speaker, as Hon. Members debate this Bill, it is of paramount importance to remember and keep in mind that the Bill has been formulated in compliance with the Constitution. The Land Bill is designed to take care of interests and aspirations of all stakeholders, which are many and varied. You should, therefore, bear in mind that it is not unusual to find that these interests are in conflict with one another, hence the need for dialogue, understanding and compromise.

Mr Speaker, during the past 22 years, drastic changes have taken place in Uganda's land tenure system, the first changes were introduced by the Land Reform Decree which came into force on the 1st of June, 1975. Prior to the Decree, Uganda had four land tenure systems, major ones, that is to say: the mailo tenure, the freehold tenure, the leasehold tenure and the customary tenure. There was however, comparatively, a minor tenure system of Statutory Tenancies known as *bibanja* which existed in Buganda, Toro and Ankole. The Decree in effect abolished the mailo land and freehold tenures and converted mailo and freehold estates into leaseholds. The Decree had a negative impact, in that, apart from abolishing absolute ownership, the protection which was given to a customary tenant under the Public Land's Act and which the mailo and freehold tenant enjoyed, was removed by reducing the tenant to a mere tenant at sufferance. Henceforth, the Uganda Land Commission could alienate land occupied by a customary tenant without his or her consent.

Secondly, a customary tenant could be evicted on terms imposed by the Commission and approved by the Minister. "*Bibanja*" holders were not secure either. The Decree in effect introduced insecurity of tenure. The Decree could not be enforced and it remained a dead letter on the Statute book.

Mr Speaker, there were efforts to reform our land tenure system prior to the 1995 Constitution. The first serious attempt to reforming the country's land tenure system, in fact, started way back in 1983 as part of an overall study of the Agricultural Policy to rehabilitate and develop the Agricultural Sector. Consequently Sir, a high powered Agricultural Policy Committee was set up to formulate, co-ordinate, direct and review policies and programmes in the Agricultural Sector.

After preliminary studies, the Committee appointed Makerere Institute of Social Research in collaboration with Land Tenure Centre of the University of Wisconsin chosen in US, to undertake two studies, one of which was on land tenure and agricultural development. The Report of the study was discussed at a workshop in Jinja on the 18th and 19th May, 1989. As the study had not covered the entire country, the workshop recommended the setting up of a high powered multi-discipline technical committee to undertake a further study of land tenure issues throughout the country. Government set up a technical committee which undertook the study between 1990 and 1993 and covered the entire country.

However, as the Constituent Assembly was preoccupied with discussing sensitive land issues, Government thought it prudent to delay the legislation on the land matters to avoid biasing the Constituent Assembly debate on land. Suffice to say, Mr Speaker, that the Odoki Commission shared information on land issues with the Technical Committee and that the Committee's Report and Draft Bill provided useful information for many Constituent Assembly Members.

Mr Speaker, I would like to turn to reform introduced by the 1995 Constitution. The promulgation of the new Constitution brought about fundamental reforms to the ownership, tenure and management of land in Uganda against the background of what I have just explained. These reforms may be itemised as follows:

(a) The vesting of land in the citizens of Uganda as opposed to vesting it in the State, as was the case under the Public Lands Act, 1969 as amended by the Land Reform Decree of 1975.
(b) The introduction of four land tenure systems as opposed to the two tenure systems introduced by the Land Reform Decree. That is to say, leasehold and customary tenure.
(c) The fact that customary tenants on former public land now own the land they occupy.
(d) Restoration of the mailo and freehold tenures and estates which had been abolished by the Land Reform Decree.
(e) The Constitution's recognition and protection of lawful or bona fide occupants on registered land. That is to say, mailo, freehold and leasehold; and accordingly the requirement of Parliament to make a law regulating the relationship between the lawful or bona fide occupants and the registered owners of the land and also providing for the acquisition of registerable interests by the occupants.
(f) In the event of compulsory acquisition of land by Government or Local Government, which is provided in the Constitution, the requirement to pay compensation prior to the taking of possession or acquisition of the land.
(g) Finally, the decentralisation of land management to the District.

Mr Speaker, an attempt has been made to make provision in the Land Bill to operationalise these Constitutional Reforms as follows.

(a) The vesting of land in citizens of Uganda is provided for in Article 237 (1) of the Constitution and it will be operationalised. In Clause 3 of the Bill it is being proposed that this should be operationalised.
(b) the introduction of four land tenure systems which is dealt with by Article 237 (3) of the Constitution. It is being proposed that this should be operationalised, as in Clause 4 of the Bill.
(c) The fact that customary tenants on former public land now own the land they occupy and that they may acquire certificates of ownership as stipulated in Article 237, Clause 4, paragraph (a), is treated in Clause 4, of the Bill.
(d) The restoration of mailo, freehold tenures and the estates provided for under Article 237, Clause 3, is being operationalised in Clause 3, sub-clause 2 of the Bill.
(e) The Constitution recognition and protection of the lawful or bona fide occupants on registered land under Article 237, Clauses 8 and 9 is being dealt with in Clauses 10,11,12 and 14 of the Bill.
(f) In the case of compulsory acquisition of land by Government or Local Government, the requirement to pay compensation up front before taking possession of one's land as provided for in Article 26, Clause 2 and Article 237, Clause 2, will be implemented as stated in Clause 18 of the Bill.
(g) Finally, the decentralisation of land management dealt with in Articles 240, 241 and 243 of the Constitution will be implemented or is being proposed to be implemented as indicated in Clauses 32, 40, 44, 50 and 56, of the Bill.

Mr Speaker, a word about consultations relating to the Land Bill. There has been a lot of talk that Government has not consulted sufficiently before formulating the Land Bill and that the Land Bill is being rushed through because Government has a hidden agenda. The truth is, Mr Speaker, apart from the Constitutional stipulation of a deadline for the passing of the law, there have been adequate consultations. Sir, it is public knowledge that land issues were some of the major issues extensively investigated by the Constitutional Commission chaired by Justice Odoki. It is also common knowledge that the Commission went to the grassroots to consult on the land issues and made a Report. Ugandans had the opportunity and they did use that opportunity to express themselves on the various issues relating to land. The Constituent Assembly debated the Report, which is Chapter 15 of the Constitution.

Mr Speaker and Hon. Members, I have already made reference to the extensive consultation by Government under the auspices of the Agricultural Policy Committee and the Odoki Commission. Permit me therefore, to add that in the course of drafting the Bill, further consultations were made with stakeholders, individually and collectively; workshops and public lectures. The interest groups targeted included landowners and tenants, women's groups, Uganda Law Society, Uganda Land Alliance, and the Mengo Lukiiko.

When considering the Land Bill, Mr Speaker, Cabinet deemed it necessary to consult and satisfy itself of the contentious issues involved. A Cabinet Committee was set up and visited various areas where the issues were more pronounced and contentious. The contentious issues revolved around the following:

(a) The relationship between the lawful or bona fide occupants of mailo land, freehold or leasehold land and the registered owners of that land. That is the relationship which is envisaged in the Constitution. It was one of the contentious issues the committee came across during their consultations.
(b) The acquisition of a registrable interest in the land by the lawful or bona fide occupant.
(c) There was what has been commonly known as the Kibaale land question, it was a contentious issue, as the committee consulted.
(d) The land rights of women and children also became a contentious issue.
(e) Customary land ownership and communal land ownership, which really is a variation of customary ownership.

....

Mr Speaker, on the basis of these consultations, there are proposals to resolve the issues I have referred to in the manner provided for in the Bill. Mr Speaker I beg to move.

****

Parliamentary Committee Report

***Report of the Committee on lands, water and environment* (Parliament of Uganda Parliamentary Debates (Hansard), 20 June 1998, pp. 4044-*4059*)**

Mr Bennedict Mutyaba (Chairman, Sessional Committee on Lands, Water and Environment) (Makindye East, Kampala): Thank you Mr Speaker, Hon. Members. This is the report of the Parliamentary Committee on Works, Transport Communications and Lands, Housing and Physical Planning, on the Land Bill 1998. Mr Speaker, the committee was mandated by the August House under the Rules 99 sub-rule 5 and Rule 143 (c) of our Rules of Procedure to examine the Land Bill and advise Parliament on its provisions and implications. ....

Mr Speaker, Hon. Members, ... allow me to take the unprecedented step to ask and also to answer the questions on whether we need to pass the land law. In our consultations, this was a re-occurring issue.

In order for us to answer the questions whether we need to pass a land law, a re-statement of certain major features of our land situation is a necessary preliminary to the arguments in this report.

Mr Speaker, the problem of land is not new to our politics. The wars that have traversed this country since our forefathers decided to make this stretch of land their home, have been caused to a great extent by the desire to have more land under one's control. Land is such a special and tangible thing that out of all one's property, it is called "real". It is a store of wealth, a source of riches, a factor of production and the basis of our very existence as a human race.

In Uganda, the economy is heavily dependent on agriculture, forestry and fishing, which presently provide nearly 50 per cent of the real GDP. In terms of rural areas, however, over 80% the population rely on the land for their subsistence. Even with optimism of rapid industrialisation, it must be unequivocally stated and admitted that in the foreseeable future, land will remain the primary source of wealth for our people and the backbone of our economy.

It is therefore essential that we develop a land-holding system that is capable of responding to the above realities and ensures equity and social justice to all the people. The productivity of land and the social advancement of people are dependent as much upon an evolution of sound systems of land tenure as upon the development of improved agricultural practice. ...

The 1995 Constitution, in Article 237, provides the framework for reform of land tenure. The Constitution introduced a number of reforms: again I will go through them.

(a) The vesting of land in the citizens of Uganda. It is clear that the word 'citizens' here is used in its global and individual sense. It would therefore, be safe to conclude that the land was vested in the citizens as a group and also as individuals.
(b) The introduction of the freehold and mailo tenure system.
(c) The recognition of customary ownership on the same lines as the freehold, mailo, and leasehold tenure.
(d) The recognition and protection of bona fide occupants on registered land.

The Constitution requires Parliament to pass laws which would enable leasehold owners to convert their tenures into freehold and regulate the relationship between the lawful and bona fide occupants and the registered owners of land; and also the acquisition of registrable interests by such occupants.

The argument has been that it is only on the last item that Parliament was required to pass a law within the first two years of its existence. This is true, but it does not remove the need to have a comprehensive law to give full effect to the provisions of the Constitution which made redundant and unenforceable the existing legislation on land - the Public Lands Act 1969 and the Land Reform Decree 1975. There is, therefore, a vacuum which needs to be filled and filled fast, in order to give clear guidance to the people who may want to invest in the land or to carry out development. The impasse created by the Constitution between the lawful and bona fide occupant and the registered owner, needs to be resolved. The definition of a lawful and bona fide occupant needs to be addressed; the issue of management of land, which is still held on account for all the citizens, must be resolved.

From our own experiences, during the public consultations we held, it was apparent that people's indignation with the Bill was because of their ignorance of its contents and its aims, while we are told that consultations on reforming the land tenure system started as far back as 1993, taken to sensitise the general population about the aims of government. Studies made by technocrats can only be useful if they are well explained to the people.

It is true that the greatest impediment to progress towards modern land tenure policy is suspicion. Africans, and forgive me for saying this, are naturally attached to their traditional practices and regard all interference by Government as a prelude to some policy designed to deprive them of their land.

It is therefore, imperative that the Government should, before introducing any law, make wide-spread consultations with the people, and get their trust. As one eminent lawyer said, "if you do not trust the messenger why should you trust the message."

In this case this was not done and last minute, frantic, and unco-ordinated efforts by Government to explain the Bill came too late to allay people's fears that there is something sinister behind the Land Bill. It is hoped that this has been a learning experience and that the next time around the Government will be more organised. It is, however, disappointing that most of the heated debates about the Land Bill dwelt on historical events whose relevance and applicability is no longer current. Debate has centred on narrating these historical events without analysing the conceptual issues surrounding them. We trust that this House will not relegate itself to this untenable position.

The Land Bill

We have already noted the capricious way in which this Bill was initiated. Our observations are borne out by the inadequacy of the Bill itself. The Bill is supposed to provide for the tenure ownership and management of land: to amend and consolidate the Law relating to tenure, ownership, and management of land and to provide for other related incidental matters.

In the majority of its provisions, however, it leaves lingering doubts and uncertainties on what its intentions are. In many cases it restates the present position in others it brings back the old Law in a poorer form from the point of view of practicability.

It will be unfair for Government, however, to sound totally negative. The positiveness of the Bill lies in the fact that, irrespective of the muddled way it was presented it makes a break with the past, by recognising the general rights of the citizens in the land and it builds upon this foundation, the individual interests including derivative interest in land.

The Committee has therefore made many amendments to the Bill to bring it in line with what we assumed are the objectives of Government. We shall however, in this section, deal with the most contentious issues...

LAND HOLDING

The first part of the Bill deals with the various tenures under which citizens may own land. The system of freehold tenure and mailo which had been abolished by the Land Reform Decree are restored in Clause 3 of the Bill in addition to customary and leasehold tenures.

We shall deal with each tenure system separately:

Customary tenure

Clause 4 of The Bill empowers a person holding land under customary tenure, on former public land to acquire a certificate of customary ownership. By mentioning former public land, the Bill excludes the tenants occupying mailo land who had also been turned into customary tenants under the Land Reform Decree. This provision entrenches Article 237 (4) of the Constitution which is similarly worded.

The Bill, however, does not resolve the controversy surrounding customary tenure that says that it is inferior to the other types of tenure. We should have assumed that by empowering customary tenants to acquire certificates of ownership, the Bill was recognising that this system was at par in prominence with the modern tenures.

By providing that a certificate of customary tenure may be converted into freehold, the Bill like the Constitution keeps customary tenure where it is now, an inferior tenure which lacks the security modern tenures afford to their holders.

The truth is that customary tenure retains widespread legitimacy in the rural areas and offers some safeguards for the poor and the vulnerable. It recognises some degree of gender rights, where women can secure access to farm plots, and it provides a cheap mechanism for settlement of disputes. In terms of response to development it is even more desirable than freehold. In the customary system, land as such, has no value, but it is the productive effort of the individual, his wives and children which gives value to land. The landholder's rights to the land he clears are secured, as long as he cultivates his piece.

Granting certificates of ownership to land which does not have cadastral mapping will not achieve one of the aims of the Bill – affording the customary owner access to productive credit – because many financial institutions will not extend credit on the basis of a certificate of ownership, the dimensions of which cannot be easily verified.

Studies carried out in Kenya, on land registration, suggest that on the balance, the cost-benefits of land titling can be negative, resulting into increased landlessness and vulnerability for the poor, while having a minimal impact on credit and productivity for the majority of stakeholders. Furthermore, the registration exercise is extremely expensive, it requires paying for the surveys, mapping and administration.

The idea of freehold titling, which was experimented in the late 1950s by Wilson Rwetsiba in the areas of Bushenyi, Ntungamo and Rukungiri, was originally heavily subsidised and people rushed for it. When the subsidies were, however, removed, the process became so cumbersome that some people who applied for titles in 1961 did not get them until 1968. I believe Hon. Kaijuka will bear me out.

In terms of structural basis, the customary tenure is akin to freehold in that it is for an indefinite period and it is inheritable. The ultimate title, however, resides in society. We have, therefore, come to the conclusion that the customary certificate of title should be equal and at par with a freehold title, with a difference in just one aspect, the usual rights of the individual in customary tenure are subject to the general good of the community.

The Bill says little on the process of application for a certificate of ownership. The Committee has, therefore, come up with elaborate provisions on how the process may be initiated; and the functions of the Parish Land Committees have been made more detailed.

The Bill also makes a big oversight, in that it provides no law for the traditional institutions. When I say traditional institutions I do not mean as defined in the Constitution, but those referred to as the village headmen, leaders, elders, those are the ones I am referring to. As long as the tenure remains customary, these institutions must continue to play a role. It is them, that may advise the land committees on the customary rights of the applicant, or the right claimant, where there are competing applications. In many customary systems there are areas of land which are owned and utilised by the community as a whole; on this common land, all members of the group or community have equal and non-exclusive rights, an example of this is, common grazing land. The most important characteristic of this system is that it aims at maintaining that unit against strangers. The Bill recognizes this type of tenure in Clause 6; such groups are also empowered to have customary certificates of ownership and convert them into freehold. The group may appoint trustees to look after the land and communally owned land, which may be used by individuals. I hope you get me.

The law of trustees, which is part of the common law and which Clause 6 seeks to apply, is a complex system which is not well suited for customary tenure as envisaged in the Clause. The Committee believes that the formations of communal land associations would be a more practical development. Such associations have been provided for in many African countries. In South Africa, the South African Communal Property Act was enacted in 1996, the Committee borrowed heavily from that statute and from the Tanzania Land Resettlement Bill 1997, to make elaborate changes to Clause 6 of the Bill. We do, however, agree with the provisions of the Clause which allow an individual who wishes to own his own piece of land, to be allowed to do so where it is possible. We have accordingly provided for more detailed provisions on how this may be accomplished.

It may still be necessary, even after individualisation, to keep some areas for communal use for example, forests for wood fuel. We have accordingly made provisions for this situation in our amendments. Hon. Members, when you are considering our proposals under this section, you must appreciate that it is the tenure security which can be delivered by both customary and formal systems of tenure, not the formal land title, which is a relevant [sic] for investment and improved efficiency in agricultural land use.

The charge that widespread titling of small plots may lead to land fragmentation must also not be discounted. If we think that customary tenure systems are relics of primitive society, let us borrow a leaf from Zimbabwe. In 1993 the Government of Zimbabwe formed the Commission of Inquiry into appropriate agricultural land tenure systems. One of the recommendations of the Commission, which has been accepted by the Government, is the restoration of customary systems of land allocation; and that communal area households should continue to benefit from the systems of traditional freehold tenure under customary law. By maintaining customary [land tenure] and improving on it, to conform with modern developments, we shall be empowering our rural communities to develop their potential, by giving them security of land tenure. This will avoid situations where a free market reduces them to cheap labour supplemented by subsistence production.

Conversion of leases into freehold

Article 237(5) of the Constitution allows leases, which were granted on former public land to be converted into freehold. The process is, however, optional. Clause 9 of the Bill, however, provides for the automatic conversion of leases into freehold. The argument here is that, article 237 of the Constitution vests land in the citizens.

The Committee found this Clause to be one of the most contentious in the Bill. In fact most of the representations received from the Public are against this conversion. The majority of the Committee agrees with the public. Article 237(1) of the Constitution must not be interpreted restrictively. When it vests land in the citizens, it means citizens as society and as individuals. Legal scholars have now agreed that the ultimate title to land is invested in the society with the individual only enjoying the effective title. While the Constitution abolishes public land, it does not stop local authorities, for example district land boards, from holding this land in trust for the citizens in the districts.

It has been argued that the great disservice the British did to Buganda was on the allocation of land. It has been argued that half of the land in the Kingdom was allocated to 4,300 persons, in an area with a population of nearly half a million. If we believe that this act was wrong, we would be committing a bigger crime, if this enlightened Parliament were to do the same, by allowing a few people who have leases over stretches of land to convert them into freehold automatically.

The leasehold system gives Government the powers to intervene where the owners are holding land for suspicious purposes. Leaseholds lead to improved land use and planning, through the establishment of a direct and a personal relationship between society and the leaseholder. It may be necessary, however, to increase the leasehold term to a longer period, even over 199 years.

Of course one may argue that the freehold system gives the land the quality of an unrestricted disposition which in a free market would allow mobility in the transfer and disposition of land; and the psychological sense of responsibility flowing from security in ownership, that is the argument. These arguments are valid when considered from the standpoint of social justice. There is no evidence that productivity on freehold land is higher than that on leasehold or customary land. In fact, over 90 percent of the agricultural production is by small farmers on customary land.

There is danger that if we allow the creation of individual freehold ownership at this moment in time, we may encourage the growth of a class of rural proletarians, depending on the decisions of landowners for their existence. There is now a generally accepted notion that, in Africa, land belongs to a great family for which many members are dead, some are living, but the larger number is yet to be born. Even if we were to allow freehold conversion, logic would demand that this should be done selectively, after inquiring into the sustenance of the lease – for example, whether the leaseholder has fully developed his or her land, has paid ground rent regularly, whether there is no pressure for land from surrounding areas etc. Furthermore, it would still require the leaseholder to pay market rent for a reversion, depending on the balance of the term of his or her lease, rather than giving it to him on a silver plate. Proponents of conversions of lease into freehold must realise that the Constitution leaves it to Parliament to decide on the right moment to enact a law for that purpose. Our argument is that for a long time to come our society will remain agrarian and poor and the demand for land will continue. Maybe the position will have changed 50 years from now, and then, Parliament will be entitled to enact such a law.

Having agreed that the freehold title vests in the people, the Committee recommends that the reversions should be held by the district land boards, in trust, for the people. This does not give the boards the beneficial ownership. The Committee is echoing the recommendations of the report of the Uganda relations commission called the Master Report of 1961 which says that former public land should be administered by the local authorities. The primary objective here is to counteract suspicion and to push the ownership and administration of land into the hands of authorities which are accessible and familiar to landowners of every class. In view of what we are recommending above, Parliament at an appropriate stage may need to re-address itself to the various incidents of tenure provided for in article 237 of the Constitution.

Lawful and Bona Fide Occupants

Mr Speaker, as already discussed, the land reform decree had removed security of tenure from the tenants on mailo and freehold land. The 1995 Constitution however, re-introduces this security but in restrictive terms. It provides in article 237(8) as follows:

> Upon the coming into force of this Constitution, and until Parliament enacts an appropriate law under Clause 9 of this article, the lawful or bona fide occupants of mailo land, freehold shall enjoy security of occupancy on the land.

The security granted by the Constitution therefore expires the moment Parliament passes the law regulating the relationship between the tenant and a registered owner. Accordingly, the Land Bill, in Clause 10, provides for the security of occupancy of the above said category of occupants. The Bill goes further than that and turns such occupants into statutory tenants. The Constitution does not define the term "lawful" or "bona fide occupants" and in all good sense, it is difficult to envisage the special group of people the Constitution was referring to, in the absence of an interpretation by a Constitutional Court. The Bill nevertheless has its definition of the two types of occupants.

The Bill defines a lawful occupant as:

(a) a person occupying land by virtue of the repealed Busuulu and Envujjo Law of 1928, the Toro Landlord and Tenant Law of 1937, the Ankole Landlord and Tenant Law of 1937 and then;

(b) a person who entered the land with consent of a registered owner and includes a purchaser; and then;

(c) a person who had occupied former public land as a customary tenant but whose tenancy was not disclosed or compensated by the registered owner at the time of acquiring the leasehold certificate of title.

More light needs to be shed on item (a) of the definition.

In 1900 and 1901 ... the Colonial Government entered into agreements with Buganda, Toro and Ankole where parts of land were allocated and their ownership transferred to individuals. Most of this land had peasants who had occupied it for generations under the trust of the Kings and Chiefs. As the Colonial Government introduced cash crops and thus a market economy, the new owner imposed rent on the cultivators. There was, however, no security of tenure, nor formal recognition of the tenant's rights. Increasingly also, the owners started demanding excessive *envujjo*, which is a tribute – a form of tribute which the peasants had to traditionally pay to their landlords. It is said that at one time, for every three bags of cotton produced, the landowner would demand one bag. This state of affairs led to discontent, bordering on an open rebellion. A commission set up by the colonial government in Buganda, was persuaded to pass the Busuulu and Envujjo Law in 1927. This law recognised the rights of the landowner and granted safeguards to peasant occupiers. Similar registration was passed in 1937 in the Landlord and Tenant Law in Toro and Ankole.

It is the above group of occupants together with those in items (b) and (c), including their heirs, whom the Bill classifies as lawful occupants.

Bona Fide Occupants

The Bill defines a bona fide occupant as a person who, before coming into force of the Constitution:

> (a) had occupied land which lawfully belonged to another person, but which the occupant occupied and utilised or developed genuinely, believing that no registered owner or agent of the registered owner was available, from whom the occupant could obtain consent to occupy or utilise or develop the land.
>
> (b) had occupied and utilised or developed any land unchallenged by the registered owner, or agent of the registered owner, for 12 years or more.
>
> (c) had been settled on land by Government or agent of Government which may include a local authority.

These three definitions need to be addressed very cautiously. The Latin maxim 'bona fide' is equivalent to the phrase 'good faith', in English. According to the law, however, a person who enters another person's land without his permission is a trespasser. It is irrelevant and immaterial what a trespasser's state of mind was when he committed the offence. Adopting this definition would be contrary to Article 26 of the Constitution which guarantees the right to property and further provides as follows:

> No person shall be compulsorily deprived of property or any interest in, or right over property of any description, except where the following conditions are satisfied.
>
> (a) The taking of possession or acquisition is necessary for public use or is in the interest of defence, public safety, public order, public morality or public health; and

(b) The compulsory taking of possession or acquisition of property is made under a law which makes provision for; (i) prompt payment of fair and adequate compensation, prior to the taking of possession or acquisition of the property. (ii) A right of access to a court of law by any person who has an interest or right over the property.

The provision in the Bill does not even require innocence. A person could occupy what he or she knows belongs to another person and plead that the owner was not available. Furthermore, it is very difficult to determine the genuineness of the occupant, since that is an issue of the mind.

The second definition requires that the person must have been on the land for more than 12 years. Under the law, this is referred to as title by prescription. In order to prove prescription, however, the occupant must prove that he came to the land openly, without force and without permission. The Limitation Act provides that no action for the recovery of land shall be brought after the expiration of 12 years from the time such right of action arose. It must be clearly understood that the Limitation Act does not transfer title to the occupant but merely stops the owner from suing for relief. By implication, however, it comes to the same thing. If you cannot get me off your land, I can stay as long as I want. In effect, the land becomes useless to you the owner. The committee, because of the above reasons, agrees that this definition missed the test of bona fide occupant.

During our tour upcountry, some members of the public were uncomfortable with the period of 12 years because it coincides or corresponds to the period, since 1986, when the NRM came to power; and it is seen as a ploy by the Government to give legitimacy to the people it settled on other people's land. We do not think that this is true, it may just be a coincidence, in any case, the Committee was satisfied with the legal base for the definition. Furthermore, the period of 12 years must be unchallenged by the owner, evidence of even a single challenge re-establishes the owner's rights on the land. It must be understood that under the general law, the period of 12 years does not apply where the person having the right of action was under legal disability. One good example, in our case, is a person who goes into exile because of persecution, he abandons his land because of insecurity or war. There are however some people who have occupied land for less than 12 years, these, of course, are not covered by the prescription. The committee is of the view that, instead of evicting such people en masse, a compromise could be worked out which would allow such people to make a case with the landowner as to why, notwithstanding the fact that they have not occupied land for 12 years, they should nonetheless be granted security

The third definition of bona fide occupant, as given in the Bill, is clearly unconstitutional. We have already seen that under Article 26 of the Constitution, the only way Government can take away someone's land is on a 'willing seller willing buyer' basis or through compulsory acquisition, in public interest. The present definition in the Bill is silent on the issue of whether the land had been compulsorily acquired. We had assumed that this is not the case. On the basis of that assumption, the occupants on such land cannot be bona fide occupants, strictly speaking. We must, however, appreciate the fact that the person to blame is not the occupant but the Government. The occupant innocently believed that he or she was being settled on land over which the State had authority.

In the circumstances, we recommend that such occupants should qualify as bona fide occupants because of their peculiar circumstances. This, however will be conditional, it will depend on Government paying fair and adequate compensation to the owners whose land was settled on. It may be necessary to mention the issue of ranchers here.

Under the Government ranch-restructuring scheme, the Government allows pastoralists to settle on the ranches. Most of the land on which the ranches were leased is former public land. Under the lease agreements, the ranchers were obliged to develop the ranches in accordance with directives of the commissioner of veterinary services. Some ranches were already being used by nomadic people as grazing areas, consequently, they had to be evicted. Many of the ranchers developed their ranches but there were a big number who became parasite owners. They never stocked the ranches and instead hired them out to the very people who had been evicted.

The Committee has learnt in some areas, ranchers were demanding 20 heads of cattle per year for every 100 heads of cattle grazing on the ranch. It is however true, that in its quest to resettle landless people, the Government did not distinguish between those ranchers and the parasites, this resulted into a situation where some progressive ranchers lost part of their ranches.

The Committee feels that the genuine ranchers who lost their stock and infrastructure as a result of the restructuring, should be compensated because any Government intervention which was not in accordance with the lease agreements was in breach. Since this was former public land, the occupants would now transform into customary owners and be dealt with as previously provided for in the Bill, with regard to customary tenure, I am talking about people who were settled by the Government.

The Bill provides that the lawful or bona fide occupant shall be a statutory tenant of the registered owner. The effect of this provision is to prohibit a landlord from exercising the right to recover possession, against the tenant who is prepared to go on paying rent. The tenant ceases to have a contractual tenancy and gets a tenancy which continues, so long as he continues to pay rent. Adopting this provision, however, would cause some difficulties.

The Bill has provided, in Clause 13, that a tenant who leaves his or her occupancy for more than three years is taken to have abandoned it, yet the effect of Clause 10(2) is that it does not matter whether the tenant is on the land or not, as long as he continues paying rent.

Furthermore, some of the lawful tenants could have been granted occupancy under specific contractual terms, under a willing landlord willing tenant basis. It will be unfair for the law to disregard this personal relationship and make its own presumptions. Since the Bill does, in other clauses, safeguard the rights of the tenant, Clause 10(2) is not necessary.

Mr Speaker, the Bill provides for payment of ground rent of 5,000/= or 0.25 currency points by the tenant, irrespective of the size of the land. There is indeed a necessity to limit the ground rent paid, especially for those occupants on mailo and freehold land who were on the land when it was originally being allocated. The repealed Busuulu and Envujjo Law of 1927, Toro Landlord and Tenant Law 1937, also provided for nominal rent, however, in cases where the use went beyond subsistence, an extra shilling per acre was levied. The small farmer was, therefore, protected from excessive rent, while the landlord could get some extra income from the commercial farmers.

There is also a problem of land values. In Kampala for example, the value of an acre is about shs. 10 million, in Karamoja or Mubende, an acre may not be more than 200 or even 50,000/=. It would be unfair to both the landlords and the tenants, if the rent for these areas were to be uniform. The Bill also needs to consider the case of a landowner who having empty land, allows a person to occupy it, on the basis of some agreed specific ground rent. The terms of that type of occupancy should be upheld.

The Committee is therefore proposing that the rent be varied from region to region and should be fixed by the District Land Board. The Bill provides that, in the performance of its duty, the Land Board will not be answerable to anybody, we want to maintain that independence and remove the approval of the District Council. Control by the District Council will come when they are considering the annual report, which the Board will be obliged to submit to the council every year, as we are providing.

The Bill also needs to consider the case of a landowner. Mr Speaker, one of the most important aspects of the Land Bill is the introduction of the certificate of occupancy. One of the criticisms raised about the present and previous systems is that the rights of the tenant and the boundaries of his or her occupancy, could only be given through oral evidence and in many cases, it became a bone of contention between the landlord and tenant. Although, under the Busuulu and Envujjo tenants were issued receipts, these were only relevant in so far as payment of rent was concerned and did not verify the physical boundaries of the occupancy. It will now be possible for the Land Committee to verify the boundaries of the land, in which respect the certificate is to be granted.

The Bill also provides that the occupant will be able to acquire a certificate from the District Land Board without requiring the consent of the registered owner. The above provision is clearly unconstitutional and contravenes Article 26 of the Constitution. Since the certificate of occupancy is going to be an encumbrance on the landowner's title he should give his consent. This consent should come as a matter of course; where the landlord withholds consent, he must give very good reasons and the tenant has a right of appeal to the land tribunal. The Committee recommends a standard certificate of occupancy which should be available in any average shop or with the Committee. A tenant shall be able to buy that certificate and take it to the landowner to sign.

The Bill also tries to harmonise the relationship between the landowner and the tenant by giving the right of pre-emption in event one of the parties wants to sell his or her land. This provision is very welcome, as it allows the parties to negotiate on a willing seller willing buyer basis and helps to prevent future controversy.

The Committee, however, found it difficult to accept Clause 10(10) of the Bill which entitles the tenant to put a caveat on the title of the owner. The effect of a caveat is to require the buyer or dealer in any piece of land to give notice and seek consent of the caveator. We believe that a mere endorsement of the certificate of occupancy on the certificate of title, is adequate; the tenant cannot stop the owner from selling or mortgaging land as long as the person entering into such a deal knows that his or her rights are subject to those of the tenants.

The Committee further believes that it may be impossible for the holder of a certificate of occupancy to mortgage his or her certificate under the present law of mortgages, since he has only a user right. It may be necessary for Government to revisit the Mortgage Decree, to bring it in tune with these new developments.

Acquisition of registrable interest by the occupant

The Constitution requires Parliament to pass a law under which the occupant may acquire registrable interest. The Bill does not, however, change the present status in relationship between the owner and the occupant. The acquisition is based on free negotiations and the owner is not obliged to sell his land to the occupant. ...

Acquisition of land by non-citizens

The Committee agrees with the provision in the Bill which restricts non-citizens to 99 year leases. It is however, difficult to accept Clause 16(5) of the Bill which allows non-citizens who were holding freehold or mailo before the coming into force of the 1995 Constitution to continue to hold such estates. We know that before 1995, all land in Uganda was public land, by virtue of the Land Reform Decree, it was vested in the State. So there was no freehold. In any case, it will be double standards to allow such a person to continue with freehold and not to allow a Ugandan citizen who loses his citizenship but holds freehold and mailo land, not to continue holding such estates. The Constitution provides that all land is vested in the citizens of Uganda. Non-citizens are only welcome to lease this land.

The Land Fund

Any land reform policy which does not entail the facilitation of occupants to acquire registrable interests is doomed to fail, not to jail. The current impasses on freehold land can only be resolved by empowering the tenant to acquire ownership or the owner to buy off the occupant. While, however, the owner has a title which he may mortgage, the occupant has nothing. In these circumstances, the obligation is on the State to create this facilitation. The creation of the Land Fund is thus a welcome idea. It is nevertheless not desirable that particular areas must be spelt out for grants while others will only obtain loans. From the Committee's tours, it is apparent that if such a situation is maintained, it might lead to social anarchy and disintegration of the State. It is also doubtable that the Government can provide enough funds for everybody who wants to purchase his occupancy.

In order to encourage the occupants to work hard, Mr Speaker, we changed this. We have now agreed that in addition to the fund being used to give loans, it can also be utilised by Government to acquire registrable interests so that they can be distributed to occupants. In addition, the fund will be utilised to give loans to lawful or bona fide occupants who want to buy registrable interests so that they can do so. It will also be utilised by Government to acquire registrable interest and distribute these to the occupants.

The creation of the fund does not however mean that the landowner should be forcefully dispossessed. The parties should instead be encouraged to meet together and try to negotiate a method of settlement, which is fair to all and enables the land to be used productively. It will therefore, be necessary to have a neutral party who will mediate between the landowner and tenant in areas where this is possible. Accordingly, in the amendments, we have provided for the creation of the office of a mediator. The Committee would, however, discourage a situation where one section of society, because of what happened in history, is seen to be victimised without taking into account their Constitutional rights.

Control over land use

While the ownership of land is vested in the citizens by the Constitution, there is always need for the State to regulate the enjoyment of the right to property, including imposing restrictions or taking over management of some areas for the benefit of society.

In Article 237(2) of the Constitution, the Government is granted powers to take over the management of forests, water systems, swamps, national parks and gazetted areas, in trust for the people.

There is also need to provide for adjudication machinery which shall allow disputes to be resolved with minimum expenses and delay. The Bill accordingly provides for the establishment of agencies at both the central and district levels, for the better use and management of land. Some of these agencies like the Uganda Land Commission and the District Land Boards have been in the existence.

Decentralisation of land administration

Uganda Land Commission

Under the new arrangement, the Uganda Land Commission having lost its jurisdiction over public land, will mainly hold and manage land which is vested or acquired by the Government in accordance with the Constitution; and generally speaking, real property owned by the State anywhere in the world. The Commission shall also be responsible for carrying out surveys and obtaining certificates of titles for Government land.

The District Land Board

The District Land Board is created as an agency of the District Council but independent of it, in the performance of its duties. The functions of the Board are to hold and allocate land in the district, which is not owned by any person; to facilitate the registration and transfer of interests in land; to take over the management of former statutory leases to non-citizens; to carry out surveys and mapping of land and also determine the rates of compensation payable in respect of development on land.

The Board, as we have seen, is not accountable to the District Council. However, there is no reason why they should not produce an annual report which the Council should consider. It is also necessary that since the Council is the appointing authority, the Board should have regard to any views of the District Council on its report.

Land Committees

In order to ease the work of the Boards, the Bill creates Parish Land Committees whose role is to advise the Board on matters relating to land. The Committee will be responsible for ascertaining the rights on land, including inspection and verification of customary land, in collaboration with traditional institutions. ...

Land Tribunals

The Bill provides for the creation of Land Tribunals at both the Districts, sub-county, and gazetted urban area levels. These will be specialized quasi-courts whose functions shall include the determination of disputes relating to dealings in land; the determination of any disputes relating to compensation where land is compulsorily acquired by Government.

It is, however, necessary to provide for the general judicial powers of tribunals. It is suggested that in the case of District Land Tribunals, these could be specifically based on the general civil jurisdiction of Chief Magistrates Court.

The Sub-county Land Tribunal should have limited general powers equivalent to the jurisdiction of Magistrate Grade II. They should not have powers to issue Decree of specific performance.

As already suggested there is a proposal for a specific provision to give recognition to traditional dispute settlement mechanisms, to provide for mediation and to be encouraged as a way of settling disputes.

The Committee is, therefore, recommending the establishment of the position of a Mediator, who shall be a person of proven integrity and skills and shall be trusted by both parties. His role will be to negotiate agreements between landowners and tenants and to ensure that existing provisions for market transactions between such persons can be made to work.

Recommendations

1. The Bill should, after it is passed into law, be delayed from becoming effective for a period of six months, during which the political leaders should explain its contents to the citizens. This would help in raising people's awareness of the law and ease its implementation.
2. Customary tenure should be ranked at par, in value and substance, with other types of tenure. Persons applying for certificates of ownership should be allowed, therefore, to carry out cadastral surveys and mapping of their land.
3. Communal Land Associations should be allowed for those areas which still want to be governed by customary law and are owned by communities for joint use.
4. No automatic conversion of leasehold into freehold should be allowed. People owning leases should continue owning those leases until such a time as a law detailing conditions under which they may be converted into freeholds or otherwise, is passed by Parliament.
5. Former public land should be held by the District Land Boards in trust on behalf of the citizens. Until a law is passed providing for conversion of leases into freeholds, the reversionary interests in such land should rest in the Board. The Board shall exercise the powers of the controlling authority with regard to granting and renewal of leases, charging of premium and ground rent, and putting conditions.
6. Only those occupants who have occupied land for a period of more than twelve years, unchallenged by the registered owners, and those settled by the Government, should qualify as bona fide occupants.
7. In cases where the Government settled people on land belonging to an individual, they should pay him/her adequate compensation, in accordance with Article 26(2) of the Constitution.
8. Occupants who do not qualify to be bona fide occupants may approach the registered owner with a view to regularising their occupancy on a willing landlord willing tenant basis, but no landlord should be compelled to grant occupancy to such individuals.
9. Bona fide and lawful occupants should exclude licensees who were granted temporary use of the land by the registered owner.

10. Lawful occupants who entered the land after the coming into force of the Constitution shall not benefit from the provisions of the Bill which will deal with the payment of ground rent. Relationships entered into with the landowner, by such people, shall be governed by the general law of contract.
11. Persons who entered someone's land without that person's permission and do not qualify as indicated above are trespassers and should not be protected by the Bill.
12. People who were settled on ranches by Government under the Ranch Restructuring Scheme should be taken as bona fide, but the Government must pay fair and adequate compensation to the ranchers for the loss of the land developments and any damage done to their infrastructure.
13. The payment of ground rent should be left to the District Land Boards, which, however, shall be obliged to charge nominal rent taking into account the variation in values of land in different regions.
14. The certificate of occupancy should be granted by the registered owner. In cases of non-consent the occupant should appeal to the Land Tribunal to make a decision on the matter.
15. Instead of the occupant placing a caveat on a title of a registered owner, the occupancy should be endorsed as an encumbrance on title, to give notice to a third party who may want to have dealings in the land.
16. The consent of minor children and children of majority age should not be required before any dealings in family holdings.
17. Non-citizens should only own leases to the maximum of 99 years.
18. The proposed Land Fund should be applied universally to enable tenants by occupancy to obtain registrable interests and also assist persons who may want their land surveyed and mapped.
19. In the settlement of disputes on customary land, the traditional leaders should continue to be involved, in conjunction with the former systems of the land tribunals....

Mr Speaker and Hon. Members, this has been an exhausting and energy sapping exercise. We however, have proceeded as a Committee with the enthusiasm and dedication expected of us, knowing very well that the future of our Nation is at stake. While we are debating this Report, let us try to keep our emotions at minimum. Let us debate and pass a law which will strengthen the unity and amity of our people. During the debate there must not be any winners and losers. It is said that politicians say what people want to hear, and that leaders tell what is right, even if it is a bitter pill. I implore you to become leaders because this law is not about politics.

****

4
Customary Land Tenure

DEFINITION OF CUSTOMARY TENURE

Customary land tenure is one of the four-land tenure systems recognised by article 237(3) of the Uganda Constitution. Section 4(1) of the *Land Act,* defines customary land tenure as a form of tenure:

(a) applicable to a specific area of land and a specific description or class of persons;
(b) subject to section 28[7] of this Act, governed by rules generally accepted as binding and authoritative by the class of persons to which it applies;
(c) applicable to any persons acquiring land in that area in accordance with those rules;
(d) subject to section 28 of this Act, characterised by local customary regulation;
(e) applying local customary regulation and management to individual and household ownership, use and occupation of, and transaction;
(f) providing for communal ownership and use of land;
(g) in which parcels of land may be recognised as subdivisions belonging to a person, a family or a traditional institution; and
(h) which is owned in perpetuity.

Outside Buganda and urban areas, most land in Uganda is owned under customary land tenure. The specific tenure system varies according to the ethnic group and region of the country. However, due to several factors such as government intervention, migration, inter-tribal social-economic interaction, and population pressure on land, many customary systems have similar characteristics.[8]

CLASSIFICATION OF CUSTOMARY TENURE

In the following extract the writer identifies major classifications of customary land tenure systems in Uganda.

****

Obol-Ochola: *Customary Land Tenure and the Economic Development in Uganda,* LLM Dissertation, University of Dar es Salaam, 1971

Traditionally land tenure systems in Uganda fell broadly under three systems, namely: communal or tribal tenure where ownership was vested in the ruler either as owner or trustee – this tenure prevailed mainly in the Kingdom areas of Uganda (Buganda, Toro, Bunyoro and Ankole) which were usually referred to as the lacustrine Kingdoms. They had centralised and feudalistic systems of administration.[7]

Secondly, clan tenure was the common tenure in the nilotic, nilo-hamitic and Bakiga communities – some of these tribes had traditional chiefs, but with decentralised systems of administration in which clan leaders and elders had great influence on the Chief. And thirdly, what may be described – for lack of better terminology – as nomadic tenure prevalent in Karamoja district.[8] Under this system grazing right was vested in the entire members of the tribe with no

---

[7] Section 28 prohibits any customary practice that discriminates against women, children and disabled persons. See Chapter 5.

[8] Obol-Ochola, *Customary Land Tenure and the Economic Development of Uganda,* (LLM dissertation, University of Dar es Salaam, 1970) p. 75.

specific rights vested in the individual. However, restrictive claims to certain pastures or wells are permanently or seasonally enhanced. In both the tribal and clan tenure systems – these were simple agricultural societies – individual rights to field agricultural products, trees, trapping sites etc. did exist. Again in the tribal and clan systems cultivated fields and homesteads were owned corporately, but within this clan and tribal umbrella there were specific rights of individuals attached to the fields, agricultural products and the homesteads. However, grazing lands, forests and virgin uncultivated grasslands within the clan or tribal boundaries were communally owned by the clan or tribe, in the sense that no specific rights, estates or interests were vested in the individual members of the clan or tribe....

The present customary tenure in Uganda is a result of many contemporary social, economic and political forces. ...

Tribal tenure

Tribal tenure where ownership [was] vested in the rulers or kings ...is now defunct. Some elements of feeling by members of a tribe that the land within the tribal boundary is owned collectively or communally by the tribe still exists. Clan, village and family tenures are still predominant, but in the densely populated areas there is a general trend towards individual tenure. ... This trend is mainly because of demographic pressures on land.

Clan tenure

Clan as corporate land holding unit is by far the most important in Uganda customary land law today. This statement is buttressed by an assertion of K. K. Labwoni who was then a Bunyoro Saza Chief:

> From the time people first settled in Bunyoro, the clan system has been the force which has united them; for although rulers rose and fell, the clans have remained. The basis of the clan system is the land. The greater the clan, the more land it would possess. Each clan held sufficient land for the permanent food crops such as plantains, for the annual crops, for its grazing and for the needs of the future generation.

He then continued to comment on the nature of clan tenure in the following words:

> Inside the boundaries of the clan land, each family would have its own recognised area in which the householder's sons would settle and increase the numbers of the family. A householder had the right to allocate land to his children within his family area, but if there was no available land at his disposal, the sons had to apply to the head of the clan to give them unoccupied portion of the clan lands. The head of the clan has authority to allow a person who is not a member of the clan to settle and build on the clan lands. Any children born to that man are reckoned as belonging to the clan, are subject to the rules of the clan and are called members of the clan.

...

Rights of the clan

What is the nature of control of the clan over individual landholders within the clan unit? We should attempt to answer this question by looking at a few clans picked at random from three of the regions of Uganda. We believe that from these examples we shall get a clear picture of the quantum and nature of control exercised by the clan and its land controlling agencies. For this purpose we shall examine the practice and custom in Acholi, Bugisu and [Teso]. Under customary law a clan is a corporate legal entity with perpetual succession.

[Acholi]
We would look at the custom in Acholi first.... For instance, the clan of the Panyinga has a clearly defined area of land in Padibe. The boundary of the clan is demarcated by [a] river ...a small hill ... by the limit of the gardens.... The land within the boundary is exclusively for use of the members of members of Panyiga clan. The man in charge of allocation and controlling the use of land is known as Rwot-Kweri (the chief of the Hoe). Plots which are allocated to individual members remain theirs unless they abandon it. Each member has an absolute title to his agricultural products. Cultivation is normally carried out communally in consideration for food and beer. Once a piece of land has been cleared by individual efforts and used as a garden the improvement thereon may be sold but only to members of the clan.... Members of the clan, including assimilated strangers, communally enjoy rights over grazing land, forests, grass, wells and water from [the] river ...and clay deposits for making pots and the various paths to and from Panyinga.

[Bugisu]
It has been pointed out by G.K.A. Gayer [in Lawrence (ed) *Land Tenure in Uganda*, 1957, at p 10] that in Bugisu the clan exercised the following rights over its land: to settle land dispute within the areas of. its control; to exercise a right of option to buy land offered for sale and to declare void any land transaction which has not received its approval. The community has grazing rights, free use of water, firewood, clay deposits and grass for thatching. He suggested that these rights by the clan should be referred to as mere safeguards.

[Teso]
In Teso, the allocation of land lies in the hands of the clan leader or extended family head within the group, which traditionally has authority over the area. Land rights may be acquired by members of the extended family either by inheritance or gift by breaking new ground. These rights are stated by Lawrence [Lawrence (ed) *Land Tenure in Uganda*, 1957, at p 24] to be "nearly amounting to full ownership. In particular, they imply the right to cultivate, to excavate, to build, to bury the dead, to cut trees...to sub-divide and bequeath the land or any part of it. They do not imply the right to sell or rent the land". A stranger, on the other hand, does not, at any rate for a considerable time by the end of which he has been absorbed into the community, obtain rights so approximate to full ownership. He must first find a sponsor who might speak before the allocating authority as to his character, and if the authority is satisfied he will then be allocated land which he may cultivate, but only so much land as he is able to cultivate and after the first harvest he is expected to provide beer and food for the clan leaders. In the course of time a stranger may acquire the full rights possessed by a local person, but until he does he has merely the right of user which are not strictly speaking inheritable, and he may under certain circumstances, for instance if convicted of witchcraft or theft, be liable to eviction by the land authority; furthermore he forfeits his rights if he leaves the land.

Individual interests in clan land

It is important to state that the individual is rapidly being emancipated from the clan yoke or group control. We should therefore next look at the nature of rights of an individual within the umbrella of clan tenure. The individual acquires the right to occupy and use clan land by any of the following modes, namely: first as a clan member he may be allocated any clan land over which no other member exerts a claim; secondly, he may inherit land from his father; thirdly, he may acquire usufructory interest in land as a result of a right of a gift; fourthly, it is common now for him to buy land from other clan members ... Once the individual has a valid claim over the clan land he enjoys the following rights: to utilise his land as he thinks best; to lend the land for temporary purposes; sell the improvement or the land; dispose of it according to customary law of inheritance; prohibit grazing near his homestead; fence his homestead; and he is entitled to enjoy the benefits of the subsistent and cash crops he grows on the land allocated to him. In some districts in Uganda he may even rent his land. All these modern forces tend to introduce flexibility in the acquisition, use and occupation of clan land as between members and even by strangers.

....

Inheritance

...

[I]t seems possible to summarise the following as being the basic principles of customary inheritance. [F]irst it is to be noted that all Ugandan societies are partrilineal; secondly, following from the first point, women do not inherit land; thirdly, a boy usually takes over the land allocated to his mother for her use and care; fourthly, a brother of a deceased father looks after land of a minor until the minor comes of age; fifthly, customary inheritance normally operates within an automatic and built-in functional system and testamentary disposition is infrequent; sixthly, inheritance cause serious land problems in areas where population is dense and leads to serious fragmentation, but in the less densely populated areas, inheritance of land does not present social problems; and, finally, it is to be noted that customary inheritance is the greatest single enemy of individualisation of land interests, since the self-acquired land may devolve into family property.

...

Village tenure

Village tenure is one of the important systems of land holding under customary law. ...[I]ts nature and incidence are similar to clan tenure. The institutional controls by members of the village through the leader or the Chief ... are the same ...[as] in case of clan tenure. The quantum and nature of right of the individual within the village tenure are also the same as those of an individual in the clan tenure. The only point of departure is on the basis of membership. On the one hand, only members of a clan and accepted strangers enjoy the usufruct of clan land. A person becomes a member of a clan by tracing his descent patrilineally to the founder of the clan. On the other hand, a village is a land tenure, and sometimes also an administrative unit, constituted by members who may not be blood relations. They are normally people who have settled around the trading centres, schools, churches, water pump stations, dams, and at the local government administrative headquarters. Although they may be from a different clan they invariably live in a social unit.

...

Individual tenure

How far can we meaningfully talk about individual tenure in Uganda today? ... Indeed, how far is an individual free to exert exclusive claim of ownership under customary law? This is a sensitive, controversial and politically explosive issue in Uganda on which one must avoid impetuous generalisations or under-estimates.

....

[The author cited a number of writers who claimed that individual customary landownership existed in various parts of Uganda, and continued]. Apart from Kigezi, it is submitted that the popular view among the Africans is opposed to the idea of individual interest in land and they tend to treat it with suspicion and hostility. ... Indeed, it might be more accurate and satisfactory to [state] that generally there is a trend or a transitional phase towards individual tenure, though the feeling of clan tenure is still rampant. [Due to diverse social, political and economic factors the level of change towards individual tenure is not uniform]. In Kigezi District, for instance, where there is a real shortage of land the individual has naturally tended to be more demanding and assertive of his rights. In the sparsely populated districts, e.g. Acholi and Madi, individual tenure is a largely strange and unintelligible idea.

****

Questions

1. Compare and contrast the customary systems of land tenure discussed by Obol-Ochola with your customary system of tenure or other customary tenures you have observed.
2. Obol-Ochola talks of 'usufructuary' rights as opposed to individual title. What are 'usufructuary' rights?
3. To what extent, if any, does the *Land Act*, 1998, alter the rights of individual holders under the customary tenure systems described by Obol-Ochola? See, for example, sections 5 – 9.
4. Do you agree that a change to individual tenure is inevitable? Discuss with reasons.
5. Alice is an aspiring Member of Parliament. She has five siblings, all male. Alice's father died recently. In his will he devised his land, which he owned under customary tenure, to Alice. However, the clan elders have refused to recognise her title because, according to the clan customary land tenure law, women are prohibited from inheriting customary land. The clan elders have instead decided to recognise Alice's brothers as the joint owners of the land. Advise Alice. (Refer to the *Land Act* and the Constitution).
6. It is a truism that customary law – including customary land tenure – is dynamic. Discuss the forces that contribute to this change and why.

****

CUSTOMARY LAND TENURE AND ECONOMIC DEVELOPMENT

Is customary land tenure a constraint on Uganda's economic development?
During the debates of the Land Bill, President Museveni reportedly 'rubbished' customary land laws and said that they were backward and should not be encouraged in the new bill. Museveni said, 'Customary laws refused to operate when we were still under populated in 1956 with a population of only 4 million. How can it operate now with a population of over 20 million? Don't use land in the context of backwardness, use it to increase production'. The President stressed that the law must change to increase production and transform society. (*Monitor* Newspaper, 25 April 1998).

****

Obol-Ochola, Customary Land Tenure and the Economic Development in Uganda.[9] 'Customary Land Law and development: a theoretical and normative consideration and critique

General remarks

The conception of this thesis has been prompted by two reactions. On the one hand, a protracted study of the subject of customary tenure has led us to the conclusion that to study rules of law without paying attention, or relating such rules to the policy behind the rules is a reactionary and negative scholarly gymnastics, which should be discouraged. On the other hand, following from the first point, one of our fundamental assumptions in this work is that we are anxious for economic development and social transformation. This is our first imperative; and, since we have had a sustained interest in land law, we attempt herein to relate the subject of customary tenure to the serious issue of development in Uganda. The question is, taking it for granted that we must

---

9 Some of the footnotes have been omitted.

develop, does customary tenure frustrate and keep our efforts stagnant? If it does, a normative question follows: how can we make customary law facilitate development policies? If it does not, why has the traditional system of land holding been subjected to such vehement strictures?

On the other hand, this thesis was a result of our reaction to the bitter fact that at the moment there seems to be very little development in the rural communities. On the second point, we observed that the life and the appearance of the peasant cultivator has remained the same for a long time now. The same inevitable question then is why has the peasant economy entrenched itself so much in Uganda? Is customary tenure the culprit? If it is true that customary tenure is responsible for this sluggish, or almost static rate of economic development, why can we not remove it for retarding our very much wanted progress? Of course we realise that the obstacles to development could be many and customary law may just be one of them. That may be true. However, we should restrict ourselves here to the discussion of the relevance of this subject to development programs and aspirations. Others may, from the point of view of their disciplines, identify other obstacles and they are also entitled within their own fields to look for the relevant and effective therapy or panacea.

We are conscious of our limitations to discuss the subject competently with the sharp and shrewd and business-like eyes of the economist. McAuslan has correctly pointed out "that it is with some trepidation that I step into the unfamiliar territory of-the economist." However, it is generally agreed now that the problems of agricultural development and land tenure are related. It is an obvious fact that before a farmer can plough and sow seeds on a piece of ground, he must first have got or get a lawful and peaceful access to it. Land tenure may bar him from getting access to arable land or give a very small and economically unviable unit. At the initial stage of getting access to the land the economist may allow us to have a say. This is the first reason why we consider that these topics - land-tenure and agriculture - are related. Secondly, after having acquired a piece of land a farmer would like to ensure that in the course of his farming, he is not molested or evicted from the farm. This involves security of tenure, which, too, is within a lawyer's field. Indeed, even some of our indigenous progressive farmers feel very strongly about land title and security of use as part of and necessary conditions to their agricultural activities.

...

The legal implications of economic developments and programmes of modernisation, as pointed out by Professor Allot, are that any major change in social and economic arrangements which a government wishes to introduce has to be procured by a revision of the law and the law may also be changed as a stimulant to economic development. Law is therefore both an instrument of economic change and it is also a lubricant which facilitates the realisation of economic goals. Does customary tenure obstruct Uganda's development policies and aspirations?

Criticisms levelled against customary tenure

Customary tenure has been a common target of academic sceptics, agricultural opportunists and Commissions with different motives and ideologies. We should only examine a few for purposes of this chapter.

The negative views expressed against customary tenure started with colonialism. However, owing to the British policy of gradualism and indirect rule, nothing official was done to change the nature and status of customary land-law. In East Africa the official attitude was focused to this subject after a report by the East African Royal Commission.

On the lst January 1953 a Royal Commission was appointed to enquire and make recommendation for the better economic development of the land in East Africa, including the modification of the tribal traditional system of land tenure. As a result, a very comprehensive report was published in June, 1955. The following principal recommendations were made under the chapter entitled 'Tenure and disposition of land':

(i) Land policy which aims at individualisation of land ownership and mobility in the transfer of land, without ignoring existing property rights, will enable access to land for economic use.
(ii) Land tenure law cannot be left to evolve under the impact of modern influences. A lead must be given by government to meet the requirements of the progressive elements of society by applying a more satisfactory land tenure law.
(iii) Existing property rights must not be arbitrarily disturbed. Exclusive individual ownership of land must be registered and government must not dispose of the land without an established legal process of adjudication and registration of all interests in land.
(iv) There should be prohibition on the registration of subdivision of land below a certain size.
(v) Land tenure rules to meet local circumstances must command a measure of local support, but no rules should be made which are inconsistent with the territory-wide policy and which would obstruct the eventual individualisation of land ownership and access to land in the interests of the territory as a whole.
(vi) Local Land Boards should be established to assist in interpreting and guiding views and actions concerning land tenure.
(vii) Finally, in so far as barriers to free land exchange are not removed, to that extent will the prosperity of the people of the territories of East Africa be retarded.

The above recommendations were made on the assumption of the following endemic ills of customary tenure: it did not allow mobility in the transfer and disposition of the land; ownership of land under customary tenure was not recognised by financial institutions for purposes of loan and this was a big impediment to development; the advisory system of customary inheritance coupled with expansion of population lead to fragmentation and subdivision of holding; finally, in the cattle-keeping communities, customary law permitted communal grazing which leads to absence of proper pasture management and the deterioration of the pasture eventually resulting in soil erosion.

An economic survey mission to Uganda in 1962 in its report also came out strongly against customary tenure. The report of this Survey Mission supported the recommendations of the East African Royal Commission and castigated customary tenure as an impediment to economic development of Uganda.

In its own words, the report of the Survey Commission, went on to say the following which we quote at length because of their of their importance and relevance to this work:

> Apart from mailo land in Buganda and limited areas in Western Province, land is held under customary forms of tenure by Africans. Their forms vary, but their major characteristics are that there is no private ownership of land (land is neither surveyed nor registered) and the allocation of rights to land depend on clan relationship and in some instances on tribal or district Councils. There is no security of tenure, no title and no market for the land, consequently there is no incentive to invest in land, to increase its productivity or its capitalised value. As the Royal Commission pointed out, the major criterion for distribution of land is land need rather than land use. Customary tenure is based on the needs of a simple subsistence economy and the social relationships that are associated with land use in such an economy.

The Survey Commission concurred with the Royal Commission's recommendation that land use rather than land need should be the criterion for land rights and the market should be the arbiter of these rights. If there was to be a market for land there will have to be individualisation of titles and tenure and this would require survey, adjudication of rights and registration of titles.

However, in the short run, changes in the system of land tenures should be modest and largely based on modifying rather than altering the fundamental structure of land system. Such modifications should take account of the changing political and economic conditions in Uganda and be considered as part of the general programme to increase productivity and encourage the flow of capital into agriculture.

Here again then we had an instance where communal customary tenure was singled out as the impediment to development for the following defects: absence of private ownership; land under customary tenure being neither surveyed nor registered, absence of security of tenure; and this kind of tenure being devoid of title and market for land. Above all, customary tenure was inhibitive to incentive to invest in land, to increase its productivity or its capitalised value.

As pointed out by Prof. R. W. James, one of the arguments against customary communal tenure is based on psychological assumptions. It is contended that individual sense of responsibility flows from security in ownership. The argument comes out in a dramatic form in the famous words of Arthur Young:

> the magic of property turns sand into gold....Give a man the secure title of a bleak rock and he will turn it into a garden. Give him a nine years' lease of a garden and he will convert it into a desert.

The FAO Africa Survey Report was also against customary tenure and in favour of individual ownership of land:

> In much of the territory, the right to occupy land is considered irrevocable. In many areas it is the fact of cultivation the establishment of tree crops or the construction of a house which guarantees individual use for as long as the signs of individual activities persists.

In spite of all these strictures against customary communal tenure, it would seem to us that the shortcoming recently pointed out by McAuslan is most important and it is a point we should emphasise and discuss seriously in the concluding part of this chapter.

> Fourthly, and lastly, the commercial banks, both state companies dealing with farm equipment and the like, will not readily accept that a customary title in land can be as good a security for loan as a registered title. This may be unfortunate, but it is one of these existing facts, which it would perhaps be better to learn to live with than try to alter. Efforts to do so are 50 years too late.

Indeed, the factors which have precipitated the arguments against customary system of land holding could be epitomised as follows: insecurity of tenure, communal tenure, uncertain boundaries, poor farm and pasture managements, and fragmentation and sub-division owing to customary system of inheritance, lack of capital value, and individual incentive for developments. Next, we should have a look at some of the arguments in favour of customary tenure.

Objections to criticisms

Customary tenure has been in the dock for so long that it has won the sympathy of a few observers. Human psychology tends to be against excesses either for or against and spontaneously sympathy is usually meted out against an institution or person being seriously scolded. Indeed, basic human sympathy calls for justice. Justice in turn demands fair hearing. Have we given a fair chance of hearing to customary tenure? This is the question which seemed to have provoked recent support for traditional tenure and the subsequent transfer of the blame for static development from customary tenure to some other variables or agencies.

The first argument against customary tenure was that it perpetuates communal tenure. It has been pointed out that this is a fallacious argument based on the wrong a priori assumption that African land law is static and does not adapt itself to changing conditions, and circumstances. Although there are vestiges of communal "safeguards" over tenure, there is a trend set towards individual tenure. C M White comes out clearly that "the sum total of rights which make up the system of African land tenure can only be regarded as equivalent to individual tenure."

Professor Bentsi-Enchill had this to say:

> This is substantially the position in a large number of traditional African politics where the allodial title is regarded as being in the community as a whole or the chief as trustee for the whole people. Beneath the umbrella of this group title is a progressive *individualisation* of interests specific to particular portions of group owned land and vested in sub-groups and individuals. It is the unapportioned area which, like public land everywhere remains under the direct supervision of the group.

He therefore stresses that there is individual ownership of land, some of these equal, some less, some more in quantity than the Anglo-American fee Simple. Asante has also pointed out that the courts in Ghana have established a trend of transforming traditional usufructs into individual rights over land. In East Africa sale, pledging and leasing land under customary tenure are not just practised but they are now recognised and enforced by the courts. It is thus clear that sufficient doubts have been cast on the charges against the backward communal African tenure.

The second argument against African tenure was that there is no security of tenure and there was no land title. Chango Machyo has rebutted this contention by pointing out that there has never been insecurity of tenure in East Africa. Today its prevalence is due to conditions which could be remedied by legislation. He went on that both 'land speculation and hoarding are not characteristic of communal tenure. In fact, the latter system is the best safeguard against these evils.' Richards has also pointed out that 'what they envy is not the security of a peasant on his plot, for their own system of land tenure gives the peasant the security he requires. On the contrary, they envy the Gandas' power of raising large sums of money for sale or mortgage.' Indeed, it seems, possible to argue that in the traditional African system of tenure there was security of tenure. However, increase of population and subsequent increasing pressure on the land has introduced boundary disputes in the densely populated areas.

The third conventional argument against traditional tenure was that, under it, land is not treated as a marketable commodity and therefore land has no market value. Under this system there is no sale, leasing, mortgaging and other commercial dealings in land. It has been pointed out now a number of times that there have been sales of land in Africa in many communities before the advent of Europeans and in the present time where there is economic pressure on the land contracts for sale of land are common; such lands have acquired economic value. Consequently sale, mortgage and other dealings in land have been adopted by customary law. It was wrong to blame customarytenure for this. Recent experiment in Kigezi District has proved this assumption misleading:

> Moreover the Uganda Government's experience in the pilot schemes for the registration of land titles in Kigezi and Ankole seem to indicate that what peasant farmers were most concerned with was not the paper title as such but safety from those who might grab their land. They are more concerned with having boundaries of their plots properly defined so that they will feel adequately secure.

Although it may be argued that it is too early to properly and objectively judge or evaluate the economic results of these pilot schemes, it would seem seriously misleading to maintain the argument that traditional tenure was responsible for subsistence economy and it is the same factor which is maintaining this economic structure. This kind of argument takes us to the "egg-and chicken" logic and therefore detracts our attention from serious problems facing us. Land tenure cannot determine the question of when land will acquire market value in a given society.

We have pointed out that by far the most cogent argument against customary tenure is that it does not enable customary landowners to raise capital from financial institutions - an existing fact we have to learn to live with. This suggestion has been subject to a number of subsequent scrutinies. Quite a number of writers seem to be zealous to exonerate customary law from this charge. It was pointed out that in theory the idea of raising capital is very plausible. However, experience has shown that it does not work wonders in a peasant or small-scale agriculture. To raise enough capital by sale will depend on where the land is situated and on its potential value for either agricultural or industrial use and on the acreage to be sold. If it is miles away from factors which determine its value, then the proceeds might not even be enough to pay for fertilisers.

Moreover, Kyesimira has pointed out that traditionally the banks are very reluctant to grant loans to farmers and this basically has nothing to do with customary tenure - the security of tenure is merely used as a cover up. Dr Van Arkadic also pointed out that it was not bank loans to smallholders that were the most significant sources of agricultural credit in East Africa. Furthermore, it has been contended that to give a loan to a peasant farmer does not mean necessarily that he will change the economic status from subsistent to cash economy. As a matter of fact, the mortgage system has been cursed by the peasant farmers. Liversage said:

> When the capital is borrowed, however, the trouble arises out of the rigidity of the debt compared to the returns which are always fluctuating. ...Sooner or later returns fall below the level at which the obligations were contracted, the debtors working capital becomes reduced and his economic efficiency impaired. The farmer is thereby placed in a vulnerable situation in which he runs the risk of being dispossessed with the loss of the greater part of his equity in the farm.

Liversage thus suggested that borrowing was no remedy for low average income. It only aggravates the evil by increasing the peasants' cash obligation. For there was an ever present temptation to borrow, in order to maintain a preconceived standard of living.

Both the Royal Commission and the economic Survey Commission were implicitly stating that-it would be a good idea if lands were accumulated in the hands of the most progressive people in society. This has also been strongly objected to on political, social and economic grounds. President Nyerere has said that even if there were no rich foreigners in this country there would emerge rich and clever Tanganyikans. "If we allowed land to be sold like a robe, within a short period, there would only be a few Africans possessing land in Tanganyika and all the others would be tenants." Professor Rudi went on that in such a situation "Land ownership then becomes the organiser of wealth and the arbiter of social values. Land speculation and absentee landlordism follow as a matter of course and present not only social problems but also provide an obstacle to development."

Chango Machyo presses the point even further by stating that experience in countries like Egypt, and most of the Middle East and Latin American countries has shown that private land ownership has a strong tendency to induce unbalanced distribution of income. The result is that as the landlord becomes richer through rents collected from the peasant farmers and share-croppers, the latter become poorer and poorer. Therefore their purchasing power is diminished and this has a negative effect on the economic development in general.

The above then are the counter arguments normally advanced against individualisation and hence in support of traditional land tenure. We are therefore apparently at a loss. All the arguments for and against traditional tenure have got supporters. The only conclusion we are, therefore, logically led to, as pointed out by the East African Royal Commission Report, is that from the land usage angle there is nothing necessarily associated as more beneficial either with communal or an individual approach. Neither individual tenure nor co-operatives nor collective farming makes crops grow better.

Indeed, armchair arguments for or against customary tenure does not seem to take us far. The glaring practical fact remains the same. It is that the rate of economic development and social transformation within the peasant sector is irritatingly slow. What should we do about it? Blaming or praising customary law does not seem to solve the problem. It should indeed be noted that too much realism leads to infertility and detracts from one's original creativeness. Too much idealism also lends to ineffectiveness. We must therefore, in the next section of this chapter adopt both a functional and conceptual approach and assumption in order to tackle the problem and provide possible solutions to the hitch provided by customary land law in relation to development.

Appraisal of the conflicting views

From the outset it should be pointed out that this section of the chapter will be discussed with the following basic commitments and pre-suppositions:

(i) Uganda is resolutely committed to developing a united socialist state at an accelerated speed.
(ii) We have to be realistic and it would be preposterous to expect modern changes to emerge out of the blue in one day.
(iii) Land is the most important national asset and should be used in the best possible ways to serve and promote national or public interest. It therefore follows that landownership, use, occupation and development should be determined by national policies and aspirations.
(iv) Since development constitutes our basic theme and commitment, all possible land must be put to effective use. Ownership should be determined by effective use. Lands not being properly used according to national priorities must be forfeited.
(v) Finally, it is platitudinous to state that Uganda is now an independent sovereign African state. The majority of the citizens in the Benthamite sense are Africans. The interests and progressive African concepts should be paramount. We should no longer tolerate a situation where Africans' net interests, rights and conceptions are treated as inferior and backward. We have had enough of that kind of treatment during the colonial period. There should be no more of it.

With the above five basic assumptions, we should now proceed to appraise the defects and the peculiar strength of customary land law with a view to postulating some possible solutions on the best course of action necessary to make customary tenure facilitate rather than retard our programmes of modernisation and development.

The first and most important issue involving customary tenure is the question of individual versus communal tenure. We have seen as a fact ... in some Uganda communities tribal awareness, and clan tenure in relation to land still exist. McAuslan has warned that this problem is discussed in non-legal literature and is not in fact susceptible to a legal answer. With due respect we do not agree with this watertight division of intellectual role. It is conceded that, from an economic standpoint, the type of tenure does not necessarily lead to rapid economic development. However, the choice between individual and communal tenure raises fundamental problems relating to the kind of society we want to build. This is a matter of basic policy and commitments. We are committed to socialism. Therefore fundamental socialist doctrines should determine whether or not we shall favour one or the other type of tenure.....

Indeed, now that we are committed to socialist principles the issue of individual and communal tenure is very relevant. We should not establish or continue to have a tenural system which willfoster and perpetuate exploitation, social and economic injustice and disparity. Because of these ideals we have already suggested that in this conflict both customary communal tenure and individual tenure advocated by the two commissions be improved upon or abandoned - but on different grounds. We have submitted that in a socialist state the executive must formulate and implement the necessary development policies and programmes. The executive must be in a position to control the citizens and enforce its policies effectively. On the basis of this argument we have proposed that radical title be vested in the State. Ownership should, in the words of R. W. James, be nationalised. The issue of individual ownership and communal ownership, therefore, becomes irrelevant and redundant. As a matter of idle policy both customary law and the freehold should be carefully examined. Customary law communal proprietary interests tends to foster parochial and anti-national aspirations and ideas and may therefore impede free access to land for developments. Freehold ownership is bad because it will make us continue to suffer from exploitation of man by man and perpetuate social and economic disparity in Uganda.

Having submitted that ownership be nationalised the next question is what interest or estate should be vested in landholders. We have already indicated that we prefer leasehold estate - preferably on communal basis. Individual leaseholds of certain maximum acres may also be permitted but this must be subjected to proper and effective anti-exploitation institutional set-ups or structures, and vigorous development conditions.

The next important issue is the question of loans to customary tenants. We have seen the arguments for and against this institution. It would seem to us that there are two problems here, namely, first the question of good security for such loans by peasant farmers, and secondly the problem arising from traditional or orthodox attitude of the bank. We should look at the question of good security first. We begin from the unavoidable premise that a bank cannot lend money without a good security. Unless it takes a good security it will collapse. The second point is also a hard nasty fact: most of the rural lands under customary tenure have poor market value and no one would be interested in buying them in event of a fore-closure of a mortgage. Indeed, to simplify this argument it would be submitted that the rural lands held under customary tenure cannot provide security which would be acceptable to even a modest and progressive bank. This is a bleak fact and we cannot in any way pretend or shy around it. The third point is that we do not want the rich Ugandans to buy the land of the poor peasants in the would-be multifarious processes of mortgages. This would defeat our purpose and it does not solve our problem – the economic progress of the Common Man in the rural sector. To develop, he needs capital. It is seriously submitted that we should abandon this argument in support of transformation and raising the status of customary tenure so that it acquires a secure title, which will enable peasant farmers to get loans from the bank. It cannot work and produce the wonders attributed to it. The customary tenants will not get the loan. If we think they will, we are unrealistic, hypocritical and not honest in searching for the best solution in the unique circumstances of the case. It occurs to us that the only solution is for us to look for other alternative securities. Other alternative securities which could be pledged to the banks are: livestock (cows, goats etc), government guarantees, and an insurance system of security for loans. The details and the economic implications of these proposals could be worked out by relevant experts. However, we feel duty bound that the pressing need for development and modernisation, on the one hand, and realism, on the other, calls for open-mindedness and serious search for possible alternatives. As for the banks, it has been noted that they are reluctant to lend money to peasant farmers and they use the security issue merely as a shield. To force the banks to do something wrong is stupid. At the same time we should not tolerate a bank which is basically unco-operative, negative and unsympathetic to our national problems. If we are convinced that we are taking the right course of action, the banks should move along with us without any question. The control and powers the banks enjoyed during the colonial period should immediately come to a halt. We must give way and clear the stage for purposeful national growth and development. This calls for an immediate investigation of what the banks hitherto have been up to and positively correcting the situation.

The third point we would like to comment upon briefly here is the question of security of physical land boundary. If leasehold estate is taken as the standard interest it becomes necessary for such a holder of the leasehold estate to have a safe boundary. Customary boundaries demarcated by trees, ends of gardens, ant hills, hill, etc, are not reliable. [In densely populated districts such as] Kigezi, Bugisu and Bukedi they have led to multiple complex and endless litigations, encroachments and boundary disputes. In such areas there is a real need to establish permanent unchallengeable boundaries. However, land adjudication and scientific boundary registration should be introduced on an ad hoc basis in the areas where there are multitudinous boundary disputes. In the sparsely populated areas where there are not many boundary disputes there is no immediate need for the introduction of the expensive registration of titles.

By far the greatest weakness of customary tenure in relation to development is the system of inheritance which leads to land fragmentations and divisions. So long as our economic structure in Uganda remains basically subsistent the problem of availability of land and inheritance will continue to be stupendous. ....

....

One of the alleged blemishes of customary law is that this system of land holding is not conducive to increase of production and productivity. This charge, however, is denied by some writers: 'On the question of productivity it could be shown that the productiveness of land does not depend on the system of tenure but rather on factors some of which are beyond man's control, and others like the size of farm and the method of agricultural organisation. In Uganda we have good example of productivity and land tenure. In Busoga there is no private land ownership but there is security of right of use. In Buganda there is individual ownership but no agriculturalist will tell you that Buganda is more productive than Busoga and vice versa because of the system of landholding.' Indeed, increase in productivity of land held under customary law requires a compendiously conceived agricultural project involving proper farm education, effective and adaptable extension services, constant supervisory exhortation and, guidance of the farmers. All these programmes must be preceded by proper and thorough research on the soil climate and rainfall reliability, and socio-economic environments and attitude of the people. These problems can be legitimately dumped on the lap of the Agricultural department in Uganda to wrestle with. It should not occupy our time here.

****

Note

Obol-Ochola wrote the foregoing materials more than thirty years ago. Arguably, Uganda's social, political and economic circumstances have changed. For example, the country's population has almost doubled and the country no longer aspires to develop as a socialist state, if it ever did. Is the writer's basic thesis still valid? For further reading see Irving Gershenberg, "Customary land tenure as a constraint on agricultural development: a revaluation", (1971) *East Africa Journal of Rural Development* 51; David Atwood, 'Land registration in Africa: the impact on agricultural production', *World Development*, vol. 18 No.5 (1990) 659-671. See also Mutyaba MP's Parliamentary speech, see excerpt in Chapter 3.

****

REFORM OF CUSTOMARY LAND TENURE LAW UNDER THE *LAND ACT*

Summary of the reform measures

Section 5 of the *Land Act* provides that persons occupying land under customary tenure may obtain a certificate of customary ownership as documentary evidence of their entitlement. Sections 6 – 8 prescribe the procedure to be followed by applicants, which includes a process of adjudication and demarcation of boundaries and rights in the land conducted by Parish Land Committees (PLC) and District Land Boards. Third party rights in land will also be recorded at the time of adjudication and protected (s 9(1)). Certification of customary rights is entirely voluntary and no specific provision is made for systematic certification.

Section 9(2) provides that customary owners may undertake the full range of transactions in land both commercial (sale, lease, pledge, mortgage) and family (gifts, devises). Where certificates of customary ownership have been issued, they will be the medium of transactions which to be valid will have to be recorded in the register (9(4)).

Section 16 provides for persons wishing to own and manage land (under customary or any other tenure) on a communal basis to form themselves into a Communal Land Association, which will be able to hold and manage the land in accordance with the rules agreed to by the members. (See also sections 17 – 27.)

Persons owning land under customary law may, instead of applying for certificate of customary ownership, proceed to apply for a freehold title (s 10). In that case, the demarcation of boundaries, measurements and registration will be subject to the provisions of the *Survey Act* and *Registration of Titles Act* - a much longer and more costly process than obtaining a certificate of customary ownership. Freehold ownership may be granted subject to conditions, which will be designed to protect third party rights (s 10(5)).

****

Questions

1. David Atwood, 'Land Registration in Africa: The Impact on Agricultural Production', *World Development* vol. 18 No 4 (1990) 659, critically examines the proposition that registration of customary land titles increases efficiency and productivity in cropped land. He concludes (at pp. 668-69) that:

   The conventional and largely erroneous view of land registration's impact on agricultural efficiency and productivity in Africa stems from a failure to take adequate account of the extra-legal, informal, local institutional environment through which most rural Africans continue to acquire and maintain their claims to land. Establishing a land registry or land titling system does not lead to a wholesale change from traditional, informal set of property rights and rules to a modern legal one. It is more likely… to simply create one more source of opportunities and uncertainties, among several others already existing in many areas, for establishing and maintaining one's land claim. It is not at all certain that the net effect on either productivity or equity is positive.

2. Discuss Atwood's conclusion with reference to the provision for registration of customary land titles under the *Land Act.*

3. Elsewhere in Atwood's article he speaks of 'alternatives' to registration being tried in some jurisdictions and which appear to be suited to certain circumstances. Does the *Land Act* provide for 'alternatives' to land registration? If so, name them.

****

IMPLICATIONS OF THE *LAND ACT* ON CUSTOMARY TENURE

The following is an excerpt of the research finding by Marsh and Laker, on how the changes in the status of customary land tenure introduced by the *Land Act*, affect or are likely to affect customary landowners and users.

****

Marsh and Kego Laker, *Land Act Implementation Study: Social Appraisal, Annex 3*, Draft Report, 6 August 1999

The Act is not explicit on the policy context of its provisions. A review of policy documents appear to suggest that the underlying motivation for the shift in the legal status of customary land is based on the assumption that customary land tenure is insecure and inferior, and that individual private land rights are the basis for development. This is a simplistic view of development, and does not take account of complex relationship between land tenure and development and the contribution of customary tenure systems to sustainable livelihoods and development.

In all the districts visited, customary land holders generally felt that they had security of tenure. Generally, when asked about the main barriers to investment and productivity on their land, lack of markets, unemployment, crop pests, soil infertility, lack of transport, lack of storage facilities, lack of credit and general poverty were cited as the main inhibiting factors. This was also the case for mailo tenants interviewed in Nakasongola, Kibaale and Bushenyi. Tenure insecurity as a factor limiting development was only mentioned in mailo areas with regards to construction of permanent structures and the planting of high value trees such as the *muvule* which landlords were opposed to. …

The concept of land registration and formal survey methods appeared to be too bureaucratic and 'official' to customary land users interviewed ... Respondents opposed the payment of fees for registration of customary land, and were sceptical about the benefits of conversion into freehold tenure. The feeling was that although conflicts over land were common and inevitable, there were well functioning rules and regulations on customary land ownership and dispute resolution which worked well for them. These views complement studies done elsewhere which indicate that customary landholders generally feel they have security under customary tenure. One observer has pointed out that western survey requirements are demonstratively unhelpful to rapid registration and are even inappropriate to situations where the most important requirement is that boundaries may be immediately known and recognised in the local vicinity and do not require re-survey to be sure of their location.

The only group of customary land users in Uganda that are likely to take advantage of this shift in the law in the immediate future are customary tenants on land close to urban and peri-urban areas whose land rights are potentially under threat from urban expansion programmes by municipal councils or commercial interests. Their land rights would be protected by formal registration of their landholdings.

In terms of the likely social impact of the shift in the legal status of customary land this study makes a number of observations:

- The registration of customary land provided for by the Act is unlikely to lead to widespread registration of customary land in the short and medium term except in areas already referred to above. Even then, the motivation to register will depend on factors such as the economic value of the land, the perceived or real threat to people's land tenure security and their ability to meet the costs of registration.
- The poor and vulnerable are unlikely to embark upon land registration in the short term because the process appears to be complicated and might involve unaffordable costs to the poor. In this regard, registration requirements should be reconsidered in favour of a single application process, which removes the need or cost of conversion processes, without significant loss or liability.
- To protect the land rights of the poor and vulnerable who might not have an interest in taking up formal land title, the Act will need to be amended to include a declaratory provision that whether registered or not, land acknowledged as owned by a person, or group, is recognised as privately owned land, and equivalent in the right it endows, to freehold ownership.
- Legalising customary land title on its own is insufficient. Customary tenure is multidimensional and involves rules relating to inheritance, religious and other cultural rights. There is a need to harmonise customary and statutory tenure systems so that land laws provide a framework to guide change and avoid conflict.

****

Note

During the Parliamentary debate of the Land Bill, several members, especially women members of Parliament, criticized customary land tenure. They claimed that it discriminates against women. See Chapter five for discussion of this topic.

Questions

1. The writers seem to play down the significance of the land tenure law reforms with respect to customary land tenure, do you agree with their views?
2. Suggests laws that need to be amended or enacted in order to 'harmonise' customary and statutory tenure.
3. 'It is becoming clear in some areas of Kenya that titling has not prevented a convoluted dispute settlement process, since legislation now states that title is only one piece of evidence regarding ownership rights, and that the testimony of local elders will have weight in settlement of land disputes'. (David Atwood, 'Land Registration in Africa: the impact on agricultural production', *World Development* vol. 18 No 4 (1990) 659 at 667). Discuss the possible advantages and disadvantages if such a provision were enacted in the *Land Act*. On balance, would you advocate for its inclusion?

****

5

Land Rights of Spouses and Children

INTRODUCTION

Article 33(1) of the Constitution declares that men and women shall be treated equally. However, Article 33(5) states that: 'Without prejudice to article 32 of this Constitution, women shall have the right to affirmative action for the purpose of redressing the imbalances created by history, tradition or custom'. The principle of affirmative action is further entrenched in the Constitution by article 32(1):

> Notwithstanding anything in this Constitution, the State shall take affirmative action in favour of groups marginalised on the basis of gender, age, disability or any other reason created by history, tradition or custom, for the purpose of redressing imbalances which exist against them.

Article 33(6) prohibits 'laws, cultures, customs or traditions which are against the dignity of women or which undermine their status'. By Article 31(2) Parliament is required to make appropriate laws for the protection of the rights of widows and widowers to inherit the property of their deceased spouses.

The rights of children are protected by Article 34 of the Constitution. Relevantly for present purposes, Article 34(1) enjoins parents or guardians to care for their children. Article 35(1) imposes an obligation on the State and society in general to take appropriate measures for the protection of people with disabilities and to ensure that they realise their full potential.

Article 2 of the Constitution declares that the Constitution is the supreme law of Uganda and that if any other law or custom is inconsistent with any of its provisions, that law or custom shall be void to the extent of the inconsistency. Accordingly, when interpreting provisions of the *Land Act* or any other law (including customary law) affecting land one should be mindful of the constitutional provisions mentioned above. In addition, it is important to bear in mind Article 26 of the Constitution. That article gives a right to individual ownership of property and protection from deprivation of property.

In this chapter the excerpts of Parliamentary debates deal with sections 28 and 40 of the *Land Act.* The former provisions concerns rights of women, children and people with disabilities with respect to customary land. Section 40 deals with protection of family members in respect of family land.

Discriminatory customary practices

Section 28 of the *Land Act* provides that:

> Any decision taken in respect of land held under customary tenure, whether in respect of land held individually or communally shall be in accordance with the custom, traditions and practices of the community, concerned; except that a decision which denies women or children or persons with disability access to ownership, occupation or use of any land or imposes conditions which violate articles 33, 34 and 35 of the Constitution on any ownership, occupation or use of any land shall be null and void.

******

Demand for recognition of women's land rights

***Parliament of Uganda Parliamentary Debates (Hansard)*, 23 June 1998**
Mrs Matembe: (Woman Representative, Mbarara) [*Hansard*, pp.4097- 4098] … The Bill has been and continues to be controversial. It has attracted a lot of enthusiasm and emotion in many categories of people. Mr Speaker, as you always know, I wish to restrict my contribution to that subject nearest to my heart: women and land rights. I can rank women as third in the level of interest and enthusiasm in this topic maybe next to Baganda and Banyoro, as the interests arose. Women are now alert and alive to their rights. Knowing that they mostly till the land, they mobilised and educated themselves about this issue and its importance, they therefore gave very concrete and specific provisions on women and land rights.

I wish to thank the Committee for putting some isolated provisions in the Bill to cater for women's interests. I, however, regret the inadequacy of these provisions because they fall short of specifically providing for rights of women over land. I wish to regret the emphasis placed on customs and culture as noted in Article 4(b). We all know that customary and cultural practices are the major offender of women's rights. I wish to note, however, that Article 5 purports to protect the women's rights under the guise of the family. I wish also to note Article 21 [s 28, *LA*] categorically entitled, 'Rights of women and children' notwithstanding its prominence on custom and culture. In my view, it should have been entitled, 'The Rights of custom and culture', not the rights of women yet, Mr Speaker and Hon Members, there are many reasons why rights of women over land should be categorically and specifically stated in this law.

There are two ways through which one can acquire land, either through purchase or inheritance. As you all know, both these methods are not conducive to women's acquisition of land because of historical injustices. Women form more than 50 per cent of the population of Uganda and they are responsible for 85.79 percent of the agricultural production yet, where are their rights over land? The reason why women should categorically and specifically be mentioned as owners of land is because of productivity. If this land law is to modernise and increase productivity, the rights of women must be categorically stated for the purpose of motivating them to produce more and for the purpose of enabling them to take proper decisions in agricultural production…. Mr Speaker, I have examples in Mbarara when women plant trees for environment, they have no opportunity or right to sell them and raise money. The men sell them and take the money; therefore these women have been demotivated to do this kind of good activity. For increased productivity, we need to categorically express the rights of women.

For political reasons, Mr Speaker and Hon. Members, the country Uganda, is high up on the international arena for being committed to the equality principle and non-discrimination. This has earned it international repute. It has been doing this by establishing this principle of gender equality in the Constitution and in the policies that govern this country, therefore it is only prudent that the principles of equality be expressed in the laws that we are making right now. Politically, by the way, women are the majority voters. Hon. Members, you come here through women, you use them as stepping stones, how can we arrive here and fall short of providing for their rights? Would it not be a betrayal of the confidence they put in us? Mr Speaker and Hon. Members, legally, women's rights over land should be expressed because the provisions under the constitution categorically express the principle of affirmative action and the principle of gender equality. …

Mr Speaker, … at a later stage, … I will… put forward specific provisions like the one seeking for joint ownership of the land that is used for the home maintenance, so that it is clearly stated here. I will bring up amendments to this effect. … I will make my conclusions by saying that the principle of affirmative action which is supposed to redress the historical mistakes, should be reflected in the laws made under the Constitution. You know that we have been historically denied the right to own land and the Constitution says that affirmative action must be taken and Parliament will take other measures to redress the historical imbalances as we make this law; these historical imbalances that deny women the clear right to ownership over land should not come in. I can assure you Mr Speaker the principle of equality between men and women as expressed by the Constitution, if not expressed in the laws particularly this one ... will remain meaningless to the rights of the women and it is in this regard ... that at a later stage, I will bring amendments to clearly state the rights of women over the land.

Therefore, I am using this general debate to lobby you Hon. Members, so that when this provision comes in, please, embrace it for your sisters, for your daughters, for your mothers. You could forget your wife for the time being, but those people - *(Laughter)* - I think you should be interested in giving them the rights over the land. That is when we shall move together for equality, peace and progress.

****

***Parliament of Uganda Parliamentary Debates (Hansard)* 23 June 1998**

Mrs (Prof.) Mwaka: (Woman Representative, Luwero) [*Hansard*, p. 4099]: ... I go to land management, Mr Speaker. As Hon. Matembe said, women make up 50 per cent of the population. I say this as a reminder, the 30 per cent representation of women should be respected in the Districts. On the Land Board, on the Land Committees and on the Land Tribunals 30 per cent of the members should be women. I say this because, one time I visited parts of my constituency and there was only one woman on the Executive. I asked the Chairman whether he had not read that part of the Constitution that said 30 per cent should be women. He said, 'you know I am still looking around, among all the women there is no one who is really up to the standard.' I told him to choose her, bring her to me and I will teach her and then she will come to that standard. They all laughed but I had made my point. So, Mr Speaker, the 30 per cent representation should be respected on these Land Boards.

Lastly, on the Land Fund, we again have the problem of the marginalised groups, that is the women, the youth and persons with disability. Some of these people have very good ideas but because of historical accidents, they are unable to acquire land. They do not have the money to invest, but they have very good ideas. They should be allowed to write out projects and if these projects are viable, they should be given loans to buy land and use that land to put on them up [sic]. I think that can be done. They should be empowered to purchase land on which to carry out their activities, this is some kind of affirmative action, which all of you ... say is a good idea.

****

(Parliament of Uganda Parliamentary Debates (Hansard) 23 June 1998

Miss Winnie Babihuga: (Woman Representative, Rukungiri) [*Hansard*, pp. 4114-4115]: ... From my understanding, this Bill aims at addressing historical mistakes which have been perpetuated in this country regarding the ownership of land; amongst those I would like to really support my colleagues who have brought out the issue regarding land ownership for women. I am proud of being a product of affirmative action which affirmative action was stipulated by the Constitution.

In the same vein, I would like to bring out what is in Article 33, which talks about the responsibility for this country to accord equal dignity toward men and women, not only in representation in local governments and Parliaments, but also ownership rights of land. I would like to remind the Members that amongst our many roles as representatives of the people, our key role should be to speak for the silent majority who have been oppressed throughout the generations. They would like us to be brave enough and affirm that this is the time to put down a law that will protect the women regarding the right to own land.

I would like to thank the Committee for attempting to address this matter; and would like to refer to their report. They have rightly said that customary tenure retains widespread legitimacy in rural areas. They also go ahead and say that this system recognises some degree of gender rights, but I would like to say that, to a bigger degree women's rights to own land have been marginalised by virtue of our customs and cultural practices. It is a mere shame to note that, even the Committee recognises that in the customary system, land has no value and yet within their recommendations for amendment they boldly say that the rights of women and children are embedded in customary ownership. Ownership which is looked down upon, which has suppressed the rights of women over the ages, over time immemorial and of course, which gives them no opportunity to have value in land rights.

I would therefore like to plead with the House, to gently support us on this matter and bring in a new clause. A clause which will make it crystal clear and provide categorically that women have an equal right to ownership of land that is jointly held with their spouses. (*Applause*) Why do I say this? I would not like to displease our colleagues the men. When we say, women should have a right to ownership, they think that women want to come out and grab property; that they have not contributed anything to this property. Men forget that the majority of them started with their spouses with nothing. We need to address the historical distortion where women have continued to toil in unpaid family labour. Statistics has it that 65.7 per cent of the Ugandan women toil away in unpaid labour. If this labour was to be priced in monetary terms, I believe the women of Uganda would be the richest even in terms of land ownership.

Hon. Members, I would therefore like us to gently bring in the women folk of this country so that we can affirm Article 33 and see that Women are accorded equal dignity of person in such matters as land ownership. When you go to Article 33 sub-section 6 of the Constitution it says that, any law against the dignity, welfare and interests of women is against the Constitution. I would like to say that, this land law that we are debating now, in as long as it does not categorically give women the rights to land ownership, will be working against the interests of the majority of the women in this country whom we represent.

****

The 'lost amendment' saga

During the Parliamentary debate, at the committee stage, of what subsequently became s 28 of the *Land Act*, 1998, Mrs Matembe MP proposed an amendment to the Bill in respect of land acquired by the spouses in their individual capacity before they were married and during marriage. Mrs Matembe wanted to make it clear that married women had equal rights with their husbands to such land. The discussion that ensued raised several other issues including whether such a provision if enacted would not violate Article 26 of the Constitution, which gives a right to own property individually and prohibits deprivation of property except in the circumstances mentioned in the Article. Below are excerpts of the debate.

****

***Parliament of Uganda Parliamentary Debates (Hansard),* 23 June 1998**
Mr Mutyaba: [*Hansard* p. 4198] Mr Chairman, I beg to move the... following...Clause...

> Section 21: Rights of Women and Children Regarding Customary Land.
> Any decision taken in respect to land held under customary tenure, whether in respect to land held individually or communally, shall be in accordance with the customs, traditions and practices of the community concerned; except that a decision which denies females, or children access to ownership, occupation or use of any, or imposes conditions which violate Article 33 and 34 of the Constitution on any ownership or occupation of any land shall be null and void.

Mrs Matembe: [*Hansard* p. 4198] Thank you, Mr Chairman I wish to move that before that section which has been read, we insert a new clause reading as follows:

> Where land is acquired by either spouse before or during a marriage, on his or her behalf and where that land is not normal abode of the family, then it will be regarded as the land of the spouse who acquired the land.
> Where land is held or acquired for the joint occupation and use of the spouses, the spouses will hold the land as joint owners and the recorder shall register the spouses accordingly.
> In case of polygamous unions, each wife shall jointly own with her husband the piece of land on which she resides and works.
> In case where the wives occupy and work on the same piece of land, they shall hold the land jointly with their husband.

Mr Chairman, the reason I am bringing this up is because it is in line with the Constitutional provisions. As I said when I was laying a preamble to this provision the other day, in accordance with the principle of equality as established in our Constitution, and in accordance with the principle of affirmative action which is intended to redress the imbalance and mistakes caused by history, there is an urgent need to declare specifically in this Land Bill, that women do own land.

Mr Chairman, I have noted that several provisions, including the one the Chairman has just read attempt to protect the interest of women. I appreciate them but Mr Chairman they fall short of specifically saying that women, also are citizens in this land, own land.

Mr Chairman, in the District where I come from, I have seen many women suffering. They do not own land anywhere. At their home, the land belongs to the men, even when it is being bequeathed; it is given to the brothers. When she gets married she reaches there; she tills the land for 20-30 years. When she is exhausted the cruel man says, 'Hallo, go back you are no longer useful' and she is just nowhere. During the time I have been a Member of Parliament, that is since 1989, I have had to cry about women being chased and belonging nowhere.

So Mr Chairman, at this time when we are attempting to implement our Constitution, when we want to give real rights to the people of this land, I beg you kindly ... that we include these provisions for the security and for the safety of women, so that women in this land can feel they also belong to this nation. ...

I sincerely hope that you are well aware that those women gave you votes to come here and think about them, to come here and defend their rights, to come here and be considerate to their problems ...

The Minister, Office of the President (Mr Ayume): [*Hansard* pp. 4198-4199] Thank you Mr Chairman. I have the benefit of having a copy of the proposed amendments, they are four of them.

The first one, if I may repeat says 'where land is acquired by either spouse before, or during marriage, on his or her behalf and where that land is not normally where the spouses live as a husband and wife', I suppose or as a family or the main source or it is the main source of production supporting the family, 'then it will be regarded as land of the spouse who acquired the land in the first instance'.

Mr Chairman, I think there is no problem with that because whoever acquired remains to own it, unless you want to share it with somebody else, that should cause no problem.

Amendment 2, Mr Chairman, is where the land was held or acquired, held or acquired I want to emphasize this, held or acquired for the joint occupation and the use of the spouses. The spouses will hold as joint owners and the recorder shall register the spouses accordingly.

I would like to be assisted by the Mover of these amendments. When we talk of held or acquired by whom? Is it by either? Because it is acquired jointly, one person or both must have acquired it. Now, if I acquired the land, probably registered in my name, alright it is mine and the Constitution says it is mine and it belongs to me. I may have acquired it and registered it in my name for purpose of looking after my family. Does it mean therefore, that this land is jointly owned?

Number three; in the case of polygamous unions, a wife shall jointly own with her husband a piece of land on which she resides and works.

Mr Chairman, subject to refinement by the draftsmen, I would also have no problem with these two provisions. My problem is clarification in the case of the second amendment. I thank you Mr Chairman.

Mr Ongom: Thank you Mr Chairman. I just want clarification on number one where you acquire these pieces of land separately and you regard them as belonging to you separately as spouses.

According to this, if we pass it, the law will say, it will belong to you separately. Is there no case for spouses to say: although I acquired these and they are separate, they are far apart, we are not depending on them basically but we would like to agree to hold them jointly, is there no case for that? Because according to this, it will regarded as belonging to each separately. Must the law be like that? Is it there no responsibility for the two to agree that although they do not live on the same land, they can actually own it jointly? That is the clarification I would like to get.

The Chairman: [*Hansard* p. 4199] We have to get some terms clear. Joint ownership of land means, according to the law, that the land is not divisible, it is indivisible; and automatically upon death of one of the joint tenants in transmits, the language is transmit. Transmit to the surviving spouse by operation of the law, you do not have to do anything about it.

Tenancy in common, the shares of either are identifiable and if you die your inheritance can actually inherit your portion of that particular piece of land on which you were. So that if a man and his wife, own in joint tenancy and one dies the survivor takes the whole of it.

With tenancy in common if one of the spouses dies and has left a will behind, whoever is benefiting under the will, benefits to the extent of the share in that piece of land. But where [sic] is not such thing and the land is clearly identifiable and is registered to belong to so and so, you do not have to say it as, who it belongs to because it belongs to whoever owns it, hence I do not see the need of 1.

There is no need; you do not have to say it. But 2 is where you are saying, the land is held or acquired for joint occupation. Now, the joint occupation has no legal – it can cause confusion. What you are saying is that, where any land is a matrimonial home, being the home of spouses, you do not have to go [sic] one to spouse or the other. If it is a matrimonial home of course, then we have a problem of whether marriage and custom also attract that definition.

If it is a matrimonial home, what do you mean by use? Is it for digging? Where the land is held or acquired for the joint occupation and use of the spouses. What you are saying, that if the land is a matrimonial home the parties to the marriage shall be joint tenants in respect of that land? You do not have to say more. Because if it is a matrimonial home the implication is that, that is their home. And if they are joint tenants whoever dies the other one takes. If they divorce the court will order that the land be sold as part of a settlement, so that you share the money and go and start your new lives. If you have children who are dependent the court may decide that one party vacates the matrimonial home and benefits from the other joint property or common property so that the home may be retained for the spouse who has been given the custody of the children. So it is more complicated than it appears on the face of it.

Mr Bidandi Ssali: Thank you, Mr Chairman. I understood the amendment by Hon. Matembe to say that there is a situation where there is land on which the matrimonial home is situated but the land which is the source of their livelihood has a different land title, it could be in the same vicinity but different.

So if you limit it, Mr Chairman, on the basis of the clarification you have made, the land which is the source of their livelihood, will belong to one spouse and you are only limiting it to this land where the actual home is located.

The second part, as I understood, this being a new law, it is going to find a situation on the ground; and I think provision No. 1 and amendment No.1 sort of serves a situation for avoidance of doubt. If you do not place it so one of the spouses will claim joint ownership even in a situation of a piece of land which is anticipated in amendment No.

So, in order to avoid wrangles in society, amendment No.1 is vital and so is the part which talks about the land in regard to the home and the land in regard to the source of livelihood. Thank you, Mr Chairman (*Applause*)

The Chairman: [*Hansard* p 4200] I restricted it to the home because of the way 2 is written; and why I thought No.1 was not necessary is because of the Constitutional provision which says: *'any person in Uganda has a right to own property either individually or together with others.'*

There is a Constitutional guarantee. So if I have got a piece of land and it is registered in my name, it is mine. If I want my wife to have a share in it, I will write in a will that upon my death, it transmits to her. Or we convert our respective individual ownerships to joint ownerships; in which case then, upon death of one of us you do not have to worry about the in-laws coming to grab the house because they are just doing nothing. By the law, the house belongs to her. Therefore, there is no need to mention it in the proposed amendment 1, because the Constitution says so and it is left to the individuals to elect.

The other one is the word 'occupation', it is what made me confine to the home acquired for the joint occupation and use. If you want to specify that you are not only talking about matrimonial home but you are also referring to other land which is used for sustenance like Hon. Nkalubo yesterday was attempting to do, then you have to be exactly that specific. Then they will be joint tenants but you say joint owners, we have to do a bit of more drafting. You must write it in relation to land used as matrimonial home and we do not want to tie it to the land used for tilling. That one can also be written separately, the word land here becomes crucial because I have a law relating to condominium titles somewhere.

So someone who buys a block of flats in Bugolobi will own land, although it is air space and that also will be covered as a matrimonial home without people looking to physical land on the ground.

An Hon. Member: Mr Chairman, I want clarification. In other laws, we have been getting the provisions of the Constitution in the body of the law. The fact is that women have suffered and the fact is that we want to make sure that very law which will be the common bible in the courts, what harm will it do if we repeat the constitutional provision here as we have done in other laws? Would there be any harm?

Mrs Mukwaya: No, you only have to write it in such a way that you are referring to land because this law is not for bicycles and boats. Mr Chairman, Women can get bicycles but this is between life and death. ... That is why we are very – yes we are specific. This is something we own whether both as men and women, that is why we want to be very specific, now that we are talking about land, let us really talk about land. The bicycles can take care of themselves.

The Chairman: That is what I was trying to tell you, that you want to reproduce the Constitution. In this respect, the Constitution talks about Ugandans being entitled to own property in a very broad sense. So that is why I am saying you will have to reproduce it with the necessary modifications so that it applies to land; so that it does not extend to bicycles and other family property.

Dr Malinga: Thank you Mr Chairman. If a man or a woman acquires land before they get married, do they really have to own it jointly or should it remain as the property of that woman or man? In case of death of one of the spouses, if each of them acquired that property before marriage, pre-marital property, how do you clarify that?

The Chairman: That situation is covered by 1. It is saying before or during marriage. It does not matter. If you bought it specifically for yourself, that is yours.

I was saying if you want to bring it up for purposes of educating the reader on the law, you can say that a party to a marriage, or a spouse, is entitled to own land individually and such land shall be registered in the name of the owner. Full stop. You just want to state that. Then now they are saying, but where during marriage you acquired – this does not come out clearly. Is it customary or both?

Mrs Matembe: [*Hansard* p. 4200] Mr Chairman, if you look at that section which precedes the one which the chairperson to the Committee read, it was entitled, 'the rights of women regarding customary land'. So these provisions were brought specifically under that heading and that is how the question put by Hon. Ayume would be answered.

His concern was, if I am already registered on my land, how do you come and say that I jointly own it with you? That was his concern and he thought it might contravene the constitutional provision which guarantees right to property under which law you cannot deprive somebody of his or her property unless those exceptions are fulfilled. So I am envisaging the people in this country, like in Mbarara which I represent, many people there hold their land under what we call customary land holding. It is a system of land that is different from that one up there in the north, for instance.

Mr Chairman, these are types of land I am talking about. In my family - my husband and the other extended family - there is land where I was married, where my father-in-law lives with the children. In Ankole when a young man marries he is given independence from his parents and he is given a piece of land there. Whoever marries is given land, but the women do not get. This piece of land which is given to that young man who has married is really like freehold, it belongs to him. This is the type of land I am talking about.

Now there is the type of land like my husband and I bought when I married him. It is there, it is not registered anywhere. That is the land where he and I live, and that is what we call his land, his home; as if I just belong there and one day I will quit. ...[T]hey say you are going to Mr. Matembe's home, Mr Matembe's house and everything, but what about me? I am simply saying that the land which is currently referred to as his, let it be ours. Let the law say that where Madam Matembe has lived together with Mr Matembe for 23 years, let it cease to be his, so that he can[not] at will say, get away, like they have been doing. Let it be ours, let the law say it.

The Chairman: Okay, you have now made your point. Had you made it very clear that it was only in relation to customary tenure, it would be fine, because the other one would create complications as the Minister said.

What you actually want to say is whatever section number it will carry, you are saying that this section shall have the effect of modifying or repealing to the extent necessary, any customary practice in relation to the holding of land.

In other words, you are saying there would be, in various customary practices, ways where women are prejudiced. So you want to have the effect of modifying or repealing any customary rule, regulation or practice relating to the holding of land contrary to the provisions of this section. Then you say, in relation to land held or used for purposes of earning sustenance for the family, that land shall be held to use jointly, creates problems. You have to find the proper words. Shall belong or shall be owned by the husband or the wife.

Mrs Matembe: Precisely Mr Chairman, I may be very poor in the language but that is precisely what I want to say, so that from that day, these women will not cry all over the place looking for where to belong.

The Chairman: I thought we were just formulating principles, which can be polished up by the draftsmen. So in the first one you want to actually negative any customary practice that would otherwise prevent the situation we are trying to describe and then you describe land used for accommodation or as a matrimonial home including land used for earning sustenance for the family and that land shall be held together by husband and wife and the registrar shall record it accordingly.

Then the other one you are trying to look at is a polygamous situation. But maybe it may not be necessary to talk about polygamous situations because when the interpretation Act so that if you say spouse you mean spouses because you are talking about a customary situation...

Mrs Matembe: [*Hansard* p 4202] Mr Chairman, these provisions are actually springing from practical situation. That is why you find them coming up here. This might not be clear language but it is based on real situations.

When you go back home, you may find this good man who marries more than one wife, but he is good enough to say, go and I will find you there. I will find you there; this is your place. This one, you go in this place and they dig there with the children and Mr Chairman, what 2 is saying is, in that case where number one lives with her children and the husband finds them there; she is together with her husband. And here also, this one enjoys the other one completely with the husband. The husband is getting a lot anyway and the other one.

In the third case Mr Chairman, there is this case of a man who is not so good, who is not even rich, who does not even have much land but he is there marrying many people. He is so bad – although I am trying to protect these wives – that he just puts them one place and that is where they are being dehumanised. They live together; there is no particular demarcation.

All I am saying Hon. Members is that the law says it clearly, these three or four women rightly belong here with this man because he brought them here. Because if this situation is not clear, women have suffered. I am here to protect all women, they suffer. There is the wedded wife, who may say, now that this man is gone, I do not want to see you here. Women have been crying and coming to me because of these cases. That is why I wanted those clear situations to be indicated in this law so that all categories of women are protected accordingly Mr Chairman.

The Chairman: But you are misunderstanding my position. I am not saying that they should not be protected, all that I am saying is, you may find that all this can be summarised into one paragraph but we can regard these as drafting instructions and can approve the principles but not finally. We let the draftsmen come back tomorrow with a text. The principles are where land is occupied as a home, where land is used, it should belong to the husband and wife. Then in a polygamous situation, it should be the wives and the husband, where they work the land and reside it should belong both to the husband and each of the wives. Where they work on the same piece of land, they shall hold the land jointly with the husband. I have heard someone whisper, what about the other way round? One wife with many husbands I think that is not *–(Laughter).*

Mr Kintu Musoke: Mr Chairman, now that you raise it, I definitely share all the sentiments and facts that were raised by Hon. Mrs Matembe, but then our law recognises polygamous marriages and does not recognise polyandrous ones. But we have our poor Nakamatte, women who have children from many men.

In the Bible, somebody went and asked Jesus, which one of these will be considered the husband? Jesus, I think, was not able to answer that question but this law should answer it. This lady may be wealthy and she has children or has married, lived a number of years with this man, has had children and then the man goes away and another one comes and soon. She may have three of them. Now which one of these shares in her property? *(Laughter).* I want clarification.

Dr Wandira Kazibwe: [*Hansard* 4203] Mr Chairman, I did not know the law allows polygamous marriages and I do not know of any law which disallows polyandrous marriages. The Constitution, by inference gives equal rights and equal opportunities to all sexes. Mr Chairman, a woman or man who is married by whatever means, for him or her to be called a wife or a husband, there are rituals to be followed, whether religious or customary. If I get a child with a man and we have not gone through those rituals, whether local or imported, then that person is not my husband and I am not his wife. He is the father of my child and I am the mother of his child, his wonderful friend.

Mr Chairman, what Hon. Matembe is trying to do here – because we really caucused on this with some men – is to really help us, in legal language, to say what you also know is happening and I think the ruling you have made, with your permission, is very good for us and those men who know what is happening in villages.

This amendment is really very, very important because we are here to make laws, not to cater for those who are having a wonderful time but to make sure that we redress these available ones through the arm of the law, for those who are having a raw deal. The Constitution gives them equal rights to enjoy Uganda like any other person. Thank you, Mr Chairman.

The Chairman: As far as this is concerned, we have made a decision. It will be referred to the drafting Committee of experts and then it will come back here, for us to baptise it with a section and adopt it. Otherwise these are drafting instructions to what appears to be a popular position subject to clarification and drafting.

Now there was a new section 21 which was read out and which does not negate but rather reinforces what Hon. Matembe has been pushing, concerning rights of women and children regarding customary land.

Mr Katuramu: Mr Chairman. Yesterday, when we debated on section 6 Clause 1(g), in the amended Bill, we looked at the recognition of women, minors and persons with disabilities. It was clarified and specified that we delete the word 'disability' and replace it with 'persons with disabilities'. In this new section, that is section 21, which has been read by the Chairman, 'persons with disabilities' is omitted implying that there will not be constituency in these sections.

I therefore move an amendment in this new section on page 32 as proposed by the Committee. Mr Chairman, I think you had said women use men instead of females. Immediately after women or women, I propose we insert 'persons with disabilities' in order to avoid ambiguity. Thank you.

Mr Ayume: Mr Chairman, thank you very much. I do not know whether I have understood the concern very well, but I thought that when we made that reference in clause 15, we were covering women and men. So persons with disabilities would fall in either category. …

The Chairman: Are you saying that there are, in our customary tenure, customs, traditions and practices which deny people with disabilities or impose conditions, in relation to land. Are they in the same category as women and children under customary practice? ...

Mr Katuramu: Mr Chairman, I think this has been very common. Some of our customs have been negative to persons with disabilities. In fact some families think it is an abomination. They think it is a taboo. If you have disabled person, they feel it is a bad omen. But sensitisation is now paying its role and there are some positive attitudes coming out.

What I believe is the most significant reason for this law, is catering for the vulnerable groups in our community. The disabled persons are some of the most vulnerable people, they cannot fend for themselves; and disability cuts through age. Disability prohibits a person from fending for himself. That is why I move this amendment that, so long as one is a person with disabilities, he should have a right to this customary tenure landholding. …

The Chairman: The proposal can be affected by amending it to read: 'Except that any decision which denies women, children or persons with disabilities access to ownership, occupation or use of any land or imposes conditions which violate Article 33 and 34 of the Constitution on any ownership, occupation on any land shall be null and void'. After 33 put a comma, then put 34 and 35. There, you have achieved what the Hon. Member is pushing for, if it is acceptable to the Chairman of the Committee.

Mr Mutyaba: Thank you, Mr Chairman. Mr Chairman, I have no problem with what the Hon. Member is proposing.

****

***Monitor* 23 April 1998**

What do women want in the Land Bill?

The Uganda Women's Network (UWONET) and the Association of Women Parliamentarians (AWOPA) have submitted proposed amendments on the Land Bill 1998. Noting that women are the major land users (providing 70-80% of labour in agricultural production and contributing about 90% in food-crop production and processing) yet they own only 7% of the land, UWONET came up with the following proposals among others:

- That registration of land in all cases should specify all stake holders and beneficiaries, especially women on the certificate of ownership.
- Women and men should have equal rights on inheritance of land based on Article 33(6) of the Constitution which prohibits laws, cultures, customs or traditions which are against the dignity, welfare or interest of women or which undermine their status.

- UWONET proposed that the Bill requires at least one third of the trustees on land management committees to be women and that persons with disabilities should be represented.
- Names of both spouses should be included where occupants are married. To guarantee the rights of women, in case of the freehold, customarily held land converted to freehold should be registered in the names of both spouses or in case of polygamous marriages in the names of spouses.
- The proposal suggests that the Bill should explicitly state that a spouse or spouses are joint owners of land on which the home stands. And, therefore, one of the persons cannot transfer land without the consent of the other.
- That where land is acquired by either spouse before or during a marriage on his or her own behalf, and where that property is not the normal place of abode of the household or the main source of production supporting the family, then it should be regarded as the property of the spouse who acquired the land.
- UWONET further suggests that the Bill should provide that any land inherited by a woman may be retained as her own property to use and dispose of as she will, including the right to determine the person who will inherit it.
- The proposal emphasises that women should be given a chance to take part in the management of land and suggests that women 'must' constitute at least 30% of members of land management bodies.

'Wherever education qualifications appear as a prerequisite for one to serve on a land management body, it should be deleted," UWONET suggests in an apparent bid to make sure women are accommodated. Generally focusing on the interests of women, UWONET's proposal cautions parliament not to deny women the right to own land. 'Women need to have secure access and more control over land because these are essential elements for any adult individual to live with dignity', UWONET emphasised.

(Adapted from the 'Proposed Amendments on the Land Bill' 1998.)

****

Note

Although Parliament agreed to incorporate Matembe MP's proposal into the Land Bill and referred it to the draftsperson to put it in the appropriate legal language, when the final version of the Bill was enacted the amendment was mysteriously missing. There are various versions as to what actually happened ranging from allegation of sabotage by male Members of Parliament to 'technical' difficulties. In the event, in June 1999 the Speaker ruled that the amendment had never been passed by Parliament. Due to intense political pressure the Government promised to incorporate the 'lost amendment' in the Land Act during the next phase of amendments or insert it in the projected Domestic Relations Bill. Todate neither has been done.

Questions

1. One of Matembe's reasons for incorporating an express provision into the Act, to the effect that husband and wife were joint owners of their 'family' land, was to protect women from being ejected from the land by their 'cruel' husbands. In the absence of such a provision, is there any remedy under the current law available to women in situations instanced by Matembe?
2. Discuss possible legal and social difficulties that might be encountered if Matembe's proposals were incorporated in the *Land Act*. (See also extracts below).
3. The Minister (Ayume) expressed a view that Matembe's proposal could not apply to land over which the husband was a registered proprietor, because the courts might construe it as deprivation of the husband's property contrary to Article 26 of the Constitution, and,

therefore, it would be void. Do you agree? If so, shouldn't the same constitutional provision apply where the husband owns the land under customary tenure?

4. For 15 years, widow Namwandu and her children lived on her late husband's customary land. Recently, Sezala, her husband's father, told her that because her husband's young brothers have grown up he wants the land back, in accordance with their customary law, in order to give it to them. Assume that under customary law Sezala is entitled to demand the land back. Advise Namwandu and her children of their legal rights, if any, under the *Land Act* and any other law. Would your advice be different if the 'lost amendment' clause had been enacted?

****

Hunt and Eturu, *Land Act Implementation Study: Economic Appraisal, Annex 1,* Draft Report 6 August 1999

Likely impact of the 'lost amendment'

It was the intention of the promoters of the 'lost amendment' to the Land Act that the latter should confer increased rights in land on women: i.e. those who are usually the main cultivators of the land, but who currently have varied but limited rights over the income that it generates and/ or the manner of development of land use. If the 'lost amendment' were to be reintroduced, this might, depending on the wording of the final version, have both production and equity impacts – at least in some areas where women lack a sense of empowerment with respect to key aspects of land use and farm development, but carry prime responsibility for day-to-day farm management. ... However, as with Section 40, it seems likely that any beneficial impacts to stem from the amendment would be unevenly distributed and would depend partly on the reactions to the amendment's provisions in different districts.

We found that in Kabale and Rukungiri Districts [and presumably this also applies in Kisoro District, where population density is even higher, and average farm size consequently even smaller than in Kabale] women are responsible for farming, with little male involvement in crop cultivation, but men retain overall control of key decisions and actions relating to farm development. Male informants at parish level emphasised that women frequently do all crop cultivation and sometimes also decide what to sell and how to use the income: indeed, we were told by the same male informants in Nyaruhanga parish that 'what comes from the land is not men's business'. Yet taking action which entails initiating contact with external change agents to secure introduction of a new cash crop, or enhanced access to improved farm inputs, is apparently viewed differently – as a predominantly male concern. The passing of the 'lost amendment' if appropriately worded, might, by providing for co-ownership by spouses of at least some of the household's land, provide some rural women with a stronger incentive to take new initiatives in farm development, including in contacting external change agents. However, a clause which promotes an increase in women's formal juridical rights over land is highly unlikely to be a sufficient condition for this to occur: where women experience lack of influence over such decisions, there is usually a need for a change also in social norms regarding intra-household decision-taking authority. There would therefore be a need to back legal change with a sensitisation programme directed towards both men and women, emphasising the role of women in farming and the potential benefits of encouraging them, with their practical knowledge of the farm system and of needs for particular types of assistance, to take more initiative in making such needs known as well as in introducing new enterprises. In these two districts, men often show little interest in farm development where crop [mainly food crop] production generates only a small cash surplus. Yet there is scope for farm development, including potential for further expansion of small-scale dairying using zero grazing. If adopted, in these districts it is women who would usually be responsible for fodder production, milking and general management of the dairy enterprise. Moreover, this particular innovation can generate multiple benefit: manure production for fertility restoration on small farms under continuous cropping, improved household nutrition and increased access to cash income. This is but one of a number of developments whose uptake might be accelerated in these districts if women had a greater sense of empowerment with respect to farm development. In Kabale District, one woman informant identified the need for improved Irish potato varieties as her primary concern, but her attitude towards making this known to an external change agent was entirely passive: she did not perceive this as her role. ...

However, we did not explicitly discuss the likely impact of legal provision for co-ownership in Kabale and Rukungiri Districts and hence cannot comment on likely male response to the main intent of the lost amendment. On the other hand, discussions regarding the lost amendment were held in Soroti and Lira Districts, where men play a more active role in farming. [According to the normal division of labour, men clear and open new land, plough and also help with harvesting, especially for tubers, while men and boys do the herding and milking.] Discussions in these districts indicated a range of concerns regarding the amendment and provided indications of potentially strong male opposition to the concept of co-ownership of all or part of the land brought to a marriage by the husband. In both districts, the issues involved prompted vigorous debate. In discussion with members of the Soroti District Land Board and the District administration, debate focused on the need not to rush reintroduction of the amendment, and on some of the issues that need to be confronted first. Among such issues were: would women have co-ownership rights from the day of marriage, was it acceptable for a woman to retain rights in land which was part of that held by her husband's clan if either she left this land [for example to return to her father's home] or, following her husband's death, she brought a non-clan member to live on land that she had co-owned with her husband; whether co-ownership should be allowable at all for clan land, or only for bought land; and the importance of distinguishing clearly between the rights conferred by joint ownership on the one hand and co-ownership on the other. In Lira District, at a meeting attended both by local administrative officials working at levels LC3 - 5 and by local politicians, the predominant, but not unanimous, view was that women should have co-ownership of land with their husbands if this land was their place of residence and/or main income source. [The] debate focused partly on whether women benefiting from co-ownership with their husbands should also retain rights to land at their father's home, with many men arguing that they should not. Informally, after the meeting, some women expressed doubts as to whether the support which had been expressed for co-ownership by men during the meeting was all genuine. In both districts discussion of these issues absorbed so much time that it was not possible to consider the likely impacts of co-ownership on women as producers. However, in Soroti District we also encountered evidence that the agricultural extension programme deliberately promotes outreach to both men and women.

It seems unlikely that there will be a uniform reaction to reintroduction of the lost amendment across all of Uganda's districts. One possible response in districts where there is strong opposition to co-ownership of any of a husband's clan's land is that fathers will cease to give land to their sons while they themselves are still living, but instead will only lend it. If for prolonged periods of their adult life sons possess only use rights in land but not full ownership rights, this could in turn be detrimental to the operation of a land market and, in some cases, to farm development. Wherever the lost amendment, if enacted, becomes a major source of tension, the potential economic benefits that might stem from providing women, through the amendment, with an increased interest in farm development are also initially unlikely to [be] realised. Attempts to enforce the amendment in such areas are likely to generate increased litigation over land rights. To give another example, some brothers may use the amendment to justify denying married sisters rights in their father's land and some women may, if they can afford to, choose to fight this. While strongly sympathetic to the equity goals which underlie the lost amendment, we concur with the view expressed in Soroti and Lango Districts that further consultation on likely responses to the amendment in rural districts is needed before this is reintroduced. ... There was a widely held view among those whom we met in all four districts that there had been insufficient consultation before the 1998 Land Act was passed. This view was held in relation to all aspects of the Act's provisions, but it was made very clear in the two districts where the issue was explicitly raised – Soroti and Lira – that the 'lost amendment' in particular is a sensitive issue.

Summary

The equity goals which Section 40 and the 'lost amendment' promote may prove difficult to attain via these measures because both may prove difficult to enforce effectively. Both the strength of the case for these provisions and dominant responses to each are likely to vary between districts. Both require further consultation and, if the former is retained and the latter passed, both will need to be supported by sensitisation programmes.

****

RESTRICTION ON TRANSFER OF LAND BY FAMILY MEMBERS

Section 40 of the Land Act

Section 40 of the *Land Act* imposes restrictions on a landowner to transfer or enter into dealings affecting 'family land'. The section provides as follows:

(1) No person shall:

(a) sell, exchange, transfer, pledge, mortgage or lease any land; or

(b) enter into any contract for the sale, exchange, transfer, pledging, mortgage or lease of any land;

(c) give away any land inter vivos, or enter into any other transaction in respect of land:

- (i) in the case of land on which the person ordinarily resides with his or her spouse, and from which they derive their sustenance, except with the prior written consent of the spouse;
- (ii) in the case of land on which a person ordinarily resides with his or her dependent children of majority age, except with the prior written consent of the dependent children of majority age;
- (iii) in the case of land on which a person ordinarily resides with his or the children below the age of the majority, except with the prior written consent of the Committee;
- (iv) in the case of land on which ordinarily reside orphans below majority age with interest in inheritance of the land; except with the prior written consent of the Committee.

(2) Subsection (1) of this section shall not apply to any transfer of land by a mortgagee in exercise of powers under the mortgage.

(3) Where consent is required to be given by a person, other than the Committee under subsection (1) of this section, the consent shall be given to the Committee by the person giving the consent.

(4) Where any transaction is entered into by a purchaser in good faith and for value without notice that subsection (1) of this section has not been complied with, the transaction shall be void but the purchaser shall have the right to claim from any person with whom he or she entered into the transaction any money paid or any consideration given by him or her in respect of the transaction.

(5) A consent referred to in subsection (1) shall not be unreasonably withheld.

(6) Where the consent referred to in subsection (1) is withheld, a person aggrieved by the withholding of the consent may appeal to the Land Tribunal and the Tribunal shall require the spouse or children of majority age or the Committee as the case may be, to show cause why they cannot give consent and may, in its discretion, dispense with the consent.

(7) The spouse or children of majority age, not being the owners of any land to which subsection (1) applies, may lodge a caveat on the certificate of title or certificate of customary

ownership of the person who is the owner of the land to indicate that the property is subject to the requirement of consent under subsection (1).

(8) The Committee may, on behalf of the children below majority age or orphans below majority age and not being owners, take action similar to that described in subsection (7) of this section.

(9) In this section 'notice' means, actual or constructive notice; 'purchaser' means a grantee, lessee, sub-lessee, assignee, mortgagee, chargee or other person who acquires an estate or an interest or right in the land.

The materials below relate to the discussion leading to the enactment of these provisions. When reading the materials, note the underlying policy objectives of the provisions.

****

Family holdings

Mr Benedict Mutyaba: (Chairman, Sessional Committee on Lands, Water and Environment; MP (Makindye East, Kampala) [Hansard pp. 4055-4056] One of the issues which has been of great concern to people is rights of family members, as a group, to own property and have a say in the management of the affairs of the family holding. The report of the Uganda Constitutional Commission did highlight this problem, allow me to quote:

> The family is the basis community and school for the right and duties of citizens and for the values which must guide the nation. Whatever therefore, contributes to family stability and happiness and effectively addresses family problems should be encouraged. The family at the moment contains element of injustice in the relations between husband and wife, parents and children, nuclear family and extended family, only clearly defined family rights can eliminate such glaring injustices.

The 1995 Constitution in Article 32, 33 and 34 entrenches provisions which protect the family, women and children. The Land Bill, taking cue from the Constitution, provides for the protection of the family, women and children, in relation to land. With regard to customary tenure, females and children's access to ownership or use of the land, shall be null and void.

When it comes to family holdings, the Bill makes more detailed provisions. The effect of these provisions is to restrict any dealings in land, which is a family holding, without the consent of either spouse, minor children and dependent children of majority age. The Committee, in principle, supports this provision, however, we believe that a provision, which requires the Parish committee to give consent on behalf of children who are minors, will cause friction between the family and the land committee.

Under the law, parents have obligation to look after their children and they are in a better position to determine what is good for them, if they fail in that duty, they are liable to prosecution. We suggest that this law be effectively enforced. Rather than asking the Committee to give consent, they should effectively enforce the law which obliges the parents to look after their children. The Committee also thinks it is unfair to require the consent of adult children who should be able to fend for themselves and who, under the law, parents no longer have a legal obligation over.

****

Mrs (Prof.) Mwaka: (Woman Representative, Luwero)[*Hansard*, pp. 4098-4099] …I go on to restriction on transfer of land by family members. I agree this is a very good provision but there is one point I want to raise and that is on section 15(b) and (c). We did not see the logic behind the inclusion of these. I think these were included because of the single parents, especially (b); *'In case of land on which the person ordinarily resides with his or her dependent children of* *majority age except with the prior consent of the dependent children of majority age'.* We have a situation, here, where the man dies and leaves behind a widow, he had older children but the widow is the young wife with two small children. That lady can easily, with due respect to the ladies, sell off the land, take her children and get married elsewhere leaving these old children destitute. So, that was the logic behind the inclusion of that section.

Let us now go to (c). This is in case of land on which a person ordinarily resides with his children who are minor. This goes mainly to the men. The woman may have gone away and is married elsewhere, the man will tell the children to go where their mother went then he will sell off the land, migrate and go elsewhere, the children will remain destitute. That was the logic behind putting in these two provisions. ...

Then we go to (a) which refers to wife and husband. How about a situation where a man [has] ... four or five wives under the same roof. I can see a problem of divide and rule. The husband will either consult the favourite wife or the first wife. He will confuse the others, pretend to sack them and then we shall have a problem. There should be a provision in case of polygamous marriages. What should be done, if the five women cannot agree? One may say yes and the other four say no, whose word will be taken? I think that has to be addressed.

****

Miss Winnie Babihuga: (Woman Representative, Rukungiri) [*Hansard*, p. 4115] Mr Speaker and Hon. Members I would like to support the cause of the children in the proposed Bill, clause 15 part (c), regarding the welfare of the minors. From the report the Committee had recommended that this section be deleted, but I see a big danger in this, regarding the property rights for minors. We see this danger in all our own constituencies. Even when the spouses would still be alive, if they are not committed to the welfare of their children and are selfish, the future [of] these children can be bleak; no wonder we have so many children on our streets now. I would like to... beg that we work in the spirit of the Constitution to protect the welfare of the children so that there is a piece of legislation which is laid down to protect the rights of the children. Before land on which the family is settled is sold, a land Committee within the parish should consent that there is adequate provision for the children.

****

Consent of wife and dependent children

Mrs Mpanga: [*Hansard* pp. 4121] ... Mr Speaker, people have argued that they should not consult women; some people on the Floor have advanced that argument. I would like to congratulate the Committee for accepting that women should be consulted. I would like to go further and say that this consent from the wife or from wives should be in person, because, if it is in writing, one can be beaten, can be flogged, can be coerced, to sign. It is better when the wife actually comes and when she feels protected by the Committee; then she can give her consent. If there is more than one wife, some agreement must be reached so that majority is taken care of. ...

People have said, people who are 18 should look after themselves, but dependent children are dependent children. If you take your 18 year old to be dependent on you, it is because:

(a) He or she is still going through school and you may disinherit her or leave her homeless while she is pursuing her education or;

(b) She may be disabled or somehow unable to earn an independent living.

Otherwise, when a child becomes of majority age, he/she starts a family of her own and is not considered. But we should protect the right of dependent children. In the case of single parents, we should protect the children, because most often the fathers lose their wives. Suppose the wife died ... he may get married or not but these other children are disinherited or somehow they are abandoned. In case the husband dies, the uncles may come and sell the land, not taking into consideration the children.

****

Consent of dependent children of majority age

The Minister in the President's Office (Mr Ayume): [*Hansard* pp. 4132 – 4133] ... Mr Speaker, recommendation No 16, relating to the protection of women and children.. The Committee in effect recommends as follows: there should be no reference, for purposes of obtaining consent, to either children of minority age nor of majority age. In other words, the Committee is saying, you deal with women and stop there. Government does not accept this recommendation, as it is dangerous to society. Children of minority age and majority age are dependent, and they should be protected. Let me give a distinction here; the children of minority age are obviously, according to law, not supposed to speak and contract for themselves. That is why this is being proposed. They are not even capable of consenting in law. That is why provision is being made in the Bill for the [Parish] Committee from that area ... to handle the matter. Now, as to why we should refer to children of majority age, whom you can even describe as adults, the argument is that they can fend for themselves. Mr Speaker, the operative word there ...is *dependent child.* A child may be an adult, but it could be an invalid, is it not? It could be an invalid, it could be incapacitated, but it is an adult. Tomorrow a capricious parent, an unreasonable parent who is fed up with nursing and nurturing this invalid might say 'ah, let me just sell the house and let him go and suffer'. These are situations the Bill seeks to protect.

****

Hunt and Eturu, *Land Act Implementation Study: Economic Appraisal, Annex 1, Draft Report 6 August 1999*

Potential economic impacts of Section 40

The potential intra-household economic impacts of the Land Act relate primarily to impacts on the relative strength of rights in land of different household members and the economic consequences of these impacts. Potential impacts of this type may be expected to stem from Section 40 [the consent provisions] and from the 'lost amendment' if it is reintroduced and passed.

Section 40 of the Land Act states that no person shall contract to sell or in any other way transfer land on which that person normally resides with his or her spouse and/or adult children without the written consent of these persons; the same provision also applies to land from which a person and his/her spouse derive their sustenance. The rights of minors who reside on such land, and of orphans with an interest in its inheritance are also protected through the provision that land on which they have such claims cannot be transferred unless the consent of the relevant Land Committee has first been obtained on their behalf. Section 40 can be expected to have positive welfare impacts by providing increased economic security to household members who in the past have had no secure control over land disposition. The positive impact that this clause might have on the welfare of some women and children was emphasised by several of those to whom we spoke in Kabale and Rukungiri Districts, including the Deputy Chief Administrative Officer in Rukungiri District and the Chairmen of both the Parish Land Committee and of the LC2 in Nyaruhanga parish, Ikumba sub-county, in Kabale District. Each expressed concern at the frequency of irresponsible land sales. On the other hand, at a meeting with District officials and politicians in Soroti District, in the office of the CAO, those present expressed ignorance of Section 40 and, when the section was read out, stated that traditions of male land ownership [enforced by men] would prevent its implementation. While the CAO affirmed that there was a lot of work to be done in the district to give equal rights to women, it also appears that irresponsible land sale is not equally prevalent in all parts of Uganda: in both Lira and Soroti Districts the land market in most of the rural sector is much less active than in Kabale District, where the rate of land transactions appears to be exceptionally high. In neither Lira nor Soroti was irresponsible land sale singled out as a problem. It appears that if the provisions of Section 40 can be effectively enforced, the benefits will be unevenly diffused, being concentrated chiefly in areas of high land market activity.

However, a number of questions were raised in some districts, as well as in conversations with representatives of commercial banks in Kampala, concerning the enforceability of Section 40. One member of Soroti District Land Board thought it likely that the granting of consent for sale on behalf of minors would be treated as a formality. There is also a risk that many rural women, especially those with little formal education, may be manipulated by their husbands when their written consent to sale is required. It may therefore be necessary, in the Land Act regulations, to require that this consent should be given in the presence of representatives of the relevant Land Committee, who should check that those giving their consent understand its significance, and/or for the Committee itself to assess the likely economic fall-back of land sale on the seller's dependants.

A further qualification to the support for Section 40 that was expressed in some districts concerns the rights and responsibilities of children aged 18 and over. In Rukungiri District a number of those with whom we discussed Section 40 expressed the view that many parents invested in their children's education, sometimes even selling land to do so, but in adulthood not all of these children acknowledge their debt of responsibility for their parents' welfare: children pay graduated tax at 18 and at the same age they should become responsible for finding their own land and lose the right to influence the disposition of the land of their parent[s].

A further problem with respect to Section 40 was not raised in any of our discussions, but is suggested by experience gained in Kenya with respect to a similar protective provision, concerns another aspect of enforceability. This concerns whether many transactions in land will be reported at all. In Kenya, protection is in principle provided to the seller's dependants by the requirement that the District Land Boards check the implications of any land sale for the livelihood security of the seller's wife and children. The effectiveness of this protection depends on the reporting of all transfers but there is no way of enforcing such reporting. It appears that the same will also apply with respect to future land transfers in Uganda. Firstly, there will be no incentive under the provisions of the 1998 Act for those who transfer land to report this. For land with certificate of title, reporting will therefore depend on the purchaser's appreciation of the significance of transferring the certificate. For uncertified land most transfers are likely to remain unreported. There will be a need for a major sensitisation campaign if Section 40 is to be effective in protecting the livelihoods of those at risk from irresponsible sales, especially in rural areas.

Finally, the commercial banks expressed strong concerns regarding the likely accuracy of reporting of spouses and other dependants when land is offered as collateral for a loan and the consequent adverse impact of Section 40 on the value of the land taken as collateral. One proposal made in response to this problem was that the range of dependants from whom consent is required should be diminished. ...

Should there be circumstances in which Section 40, in either its present or an amended form, is genuinely and effectively implemented, then the clause would affect members of both rich and poor households. However, it would have a particularly important welfare significance for women and children in poor households with little land. The potential impacts on output and employment of implementing Section 40 are indeterminate. They would depend on the relative efficiency in land use of potential land buyers who are thwarted by Section 40 on the one hand, and of the current users of land whose sale is prohibited, on the other.

****

Hunt and Eturu, *Land Act Implementation Study: Economic Appraisal, Annex 1,* Draft Report, 6 August 1999

Response of the banking sector to Section 40

We spoke to representatives of three commercial banks, one foreign owned and two incorporated in Uganda, one of these representatives also being the spokesman for the Uganda Banker's Association. Those to whom we spoke voiced two main concerns: that the consent provisions in Section 40 are unworkable and that the Act has in one stroke devalued much of the land which the banks currently hold as collateral [thereby increasing overnight their risk exposure] and has likewise devalued title to land which they might in principle take as collateral in the future. Some of those to whom we spoke drew a distinction between the impacts on the value of residential land as collateral and on commercial land, although it is not clear that this distinction is invariably justified. Since most commercial bank credit is outstanding to the non-farm sector, located primarily in the larger urban centres, these are the areas where any impacts of the Act on credit provision would initially be most strongly felt. ...

The commercial banks, including the UCB and CERUDEB have in the past relied heavily on residential land as an important component of the collateral for many of their loans. Their concern is with the additional lending risks created by Section 40. The banks have no way of ensuring the accuracy of borrowers' statements concerning who has a claim on land offered as collateral. Concerns expressed included the possible existence of undeclared illegitimate children and/or of an undisclosed spouse, either of whom could, under the terms of the Act, have the right to block the sale of land taken as collateral should the bank foreclose. Concerns were also expressed concerning the lack of a clear definition of dependent orphans and concerning the definition of the property covered: if the bank were to take as security land onto which the borrower's family subsequently moved and which then became the family's main residence how would this affect the status of the land as collateral? The banks may require sworn affidavits from borrowers regarding those who have a claim on land offered as collateral, but this provides them with no real protection: if either error or falsehood in the affidavit were to be disclosed at the time that collateral was put up for sale, the only redress for the bank would be to sue the borrower but s/he, following the failure of the loan, would be unlikely to be able to pay compensation, while a prison term would hardly help the bank to recover sums due. The executive director of CERUDEB observed that the State of California also operates a consent provision. However, this is confined to a single spouse ... Children are not included. The provision thus faces none of the range of uncertainties surrounding the reliance on, and enforcement of, Section 40.

Some banks, including the UCB, already require completion of consent forms pursuant to Section 40, but senior UCB loans staff stated that they have no confidence in these forms. In the absence of the installation of the Land Committees for which the Land Act provides, the UCB has been asking LCs to verify the information given, but the bank acknowledges that it is putting the LCs and itself, in a tricky situation. To hold an LC liable for confirming inaccurate information would probably lead to loss of future co-operation. Other reactions by the banks to Section 40 have been to increase the total collateral demanded for a loan, to increase the emphasis given to past knowledge of the borrower in granting new loans, and to encourage some borrowers to create companies and transfer land ownership to the company in order to avoid the provisions of Section 40. [Legal advice obtained by the Uganda Bankers' Association following the Act's publication was also to cease lending on the security of residential land, a measure which could badly hurt first time borrowers seeking to start new businesses.] Resources devoted to avoiding the provisions of the Act might be put to more productive use. Meanwhile, officials of both the UCB and CERUDEB stated that Section 40 poses particularly serious problems with respect to new loan applicants with no proven track record. CERUDEB has already slowed down the granting of loans to new applicants for larger loans. While this is a relatively small proportion of the bank's total business, there could be disportionate impacts in terms of failure to fund potentially dynamic medium-scale enterprises.

****

Questions

1. In view of the banks' reaction would you advocate the repeal or amendment of section 40 of the *Land Act*?
2. Last year, the Uganda Farmers' Bank (UFB), lent Hamisi 10 million shillings secured by a registered mortgage over Hamisi's land. The loan, with interest, was repayable within a period of twenty-four months or upon demand; whichever was the earliest. Hamisi is in default and the UFB wishes to exercise its right to sell the land to recoup the moneys owed to it. However, it transpires that neither Hamisi's wife nor his dependent children gave consent to the transaction let alone being aware of it. It is established that Hamisi lied to the bank manager that he was a bachelor and had no dependants. Advise the UFB of the legal position and possible remedies, if any.
3. Suppose in the above problem, Hamisi was actually a bachelor and had no dependent children, but got married soon after he mortgaged the land. What would be the legal position with respect to the mortgage?

****

Marsh and Kego Laker, *Land Act Implementation Study: Social Appraisal, Annex 3*, Draft Report, 6 August 1999

Gender equity and the 'lost amendment'

In Uganda, access to land by women is generally regulated through male relations – either through marriage or kinship ties. Decision-making over land allocation and transfer lies almost exclusively with male heads of households or traditional authorities and elders. In order to address the gender inequality over land matters Clause 40 of the Act attempts to protect the rights of spouses and dependent children. It provides for certain restrictions on the transfer of land by family members, requiring the consent of a spouse for the transfer of land on which the parties ordinarily resided. The Act takes further the gender equity issue by creating a role for women in land administration. Accordingly, at least one woman is to be appointed to each Land Tribunal, Land Board and Parish Land Committee.

There is a strong case for improving women's rights over land as a result of international conventions and national laws, and also for equity and development reasons and the Act provides some ground-breaking provisions for this. However, there is no doubt that it is in this area that the Act faces it greatest challenge in terms of implementation.

Even before the Act was passed there was evident dissatisfaction that the provisions of the Act were not comprehensive enough to protect the rights of women to land. There were calls for an amendment to the Act to deal with the question of married women's rights to ownership of land. This debate is in progress and the said amendment is due to be tabled at the next parliamentary session.

On the likely impact of the equity issues raised by the Act, the following areas are considered to be priorities and needs for implementation.

While the Act is progressive in setting the legal framework for gender equity in land matters, and setting standards of good practice, the legal framework must be in touch with reality. During the field studies, the consultant found a very high level of resistance to the issue of consent of spouses over land transfers. It was generally felt that the provision was unworkable, because it contradicted cultural norms. Most women interviewed during the study stated that they had access to land once they remained married and did not feel that they needed to consent about land transfers. The general feeling among those interviewed was that enforcement of the law on consent would deter people from registration of title, which will not improve tenure security for women. This is one area where an extensive sensitisation campaign will be necessary both in the short and longer term. Details of target groups and requirements for sensitisation are contained in Appendix 1. Other action points recommended include: 1. the harmonisation of relevant legislation such as business and commercial law in order to address any contradictions and inconsistencies. 2. the Act needs to take account of the realities of the position of different socio-economic groups of women and address their needs accordingly. This can be done through small research projects or in conjunction with community based NGOs. 3. the draft Domestic Relations Bill needs to be harmonised with the provisions of the Land Act. 4 it will be worth considering collective registration in gender-neutral terms in order to lessen the vulnerability of women's tenure security.

A review of the Act and other legal statutes shows a conflict between statutory and customary law. Though the Act provides for greater security and protection for women, it is less utilised in rural areas. Women have access to land by virtue of marriage relations and kinship ties, but generally have no control over decision-making powers over land. Lack of security of tenure for females has an impact upon land usage. There is a clear contradiction between gender-equitable land laws provided for by the Act and gender inequalities under customary law. More fundamentally the gender inequities of customary law, are in breach of the Constitution. If people decide not to register their land titles which they are not forced to do anyway, the equity objectives will not be met. However, the law is enforceable for land disposals where consent is required. Sensitisation is key to changing attitudes and creating awareness of the wider developmental benefits of co-ownership and consent.

To facilitate the work of land administration bodies, sensitisation on the Act, the Domestic Relations Bill and other related legislation should run concurrently, to avoid misunderstanding among people about what the law says. This is necessary so that when land administration bodies hand down decisions, people have full knowledge of the context in which they are made.

The field studies found that although the Act provides for a gender balance of men and women on land administration bodies, this has not been achieved in some districts. In Moroto for example the whole of the Land Board was dismissed because there were no women representation. When asked, some former members stated that it was difficult to get local women to participate in meetings with their male counterparts. Support and encouragement is needed in such areas if the objectives of the Act are to be met. Training is needed as a matter of priority for members of land administration bodies on gender issues, and female members in particular will need additional training in areas such as public speaking, conducting meetings and networking with other women in other organisations to overcome their limitations. Some larger NGOs like Oxfam, ACORD and Action Aid have well developed community theatre programmes which could be useful for training. The advantage of such programmes is that they are flexible and allow for wider community participation.

The status of women is an essential concern in African land tenure policy. It is important however to consider how far the Act, and its rules and regulations may be in contradiction with discriminatory elements of constitutional laws or customary practice. It was not possible to identify any areas of contradiction during the study, but it is important to look into this as part of the research into land issues in each district.

There is a need to monitor land markets from a gender perspective. Women suffer from land markets when their spouses alienate family land. The study did not investigate this in detail, but the evidence from elsewhere suggests that this has a negative impact on women in poorer households.

Both formal and customary systems discriminate widely against women, and positive action is required to enhance women's land rights, not only through land law, but also through education, advocacy and tackling discriminatory inheritance systems. This is an area where NGOs and the government could work together. The Uganda Land Alliance, Oxfam and WLF were found to be doing valuable work on land issues. Their work needs to be fully integrated into the implementation process.

****

Questions

1. 'Section 40 of the *Land Act* should be amended to remove the requirement for consent of dependent children above the age of majority. This requirement, if left in the Act, will greatly affect transactions on land. It unreasonably fetters transactions and will make it difficult for the financial institutions to determine who the dependent adult children are and if they have been adequately consulted' (per McAuslan and Mwebaza 'Land Act Implementation Study, Annex 6, Draft Legal Appraisal', unpublished, 1999). Do you agree? Why?
2. Does s. 40 of the *Land Act* give the spouse and dependent children any 'proprietary' interest in the land?

****

Marsh and Kego Laker, *Land Act Implementation Study: Social Appraisal, Annex 3*, Draft Report, 6 August 1999

The *Land Act* and national gender policy

The National Gender Policy of Uganda (1997) recommends the protection of the rights of marginalised and vulnerable groups, in particular women, in order to harness their potential for sustainable and gender-responsive development. It stipulates mechanisms for the initiation and formulation of gender-responsive policies and programmes in all development activities. The need to take care of gender concerns through affirmative action, and the mainstreaming of gender in development programmes, and setting of monitoring and evaluation mechanisms are key elements emphasised in this policy.

Within the Land Act, there is a conscious effort to address the constitutional provisions of gender equity and National Gender Policy. Sections 28, 40, 48 and 66 of the Land Act, 1998 specifically address the issue of gender equality in transactions regarding land.

Section 40 backs this principle by more specifically requiring the written consent of a husband or a wife to any transaction that will affect the status of the land upon which they are residing. ... Notwithstanding these positive provisions in terms of gender equality, most communities still uphold gender discriminatory traditional values, which go against the principle of gender equality.

The access of women to resources of production is not matched by their control over the use of the resources and especially those generated from the sale of crops. A study done in Western Uganda revealed that 16.3% of farm holdings were controlled by women and 83.7% were controlled by men (Busingye, 1993). Land, which is a major economic resource that has direct impact on women's involvement in agricultural production, is almost exclusively controlled by men.

In addition, according to the Succession Act:

> property acquired during marriage belongs to the husband. In the event of the husband's death, the woman is not the automatic heir ... According to the formal legal system, a wife or wives get 15% of the husband's estate while the children get 75% in equal shares. The dependent relatives get 9% of the estate and the customary heir gets 1%.

An examination of the access of women to agricultural capital and credit depicts a similar scenario. Capital from either waged or self-employment is controlled by men. Female labour supply for wage work is restricted by the multiple demands of domestic food production and processing, household maintenance, child-care and health care.

The Uganda Commercial Bank (UCB) Rural Farmers Credit Scheme was launched in May 1987 with the objective of providing credit to the rural small farmers with special emphasis on primary lending to women with an anticipated target of 70% participation by women. However, the participation of women was found to be much lower than that of men. The proportion of women who received loans was only 31.7%. In reality, however, the RFS has served far fewer women than originally targeted and many of the borrowers did not benefit from it , some actually coming out of it worse off than they went in.

Women are also at a disadvantage, in terms of education with respect to men. Forty-three percent of rural women are functionally illiterate compared with 28% of rural men.

The provisions in the Land Act for women, although helpful on their own, are not enough and further provisions need to be made to lay the legal basis for gender equality in land ownership and management. Potentially, the Land Act may either make no difference to women's rights over land or even worsen their condition.

In most parts of Uganda women don't inherit land from their fathers' line since they are expected to join another family on marriage where they have partial rights in relation to property and land. The underlying assumption here is that all women will be married and will be properly catered for when they get married.

Today, as a result of changes in the socio-economic environment with the emergence of women-headed households, it is evident that most women-headed households acquire land but the element of patriarchy still dominates. For instance, Bazaara (1994) noted that in Masindi, women who acquired land passed it on to their sons but not to their daughters. Similar findings were reported in Okumu-Wengi (1990) and Kyasiimire (1996). This puts daughters in extremely precarious conditions.

Particular reference to the inheritance legislation indicates discrimination against women. For example, Section 3 of the Succession (amendment) Decree (1972) prefers the nomination of a male heir. Studies done by Okumu-Wengi (1990) and Kyasiimire (1996) examined some wills by men probated in the High Court [which indicated that in 50% of such wills *only 10%* of men bequeathed their property to their wives in trust for their children. While 90% bequeathed to their children who are assumed to take care of their mothers.

Written consent of wife or husband before a land transaction is not enough to safeguard women's tenure. Given the fact that most women are illiterate and are in subordinate marital positions, it will be difficult to ensure that the consent of women is actually guaranteed and she is not coerced to agree to the sale of land. Even after the sale of land access it may not be possible for women to access the proceeds from the sale.

The Land Act has an affirmative action for women in the Parish Land Committees *and* District Land Boards. This is positive in that women are able to participate in decision making on land issues. However, from the field visits it was reported that although there is an affirmative action in the District Councils for women, they do not influence decisions made at that level. Their performance is compromised by lack of skills in articulation and leadership, and adequate time. Sometimes, their votes are manipulated, they are ridiculed and are often not educated well enough and are burdened with heavy responsibilities, which militate against their ability to influence decisions at that level. Therefore, for effective implementation of the Land Act and the protection of women's and children's interest, the capacity of women with these land committees will have to be built.

****

Justice Benjamin Odoki, 'Experiences in the implementation of the Land Act', (unpublished paper presented at the Uganda Law Society Workshop on the Land Act, 19 August 2000)

Section 40 : Shortcomings

Section 40 … remains problematic since while nullifying the transaction entered into without consent, it goes ahead to provide for recovery of money paid under such a void contract. Not only is this contrary to the general common law position that money paid under a void contract is not recoverable but it also defeats the purpose of the reform since the same land can be attached and sold in execution of a court decree for recovery of the moneys paid. Further, it has been found that this provision has a narrow catchment area because it imposes restrictions only in respect of land where the family ordinarily resides and earns a livelihood.

The use of the word 'and' will lead some to argue and rightly so that if both or one of the elements are missing then the consent requirement should not apply. This will act unfairly in places where there is land fragmentation such that a family resides on one small plot but earns its livelihood elsewhere. A better word should have been 'or' but not 'and'. However, the women activists have argued that Section 40 should be strengthened by the "Matembe amendment" on co-ownership by spouses.

****

6

Land Disputes Settlement

ESTABLISHMENT OF LAND TRIBUNALS

From the commencement of the *Land Act*, 1998, courts, other than the High Court, ceased to have jurisdiction over land disputes.[10] Instead, for each District provision is made for the establishment of a District Land Tribunal and for each Sub-county, gazetted urban area and division of the city there shall be respectively a Sub-county Land Tribunal and Land Tribunal (see ss. 75, 76, 81 and 82). All members of the tribunals are to be appointed by the Judicial Service Commission.

The Land Tribunals have jurisdiction over land disputes relating to the grant, lease, repossession, transfer or acquisition of land whether arising under the Act or otherwise and whether between individuals or involving the Uganda Land Commission or other authorities with responsibility relating to land (see sections 77 and 85). Tribunals also have jurisdiction over amounts of compensation payable for land compulsorily acquired (section 78). District Land Tribunals hear cases on appeal from Sub-county Land Tribunals and Urban Land Tribunals. Further appeals lie from the District Land Tribunals to the High Court (section 88). Special rules of procedure are to be made for Land Tribunals by the Chief Justice (sections 79 and 86).

The establishment of land tribunals is a constitutional requirement (see article 243 of the Ugandan Constitution).

Why tribunals?

In the following excerpt the author discusses the limitations of the dispute settlement forums prior to the enactment of the *Land Act,* 1998. He concludes by proposing the establishment of specially constituted land tribunals to deal with land disputes.

****

John Kigula, 'Land Disputes in Uganda: An Overview of the Types of Land Disputes and the Dispute Settlement Fora', Research Paper 3, prepared for the Makerere Institute of Social Research and the Land Tenure Centre, University of Wisconsin, March 1993.

A review of the appropriateness and limitations of the dispute settlement fora

A number of positive aspects and tendencies in the system of land dispute management do exist in Uganda. These, however, are bedevilled by a host of variables that pose such limitations on the dispute settlement fora that the structure and mechanisms of dispute management are eventually ineffective and retrogressive. At the grassroots, as already pointed out, the informal mechanisms of dispute settlement are moribund. The semi-informal and formal systems of dispute settlement– the RC [Resistance Council] courts and Magistrate Courts respectively – are the predominant institutions that have come to handle the overwhelming majority of almost all types of land disputes. The RC courts have a number of advantages. Firstly, they are near the masses and easily accessible. They are also inexpensive in that the parties to a suit may not have to incur prohibitive

[10] Section 98 of the *Land Act*, as amended by the *Land (Amendment) Act*, authorises Magistrate's courts to continue dealing with land disputes pending before them prior to the commencement of the Act, until completion.

expenses toward the institution of a case: transportation fares to the court, hiring a lawyer, etc. The RC courts deal with matters expeditiously: in most cases instantaneously or within one or two weeks. These courts are not hampered by technical procedures, and they often are able to use the local languages. Given that the RC courts are situated within the vicinities of the litigants and the lands that are disputed, they are better equipped with background knowledge about such litigants and locals than any other forum kilometres away. This is an advantage that would, in the absence of other inhibitive variables, enable the RC courts to reach impartial decisions expeditiously.

Yet, with all these advantages, the RC courts are attended by a host of inhibitive factors. It was found that most of the committee members who sit to constitute a court were not clear on the limits of their jurisdiction. It is not rare to find an RC court seeking to entertain a dispute regarding titled land even though the dispute is outside its jurisdiction. Most of the RC courts visited did not keep proper records of proceedings and judgements. Hence, when a litigant appeals to the Chief Magistrate's Court and the Chief Magistrate calls for the proceedings or judgement of the RC court, the relevant information is not always available. This leaves many cases pending for quite a long time, sometimes for over two years.

On the other hand, there is widespread ignorance of court procedures, such as how to procure information from witnesses and how to identify key issues that would form the basis of a judgement. There is also evidence that the committee members are sometimes ignorant of the prevailing land tenure law. Prejudiced as they are, the rights of a state-lessee vs. a tenant as spelled out in the [Land Reform Decree] are not clearly understood by a large number of Resistance Committees and, therefore, the RC courts.

The lack of incentives for committee members has demoralised a large number of the RCs. Some RC members who had been elected due to their wisdom, social influence, and administrative abilities have gradually given up attending the numerous matters referred to them and have instead concentrated on their income generating activities. For example, this was found to be the case in Ihanga, Kabale District. Lack of due rewards for the exacting work performed by committee members is one of the factors that have fanned widespread corruption amongst the members. The key members and chairpersons on the RC courts have increasingly exhorted bribes from parties to a suit and these recipients of bribes subvert justice by confusing the financially weak party and taking sides with the bribing party. ... Taking into account the prevailing cost of living and the time it takes to obtain the money, the amount of money given to the RC III members hardly serves as an incentive for them to be committed to their duties. Also, the payment of RC III members discriminates against the lower levels of RCs in that the latter receive no remuneration. There is discord among the lower levels of RCs about this, especially since it is these lower RCs that handle the bulk of the disputes and other matters that come before them at the village and parish levels.

Loss of morale amongst members of most committees is also evidenced by [lack of] attendance of RC meetings or court sessions. About half the RC chairpersons interviewed decried the low levels of attendance, pointing out that in most cases they have had to co-opt other members of a Resistance Council to form a quorum and constitute a court. It was established in this study that certain members of the RC court influential by virtue of their social and economic status, do affect the decisions of the court, especially when they are interested parties in a dispute.

The Magistrates' Courts Grade I have advantages in common with the RC courts in that they are also accessible by the local people, especially since they rotate within the district at the county and sub-county levels. However, Magistrates Grade II were found to have acquired elementary knowledge of the law through long-term service and training at the Uganda Law Development Centre.

One of the major problems identified in this study is that there is duplication of the jurisdictional powers of the RC courts and the Magistrates' Courts Grade II. The litigants in the countryside are confused over where to institute their cases in the first instance. Some institute their cases in the Magistrates' Court Grade II, others in the RC court and some (as is often the case in Kabale and Kabarole Districts) institute their cases in both courts. There seems also to exist a conflict between arbitrators in each court: each ill-advising litigants and expressing negative attitudes towards the other court.

Much as they have the capacity to dispense with cases at their level of jurisdiction, the Magistrates' Courts Grade II conducts proceedings in a technical manner: using English interpreters, and more or less adhering to the letter of the Civil Procedure Rules of the Laws of Uganda. This, added to the fact that there is legal representation by advocates in these courts, serves to delay the settlement of disputes. Advocates were found to be constantly pleading for adjournments of hearings for one reason or another. In many cases, they simply would not attend court on the hearing date, especially when involved in cases in other courts.

Just as the RC court members lack incentives, the Magistrates Grade II are very poorly remunerated. While they are supposed to move around the district to the sub-county and county administrative centres to hold court sessions, the Magistrates do not have means of transport such as a bicycle or motorcycle purchased for them by government. As a result, there is alleged widespread corruption among these magistrates with a large number of them subverting justice.

The Magistrates' Courts Grade I and the Chief Magistrates' Courts, normally, situated at tile district headquarters, handle a large number of cases in addition to land disputes. The cases instituted in these two grades of courts normally involve titled land and are, in the case of tile Chief Magistrates' Courts, of the pecuniary value of shillings 5.000.000/=. The majority of the land dispute cases before the two grades of courts came on appeal from the Magistrates' Courts Grade II and the RC III courts. This study found that the available Magistrates in each of the districts visited were too few to handle all the cases effectively. Few of the Magistrates are able to visit the *locus in quo* because of the limitations in manpower. With the exception of some Chief Magistrates who were allocated Land Rovers, most Magistrates do not have means of transport. On the other hand, excessive delays exist due to technical procedures and referrals back to lower courts. It is expensive for ordinary people to have their disputes solved in these Magistrates' Courts because of the exorbitant fees for hiring a lawyer and the long distances which the parties to a suit and the witnesses must travel to reach the courts. As earlier noted in respect of the Magistrates' Courts Grade II, the advocates often seek adjournment of cases in these two grades of courts as well, thereby delaying the disposal of cases.

The Magistrates Grade I and the Chief Magistrates are also poorly remunerated. Detailed examination of the Magistrates' indulgence in corruption is beyond the ambit of this study; however, it is alleged that some Magistrates and Chief Magistrates engage in corrupt conduct and delay or subvert justice.

The High Court, on the other hand, can exercise its powers of review and revision to ensure that all courts below it perform their functions satisfactorily and ensure that justice is done. Yet, there are limitations on the High Court as a dispute settlement forum or as a watchdog institution that oversees the activities of the lower courts; one limitation is the lack of High Court Judges in most districts. There is need for increasing the number of judges and posting them up-country. While it is quite expensive for the ordinary person to litigate in the Magistrates' Courts, it is even more expensive to do so in the High Court. In the regions where there are no resident judges, it requires parties to travel long distances to the High Court in Kampala. Moreover, the technical procedures and the involvement of advocates, whose peculiar demands for adjournments often delay cases, are obstacles for parties using this forum for settling disputes.

At this stage of the study, it is impossible to provide authoritative conclusions on the appropriateness of the dispute settlement fora or to prescribe viable options to alleviate the limitations on them. While this awaits a more detailed study that will substantiate or refute some of the RRA [Rapid Rural Appraisal] findings reported here, some observations and broad suggestions can be made regarding which likely policy options would be available. It is suggested that there be established Land Adjudication Committees at the sub-county level. These should be concerned primarily with the administration of land matters within a respective sub-county. At the same time, these committees should be vested with limited judicial powers to settle land disputes currently being handled by RC courts I to III. The RC court system should be divested of land dispute settlement powers. Members of a Land Adjudication Committee would be more enlightened personalities, specialising in one aspect of social conflict: land issues. These members would be easy to train and, with time, should be able to effectively handle land disputes without causing the confusion and the delays presently being experienced. It is suggested further that a Land Adjudication Tribunal be established at the district level throughout Uganda. This would have the same advantages as enumerated above and would entertain land disputes on appeal from the sub-county Land Adjudication Committees. As well, cases of first instance will be lodged with the District Lands Adjudication Tribunal outright. Appeals from the District Lands Adjudication Tribunals should go to the Chief Magistrates' Courts. Mechanisms for providing adequate incentives to the committees and tribunals should be worked out, with the main source of funding the district itself supplemented by contributions from the central government. Mechanisms of supervising these institutions of land dispute settlement should be worked out as well.

Conclusion

... [T]his study has identified numerous instances of confusion in the RC court system as one of the agencies of land dispute management. The RC court system seems to have similar functions as those of Magistrates' Courts grade II. Litigants, in some cases, do not know where exactly to institute land cases. This RRA has established that the RC court system is ill equipped to handle land disputes. While the ultimate goal would be to reduce the incidence of land disputes, it is also worthwhile for government to promote a policy, which focuses upon improved land dispute management. For that matter, it is suggested that specialised Land Adjudication Committees be established at sub-county level, charged with general administration of land matters within a sub-county and vested with limited judicial powers to try the land disputes now being handled by RC courts. It is also suggested that a Land Adjudication Tribunal be established at district level to entertain appeals from the sub-county Land Adjudication Committees, as well as receive some land disputes. The forthcoming detailed study will seek to examine further the factors that are likely to enhance or pose limitations on the proposed tribunal system.

In order that the broad masses of the people become willing participants in the programmes geared towards reducing the incidence of land disputes and improving land disputes management, there is need for awareness programmes through which the relevant parties will be educated on the modalities and values of the set plans.

****

Questions

1. Kigula points out several limitations of the Magistrates' courts, LCs and RCs in resolving land disputes. How will the appointment of land tribunals under the *Land Act* eliminate the problems he identifies?
2. In your view, what needs to be done to ensure that the Land Tribunals resolve expeditiously, efficiently and fairly all land disputes referred to them?
3. Kigula identifies the presence of lawyers as one of the causes of the delay in the delivery of judgements. Should lawyers be banned from representing clients before land tribunals? Why? If not, what should be done to ensure that the presence of lawyers does not hinder the administration of justice?

****

ALTERNATIVE DISPUTE SETTLEMENT

In addition to Land Tribunals, the Act provides two alternative channels for dispute settlement: (a) Customary dispute settlement and (b) Mediation:

****

Customary dispute settlement

Section 89 of the *Land Act*, provides that traditional authorities may continue to exercise their functions of determining disputes over *customary tenure* or acting as mediators between the parties to a dispute. This provision was enacted after 'consultation with the local people who felt comfortable using the traditional set up in solving some of the disputes. Many of them did not want the idea of automatically going to the Land Tribunal'. (Mutyaba MP, *Hansard*, pp.4351 – 4352). Compare this with Kigula's findings in the following extract.

****

John Kigula, 'Land Disputes in Uganda: An Overview of the Types of Land Disputes and the Dispute Settlement Fora', Research Paper 3, prepared for the Makerere Institute of Social Research and the Land Tenure Centre, University of Wisconsin, March 1993.

Informal dispute settlement fora
The informal system of land dispute settlement has been reported as existing in all districts visited in this study. In the central region of Buganda, the informal mechanisms of land dispute settlement mainly features in matters of succession rights amongst the members of the extended family. The clan head or authorised executive members of the clan have often resolved succession disputes prior or just after the celebration of the second funeral rights of a clan member. [C]lan authority is diminishing, and it is now possible to find intra-familial land disputes relating to succession rights being instituted in the formal courts without recourse to or in disregard of the clan head's ruling. In the districts of Masaka, Mukono, Mubende, and Kabarole, quite a few boundary disputes are being settled with the intervention and indulgence of the village elders. While in most of the districts visited the authority of the clan, clan head, or elders as a dispute settlement institution still lingered. In Kabale district litigants did not resort to this moribund forum. This... might be explained by the high population pressure on land that has led family members and neighbours to treat each other as total strangers to such an extent that even murders occur.

Conclusion

During this [study] it was observed that there is overwhelming disregard of the semi-informal RC courts when it comes to instituting land-related cases in the first instance in the high-population-pressure district of Kabale. ... The reasons for skipping the less formal courts by litigants is not attributable to ignorance of the proper hierarchy of the courts system. It is to a certain extent attributable to the lack of overarching traditional structures of dispute settlement, and more significantly, to the high population pressure on land in Kabale. This suggests the following hypothesis: the higher the population pressure on land, the more the social control of land and land dispute arbitration shift from the informal/semi- informal institutions (that is, the extended family, the clan or the grassroots semi-informal courts such as RCs) towards the formal institutions.

On the other hand, it has been observed that, although the informal mechanisms of land disputes arbitration still exists in all the districts visited in this [study], they are not all active. In the mailo land region of Buganda, for example, the role of the clan head in overseeing property and arbitrating land disputes has diminished in value. The new generations who are parties to the disputes are participants in an ever-advancing market economy in which tribal custom and communalism become dysfunctional; these parties do not seem to acknowledge the traditional powers of the clan head. This suggests the following hypothesis: the higher the market-economy impacts, the more the social control of land and land dispute arbitration shift from the formal/semi-informal institutions towards the formal institutions.

****

Questions

1. Do you agree with Kigula's hypotheses?
2. Suppose that X and Y have a dispute over certain land. X sues Y in the village elders' court. The elders hold in X's favour. Y decides to ignore the elders' decision. Advise X of possible cause of action, if any.
3. What is the difference between a traditional land dispute settlement institution and a mediator appointed under s 90 of the *Land Act*?

****

Mediator

A Mediator may be appointed by a Land Tribunal to assist parties to a land dispute to reach an amicable settlement. A Mediator is not required to have any special qualifications. Nevertheless, she or he must be a person of high moral character and proven integrity who must exercise her or his functions in accordance with the principles of natural justice and general principles of mediation and conciliation. [See section 90 of the *Land Act*].

****

***Parliament of Uganda, Parliamentary Debates (Hansard),* 3rd Session, 1998**

The role of a Mediator in negotiations between a registered owner and lawful or bona fide occupant.
Mr Mutyaba MP: [Hansard, p. 4270] Mr Chairman, normally in negotiations between two willing parties, you do not need a third person. However, in this case because of the peculiar nature of the occupant and the registered owner, we have created this position in order to assist them in the negotiations. This does not diminish either party's rights to refuse, if he thinks that the negotiations are not in his or her best interest, to proceed with the negotiations. Because it is still on the basis of a willing seller, willing buyer.
The Minister, Office of the President (Mr Ayume): [*Hansard*, p. 4299] Mr Chairman, an institution of a mediator is created for the purpose of narrowing any differences wherever there is a dispute between the landlord and the bona fide occupant. Here we are dealing with unique situations such as Kibaale and other areas where it may be difficult to bring the landlord and bona fide occupant to the negotiating table to agree on the prices. So this mediator is there to try and bridge the gap and that is the very reason why he is brought in.
Mr Mutyaba MP: [*Hansard*, pp. 4299-4300] Mr Chairman, we envisage a situation where, in some areas, the occupant and the owner may actually be on such bad terms so that they will not be able to come together and negotiate as two parties. In those cases, we thought that it would be appropriate to have a neutral party as established by this Bill, is a mediator. A mediator is not a government agent, he is not a cohesive agent. He is not going to force the two to agree. He is just there to guide them and to make sure that they reach a good conclusion.

****

Concept of mediation

Brown and Marriott, *ADR Principles of Mediation* (London: Sweet and Maxwell, 1993), pp.108-111[11]

Principles of mediation and conciliation defined

Mediation is a facilitative process in which disputing parties engage the assistance of a neutral third party who acts as a mediator in their dispute. The neutral has no authority to make any decisions which are binding on them, but uses certain procedures, techniques and skills to help them to negotiate a resolution of their dispute by agreement without adjudication.

The term 'mediation' is often used interchangeably with 'conciliation'; sometimes, however, mediation is understood to involve a process in which the mediator is more pro-active and evaluative than in conciliation; and sometimes the reverse usage is used: there is no national or international consistency of usage of these terms. In this book, the terms will be treated as synonymous.

Mediation differs from arbitration in that the role of the neutral third party in arbitration is to consider the issues and then to make a decision which determines the issues and is binding on the parties. The neutral third party in mediation does not have any authority to make any decision for the parties, nor is that the mediator's role or function.

Even where the mediator expresses a view about the merits of the dispute, which may happen in some but not other models of mediation, this would only be a non-binding opinion, and in no circumstances would a mediator have the power to impose this view on the parties. Indeed, any such power would be contrary to the spirit of mediation, which is inherently consensual.

Use of the term 'mediation' may suggest one consistent uniform procedure; but in fact mediation comes in different models and covers different fields of activity, each with its own traditions, ethos and culture. Consequently, a mediator practising in the commercial arena may adopt different procedures and have different views and approaches from a mediator working with neighbourhood and community disputes, and both may differ from labour mediation or divorce mediation. Nevertheless, certain fundamental principles and core skills run through all the diverse forms of mediation.

Common features of mediation

There are a number of common threads which generally run through the different forms of mediation:

1. *The use of a mediator.* It may be trite, but mediation cannot take place without a mediator. Mediation brings into the dispute resolution process a neutral third party whose very presence creates a new dynamic which does not exist when only the parties themselves or their representatives undertake direct negotiation. It is this element of third party intercession which can be very helpful to the resolution process, but which also some traditional litigators find difficult to accept.
2. *The neutrality of the mediator.* Mediator neutrality and impartiality are fundamental to the mediation process. The mediator should not be associated or connected with any of the disputing parties in a way that would inhibit neutrality or effective intervention.
3. *Nature of the mediator's authority.* If a mediator has authority to make any determination which binds the parties that would be inconsistent with the notion of mediation. The mediator has no power or authority other than that given by the parties expressly or implicitly. If any party decides to withdraw power and authority from the mediator, that ends the mediation.
4. *Consensual resolution.* The only binding outcome of mediation is one on which all the parties agree. Any process under which there is an imposed binding outcome, whether

[11] Footnotes are omitted.

stipulated by a third party or arrived at in any way other than by the agreement of the parties, is not mediation. In that event the process would be arbitration or some other form of adjudication.

5. *Settlement objective.* All mediations have as their primary objective the settlement of differences between the disputants by negotiated agreement. Because of the need to reach agreement and because the process allows more ingenuity and nuances than is usually possible in the adversarial process, mediation aims for a resolution which maximises all parties' interests.
6. *Facilitation of negotiation.* The mediator's primary role is to assist the parties with their negotiations. All mediation involves some element of such facilitation, which is enhanced by the mediator's communication and other skills. If the mediator has negotiating skills, that can assist the process; however, the mediator does not negotiate with the parties, but rather assists them to negotiate with one another.
7. *Providing a secure negotiating environment.* One of the main objectives and common practices in mediation is to create conditions which are conducive to discussion, negotiation and the exploration of settlement options and possibilities. This applies to the physical arrangements, to the ambience which is created by the mediators, and to the ground rules regulating the process.
8. *Empowerment of the parties.* Empowerment in relation to the parties collectively means the increase in their ability to make their own decisions and the corresponding reduction of their dependence on third parties including professional advisers. This arises in mediation first, because the parties retain control over whether they wish to settle and on what terms. Secondly, by their involvement in the process of fact gathering and negotiation as it proceeds, they have a direct connection with the outcome and its detailed shape. In some cases, particularly in family and inter-personal issues, the dynamic of the process, the way in which communications can be improved, and the attention given to power imbalances can all have an empowering effect on an individual party, which means that such person is better able to make his or her own decisions.

   Although the empowerment aspect may sometimes be minimal especially where the parties are represented by lawyers in the mediation, they will always have control over the outcome and will rarely lose power in the way that can happen in conventional litigation representation; and consequently the empowerment aspect can be said to exist to some greater or lesser extent in all mediation.
9. *Confidentiality.* Although parties are free to agree that mediation is to be public or that the outcome is to be publicised in some way, one of the principles in all forms of mediation is that it is by nature a private and confidential process. The mediator will invariably offer confidentiality to the parties, who may be asked also to agree to mutual confidentiality.
10. *No substitute for independent advice.* Whatever model of mediation is followed, and whether or not an evaluation is made, a mediator will not ordinarily give advice to the parties, either individually or jointly, though information may well be furnished. In mediation parties are responsible for their own decisions, and where appropriate may need to take independent advice whether on legal, technical or other issues, but not from the mediator.
11. *Containment of escalation.* Whereas the adversarial system has a tendency towards a competitive approach and confrontational communications, the mediation process tends to encourage a problem-solving approach, to facilitate communications and to allow for feelings to be ventilated within a controlled and constructive forum. Consequently, mediation generally has the effect of containing escalation of issues and antagonism. This in turn means that parties in disagreement who have a relationship with one another, whether business, family or personal are generally more likely to sustain that relationship, or to vary or end it in a more co-operative way, by using mediation than through the adversarial process.

Note

The foregoing excerpt deals with the role of a mediator in a developed western legal system. A mediator appointed under the *Land Act* need not play a similar role. For example, he or she could, and most likely will, probably play a more active role in the parties' negotiations than that suggested by the authors. However, the primary tenet remains true that a mediator's role is to assist the parties to a dispute to come to some form of agreement without forcing either party's hand.

****

ECONOMIC IMPACT OF THE LAND DISPUTE SETTLEMENT INSTITUTIONS

It is, of course, still early days. However, in the following excerpt the writers discuss the likely impact of the land dispute settlement institutions on socio-economic development in various districts.

****

Hunt and Eturu, *Land Act Implementation Study: Economic Appraisal, Annex 1*, Draft report, 6 August 1999

The economic impact of these changes will be a function of: the incidence of land disputes and their real cost, the effectiveness of the new structures and the timing of their introduction. Information obtained by the economists suggests that outside areas of mailo tenure the incidence of land disputes in rural areas tends to vary positively with population density. In the high population density districts of Kabale and Rukungiri, most disputes arise between members of the same kin group and reflect the intensity of local land hunger. Most are reported to concern various forms of boundary encroachment: movement of boundary markers, planting trees in an attempt to achieve a de facto boundary shift, refusal to allow another's cattle to cross one's land, or boundary encroachment by one person's cattle onto another's pasture or crop land. Disputation is exacerbated by high levels of fragmentation and the distances between fragments, which mean that more distant fragments may not be adequately supervised. Often the areas involved are small, but some disputes concern substantial amounts of land relative to average farm size, amounting to several acres. Some of these disputes probably derive from past land transactions or relate to inheritance. In the lower population density districts of Soroti and Lira, disagreements regarding boundaries are also a common cause of land disputes, while in Soroti District, another cause involves people returning to claim the land of their ancestors [instances in which the publication of the 1995 Constitution had prompted this were cited]. District officials predicted that as those displaced by the insurgency of the late 1980s and early 1990s return to claim their land, then, if the 12 year time limit specified by the Act for acquisition of bona fides title has elapsed, this too may prompt new disputes.

In all four districts visited, a high emphasis is placed on resolving disputes without involving the formal legal system. Informal dispute resolution procedures emphasise the mediatory role of the clan elders sometimes assisted by officials from lower levels of the administration. In some instances this form of dispute resolution is reinforced by the exchange of a witnessed written agreement between the parties to the dispute. In parts of Kabale District, another dispute resolution procedure that has evolved in response to local need involves new bye-laws: individuals experiencing persistent boundary encroachment by grazing animals approach their LC 3, via their LC 2, to request a bye-law to prohibit this.

In Soroti District the relatively low incidence of disputes, combined with the perceived effectiveness of the elders in dispute resolution, led some of those with whom we spoke to predict that not many disputes would be taken to the new tribunals. In contrast, in Kabale and Rukingiri Districts predicted use will be high.

Turning to the economic impacts of the Land Act in the sphere of dispute settlement, we identified two, one actual and one potential.

By annulling the role of the LC courts in dispute resolution, while failing to immediately activate the proposed land tribunals, the Land Act has already had some, albeit unquantifiable negative impact on farm production and income generation. This stems from the standard advice now given by local mediators to disputants, which is to stop using disputed land until the dispute has been settled under the new system. There is a growing back log of unsettled disputes which was viewed with concern in all districts visited by the economists, but particularly so in Kabale and Rukingiri Districts. Other members of the Team encountered a similar problem in other districts. In Kabale and Rukingiri we were pressed to bring this issue to the attention of the government. From an economic perspective, the real costs of the present hiatus are: loss of production, income and employment from land temporarily taken out of production and the risk of resort to physical violence, with injury to persons and property, where this requirement is not observed by both disputants.

Given the nature and causes of land disputes in the districts visited, we do not foresee any significant diminution in their number following implementation of the Act's provisions regarding either dispute settlement or the issue of certificates of title. Any potential economic benefit to stem from the dispute settlement provisions could arise only from a speeding up of the legal process. Whether this will occur, it is not yet possible to forecast. The chairman of one parish land committee indicated that the probable dispute settlement rate under the new procedures at parish level would amount to a maximum of twenty per month.

THE LAND ACT AND DISPUTE PREVENTION

When the possibility was mooted that, following resolution of a dispute, a successful disputant might be attracted by the prospect of obtaining a certificate of title as further endorsement/ confirmation of the outcome, the response in Rukingiri and Kabale Districts – both at district and local level – was that there was likely to be little interest in so doing: knowledge of the outcome among local witnesses was considered to be more important in enforcing the verdict. However, in Soroti and Lira districts a dispute-related motive for taking up certificates of title was identified as the main motive for so doing.

Summary

An unanticipated consequence of the Land Act has been the short-term adverse impact on the rate of dispute settlement due to failure to activate the land tribunals. It is reasonable to assume that this has had some adverse economic impact in terms of output foregone on disputed land and, probably, some increase in the costs arising from injury to persons. In the medium term, given the nature and causes of most land disputes, we do not foresee a major diminution in their number. The main potential benefit of the Land Act would come from enhancing the speed and/or equity of dispute settlement.

****

***Government of Uganda Report of the Land Implementation Study: Government of Uganda*, 6 August 1999**

Proposal to amend the mediation provision
The Mediator function ... [was] envisaged as an open-ended and essentially private arrangement, this [has] the disadvantage that agreements reached [are] not recorded or binding in any way.... [A new structure is proposed that] allows for a more formal process of registering mediators, and recording the agreements reached with their assistance, thus reducing the opportunity for one of the parties to re-open the same dispute immediately through application to the appropriate tribunal.

Questions

1. Is an agreement reached through mediation legally binding upon (a) the parties and (b) third parties?
2. Are lawyers allowed to act as mediators under the *Land Act?*

****

7

The Potential Impact of the *Land Act*

INTRODUCTION

In 1999, a study was undertaken, inter alia, to assess the potential socio-economic and environmental implications of the *Land Act*, and the institutional, financial and technical needs of its implementation. The study involved eight study teams examining different aspects of the Act, and comprised 17 team members (representing local and international experience equally). Below are excerpts from the final report of the study.

****

Government of Uganda, *Report of the Land Implementation Study*, volume 1: The Main Report, 6 September 1999

The underlying rationale for land tenure reform in Uganda is that land is one of the major assets of rural households and is thus a significant strategic tool for poverty reduction. It is perceived that many smallholder farmers do not have secure ownership rights over land; that women generally do not have secure rights over land, and that land is not widely acceptable as collateral to credit. The policy strategy is therefore to use land ownership as a strategic tool for fighting poverty, and achieving national food security through sustainable improvements in the land use. This implies a major assumption that this can be aided through entrenching the rights of Ugandans to land.

A key task for this study was the establishment of the potential positive and negative impacts of the Land Act in these terms, and in broader relation to the key policies discussed above. Probable Economic (and Land Fund) impacts, Environmental impacts and Social impacts were appraised directly, and broadly conclude that the Land Act alone is unlikely to deliver significant benefits in any of these dimensions. There are significant short to medium term economic and social costs to be borne, and the longer term benefits are likely only to be achieved if the Land Act is implemented in harmony with, and in parallel with, the wide range of other policies aimed at achieving poverty alleviation and more general economic and social development. The Land Fund as currently conceived is more likely to adversely affect longer-term economic development goals than otherwise. The necessity for a Land Policy to establish priorities and modalities is paramount. Environmental impacts are highly variable, depending on tenure types. Short term negative environmental impacts are deemed to spring from uncertainty due to lack of public knowledge and delays in implementation, and the longer term prospects are for broadly neutral to mildly positive impacts.

It must be emphasised that, although direct economic and social benefits are not expected to be particularly significant, the Land Act, as originally envisaged by the legislators, was not expected to deliver these benefits itself. It appears that expectations have been exaggerated by the debate which surrounded the passage of the bill, and it is important to recall that the purpose of the Act is essentially to provide mechanisms for tenure administration in support of a range of other GoU [Government of Uganda] initiatives aimed at economic and social development. It would therefore be incorrect to conclude that the analysis below indicates that the reform should not proceed. This is not the contention of the study. Rather, the reform should proceed, but carefully placed in the context of other initiatives which it will complement, and with some modifications to the provisions of the Act to prevent or mitigate potential negative outcomes.

ECONOMIC APPRAISAL

The economic appraisal indicates that it would be unrealistic to expect the 1988 Land Act to generate major economic benefits over the short- to medium-term, either in the farm or the non-farm sector.

The Act cannot be expected to lead to a major expansion in credit supply to agriculture, largely due to the unwillingness of the commercial banks to lend to that sector. It also seems unlikely that availability of certificates of title will have much impact on use of land as collateral by local micro-finance institutions. The availability of these certificates might be attractive to some externally sponsored micro-finance institutions, but it is impossible to predict whether they would be able to market these on foreclosure.

The dominant concern of the commercial banks with respect to the Land Act is the adverse impact of the consent provisions in Section 40 on the value of land as collateral. The main policy recommendation to stem from consultation with the banks was that, in order to make Section 40 of the Land Act workable, the range of dependants offered direct protection by the Act should be curtailed.

Nor can the Act be expected to have a significant impact on the land market. A land market already exists in most of Uganda and restraints on the rural market which are imposed by kinship ties will not be altered by the provisions of the Act. It is part of the normal process of development in market economies that an impersonal land market evolves over time, but over the short-to medium-term the pattern of evolution may vary, with the possibility of temporary reversals in trend. In the long run, the opportunity provided by the Land Act to obtain certificates of ownership or occupancy is likely to facilitate the development and smooth operation of the land market in both rural and urban Uganda, but in the short-to medium-term the impacts of the Act on the rural land market are likely to be limited. While in principle certificates should give greater confidence to land purchasers concerning the ownership of the land that they want to buy, this will not occur if certificates, and the land register, are not kept up to date.

The Land Act is unlikely to significantly enhance investment opportunities in agriculture or to have any major impacts on farm production in Uganda through its impacts on tenure security. Firstly, the evidence does not indicate a clear-cut relationship between tenure security and farm investment. While some longer-term investment in farming has been inhibited on some farms belonging to occupants of mailo land, it is not clear that this has been a widespread phenomenon. Nor is there evidence of widespread deterrence to investment in customary tenure areas stemming from incomplete individual rights in land. Where some evidence of a possible constraint of this nature was identified, there was no reason to suppose that, on its own, the Land Act could be expected to lead to the necessary strengthening of these rights. If the Land Act leads ultimately to speedier dispute settlement, this may have some positive production impact, but it is unlikely to be large enough to be reflected in the agricultural growth rate. The consequence of this is that the Act is unlikely to make a major impact on the Government's agricultural modernisation programme. As the Act targets underprivileged groups but does not specifically target the poor in terms of absolute income and/or assets it is also unlikely to make a major contribution to the Government's poverty eradication programme.

Meanwhile, one unexpected short-run impact of the Act is that the Act has itself created new uncertainties as to the allocation of rights over some urban and rural land and that this is leading to some disruption to land use. More broadly, the impact on urban authorities' budgets from a combination of revenues lost and increased expenditure on compensation, will be substantial.

The Land Act in its current form will have a number of presently unquantifiable economic impacts in the short-to medium-term. Some of these are highlighted in Table 1 below.

Table 1 is not comprehensive as the costs and benefits listed do not take account of possible uses of the Land Fund, which are discussed separately below. It is also clear that in practice the various costs and benefits identified will not necessarily be evenly distributed geographically. The incidence of disputes, for example, is much higher in some districts than others and so, hence, will be any impacts that are felt from the new dispute settlement procedures introduced by the Land Act. Uptake by private individuals of certificate of title to customary ownership is more likely to occur where land areas claimed are relatively large and unfragmented, because low population density is likely to be associated with higher average size holdings.

Table 1: Probable short - and medium-term costs and benefits of the Land Act

Short-term	Benefits	Costs
	• Enhanced security of tenure for some occupants of mailo land [urban] and for customary and other lawful occupants of gazetted urban land previously leased by urban authorities from the Land Commission. • For some dependants, enhanced protection from irresponsible land sale [will depend on the outcome of possible review of section 40] • For some spouses, enhanced if 'lost amendment' is reintroduced and passed by Parliament. • Right to compensate for land required for public use. • Possible enhanced welfare due to speedier dispute settlement.	• Income loss &/or increased social stress rising from delays in dispute settlement. • Reduction in collateral/market value of title to mailo land lawfully occupied by third parties • Loss of revenue to local governments from leasehold [premiums and rent]. • Increased cost of land acquisition for infrastructure development and new difficulties in enforcing zoning regulations for local governments. • Outputs foregone due to unwillingness of commercial banks to extend new loans based on residential land as collateral and to delays in dispute settlement, plus opportunity cost of public sector funds so far committed to implementation • Possible unintended adverse impacts on women of reintroduction of the 'lost amendment'. • Possible suboptimal use of some land due to jointly inherited title of customary ownership. • Reduction in collateral/market value of all residential land offered as collateral for loans.

Medium-term	Benefits	Costs
	• Possible increase in access to credit for households possessing certificates of lawful or bona fide occupancy of urban mailo land. • Possible reduction in output loss from disputed land [if taken out of production] due to speedier dispute settlement.	• Continuing loss of revenue to leaseholds [premium and ground rent]. • Increased cost of land acquisition for infrastructure development and increased costs in enforcing zoning regulations for local governments. • Outputs forgone due to unwillingness of commercial banks to extend new loans based on residential land as collateral and to delays in dispute settlement, plus opportunity cost of public sector funds committed to implementation. • Continuing Land Act implementation cost. • Outputs foregone due to diversion of resources to Land Act implementation, due to any continued unwillingness of commercial banks to extend new loans based on residential land as collateral, and due to delays to urban or rural infrastructure investment arising from the provisions of the Act.

THE LAND FUND

There is very little evidence that significant social, economic or environmental benefits would accrue from the operations of the Fund as implied by the provisions of the Land Act: the scale of expenditure involved is completely unaffordable in the domestic budget, and donor involvement is extremely unlikely given the lack of identifiable benefits, and because the 'windfall' beneficiaries of land compensation payments would be landlords who are likely to be among the wealthiest people in the country.

In the short-to medium-term, there is a dramatic mismatch between the theoretical needs of the Land Fund and the actual resources that are likely to be available. The global funding needed to finance the purposes of the Act in relation to land titling and ownership transfer alone are in excess of Ush 700 billion. Even limited measures considered to have political priority such as the 'lost counties' are unaffordable from public resources.

In the long-term, there appears to be no case, measured against normal development criteria, for investing scarce public resources in land ownership transfer. The long run solution to the issue of land ownership transfer or entitlement should be dealt with through an efficiency-led, market process where land occupants buy out their land at the point at which they see the private incremental benefits of buying out to be greater than the costs. No external development benefits can be identified which justify investing public resources into this process.

The Uganda land ownership strategy should be a private savings-derived strategy. The process would be gradual and would take decades, but the strategy would be led by the real costs and returns of input and product markets, not by government intervention, ensuring that the maximum efficiency is derived from the country's scarce resources. A national savings campaign, encouraged by government and donors, but paid for by the banking sector might be appropriate. Donor support might enhance this dynamic by targeting rural savings mobilisation. But support should be about transferring ideas and knowledge rather than about material assistance such as subsidising operations.

Any attempt to introduce a government land loan scheme would carry a high risk of failure because land occupants consider the land to be theirs by traditional entitlement and would feel little commitment to repay loans since there would be little incremental productive benefit. There would, in any case, be little (if any) productive gain from which to repay a loan. There is also still a strong and widespread psychology that a government loan is a soft loan or a grant. The possible channels for disbursements are also problematic: the formal banking sector is in a state of virtual paralysis and the micro-finance sector is at an early stage of development and is not yet self sustainable. The performance of government credit and micro-finance has been poor. Finally, a government scheme for land purchase would distort the land market as buyers and sellers reacted to the prospect of external assistance to the buying and selling process.

As a matter of principle, compensation for compulsory land acquisition in the public interest should always be built into the costs of the relevant development project. This would ensure that compensation costs are transparent, explicit and fully integrated into the total costs and into the cost benefit evaluation of the respective resettlement, physical infrastructure or other project where land is compulsorily acquired in the public interest. In the short-term there may be scope to use the current year's allocation to the fund to address urgent compensation requirements which have not been provided for elsewhere.

Lending for land registration and certification should not be considered because the small amounts of money involved in obtaining a customary land ownership certificate or certificate of occupancy on mailo, freehold or leasehold land would cost more to administer than the value of the loans. It would be more efficient to allocate this money as a direct grant to the already highly subsidised registration and certification charges. For land ownership transfer and certification, the survey, registration and certification charges including the private cadastral survey, would be large enough to be considered for lending.

SOCIAL APPRAISAL

From a social perspective, the major impact of the Land Act is for the approximately 8 million customary landholders throughout Uganda. However the extent of this impact will largely depend on the extent to which these landholders previously felt that their tenure was insecure, and it is apparent that this is seldom the case. It must be stressed that, in all the districts visited, customary landholders (including mailo tenants) generally felt that they had security of tenure and cited other barriers to investment and productivity on their land.

Land certification and registration as envisaged in the Act will have a positive impact in some circumstances but not in others, as suggested in Table 2 below.

Table 2: Varying perceived impacts of certification and registration

Urban areas	Rural areas (individual)	Rural areas (communal)
•Risk of mismanagement, appropriation and corruption as a result of the rapid increase in land values. •The Act can protect the rights of poor people from land grabbing by wealthy investors in urban areas. •Under pressure of population growth, market forces, and land scarcity many customary land-holders in urban areas are keen to document.	•Complexity of land tenure systems and multiple and overlapping rights prevail. •Some respondents perceive traditional land management to be a superior system because of equity of access and the application of customary rules and procedures which were appropriate for the local conditions. • Some expressed the view that the provisions of the Act undermined the traditional values whereby land was held in trust for all the clan members, and increased the risk of land sales, leaving vulnerable households and individuals more insecure than before. •The Act may encourage enclosure and restrict traditional communal land use, disproportionately affecting the poor by reducing the numbers of domestic animals they can keep, or increasing labour constraints. It can also lead to overcrowding that culminates into serious degradation. •Communal Land Association can protect land which is communally used against individualised control. However, the proposed procedures are seen as complicated. •Some people fear that the creation of associations will provide an opportunity for unscrupulous people to seize control of the association procedures.	• In pastoral areas property ownership involves a wider spread of seasonal or resource specific access rights which do not confer any kinds of ownership or authority on the users. • The Act and the PEAP [Poverty Eradication Action Plan] are likely to encourage sedentarisation, although experience elsewhere shows that this can reinforce poverty, and increase the likelihood of conflicts between settled agriculturists and pastoralists. •Some problems and dissatisfaction exist among communities over 'protected' lands under the state jurisdiction. This is likely to cause and exacerbate conflicts. •Where land pressure is high, there are real threats to people's livelihoods for some protected lands to revert to communal property resources. • Livelihood security is also being threatened where, for example, wetlands are currently being cultivated and poor users face the threat of eviction under the Land Act and other legislation.

Poverty eradication is the main objective of agricultural development, and this is expected to be achieved partly through transformation from subsistence type to market-oriented smallholder agriculture. The assumption is that the provision of certificates to customary landowners will facilitate transfer of land from less progressive to more progressive farmers with better capacity to improve productivity. However, the complex linkages between land tenure, land distribution, economic growth, development and poverty, are not addressed in this analysis. The field studies revealed that issues of access to credit, employment, savings and markets in rural areas were the more critical problems for improving the productivity of poor and vulnerable households.

The contention that certification will enable landowners to access credit is widely repeated but not well founded in Uganda's current situation. Even if land was accepted as collateral, the more successful farmers are more likely to meet bank-lending criteria. Informal lending arrangements will be risky for the poor and might well result in loss of land on default.

The scope for conversion of customary certification to registered title provided for by the Act is unlikely to lead to widespread demand for registration in the short-and medium-term except in areas where factors, such as the economic value of the land, the perceived or real threat to people's land tenure security, and their ability to meet the costs of registration, encourage it. The poor and vulnerable are unlikely to embark upon registration in the short-term because the process appears to be complicated and relatively expensive. Again only customary tenants on land close to urban and peri-urban areas whose land rights are potentially under threat from urban expansion programmes by municipal councils or commercial interests are likely to take advantage of registration.

The lack of an interim body to handle disputes and the delay in setting up Land Tribunals has meant that many land disputes remain unresolved, causing additional conflict and social tensions among landholders. Incidents of murder, beatings and widow disinheritance are reported to have been exacerbated by frustration arising from the lack of an authority to intervene in land disputes. District officials reported that they were inundated by vulnerable people whose land rights had been infringed upon by powerful neighbours and relatives. There are also high levels of land disputes between poor tenants, town councils and powerful private interests. The establishment of affordable Land Tribunals and mediation processes is therefore seen as a matter of priority.

In Uganda, access to land by women is generally regulated through male relations – either through marriage or kinship ties. The extent to which women provide agricultural labour is not matched by their control over the use of the resources and especially over income generated from the sale of crops. Decision making over land allocation and transfer lies almost exclusively with male heads of households or traditional authorities and elders. These customary laws are in conflict with the Constitution, and Section 40 of the Land Act attempts to protect the rights of spouses and dependent children through requiring various consents for the transfer of land on which the parties ordinarily reside.

There is a strong case for improving women's rights over land as a result of international conventions and national laws, and also for equity and developmental reasons, and the Act provides some groundbreaking provisions for this. However, there is no doubt that it is in this area that the Act faces its greatest challenge in terms of implementation. Field studies reveal a very high level of resistance to the requirement for consent of spouses over land transfers. It was generally felt that the provision was unworkable, because it contradicts cultural norms. Most women interviewed stated that they had access to land while they remained married, and did not feel that they needed to consent to land transfers. The general feeling among those interviewed was that enforcement of the law on consent would deter people from acquiring title, which will not improve tenure security for women. An extensive sensitisation campaign will be necessary both in the short-and longer-term.

It is more difficult to unravel women's land rights in urban areas than in rural areas, as social relations are more detached.

ENVIRONMENTAL APPRAISAL

It is commonly stated that improved security of tenure leads to positive investment in agriculture and other resources, thus enhancing sustainable production and also enhancing environment. However, extensive research throughout Africa has not demonstrated that formalising customary tenure, in situations where people already feel secure, has a significant impact on use of land and natural resources. In some districts there are significant areas of informal tenancy on titled mailo land and also of formal freehold or leasehold tenure but most tenure in Uganda may be described as 'secure customary tenure'.

It is important to distinguish between short- and long-term motives of people in evaluating potential impacts. Some individuals, largely due to misconceptions of the Land Act, are exploiting resources only for short-term financial gain by, for example, accelerated cultivation of seasonal wetlands, cutting down trees on what is perceived as public land for sale; speculating in assumed increasing land values in urban areas. We define such short-term negative impacts as 'before implementation impacts', or potentially the continuing impacts of not properly implementing the Act. It is, however, assumed that most people are interested in long-term sustainable economic benefits and these are more likely to result after implementation of the Land Act is fully underway.

Table 3: Expected environmental impacts by tenure type

Rural mailo land	Approximately 14% of total land area. Occupied by approximately 19% of the population.	Positive environmental and economic benefits are most likely here because formalising the status of occupants will provide improved security and is likely to promote sustainable investments. ...Where space is limited, the Act could reduce environmental stress on their existing land if the Land Fund or other sources were used by individual households to acquire additional land.
Customary tenure (Individual family type)	Individual ownership with communal rights of access dominates in Uganda, accounting for an estimated 62% of the population. Population density varies greatly from district to district.	People already feel secure, so, although there have been some negative short-term negative impacts (eg increased grabbing of land), little change of use is expected and the longer-term impact of the Land Act will be either neutral or marginally positive. There is some risk that customary shared access rights may be reduced or removed, with environmentally and socially negative consequences.
Customary tenure (Communal type)	Mainly but not exclusively in northern Uganda	Transhumant gazing movement are highly fluid and customarily

		cross clan boundaries. The more fluid the better for the environment. Although there is doubt that pastoralists will seek to use the provisions of the Act, de-gazetting the relevant protected areas is likely to benefit the environment. On the other hand, neighbours may use the Act to register communal lands in an effort to exclude pastoralists. This could result in social and economic costs, but environmental impact would depend on the carrying capacity of potentially de-gazetted areas, and cannot be assessed at this stage.
Urban areas		People have already settled and established dwellings in an unplanned and environmentally destructive way in peri-urban areas. The Land Act appears to have accelerated the process by encouraging speculative settlement in the hope of obtaining future compensation. Full implementation of the Act, and a public education and sensitisation programme may reverse or slow this process.
Reserves and sensitive ecosystems		The Land Act will invoke other relevant Acts and statutes. However, most post-1994 policies and statutes recognise merits of allowing appropriate and sustainable uses of natural resources, even in reserves and protected areas. The impact may be improved by sustainable use of resources, thus giving increased benefits to local people.

Almost all rural respondents stated that they believed they were secure on their land but nonetheless would feel more secure with certificates and would therefore like to acquire them – but who would not, if they were freely available? Some district officials cited theoretical changes in land use, for example, that farmers would plant more trees or perennial crops after formalising land title. This was not confirmed by rural residents or farmers themselves, who were not able to suggest ways in which they would change land use. Farmers are already growing perennial crops, such as coffee, both on customary land and also on informally occupied mailo land. The general conclusion is that most but not all of rural Uganda is in effect under 'secure' tenure, as perceived by the occupants themselves. The Land Act will not significantly enhance security of tenure and therefore significant changes to land use or to the exploitation of natural resources are unlikely to result directly from it in the foreseeable future.

In order to dampen or mitigate the possible negative short-term effects on shared access to resources of scattered individual registrations amongst communities/villages, there might be positive benefit in either building on traditional regulatory institutions or encouraging the early formation of Communal Land Associations as provided for in the Land Act. These could influence sound management of natural resources.

Some indirect environmental benefits from implementing the Land Act could be realised through appropriate co-ordination and especially through sensitisation concerning other laws and their implications. This must closely involve all relevant local officials, not only District Environmental Officers, and could be achieved by expanding sensitisation programmes to include reference to environmental policies, laws and practical strategies for environmental impact mitigation and enhancement.

Potential problems in implementing the Act

[This excerpt is from the Executive Summary of the Report]
Progress with implementation of the Act, which was passed over a year ago, is much slower than planned. This has had very serious consequences because previous mechanisms and structures have been removed, and a vacuum exists in land administration and, especially, dispute resolution. Disputes which would previously have been settled quickly at a local level are now persisting with consequent loss of production, hardship, and, in some cases, violence.

There is widespread general understanding that every citizen now has security of tenure and can acquire a certificate to document this. The perception is also growing that these certificates can be used as collateral to facilitate borrowing. There has also been a degree of land-grabbing by opportunists in the hope of acquiring a certificate. Expectations are therefore rising and there is a major risk that demand will be stimulated beyond the capacity of any embryonic institutions.

Under the Constitution, local authorities are now obliged to fully compensate for compulsory land acquisition. This has serious budgetary implications for urban and municipal councils, most of which do not have the necessary resources.

It has rapidly become apparent that the title registration system must be developed alongside the customary certification systems, although this is not directly provided for in the Land Act. This will require an extensive development programme in parallel with the implementation of the Land Act itself.

A final emerging consequence is that, since government can no longer rely on its ability to claim land or remove citizens from land as it needs, government land holdings must be identified, rationalised and title registered. This implies an enormous task for the Uganda Land Commission in its capacity as government's property manager.

Implementation issues

Key implementation issues which form the proposed strategy are:

- The very large number of members and associated costs of the required decentralised institutions.
- Human resources capacity will be a major limiting factor, since large numbers of personnel must be found, appointed and trained.
- The impossibility of quantifying demand for registration, especially for customary tenure certificates, makes phasing and budgeting very uncertain.

- Extensive sensitisation is essential to address problems, but will stimulate demand beyond the limited capacity available to cope with this.
- The Land Fund provisions as contained in the Act appear inadvisable and unworkable, and much less ambitious proposals are needed.

The implementation needs are considered in four categories:

- The permanent institutional requirements to meet 'steady state demand' for land administration and dispute resolution over the next ten years plus.
- A flexible provision to meet bulges in demand for initial registration.
- Capacity building and set-up activities to develop the statutory and policy framework; to create and build capacity in the required institutions, and to equip the public to exercise their rights under the Act.
- The establishment and capitalisation of the proposed Land Fund.

The permanent institutional requirements and phasing mechanisms

The land administration and dispute resolution structures as provided for by the Land Act (described as Option 1) implies approximately 21,500 members of boards and tribunals; and more than 2,400 full-time paid officials. Option 2 proposes a reduction by:

- Replacing 45 District Land Offices with 18 Branch Offices of a new Land Services Agency (LSA), which provides professional registration, survey and valuation for the District Land Boards, reducing the staff requirement to approximately 60% of that required under Option 1.
- Replacing 45 District Land Tribunals with 18 Circuit Tribunals, each serving approximately 3 districts, and creating a 'President of Land Tribunals' to permit independent administration of the tribunals system.
- Relocating the Recorder function from Sub-county to District level, reducing the support staff requirement for this function to 55% of that implied under Option 1.

A third option, which removes Parish Land Committees, is unacceptable because it compromises the accessibility of the certification process to poorer rural people. Although substitution with sub-county level committees was proposed at a later stage, this would present the same problem while not significantly decreasing (and possibly increasing) costs. As a result this has not been developed further.

Option 2 still represents a very high human and financial resource burden. Phased introduction of customary certification is also proposed to distribute costs into the future where possible. To ensure that resources are only committed where necessary, a threshold demand of, say 10 applications may be set for certification systems to be established in a given parish. Where there is evidence of widespread demand, communities rather than individual households would be encouraged to apply for (less costly) systematic certification of a village or suburb. Further, Government of Uganda should consider prioritising districts (or other target areas) for gradual introduction of the customary certification system over a number of years.

As all components of the study indicate that the vacuum in dispute resolution must be addressed as a matter of extreme urgency, it is not recommended that the introduction of Land Tribunals should be deliberately phased, although phasing will be an inevitable consequence of the extensive recruitment and training process. The proposal to permit the courts to deal with land cases for a limited period while the Tribunal system is established is being actioned.

The Land Fund and the Uganda Land Commission

The study has concluded that the Land Fund is not a priority for the use of scarce resources (see above), and accordingly proposes that the short-term one-off priority for the Land Fund should be to resolve outstanding or imminent compulsory compensation cases where no provision for compensation has been made elsewhere in the development budget.

If the Land Fund is given priority for cultural/political reasons, and the prime purpose is to strengthen the rights of occupants, the second priority recommended would be to use the Fund to subsidise the (already less than full cost) cost of issuing certificates of customary ownership and occupancy on mailo, freehold and leasehold areas. This subsidy could be targeted initially to the contentious area of the lost counties i.e. in Kibaale District. The issuing of certificates of occupancy would be a cost effective and affordable first step in strengthening the rights of mailo tenants in politically sensitive areas.

Pending a policy decision from Government of Uganda on how and whether to proceed, it is difficult to be prescriptive regarding the implementation arrangements for the Fund. It is proposed that the management and administration of the Fund should be resourced from a small (specified) percentage, say, 3%, of the total funds paid into the Fund.

Set-up activities to facilitate implementation

The current infrastructure, expertise, and human and technological capacity is far from being able to deliver the Land Act services. There are therefore a number of development initiatives which are required to build the capacity of the various institutions to the point where they can be effective. The study has described and costed each of the following activities:

Pilot operations	Limited pilot exercises to test the operation of the proposed systems on the ground prior to full implementation.
Policy development	Development of national and local land policies to guide the process of tenure reform.
Legal reform[12]	Requirements to replace out-of-date land legislation to harmonise with the Land Act and other relevant modern legislation.
Technology and infrastructure	Acquisition of modern surveying equipment, and information technology (hardware, software and systems design) and communications systems. Specialist equipment/furniture. Vehicles.
Human resource development	Developing appropriate human resources management and human resources development systems, and the costs of 'initial' training for each of the implementation institutions. Also provides for development of more general professional and technical education and training to increase the pool of appropriate skills in the population.
Financial management	The development of appropriate financing and financial management policies and systems.
Sensitisation	A range of sensitisation, public information and participatory planning activities to raise awareness, selectively encourage titling where appropriate, and mitigate negative effects and abuses.
Monitoring and evaluation	Quality assurance procedures to monitor quality of service and cost effectiveness, and survey-type activities to monitor and evaluate impact.
Co-ordination	A steering Committee and Secretariat to oversee implementation.

[12] See also below for more details.

It is particularly important to distinguish these activities from the recurrent core operations described in the previous section, since these are much more likely to attract assistance from development partners, the majority of whom are not prepared to fund routine operations but will assist with initial infrastructure development and capacity building.

The study has assessed the full cost of each activity irrespective of the duration of that activity. In reality, the activities will all take a number of years. Government of Uganda and development partners would be able to make deliberate decisions to spread the costs by planning an extended *set-up period,* but this study is unable to prejudge what is essentially a policy decision.

Budgets and funding

Budgets

Indicative budgets for implementation are based on a number of assumptions which may vary as policy priorities are amended by Government of Uganda.

The budget is presented as:

- A steady-state position (which is assumed to be in about 5 years time) in respect of the normal operating costs of the two options described above.
- Land Fund capitalisation and management requirements.
- A series of set-up costs reflecting the various policy, infrastructure and human resources capacity building activities described above.

The Government of Uganda would face annual steady-state operating costs of Sh19bn if the entire implementation structure was established as described in the Land Act itself. Option 2 reduces this by about 15% to Sh16bn per year. This must be compared with the budget provision[13] which Government of Uganda has made of Sh 2.5bn, Sh 2.9bn and Sh 4.4bn in each of the current and the next two financial years.

If implemented as envisaged in the Act, Land Fund capitalisation requirements would be Shs714bn. Under the much more restricted application described above, Shs3.1bn is required.

Potential total costs of approximately Shs23bn are envisaged for set-up and capacity-building activities.

Fees and Cost Recovery

Fees for customary registration have been set at a level which will not deter people from taking advantage of the Land Act and are not based on any financial analysis.

The total net unit cost to Government of Uganda for each customary certificate issued is of the order of Shs 21.500 – two and a half times the fees charged. As demand for certification grows beyond the 'steady state' the total recurrent expenditure burden on government will grow rather than diminish, unless fees are set at full cost recovery levels.

However, since about 50% of the population is on the poverty line, increasing fees conflicts with the intention to make certificates available to the poorest. Further subsidisation or waiving fees for certain categories of occupant may not be desirable in any case since the level of demand would in all likelihood rise dramatically.

Fees for freehold titling should be set at a level which fully recovers the costs involved.

Funding sources and mechanisms

The Land Act provides that costs of District Land Boards, District Land Offices, and Parish Land Committees will be met out of District Administration funds, while Tribunals will be funded through the Consolidated Fund.

---

[13] Note that these figures exclude the provision which has been earmarked for the Land Fund.

The amount of district administration funds required in order to sustain the steady-state structures of District Land Boards and Parish Land Committees is considerable (Shs7,400m per annum), and districts do not have funds to meet these costs at present, or in the foreseeable future.

It seems unlikely that development partners will lend support to the day-to-day running costs of the Land Act, although it is to be expected that support will be forthcoming on the set-up costs involved in implementing the Act.

In the medium term at least, therefore, funding will have to come from Central Government. The implementation of the Land Act will only be successful if there is a political will to provide the funds required, if necessary by making savings on other budgets.

The recommended method of funding the land administration structure is through the conditional grant mechanism, which already exists, using a separate bank account for this specific purpose. With correctly enforced audit arrangements, this will ensure that funds are used for their intended purpose, and will enhance the stated objective of making the District Land Boards and Parish Land Committees truly independent. Tribunals should be funded, as provided by the Act, directly from the Consolidated Fund.

Next steps in the process

This report and its annexes are not intended to represent a blueprint for implementation of the Act, and should be read as a high level evaluation of the likely costs and impact of the legislation, and a broad strategic direction for implementation.

****

DEMARCATION AND PROTECTION OF GOVERNMENT LAND

McAuslan and Mwebaza, *Land Act Implementation Study: Legal Appraisal, Annex 6*, draft report 6 August, 1999

Proposal for a Government Land Act

There is a strong case for a new Act to provide for the management of Government owned and occupied land. To understand the need for such a law, it is necessary to provide a brief historical background to what is now Government land. Generally speaking, Government land has not been demarcated in the past, because prior to the 1995 Constitution, virtually all land in Uganda was public land and the Government could more or less just take what it wanted, moving people out of the way with little ceremony. There was no need therefore to demarcate the land used by Government. In broad terms, the 1995 Constitution converted public land into privately owned land and at the same time preserved Government ownership of its land. But in the absence of any clear boundaries to Government land, the mere statement that land owned by Government remained owned by Government did nothing to protect Government land from encroachment by private citizens or local authorities, either in ignorance or wilfully. The specific abolition of statutory leases to urban authorities by Article 285 of the Constitution did not help the position either. How then may Government land be protected?

First, it might be helpful to recap on the legal position of Government land. By the Public Lands Act 1962 (PLA 62), all Crown land occupied by Government for public purposes became vested for a freehold estate of public land in the Uganda Land Commission or, in Buganda, in the Buganda Land Board, and any right, title, estate or interest in land of or to which the Government was seised, possessed or entitled immediately before the commencement of the PLA 62 vested in the ULC or BLC for the same estate etc as it was previously vested in the (colonial) Government. The Public Lands Act 1969 (PLA 69) continued this provision by s 1 and vested the land in the Land Commission established by the Constitution of 1967 for the same estate etc as was the case in the PLA 62

The 1995 Constitution provides by Article 283 that all immovable property which immediately before the coming into force of the Constitution was vested in any authority or person for the purposes of or in right of the Government or in Government shall vest in the Government, *subject to the provisions of Chapter 15,* i.e., the Chapter on land. Article 239 provides for the Uganda Land Commission (ULC) to hold and manage any land vested in or acquired by Govt. So land occupied and used by Government which was vested in freehold in the ULC is now vested in Government but there is no indication as to what estate or interest is vested in Government and such land is held by the ULC. A reasonable assumption is that the title to Government land is 'statutory' freehold; i.e., freehold by virtue of a statutory provision rather than a title issued under the *Registration of Titles Act* (*RTA*).

There is then no legal problem about the *ownership* of Government land. The problems are managerial and practical:

- how to determine the extent of Government land on the ground;
- how to determine the boundaries of the individual holdings of Government land;
- what to do if Government land is found to have been encroached upon;
- how to sort out problems of conflicts between the central government and local authorities who may have laid or are laying claim to Government land;
- how to manage Government land?

A question which may be asked however is: is there any legal input into these practical problems which, while not solving them, might make them easier to solve? A preliminary question to consider is whether, if there were to be any legal input into the problems which could be devised, it could be brought forward as an amendment to the *Land Act*?

The problem here is that there is nothing in the *Land Act* about government land as such. Section 50 dealing with the functions of the Uganda Land Commission repeats in paragraph (a) the provisions of Article 239 of the Constitution and in paragraph (c) requires the Commission to 'procure certificates of title for any land vested in or acquired by Government'. It might be difficult to *amend* that section to provide for some substantive provisions about Government land.

As we understand the position, one can amend an Act even to the extent of introducing new sections if one is dealing with a matter already in the Act:: viz, Land Tribunals: One cannot however *amend* an Act by introducing provisions on a matter which isn't in the Act to begin with. One can *add* a new Part to an Act but the new Part must have some connection with the existing subject matter of the Act. To add a new Part dealing with Government Land to an Act dealing with private rights to land might not be possible. Thus on the general principles of drafting, even supposing that there were a few provisions which might help the present practical problems, amending the *Land Act* may not be the way forward.

There are larger issues here however. A broad general problem is that by repealing the Public Lands Act, 1969, there is no general body of law to regulate and govern Government land other than the residual common law of Uganda, viz, English common law as it was on 11 August 1902 plus any specific laws about land in Uganda which can be applied to Government land. A strong case can then be made that a statute needs to be enacted to provide a framework of law for the management of Government land – a Government Land Act, in other words. The development of such a law would need to be preceded by certain policy decisions. Some of these policy decisions may be flagged here:

- Encroachment or squatting on Government land: Is it practical or politic in view of the provisions of Chapter 15 of the Constitution to treat *bona fide* occupants of Government land any differently to such occupants of privately owned land; i.e., they have security of tenure via a perpetual statutory tenancy known as a tenancy by occupancy under the *Land Act.* A fortiori in respect of persons who, as in section 31 of the *Land Act*, are not *bona fide* occupants because they have not been occupying on the land for 12 years: the Mediator must help them reach an accommodation with the landowner.

- Where for some reason persons who are qualified to be treated as *bona fide* occupants are nonetheless to be moved, what is to be the responsibility of Government to such persons? Would they qualify for assistance under the Land Fund to be resettled as 'persons who have been rendered landless by Government action'? If not, what compensation, if any, are they to get?
- On the assumption – not unreasonable given that some Government land has been more or less abandoned for some years – that people who have moved in have undertaken transactions in respect of the land, what recognition is to be given to these transactions and to the current status of the land? Is it to revert to Government land or be deemed to be ... what? Freehold? Customary tenure?
- What mechanisms are to be created to handle disputes about Government land? There are bound to be disputes on boundaries, on occupancy, on use etc. Are the Land Tribunals to be given jurisdiction? Should it be possible for occupiers to require a process of adjudication of rights similar to that provided for in Part 11 of the Land Act?
- What are the principles to be used by those surveying land to determine what is Government land? Where a Government building is involved, how much land should it be assumed is within the cartilage of the building and so part of Government land? Where there is land which is contested but unused, what presumptions should be followed to determine what is Government land?
- How are disputes between local authorities and the central Government over Government land to be resolved and according to what criteria? Via Land Tribunals? A special commission?
- What should be the powers, rights and duties of the Government over Government land? Is there a need, for instance for some special 'fast track' procedure in the courts to clear unauthorised occupants off Government land or on the contrary, should the Government be under a special obligation to such persons to regularise their occupation?
- Should any law attempt to deal with the problems thrown up by the abolition of statutory leases and the difficulties urban local authorities are now facing in protecting land needed for public development?

These may not be an exhaustive list but they indicate the extent of the problems that need to be addressed before any useful legislation could be drafted dealing with the problems of Government land. None of these issues however address the immediate problem which is as noted above. As has been pointed out however, there is no legal solution. If Government wants to protect its land, there is nothing now to stop it commencing action in the courts to claim land back from unauthorised occupants. Alternatively it could place advertisements in the newspapers reminding people that the Constitution preserved Government's rights to its land and warning unauthorised occupants that they are likely to face the full rigours of the law if they do not move. At the same time, the resources of the ULC could be increased so that it could begin the inevitably very long process of mapping, surveying and registering Government land.

****

Question

Does the doctrine of adverse possession apply to Government land? See the *Limitation Act*.

****

LEGAL REFORM

[This excerpt is from the main report]

The principal legal reforms which will be necessitated by the report lie in the area of land administration. This embraces the Registration of Titles Act and the Survey Act. They provide the legal framework and backing for title registration and are seriously out of date. These acts however can only be replaced after a thorough study has been undertaken of the most appropriate systems of survey and title registration and recommendations have been made and accepted on the matter. …

The Mortgage Decree is subject to reform by the Law Reform Commission. … The emphasis is placed on the needs of banks, finance houses and other potential mortgagees. The Land Act Implementation Unit has already submitted a draft of possible provisions for inclusion to ensure that the interests of mortgagors are also given due weight.

The Domestic Relations Bill (under development by the Law Reform Commission) deals principally with marriage and divorce but as a part of the reforms to the law of divorce, issues of property rights between spouses are dealt with. These propose different rules to those being put forward to cater for the 'lost amendment'.

The present Land Acquisition Act does not accord with the Constitution. To the extent that compulsory land acquisition will become more common it is urgently necessary to draft a replacement which accords with the Constitutional principles governing both administrative action and compensation for compulsory acquisition.

Urban authorities lack the necessary planning and development control powers to control private development and plan for public development in the aftermath of the Land Act. The Town and Country Planning Act needs to be reviewed. Like the Registered Titles Act and the Survey Act, a reform of this Act should be the outcome of a review of the system of town and country planning in the light not just of the Land Act but also of modern approaches to urban planning, and in particular of the principles and precepts enshrined in the Habitat Agenda 1996 (to which the Government is a party).

Government land has not been demarcated in the past, because virtually all land in Uganda was public. The 1995 Constitution converted public land into privately owned land and at the same time preserved Government ownership of its land. But in the absence of any clear boundaries to Government land, the mere statement that land owned by Government remained owned by Government did nothing to protect Government land from encroachment by private citizens or local authorities. A strong case can then be made that a statute needs to be enacted to provide a framework of law for the management of Government land – a Government Land Act.

A further reform, to which a lower priority is accorded, is the development of legislation regulating the operations of Estate Agents. Since this is not central to the implementation of the Land Act itself, no provision has been made for it in this study.

It may now be appropriate to use the Land Act as a trigger to more fundamental land law reform for Uganda, to develop a modern law reflecting the needs of a society and economy increasingly founded on private land ownership and transactions. Malaysia, Tanzania and New Zealand might all provide useful models.

****

8
Legal Conception of Land

WHAT IS LAND?

The common law definition of land is summed up in the Latin phrase *cujus est solum ejus est usque ad coelum et ad inferos*, which, translated literally, means that a landowner owns the air space above it and everything below it.

****

Airspace

How high above the surface constitutes land? This issue is discussed in the case of *Lord Bernstein of Leigh (Baron) v Skyviews & General Ltd,* extracted below.

****

Land includes the airspace above the surface to such height as is reasonably necessary for the ordinary use of the land; above that is public domain.

Lord Bernstein of Leigh (Baron) v Skyviews & General Ltd
[1977] 2 A11 ER 902

[The plaintiff was the owner of certain premises and surrounding land. The defendants, whose business was to take aerial photographs of properties and then offer them for sale to the owners, took a single aerial photograph of the plaintiff's premises from a height of several hundred feet. The plaintiff objected to the photograph being taken without his permission and brought an action against the defendants alleging that they had wrongfully entered the airspace above the plaintiff's premises to take the photograph and were guilty of trespass and actionable invasion of the plaintiff's right to privacy. The plaintiff claimed damages for trespass and injunctions to restrain the defendants from entering the airspace and from invading the plaintiff's right to privacy.]

Griffiths J.: The plaintiff claims that as owner of the land he is also owner of the airspace above the land, or at least has the right to exclude any entry into the airspace above his land. He relies on the old Latin maxim, *cujus est solum ejus est usque ad coelum et ad inferos*, a colourful phrase often on the lips of lawyers since it was first coined by Accursius in Bologna in the 13th century. There are a number of cases in which the maxim has been used by English judges but an examination of those cases shows that they have all been concerned with structures attached to the adjoining land, such as overhanging buildings, signs or telegraph wires, and for their solution it has not been necessary for the judge to cast his eyes towards the heavens; he has been concerned with the rights of the owner in the airspace immediately adjacent to the surface of the land.

That an owner has certain rights in the airspace above his land is well established by authority. He has the right to lop the branches of trees that may overhang his boundary, although this right seems to be founded in nuisance rather than trespass ...

In *Gifford v Dent* [1926] 1 W.N. 336 Romer J. held that it was a trespass to erect a sign that projected four feet eight inches over the plaintiff's forecourt and ordered it to be removed. He invoked the old maxim in his judgement. The report reads:

> ... the plaintiffs were tenants of the forecourt and were accordingly tenants of the space above the forecourt usque ad coelum, it seemed to him that the projection was clearly a trespass upon the property of the plaintiffs.

That decision was followed by McNair J. in *Kelsen v Imperial Tobacco Co Ltd* [1957] All ER 343, [1957] 2 Q.B. 334, in which he granted a mandatory injunction ordering the defendants to remove a sign which projected only eight inches over the plaintiff's property. ... This decision, I think, has been recognised by the textbook writers, and, in particular, by the late Professor Winfield (*Winfield on Tort* (6th ed., 1954), p.379), as stating the true law. It is not without significance that in the *Air Navigation Act* 1920, section 9(1), which was replaced by section 40(1) of the *Civil Aviation Act*, 1949, the legislature found it necessary expressly to negative the action of trespass or nuisance arising from the mere fact of an aeroplane passing through the air above the land. It seems to me clearly to indicate that the legislature were not taking the same view of the matter as Lord Ellenborough in *Pickering v Rudd* (1815) 4 Camp. 219, but were taking the view accepted in the later cases, such as *Wandsworth Board of Works v United Telephone Co*. (1884) 13 Q.B.D. 904, subsequently followed by Romer J. in *Gifford v Dent* [1926] 1 W.N. 336. Accordingly, I reach the conclusion that a trespass, and not a mere nuisance, was created by the invasion of the plaintiff's airspace by this sign.

I very much doubt if in that passage McNair J. was intending to hold that the plaintiff's rights in the airspace continued to an unlimited height or 'ad coelum' as counsel for the plaintiff submits. The point that the judge was considering was whether the sign was a trespass or a nuisance at the very low level at which it projected. This to my mind is clearly indicated by his reference to *Winfield on Tort* (6th Edn., 1954), p. 380) in which the text reads: '... it is submitted that trespass will be committed by [aircraft] to the airspace if they fly so low as to come within the area of ordinary user.' The author in that passage is careful to limit the trespass to the height at which it is contemplated an owner might be expected to make use of the airspace as a natural incident of the user of his land. If, however, the learned judge was by his reference to the *Civil Aviation Act* 1949, and his disapproval of the views of Lord Ellenborough in *Pickering v Rudd* (1815) 4 Camp. 219, indicating the opinion that the flight of an aircraft at whatever height constituted a trespass at common law, I must respectfully disagree.

I do not wish to cast any doubts on the correctness of the decision on its own particular facts. It may be a sound and practical rule to regard any incursion into the airspace at a height which may interfere with the ordinary user of the land as a trespass rather than a nuisance. Adjoining owners then know where they stand; they have no right to erect structures overhanging or passing over their neighbours' land and there is no room for argument whether they are thereby causing damage or annoyance to their neighbours about which there may be much room for argument and uncertainty. But wholly different considerations arise when considering the passage of aircraft at a height which in no way affects the user of the land.....

I can find no support in authority for the view that a landowner's rights in the airspace above his property extend to an unlimited height. In *Wandsworth Board of Works v United Telephone Co*. (1884) 13 Q.B.D. 904 Bowen L.J. described the maxim, usque ad coelum, as a fanciful phrase, to which I would add that if applied literally it is a fanciful notion leading to the absurdity of a trespass at common law being committed by a satellite every time it passes over a suburban garden. The academic writers speak with one voice in rejecting the uncritical and literal application of the maxim. ... I accept their collective approach as correct. The problem is to balance the rights of an owner to enjoy the use of his land against the rights of the general public to take advantage of all that science now offers in the use of airspace. This balance is in my judgement best struck in our present society by restricting the rights of an owner in the airspace above his land to such height as is necessary for the ordinary use and enjoyment of his land and the structures on it, and declaring that above that height he has no greater rights in the airspace than any other member of the public.

Applying this test to the facts of this case, I find that the defendants' aircraft did not infringe any rights in the plaintiff's airspace, and thus no trespass was committed. It was on any view of the evidence flying many hundreds of feet above the ground and it is not suggested that by its mere presence in the airspace it caused any interference with any use to which the plaintiff put or might wish to put his land. The plaintiff's complaint is not that the aircraft interfered with the use of his land but that a photograph was taken from it. There is, however, no law against taking a photograph, and the mere taking of a photograph cannot turn an act which is not a trespass into the plaintiff's airspace into one that is a trespass.

****

Questions

1. What does Griffith J. mean when he says that the landowner's rights must be restricted to 'such height as is necessary for the ordinary use and enjoyment of his land'? Is the test subjective or objective?
2. X Ltd, a building company, erects a crane on certain land for the purpose of constructing a building. When the crane is not in use its jib is left free to rotate. As a result, occasionally, when the wind blows it hovers and encroaches 30 metres above the adjoining land where it remains suspended until the wind changes direction and blows it back. Advise Y, owner of the adjoining land, of her possible legal cause of action.

****

Below the surface

The test applied to limit the scope of landowner's claim to the airspace would probably equally apply to ownership of the subterranean.

Fixtures

The general law relating to fixtures is summed up in the Latin phrase: *quicquid plantatur solo, solo cedit.* This means that whatever is attached to the land becomes the property of the landowner. Hence, where a person attaches a fixture on another's land, it becomes the property of the landowner and there is no legal obligation to compensate the person who attached it. The following Nigerian case illustrates the rule.

****

Francis v Ibitoye
(1936) NLR 11

[The plaintiff and the defendant were negotiating for the sale of land by the defendant to the plaintiff. Before the negotiations were concluded the plaintiff, without knowledge or leave of the defendant, proceeded to construct a house on the land at a cost of 120 pounds. When the negotiations for the sale of the land fell through, the plaintiff sued the defendant for compensation for the erection of the building.]

Graham Paul J.: ... In these circumstances I am asked to hold that the plaintiff can recover from the landowner the cost of the building. I know of no authority for such a claim ... It is trite law that a building erected in the circumstances I have indicated becomes the property of the landowner without any obligation to re-compensate the builder. The maxim *quicquid plantatur solo, solo cedit* applies without qualification. The claim for the 120 pounds is obviously without justification and is dismissed.

****

Note

Section 4(4) of the *Land Act*, defines 'mailo tenure' as a form of tenure which, inter alia, 'permits the separation of ownership of land from ownership of the developments on land made by a lawful or *bona fide* occupant' (s 4(4)(b)). This suggests that fixtures attached by a *lawful* or *bona fide* occupant on mailo land remain his or her property.

Questions

1. Was the plaintiff's claim 'obviously' without justification? Is this a fair decision?
2. If this case were decided under customary law, what would be the result?
3. Suppose the defendant was aware that the plaintiff was constructing the house before the negotiations were concluded, would the outcome of the decision have been different? Why? See *Ramsden v Dyson* 1 (1866) LR 1 HL 129, cited with approval in *Runda Coffee v Singh* (1966) EA 564 and *Babiruga v Karegyesa and others* D R CA No MKA 13 of 1993 (unreported), see extracts of both cases below.

****

Estoppel

Under the principle of estoppel the court may prevent a landowner from evicting a person who carried out improvements on the land without paying that person compensation for the improvements. The following case illustrates this principle.

****

Babiruga v Karegyesa and others
D.R. CA No MKA 13 of 1993 (unreported, High Court of Uganda)

[The appellant was the owner under customary tenure of the subject land. The three respondents, his sons, cultivated part of the land and they built their houses on the land. The lower court ordered that the land be divided equally between the appellant and the sons. The appellant was aggrieved by the decision and hence this appeal.]

Karokora J: [I]f the respondents have permanent houses on the appellant's land which they built with his consent, the appellant would on the doctrine of equitable estoppel, not be permitted to ask the respondents to remove the houses from his land. The father permitted his sons to build on his land and therefore spent a lot of money it would be inequitable to permit the appellant to chase them from there save on payment of compensation to the sons for that development. So on the doctrine laid down in *Ramsden v Dyson* 1 (1866) LR 1 HL at 170 cited with approval in *Runda Coffee v Singh* (1966) EA at 364 and more particularly in *Errington v Errington* (1952) 1 All ER155 ... where Lord Denning said of persons who by permission were occupying a building in respect of which they had expended a sum of money that they had had no right at law to remain, but only in equity and equitable rights now prevail.

So on the above principle, the respondents who had built on appellant's land with the knowledge and consent of appellant have got equitable rights to be on the land which right is subject to termination on payment of compensation. However, it seems the appellant is not concerned with the land where the respondents have their houses. He is concerned with the area which they grabbed, cultivated and used without his consent. The respondents, I must repeat had no legal right to use appellant's land without his consent. They are hereby ordered forthwith to vacate appellant's land which they forcibly grabbed from him without his consent.

****

Notes

1. Under the principle of proprietary estoppel applied in *Ramsden v Dyson* 1 (1866) LR 1 HL 129, a person whose conduct creates or lends force to an assumption by another that he or she will obtain an interest in the first person's land and on the basis of that expectation the other person alters his or her position or acts to his or her detriment may bring into existence an equity in favour of that person. The principle of proprietary estoppel applied in this case lends support to the proposition that promissory estoppel may in some circumstances extend to the enforcement of a right not previously in existence where the defendant has encouraged in the plaintiff the belief that it will be granted and has acquiesced in the action taken by the plaintiff in that belief. In *Taylor Fashions Ltd v Liverpool Victoria Trustees Ltd* [1987] QB 133 at 153, Oliver J remarked that what gives rise to the need for the court to intervene was the defendants' unconscionable attempt to go back on the assumptions which were the foundation of their dealings. See also *Runda Coffee Estate Ltd v Jagar Singh* [1960] EA 564, see extract below.
2. The court determines 'the minimum equity to do justice to the plaintiff' (*Crabb v Arun District Council* (1976) Ch 179 at 198, per Scarman LJ). In that case, as in *Ramsden v Dyson*, although equity acted by way of recognising a proprietary interest in the plaintiff, the proprietary interest came into existence as the only appropriate way by which the defendants could be effectively estopped from exercising their existing legal rights.

******

Test for a fixture

A thing attached to the land does not become part of the land unless it is a fixture. The following classical English case laid down the rules for determining whether a thing attached to land is a fixture.

****

The test for a fixture is the degree of annexation and the object of annexation.

Holland and another v Hodgson and another
(1872) LR 7 CP 328

[George Mason, owner in fee simple of certain premises at which he carried on a business of manufacturer, mortgaged the premises and all fixtures to the plaintiffs. Subsequently, Mason in bankruptcy assigned all his property to the defendants in trust for the benefit of Mason's creditors. The defendants seized 436 machines and sold them. The plaintiffs sued in conversion claiming that the machines were fixtures and therefore part of their mortgage. The machines in question were attached to the floors by means of nails driven through holes in the feet of the machines, in some cases into beams which had been built into the stone, and in other cases into plugs of wood driven into holes drilled in the stone for the purpose. It was impossible to remove the machines without drawing out the nails; but this could be done and without causing any serious damage to the floor. The defendants contended that the machines were attached to the floor to make them steadier and more capable of convenient use as chattels. The trial judge held that the machines were fixtures. The defendant appealed.]

Blackburn J:... There is no doubt that the general maxim of the law is that what is annexed to the land becomes part of the land; but it is very difficult, if not impossible, to say with precision what constitutes an annexation sufficient for this purpose. It is a question which must depend on the circumstances of each case, and mainly on two circumstances, as indicating the intention; viz the degree of annexation and the object of the annexation. When the article in question is no further attached to the land then [sic] by its own weight it is generally considered to be a mere chattel ... But even in such a case, if the intention is apparent to make the articles part of the land, they do become part of the land ... Thus, blocks of stone placed one on top of another without any mortar or cement for the purpose of forming a dry stone wall would become part of the land, though the same stones, if deposited in a builder's yard for convenience sake stacked on the top of each other in the form of a wall, would remain chattels. On the other hand, an article may be very firmly fixed to the land, and yet the circumstances may be such as to show that it was never intended to be part of the land, and then it does not become part of the land. ... Perhaps the true rule is that articles not otherwise attached to the land than by their own weight are not to be considered as part of the land, unless the circumstances are such as to show that they were intended to be part of the land, the onus of showing that they were so intended lying on those who assert that they have ceased to be chattels, and that, on the contrary, an article which is affixed to the land even slightly is to be considered as part of the land, unless the circumstances are such as to show that it was intended all along to continue as a chattel, the onus lying on those who contend that it is a chattel.

... This, however, only removes the difficulty one step, for it still remains a question in each case whether the circumstances are sufficient to satisfy the onus. In some cases, such ... as of a carpet nailed to the floor of a room the nature of the thing sufficiently shows it is only fastened as a chattel temporarily, and not affixed permanently as part of the land. But ordinary trade or tenant fixtures which are put up with the intention that they should be removed by the tenant (and so are put up for a purpose in one sense only temporary, and certainly not for the purpose of improving the reversionary interest of the landlord) have always been considered as part of the land, though severable by the tenant. In most, if not all, of such cases the reason why the articles are considered fixtures is probably that ... the tenant indicates by the mode in which he puts them up that he regards them as attached to the property during his interest in the property. What we have now to decide is as to the application of these rules to looms put up by the owner of the fee in the manner described in the case.

It is established that where an article is affixed by the owner of the fee, though only affixed by bolts and screws, it is to be considered as part of the land, at all events where the object of setting up the articles is to enhance the value of the premises to which it is annexed for the purpose to which those premises are applied ... We think therefore that the judgement below should be affirmed.

****

Note

There are several guidelines used by the courts to determine whether a thing attached to the land has become a fixture. For example, in the Supreme Court of the Australian State of Victoria case, *Belgrade Nominees and others v Barlin-Scott Airconditioning (Aust.) Pty Ltd* [1984] VR 947, a landowner sued the defendants for removing airconditioning plants from a building. The defendants were independent contractors employed by a builder to install the plants in a building, which was then under construction. When the builder failed to pay for the plants (due to bankruptcy), the defendants ripped the plants from the building citing a contract provision with the builder, which entitled them to remove the plants if they were not paid within a certain period. The plaintiffs, owners of the land, claimed that the plant was a fixture and, therefore, part of the land. The issue was whether the defendants intended the plant to become part of the land. In the course of delivering his judgement, Kaye J observed (at p 951) that:

> Whether the intention of the party fixing the chattel was to make it a permanent accession to the freehold is to be inferred from the matters and circumstances including the following: the nature of the chattel; the relation and situation of the party making the annexation vis-à-vis the owner of the freehold or the person in possession; the mode of annexation; and the purpose for which the chattel was fixed ... Facts from which the inference may be drawn that the plants were intended to be affixed permanently to the building are: the very nature of the airconditioning plants; the defendant, who carries on the business of suppliers and fitters of such plant, supplied positioned and connected

up the airconditioning plants as a sub-contractor; the plaintiffs are the registered proprietors of the freeholds, the chillers were positioned on the platforms and connected up by pipes to the water pumps fitted to each platform which in turn were connected to the reticulation system of each building; and the plants, when fitted, formed an essential part of the buildings necessary for their use and occupancy as modem office premises.

****

Right to remove 'tenant's fixtures'

At common law, unless otherwise expressly agreed a tenant has a right to remove from the premises all fixtures attached by him or her, which are for trade, domestic use or for decoration. These fixtures are collectively known as 'tenant's fixtures' as opposed to 'landlord's fixtures'.

****

Distinction between tenant's fixtures and landlord's fixtures

New Zealand Government Corporation v H.M & S Ltd
[1982] 1 QB 1145 at 1157

Lord Denning MR: ... I would describe the distinction between 'tenant's fixtures' and 'landlord's fixtures'. The term 'tenant's fixtures' for present purposes means those fixtures which the tenant himself fixed into the premises for the purpose of his trade, that is, for the business of the theatre, but which do not become part of the structure itself. Instances are the seats for the stalls, or auditorium, which are fixed by screws or bolts to the floor, wall-brackets for lights which are screwed on to the wall, electric transformers fixed on to the floor, and so forth. All these the tenant is entitled to remove when his term comes to an end. Whereas 'landlord's fixtures' for present purposes means those fixtures which the tenant himself fixes into the premises so that they become part of the structure itself: see *Boswell v. Crucible Steel Co.* [1925] 1 KB. 119. Instances are improvements made by the tenant by putting in new doors or windows in place of those that were there before, or a new frontage or a new safety curtain. These improvements become part of the structure itself. The tenant cannot remove them when his term comes to an end. All this goes back to the time of Sir John Holt CJ who had before him *Poole's Case* (1703) 1 Salk 368. A soap-boiler was the tenant for years of a house in Holborn. For the convenience of his trade he put up vats and coppers and paved the backyard. Sir John Holt CJ said:

> First, That during the Term the Soap-boiler might well remove the Vats he set up in Relation to Trade, and that he might do it by the Common Law (and not by virtue of any Special Custom) in favour of Trade and to encourage Industry: But after the Term they become a Gift in Law to him in Reversion, and are not removeable. Secondly, that there was a Difference between what the Soap-boiler did to carry on his Trade, and what he did to compleat [sic] the house, as hearths and Chimney-pieces, which he held not removeable.

****

Notes

1. In the above case, at p 1157 –1158, Lord Denning stressed, with reference to fixed term leases, that as a general rule tenant's fixtures must be severed from the land before the term expires otherwise the tenant loses his or her right to remove them.
2. Whoever removes tenant's fixtures must make good any damage caused to the land, see *Mancetter Development Ltd v Garmanson Ltd* [1986] QB 1212.

Questions

1. What is the possible policy reason(s) for allowing a tenant to remove certain fixtures?
2. At common law, agricultural fixtures are regarded as landlord's fixtures. Is this good law in Uganda's circumstances?

9
Registration of Titles

INTRODUCTION

In 1922 the *Registration of Titles Ordinance* (Cap.102 of the 1923, revised edition, of the Laws of Uganda), introduced a system of conveyance commonly known as the 'Torrens system' of registration of titles. This system of conveyance takes its name from Sir Robert Torrens, an Australian, who was responsible for its development in Australia in the late 1850s. The Ordinance was based on the 1915 *Transfer of Land Act* of the State of Victoria. Section 3 of the Ordinance provided that, except so far as was expressly enacted to the contrary, no Ordinance or rule so far as inconsistent with the Ordinance should apply to land whether freehold or leasehold which was under its operation. Part III provided for the bringing of land under the Ordinance. Section 9(3) provided that no dealing with any land, however held prior to that Ordinance, should after its commencement operate to pass any estate or interest whatsoever until such dealing was registered as therein provided. The effect of these provisions was to apply the Ordinance to all land owned under mailo, freehold and leasehold tenure. Apart from a few amendments the *Registration of Titles Ordinance*, currently known as the *Registration of Titles Act* (cap 205), has remained unchanged.[14] The Act does not provide for the registration of customary land, unless it is converted to freehold under section 10 of the *Land Act*[15].

Because Torrens is an Australian system of conveyance, it is suggested that Australian case law should be of more persuasive authority in interpreting the *Registration of Titles Act*, than English case law. For this reason we have included in these materials excerpts from several Australian cases. However, it should be emphasised that the courts are not bound to interpret the provisions of the Act in the same way as their Australian counterparts.

ESSENTIAL FEATURES OF THE TORRENS SYSTEM

The Torrens System has two essential features that distinguish it from other systems of conveyance:

1. Title by registration
2. Indefeasibility of title

Title by registration

Under the Torrens ystem of conveyance interests in land are created or transferred not by execution of documents, as at common law, but by registration under the *Registration of Titles Act*. Section 51 provides as follows:

> No instrument until registered in manner herein provided shall be effectual to pass any estate or interest in any land under the operation of this Act or to render such land liable to any mortgage; but upon such registration the estate or interest comprised in the instrument shall pass or as the case may be, the land shall become liable in manner and subject to the covenants and conditions set forth and in the instrument or by this Act declared to be implied in instruments of a like nature; and, if two or more instruments are at the same time presented to the Registrar for registration, he shall register and endorse that instrument which is presented by the person producing the duplicate certificate of title.

[14] The most important include the amendments made by s 16 of the *Mortgage Decree*, 1974 (No 17), which substituted s 73, repealed sections 117-121, 129-133, and amended s 149. The *Land Act* also amended the *RTA* by repealing s 69 and paragraph (a) of s 178 (see s 97, *LA*), and by giving the Registrar of Titles extra powers (see s 92, *LA*).

[15] See s. 15 of the *Land Act*.

Section 91(2) provides that:

> Upon the registration of the transfer the estate and interest of the proprietor as set forth in such instrument or which he is entitled or able to transfer or dispose of under any power with all rights, powers and privileges thereto belonging or appertaining, shall pass to the transferee and such transferee shall thereupon become proprietor. ...

The operation of s 51, is illustrated by the following cases extracted below: *Ndigejjerawa v Kizito and Kubulwamwana* (1953) 7 ULR 31; *Lumu v Lindo Musoke* CS No 309 of 1972 (unreported) and *Zimbe v Kamanza* (1954) 7 ULR 68.

****

Title does not pass until a transfer is registered under the Registration of Titles Act.

Lumu v Lindo Musoke

CS No 309 of 1972 (unreported, High Court); [1974] HCB 19

[The plaintiff was the registered proprietor of the subject land. He entered into a contract to sell the land to the defendant. The defendant paid part of the consideration and the plaintiff duly executed the necessary documents for the land to be transferred to the defendant. When the documents were presented for registration they could not be registered because the land was burdened with a caveat lodged by a third party. Nevertheless, the defendant started collecting rent from tenants occupying the premises. Under the parties' agreement the plaintiff was entitled to collect rent until registration of the transfer. The plaintiff sued the defendant for trespass and an injunction to restrain him from interfering with his premises.][16]

Musoke J, held:

1. The agreement did not transfer any interest in the disputed land to the defendant. It merely gave him contractual right entitling him to bring an action against the plaintiff for damages or for specific performance if the plaintiff refused to execute in his favour the statutory transfer.
2. The land in dispute was subject to the *Registration of Titles Act* ...section 51 and 91(2)... As the law stood, the land in dispute belonged to the plaintiff and it followed that the defendant's collecting of rent from the people staying on the land and the purported sale of one plot were illegal acts.

The acts of the defendant in going to the disputed land without the plaintiff's permission for collecting rent or land dues amounted to trespass.

Defendant ordered to stop interfering with the land in question, hand over the rent collected to the plaintiff and Shs.400/- damages for trespass awarded against him.

****

Note

With respect, it is submitted that Musoke J erred when he held that the defendant's acts 'in going to the disputed land without the plaintiff's permission for collecting rent ... amounted to trespass'. The primary requirement of trespass to land is that the plaintiff should be in actual possession of the land at the time of the defendant's act (*Cooper v Crabtree* (1881) 19 Ch D 193). In the instant case, since the plaintiff had rented the premises he was not in possession, therefore, he could not sue the defendant for trespass. It is also submitted that His Honour's statement that the 'purported sale of one plot' was an 'illegal' act, is not quite correct. While His Honour was right in his holding that the defendant had no *legal* title, in our view he had an *equitable* interest

[16] The facts of the case and the holding are based on the High Court Bulletin digest.

in the land which he was entitled to dispose of as he wished (*Katarikawe v Katwiremu & another* CS No 2 of 1973; [1977] HCB 187).

****

Title is transferred by registration and not by execution of documents.

Ndigejjerawa v Kizito and Kubulwamwana
(1953) 7 ULR 31

[Kizito was the registered proprietor of the subject land. By a written contract, Kizito agreed to sell the subject land to Kubulwamwana. Four days later by another written agreement, he purportedly sold the same land to Ndigejjerawa. The latter lodged with the Registrar of Titles certain documents for the purpose of transfer of title. However, the transfer was not registered because the documents were not in order. Later, Kubulwamwana submitted documents to the Registrar for the title to the land to be transferred in his name. But the transfer was not registered because the documents he too submitted were not in order. Accordingly, at the time of this action neither man had a registered title. The lower court held that Kubulwamwana had a better title because he purchased first from Kizito. Ndigejjerawa appealed arguing that he was the owner since he lodged his documents for registration before Kubulwamwana lodged his.]

Ainley J: ...I do not wish to be over-technical in my approach to this case, but I must point out that the question which should be asked in this case is not 'Who is the owner of the land?' but 'Who is entitled to the execution and registration of a statutory transfer of the land?'

It must be remembered that mailo land (and any land which is subject to the *Registration of Titles Ordinance*) can be transferred only by the execution of an instrument which fulfils certain statutory requirements and by the registration of that instrument. No document or instrument can be registered unless it fulfils certain requirements, and no instrument (however perfectly it fulfils the statutory requirements) is effectual to transfer any interest in land until it is registered.

It must now be pointed out that neither of the documents relied upon in this case fulfilled the statutory requirements of the *Registration of Titles Ordinance* and that accordingly neither document was capable of registration. It must now be pointed out that, contrary to a common belief fostered to some extent by the *Land (Agreements) Law*, 1939, the lodgement with the Registrar of an unregistrable document is not the registration of anything, and is not the equivalent of a registered transfer. ... [His Honour made the following observations:]

(a) Neither Ndigejjerawa nor Kubulwamwana achieved a transfer of the land to himself by the execution of his document or by paying the purchase price.

(b) Neither Ndigejjerawa nor Kubulwamwana achieved such a transfer by lodging his document with the Registrar of Titles. (What each achieved by his agreement with Kizito was a contractual right against Kizito.) Both have a remedy in damages against Kizito if Kizito fails to fulfil his promise to transfer the land by means of a statutory transfer. But plainly one only has gained the right to compel Kizito to transfer by a suit for specific performance. And what each party is really saying in this case is that he has the right to insist upon the execution by Kizito of a statutory transfer and to have that transfer registered.

Had there been no lodgement of documents, and had the parties claimed simultaneously the equitable remedy of specific performance no difficulty would have arisen. Kubulwamwana's equity having been created earlier than that of Ndigejjerawa would obviously have prevailed.

The question is whether the lodgement of the documents affects the position, I cannot see that the lodgement affects the situation in any way at all, it being remembered that neither of the documents was registerable. ...

Turning to the *Registration of Titles Ordinance*, rules are laid down as to the order in which instruments presented for registration shall be registered. The curious interpretation of ("excepting a transfer)" after "Every instrument in section 44 (1) raises some difficulty in determining what our rules in the case of transfers are. In some of the Australian statutes (see the Victoria Statute section 55) the bracketed words occur after the words 'may be in duplicate' and one almost suspects careless copying by our draftsman. But I do not really doubt that the general rule is that instruments of transfer are to be registered in order of production for registration. Yet any rules contained in the *Registration of Titles Ordinance* must, I think, have reference only to instruments which are registrable. I entirely fail to see how a man by merely producing at Registry an instrument which is not registrable, can (a) impose any duty on Registrar to do anything whatsoever or (b) create any equity in his own favour.

Very different of course is the case of a man who produces to the Registrar an instrument which is capable of registration. He no doubt gains priority over a competitor who comes later to the Registrar with an instrument of any kind. But I think that in the circumstances of the present case the order of lodgement of documents is irrelevant. What is relevant is the date at which the contracts were made. Kubulwamwana first gained the right to compel Kizito to transfer and I think that the learned Judicial Adviser correctly decided this case, and I dismiss the appeal.

****

Note

The case of *Ndigejjerawa v Kizito and Kubulwamwana,* supra, is also authority for the proposition that the equitable rules for determining priorities apply to competing unregistered interests over land the registered under the *Registration of Titles Act.* In that case the court applied the rule propounded in *Rice v Rice* (1854) 2 Drew 73; 61 ER 646.

****

In the absence of fraud, title of the first person to be registered prevails over that of a person to whom the land was sold first, but did not register his or her title.

Zimbe v Kamanza
(1954) 7 ULR 68

[In this case, land was sold to two different persons. The appellant, who purchased later, had his title registered. The lower court held that though the respondent's title was unregistered it prevailed over the appellant's title. This is an appeal to the High Court.]

Ainley J: ... In this case two men have tried to buy the same piece of land. Both have paid for the land, and the seller, who is now dead, was no doubt a rascal.

The respondent got his home-made agreement first, and in fact lodged it with the Registrar first, but he never achieved a statutory transfer of the land, and probably never could have done so without a great deal of trouble, because his home-made agreement bore the wrong Final Certificate number.

The appellant got his home-made agreement of sale some ten months later. His agreement bore the correct Final Certificate number, and with commendable promptitude he obtained the registration of a statutory instrument of transfer. There is not the slightest doubt as to the boundaries of the land caused by that registered transfer. It is the very land which the respondent claims.

Now the appellant can only be ousted from that land if it be shown that he obtained registration by fraud, his own not the seller's fraud. The onus of proving fraud has always lain on the respondent and it is a heavy onus because after all the Register at Entebbe is there for a purpose. It is there to enable persons like the appellant, who may be in some doubt as to whether the land they want to buy has been sold, to discover whether indeed the land they want has been sold. Such persons are entitled to rely on the Register. This appellant did go to the Register and he found nothing there to indicate that the respondent was the owner of this land. In fact, the respondent was not the owner of the land when the appellant registered his statutory transfer. No man can become the owner of land until a statutory transfer of the land to him has been registered. The appellant was entitled to rely on what the Register revealed. He was not required to make further enquiry. Now the respondent before the Principal Court made no serious attempt to prove fraud on the part of the appellant, and the Principal Court, quite rightly in my opinion, found for the appellant. They realised that their decision was hard on the respondent, but they said that the respondent had been foolish and negligent about his own affairs and had to pay the penalty for that. The learned Judicial Adviser suspected that the appellant was guilty of fraud in that he probably knew, when he registered his transfer, that there had been a previous sale. With the greatest respect, I think that he allowed his suspicions, and his desire to do justice, to take the place of convincing evidence. I have read his judgement and the record of the evidence which he called before him with great care, but I do not think that by combining the evidence before him with the evidence before the Principal Court one can fairly say that the respondent has ever proved satisfactorily that the appellant was party to a fraudulent scheme with the seller. ....

For these reasons I think the appeal should be dismissed.

****

Note

The case of *Zimbe v Kamanza*, was cited with approval by the Supreme Court in *Hotel International v The Administrator of the Estate of the Late Robert Kavuma* CA No 3 of 1995 (see extract below).

****

Title of a proprietor is indefeasible against unregistered customary rights to the land

Obiero v Opiyo and others
[1972] EA 227

[The plaintiff was the registered proprietor of the suit property under the Kenyan *Land Registration Act* (cap 300), and no incumbrances were noted on the register. She sued the defendants for possession and an injunction to restrain them from trespassing on her land. The defendants claimed to be the owners under customary law and to have cultivated the land from time immemorial. They also claimed that the plaintiff's registration, which was a first registration, was obtained through fraud.]

Bennett J:... The [main] issue ... is whether, despite the fact that the plaintiff is the registered proprietor, the defendants have any right to occupy or to cultivate the land under customary law. I am not satisfied on the evidence that the defendants ever had any rights to the land under customary law, but even if they had, I am of the opinion that those rights would have been extinguished when the plaintiff became the registered proprietor. S. 28 of the *Registered Land Act* confers upon a registered proprietor a title 'free from all other interests and claims whatsoever' subject to the leases, charges and encumbrances shown in the register and such overriding interests as are not required to be noted in the register. There are no encumbrances noted on the land certificate and according to the evidence of Mr Adongo, the plaintiff's title is free of encumbrances. Rights arising under customary law are not among the interests listed in s 30 of the Act as overriding interests. Had the legislature intended that the rights of a registered proprietor were to be subject to the rights of any person under customary law, nothing could have been easier than for it to say so. In my judgement, the defendants ceased to have any rights over the land in dispute if indeed they were ever entitled to any interest in it, when the plaintiff became the registered proprietor. It is plain from the evidence that they have been cultivating the land in dispute or part of it without theconsent of the plaintiff since she became the registered proprietor in January 1968. The plaintiff has proved to my satisfaction that she is entitled to the relief which she seeks.

There will be a perpetual injunction to restrain the defendants, their wives, servants or agents, from trespassing or continuing to trespass on the land in dispute.

****

Notes

1. In the case of *Lukwago v Bawa Singh and another* [1959] 282, it was held that customary rights of *bibanja* holders constituted overriding interests over mailo land. Section 4(c) of the *Land Act*, 1998, expressly recognises *bibanja* holders' customary rights over mailo land.
2. Subject to the *Land Act*, 1998, the case of *Obiero v Opiyo and others*, is of persuasive authority in interpreting s. 61 of the *Registration of Titles Act* (cap 205). It is suggested that, except for rights of a tenant by occupancy, customary rights unless endorsed on a certificate of title do not constitute overriding interests. For example, s 15(3) of the *Land Act* provides that where a landowner under customary tenure converts his or her title to freehold and it is registered under the *Registration of Titles Act*, the Registrar must endorse on the certificate any encumbrances ordered by the Land Board. It is submitted, that except in case of fraud, upon registration of converted freehold land any unregistered customary rights over the land cease to be binding upon the registered owner and his or her successors in title.

****

Effect of unregistered instruments

Although under s. 51 of the *Registration of Titles Act*, an unregistered instrument is not effective to create or transfer an interest in land, it is not necessarily devoid of legal efficacy, as the case below illustrates.

****

An unregistered instrument operates as a contract, which is enforceable as between the parties.

Souza Figueiredo and Co. Ltd. v.Moorings Hotel Co Ltd
[1960] E.A. 926 (U)

The respondent was the sublessee of the suit property. By a written agreement, it sub-sub-leased the property to the appellant for a period in excess of three years. The Registrar refused to register the transaction because it was his office practice not to register a sub-sub-lease. In any case, the document was not in a registerable form. Nonetheless, the appellant entered into possession and remained there for two years. Thereafter the appellant abandoned the premises without paying rent for the period that it was in possession. The High Court ordered the appellant to pay outstanding rent to the respondent. On appeal, the appellant argued that since the sub-sub-lease was not registered as required by the *RTA*, there was no lease created under the agreement and, therefore, it had no obligation to pay rent.

Sir Kenneth O'Connor: This is an appeal from the High Court of Uganda. ... The defence was that the agreement operated by way of present demise and, being a lease for more than three years, required registration under the *Registration of Titles Ordinance*; and, not having been registered, was ineffectual to create any estate or interest in the land. The appellant averred that, as the consideration for the agreement, namely the appellant's expectation of the grant of a valid term, had (for lack of registration of the agreement) wholly failed, the covenant to pay rent, which was inseparable from the lease, was unenforceable. ...

Mr Khanna [for the appellant] argued ... that a covenant to pay rent contained in an agreement which operates as a present demise of land for upwards of three years is unenforceable if unregistered. Mr Khanna summarised his argument on this question in this way: Section 3, s.9 (3) and s.51 of the *Registration of Titles Ordinance* (Cap. 123 of the Laws of Uganda) prevent legal or equitable estates in land from arising out of unregistered instruments. The covenant in the agreement to pay rent is so bound up with the land that it cannot have effect unless it is part of a registered lease. Section 9 of the *Registration of Titles Ordinance* strikes even at estates arising by estoppel, but not at pure contracts. There is a distinction in this respect between e.g. the personal covenant to repay contained in a mortgage and a covenant in a lease to pay rent, because rent issues out of the land and is bound up with the estate in land which the lease creates. The consideration for the sub-sub-lease sought to be created by the agreement was the grant of a valid term and, that having failed by reason of non-registration, the consideration for the agreement wholly failed and the covenant to pay rent was unenforceable.

Section 3 of the *Registration of Titles Ordinance* (Cap. 123 of the Laws of Uganda) so far as material, reads:

> 3. Except so far as is expressly enacted to the contrary, no Ordinance or rule so far as inconsistent with this Ordinance shall apply or be deemed to apply to land whether freehold or leasehold which is under the operation of this Ordinance.

Mr. Khanna contends that that 'rule' in this sub-section includes a rule of equity, a point on which I feel considerable doubt, but which I find it unnecessary to decide.

Section 9 (3) of the *Registration of Titles Ordinance* occurs in Part III of the Ordinance of which the heading is 'Bringing Land Under the Ordinance'. It reads:

> (3) No dealing with any land however held prior to this Ordinance shall, after the commencement of this Ordinance, operate to pass any estate or interest whatever, until such dealing is registered in manner herein provided.

It will be observed that this sub-section relates only to dealing with land and to passing estates or interests in land.

Section 51 of the Ordinance, so far as material, reads:

> No instrument until registered in manner herein provided shall be effectual to pass any estate or interest in any land under the operation of this Ordinance or to render such land liable to any mortgage: but upon such registration the estate or interest comprised in the instrument shall pass or (as the case may be) the land shall become liable in manner and subject to the covenants and conditions set forth and specified in the instrument or by this Ordinance declared to be implied in instruments of a like nature.

It will be observed that what s.51 says is that no instrument until registered shall be effectual to pass any estate or interest in land; ... but upon registration the estate or interest in the land shall pass or the land shall become liable in manner and subject to the covenants and conditions set forth in the instrument. That is to say that no estate or interest in land can be created or transferred by an unregistered instrument, and land cannot be made liable to the covenants in an unregistered instrument; but s. 51 does not say that an unregistered instrument cannot operate as a contract inter partes. Similarly s.9 (3) (assuming without deciding that that section applies generally and not only to land which has been brought under the Ordinance for the first time) says that an unregistered dealing in land shall not operate to pass any estate or interest; but does not say that an instrument purporting (ineffectually) to create an interest in the land and containing contractual terms cannot operate as a contract between the parties to it.

Mr Khanna pressed upon us that by s.15 of the *Uganda Order-in-Council*, 1902, the doctrines of equity are only applied to Uganda in so far as they are not modified, amended or replaced by the provisions of any Ordinance of the Uganda legislature, and that no equity can override the terms of the *Registration of Titles Ordinance*. No doubt that is right, but there is no question here of an equity overriding the terms of the Ordinance. As already stated, that Ordinance avoids the creation of an estate or interest in land by unregistered instruments, but there is nothing in the Ordinance which renders such instruments ineffectual as contracts between the parties to them: there is nothing in the Ordinance to say that an unregistered document purporting to be a lease of, or an agreement to lease, land which is subject to the operation of the Ordinance for more than three years is void. In my view it can operate as a contract inter partes and can confer on the party in the position of intending lessee a right to enforce the contract specifically and to obtain from the intending lessor a registerable lease. That is not to override the provisions of the Ordinance, but to act in conformity with them. The same principles apply to sub-leases. In England, since equity treats as done that which ought to be done, the intending lessee would be a lessee in equity and would have an equitable estate in the land: *Walsh v. Lonsdale* [1882], 21 Ch. D. 9. In Uganda he cannot derive any estate (whether legal or equitable) in the land from an unregistered instrument, because s.51 so says. Accordingly, as the intending lessee has no estate in the land, he would not have anything to assign or sub-let until his lease was registered, and he would be postponed to any subsequent lessee from the landlord who took without notice of the unregistered document and registered his lease; but, as already stated, there is nothing in the Ordinance which prevents the document operating as a contract between the parties to it: the document, as I have said, is not avoided by the Ordinance and must be construed *ut magis valeat quam pereat.*

The case of *Ariff v. Jadunath Majumdar* (2) (1930), 51 Cal. 1235, though decided on a different statute, is in point. In that case, the appellant, having in 1913 orally agreed with the respondent to grant him a permanent lease of a plot of land at Rs.80 per month, let him into possession. Shortly afterwards, the respondent, with the knowledge and approval of the appellant, erected structures on the land at a cost of over Rs. 10,000. In December, 1918, the appellant definitely refused to grant the respondent the agreed lease, and, in 1923, sued to eject him after a month's notice to quit. Under the Indian Limitation Act, 1908, Schedule 1, art. 113 the respondent's right to sue for a specific performance of the oral agreement was barred in December, 1921. It was held that there being no lease made by a registered document, as required by s. 107 of the Transfer of Property Act, 1882, the appellant was entitled to eject the respondent with liberty to him to apply to remove the structures; had the respondent's right to sue for specific performance not been barred, he could have claimed the execution of an instrument, which he would have registered, the appellant's suit being stayed in the mean time. Even (their lordships said) if an English equitable doctrine should be applied in any case so as to modify the effect of an Indian Act, which might well be doubted, the English equitable doctrine of part performance, referred to in *Maddison v. Alterson* (3) (1882), 8 App. Cas. 467, affecting the provisions of an English statute as to the right to sue upon a contract, could not be applied, so as to create, without writing, an interest, which s. 107 of the Transfer of Property Act enacts can be created only by a registered instrument: the principle laid down in *Ramsden v. Dyson* (4) (1886), L.R. 1 H. L. 129 appeared to be based solely upon the doctrine of part performance; but, even if it was intended to cover anything beyond that, it did not apply to *Arrif*'s (2) suit, as the only contract to which the erection of the structures could be referred had since ceased to be enforceable and as there was no representation of fact giving rise to an estoppel by s. 115 of the Indian Evidence Act, 1872. Their lordships held further that *Walsh v. Lonsdale* (1) did not apply, as the respondent's right to sue for specific performance was barred.

At p. 1241 Lord Russel L of Killowen, delivering the judgement of the judicial committee, said:

> Now it is clear that the verbal agreement alone could confer upon the respondent no such right. By s.107 of the Transfer of Property Act, 1882, it is expressly enacted that 'a lease of immovable property from year to year, or for any term exceeding one year, or reserving a yearly rent, can be

> made only by registered instrument. All other leases of immovable property may be made either by a registered instrument or by oral agreement.' This amounts to a statutory prohibition of the creation of such a right as is claimed here by the respondent, otherwise than by a registered instrument. ... No registered instrument exists: therefore, the respondent can have no such right as he claims, unless he can establish it by some means operating independently and in violation of the statute.

At p. 1245 Lord Russel says that the English equitable doctrine of part performance is inapplicable to modify an Indian statute and continues:

> Their lordships find themselves in agreement with the High Court in the view that *Walsh v. Lonsdale* [1882], 21 Ch. D. 9 has no application to this case, owing to the fact that the respondent's right to enforce the verbal contract had been barred long before the commencement of the present suit. The respondent was not in a position to obtain specific performance of the agreement for a lease from the same court and at the same time as the relief claimed in this action. Had he been so entitled, the position would be very different, for then the respondent could claim to have executed in his favour by the appellant an instrument in writing which he could duly have registered, the appellant's ejectment action being stayed in the meantime. In these circumstances, the respondent would obtain complete protection, but consistently with and not in violation of the provisions of the Indian statute.

Arrif's case, makes it quite clear that notwithstanding that under the Indian statute an oral agreement to lease land for more than one year or an unregistered document could not operate as a lease, it would (but for the question of limitation) have operated as a contract capable of specific performance and entitling the intending lessee to call for a registerable instrument. Notwithstanding that the statutes are differently worded, that is precisely the position in the present case.

A similar though not identical position obtains in various jurisdictions where a Torrens system of registration of title is in force. For instance, s.40(1) of the Transfer of Land Act, 1954, of the State of Victoria, Australia, provides:

> Subject to this Act no instrument until registered as in this Act provided shall be effectual to create or extinguish or pass any estate or interest or encumbrance in or over any land under the operation of this Act, but upon registration the estate or interest or encumbrance shall be created or extinguished or pass in the manner and subject to the covenants and conditions specified in the instrument or by this Act prescribed or declared to be implied in instruments of a like nature.

This, though the wording is slightly different, does not differ in substance from s.51 of the *Registration of Titles Ordinance*. It has, however, been held under it that an unregistered agreement for sale though inoperative at law until registered, may create equities between the parties to it: *National Bank of Australasia v. United Hand-in-Hand and Band of Hope Co* (1879), 4 App. Cas. 391, 409 (P.C.). Fox in his treatise on the Transfer of Land Act, 1954, at p.34, writes:

> Equitable claims and interest in land are recognised by the Act and unregistered instruments may confer such equitable claims or interests. ... An instrument which is unregistered will be regarded as an agreement binding on the parties to it: *National Bank of Australasia v. United Hand-in-Hand* etc., Co. (1879) A. C. 391; *Methieson v. Mercantile Finance, etc; Co. Ltd.* (1890) 17 V.L.R. 271.

At p.69 Fox writes:

Unregistered leases, effect

> No instrument (which includes a lease, s.4 ante) until registration is effectual to pass any interest in land under the Act (s.40 ante). ...
>
> By virtue of the effect of the Judicature Act an unregistered lease of land under the Act for more than three years operates, not merely to create contractual rights and duties, but creates an equitable term of years . . .

> Consequently in all the Australian States except New South Wales, where the Judicature Act is not in force, by the provisions of that Act and of the doctrine in *Walsh v. Lonsdale* [1882], 21 Ch. D. 9 a lessor is, as against his lessee, in as good a position to enforce the covenants in the lease when it is under seal and unregistered or even when it is in writing and unregistered and susceptible of specific performance as when it is registered in accordance with the provisions of the Act. In a matter resting on covenant it is the contract and not the estate which is the determining factor: *Hallen v. Spaeth* (1923) A.C. 684, at p.690; *Firth v. Halloran* (1926) 38 C.L.R. 261 at p. 269."

The learned authors of Kerr on the Principles of the Australian Lands Titles (Torrens) System at pp. 129, 130, 131 and 132 and 132 write:

> ... 246 An instrument in statutory form until registration operates as a contract inter partes. In this respect it stands on the same footing as a document, which, owing to its being in a form which will not be accepted by the registrar, is incapable of registration. The mere execution of a registrable instrument transfers no interest in the land, but merely gives a right in personam. ...
>
> 248 An unregistered lease in statutory form operates inter partes in like manner as an agreement for lease does under the general law.
> Whilst at law the lessee is a tenant at will only, yet in equity the unregistered document is binding and effectual as between the parties to it, and an action lies on the covenant for payment of rent, and the landlord's ordinary remedies, such as distress and re-entry would be open to him. ...
>
> 255 There is nothing in the Torrens Statutes to prevent registered proprietors being compelled by courts of equity to fulfil their contracts. The holding of a certificate of title does not as between the immediate parties to a contract alter their rights and liabilities to each other.

In my opinion, all the above quoted extracts would be applicable in Uganda except the statement that an unregistered lease operates to create an equitable term of years. I would not agree that in Uganda any estate or interest in land is created by an unregistered lease. Such a document may, however, give a right to require a registrable lease and its terms may be enforceable as a contract....

The High Court of Uganda is of course entitled and bound to apply the doctrines of equity to the extent mentioned in s.15 of the *Uganda Order-in-Council*, 1902, and, as I have already said, to give effect to the agreement as a contract is not to override the Ordinance by inequitable rule, as Mr. Khanna suggests, but is merely to apply an equitable doctrine to the extent that is applicable without creating an estate or interest in the land or infringing the provisions of Ordinance. So far as I can ascertain, it has been uniformly held in many, if not in all, jurisdictions subject to Torrens systems of registration of title where the court has jurisdiction to apply equitable principles, that an agreement for a lease or an unregistered lease operates as a contract inter partes. That does not (as Mr Khanna suggested) depend upon express provisions to that effect in the legislation. ...

It seems that even at common law entry under the unregistered lease for more than three years creates a tenancy at will. A tenancy at will involves no definite interest in the land, but merely a personal relation for which, however, a rent may be reserved: *Baalman, supra, and Hill and Redman of law of Landllord and Tenant* 11th (Edn.,) pp.20-22.

Whether, therefore, the covenant to pay rent contained in the agreement be looked at as a contractual stipulation in a document of which specific performance could be obtained in equity or as a term of common law tenancy at will, it is, I think, enforceable.

The appellant could have required from the respondent a registrable sublease (as in fact the appellant did on June 29, 1956, and March 11, September 17, 1957). Not having received a registrable sub-lease, the appellant could have brought a suit for specific performance of the agreement for a registrable sub-lease, in which suit, if necessary, the Registrar of Titles could have been joined. I may here mention, with respect to the Registrar of Titles ...that I think he was wrong in saying that no 'sub-lease could be registered under the Ordinance'. (A 'sub-lease' is a sub-lease); and s.111 of the Ordinance applies the provisions of the Ordinance affecting leases, lessors and lessees to sub-leases, sub-lessors and sub-lessees. Accordingly, s.108 and the form in the Tenth Schedule to the Ordinance (with any necessary modification: see s.209) would apply to 'sub-sub-leases' .:. If the agreement was not registrable in its existing form, the lessee could have called for a sub-lease in a form which was registrable, and, if he did not get one, he could have sued for it. The Registrar of Titles is, as he himself pointed out, subject to the jurisdiction of the court, and could have been compelled to register a 'sub-sub-lease' in proper form. The appellant chose, however, to surrender possession of the premises. It was suggested in argument that he did this because he could not get a registered sub-lease. There was no finding on this point; but I think that on the evidence and the correspondence, in particular the letter from the appellant's solicitors dated August 16, 1958, and the evidence of Mr Thomas, the appellant's accountant, that up to March, 1957, the accounts of the club showed heavy losses, there are strong probabilities that the appellant surrendered possession of the premises because the club was unprofitable and not because the appellant could not get a registered sub-lease. The appellant's accountants had been told by the Registrar of Titles that there was no necessity to register the agreement: the appellant had possession and enjoyment of the club premises and no one was disputing its right thereto. The balance of probabilities is heavily in favour of the premises having been surrendered because the club was unprofitable and not because of any failure to obtain a registrable sub-lease.

Of course, the agreement could not be given effect to as a contract if there was no consideration to support it; but there was consideration. The appellant took possession under it and remained in occupation and enjoyment of the premises for a very considerable time.

Mr Khanna argued that because the respondent, at the date of the agreement, had itself no registered title and did not register its transfer of the sub-lease until September 15, 1958, the agreement was not specifically enforceable. Before that date, he argued, there was no co-existence of privity of estate and privity of contract between the appellant and the respondent and both must exist before the agreement could be specifically enforced. He cited as an authority for that proposition *Purchase v. Licinfield Brewery Co.* (1951) 1 K. B. 184. That, however, was a case of an assignment where the assignee had neither privity of contract with the landlord, nor privity of estate. Here there was privity of contract between the appellant and the respondent. The respondent could have registered its transfer from George Burloyanis at any time and had it registered before the action was brought. In a suit for specific performance of the agreement by the appellant at any time after the date of the agreement, the respondent could (subject to any question of limitation) have been compelled to register its transfer and give a registrable sub-lease to the appellant: *Ariff's* case.

I think, therefore, notwithstanding the able and persuasive argument of Mr Khanna, that his contention that the covenant to pay rent contained in the agreement is unenforceable fails.

I will now consider the other grounds of appeal *seriatim*. Mr Khanna contended (ground 1 of the memorandum of appeal) that the respondent had disentitled itself from suing for specific performance by conduct; for instance by re-taking possession, attempts to re-let the premises, election to sue for damages and the like. In my opinion, provided that an unregistered lease or sub-lease can be specifically enforced, it may operate as a valid contract to grant a lease or sub-lease whether a suit to enforce it is actually filed or not. In the present case the respondent is not suing for damages for breach of the agreement, but is suing to enforce a term of the agreement: the respondent's claim is for payment of the amount which the respondent says is due under the agreement for the period during which the appellant was in occupation and enjoyment of the premises. Except in respect of the last quarter, the claim is a claim for payment of the sums due under a contract to pay rent (or under a tenancy at will on agreed terms) for a period during which the appellant had had possession and enjoyment of the property. As in *Hallen v Spaeth* (10), [1923] A.C. 684 at p. 690.

Ground 2 of the memorandum of appeal avers that no contract inferable in equity was ever pleaded and avers that it was never pleaded that the agreement was capable of specific performance or that the respondent was at the date of the suit ready and willing to perform all the obligations under the contract. The respondent pleaded the agreement ... and sued for rent under it. Not only had the respondent been ready and willing to perform the agreement, but had part performed it by giving the appellant possession of the premises. That was pleaded. In my opinion, that was a sufficient pleading in the circumstances of this case.

Grounds 6 and 7 of the memorandum of appeal aver that

> no equity can take the case out of the statute such as the *Registration of Titles Ordinance* and that no equity can co-exist with s.3 and s.51 of that Ordinance.

As I have already indicated, there is no question of equity conflicting with s.3 or s.9 or s.51 or taking the case out of the *Registration of Titles Ordinance* so as to create an estate or interest in land which the Ordinance says may not be created. The question is not the creation of an estate or interest in land but whether a term in a contract or a term of a tenancy at will can be enforced. Of course, an equity can co-exist with the provisions of s.3 and s.51 of the Ordinance so long as the equity is not inconsistent with these sections.

Ground 8 of the memorandum asserts that the learned trial judge held that equity could override s.3 and s.51 of the Ordinance. I do not think that he did. I think that he was right in treating the agreement as a contract which was specifically enforceable.

In my opinion, grounds of appeal Nos. 1, 2, 3, 5, 6.7 and 8 of the memorandum of appeal fail.

(Gould and Crawshaw JJA, concurred.)

****

Notes

1. The case of *Souza Figueiredo & Co Ltd v Moorings Hotel Co Ltd*, supra, is cited in several cases for the proposition that an unregistered lease constitutes a contract *inter partes*. See for example, *City Council of Kampala v Mukiibi* [1967] EA 368 (U); *Somali Democratic Republic v Anoop Syndirial Treon* CA No 4 of 1988 (unreported); *Clake v Sondhi* [1963] EA 107.
2. In his judgement O'Connor P said, with reference to certain principles in the extracts he quoted from several Australian authorities dealing with the counterpart of s 51, *RTA* that they would be applicable to Uganda except the statement that 'an unregistered lease operates to create an equitable term of years'. With respect, it is submitted that the Australian legal position is not quite as stated by the learned President. The view generally held in Australia in this regard was affirmed and explained by the High Court of Australia in *Chan and another v Cresdon Properties Ltd* [1989] 168 CLR 242:

> [Section] 43 of the [*Real Property Act* 1861 (QLD)]... provides, in relation to land under the Act, that, until registration, no instrument of transfer shall be effectual to pass an estate or interest in the land. Notwithstanding this provision, it has been said from time to time that unregistered instruments may confer equitable estates and interests. ...These statements need to be read in conjunction with the remarks of Isaacs J. in *Barry v. Heider* (1914) 19 CLR 197. His Honour, in the context of s.41 of the *Real Property Act* 1900 (NSW), the counterpart of s.43 of the Act, said (at p 216):
>
> > (S)ec.41, in denying effect to an instrument until registration, does not touch whatever rights are behind it. Parties may have a right to have such an instrument executed and registered; and that right, according to accepted rules of equity, is an estate or interest in the land. Until that instrument is executed, sec.41 cannot affect the matter, and if the instrument is executed it is plain its inefficacy until registered – that is, until statutory completion as an instrument of title – cannot cut down or merge the pre-existing right which led to its execution.
>
> The point made in this passage is that, though the unregistered instrument is itself ineffective to create a legal or equitable estate or interest in the land, before registration, the section does not avoid contracts or render them inoperative. So an antecedent agreement will be effective, in accordance

with the principles of equity, to bring into existence an equitable estate or interest in the land. But it is that antecedent agreement, evidenced by the unregistered instrument, not the instrument itself, which creates the equitable estate or interest. In this way, no violence is done to the statutory command in s. 43.

In *Brunker v. Perpetual Trustee Co.* (Ltd.) (1937) 57 CLR 555, Latham C.J.. in dissent, though not on this point, speaking with reference to s.41 of the *Real Property Act* (NSW), said (at p 581):

> Thus the instrument of transfer in itself cannot be effectual to vest in the defendant either a legal or an equitable interest in the land (See *Williams v. Papworth* ((1900) AC 563, at p 568)). But where there is a transaction for value which is recorded in a contract followed by an instrument of transfer, or where there is a transaction for value which itself is recorded in a transfer, ... then 'the transaction behind the instrument' and upon which it rests may create an equitable interest in the land which will be recognised in the courts. ...

3. In *Katarikawe v Katwiremu and another* CS No 2 of 1973; [1977] HCB 187 (unreported), Ssekandi J held that though in a contract of sale of land an unregistered instrument of transfer is not effective to transfer title, the purchaser acquires an equitable interest in the land. See also *Alibhai and others v Karia and another* CA No 53 of 1995 (unreported); *Popatlar Hirji v I H Lakhani & Co (EA) Ltd* [1960] EA 368 (U); *Somali Democratic Republic v Anoop Syndirial Treon* CA No 4 of 1988. It is suggested that the contract, if enforceable by specific performance, creates an equitable interest in accordance with the principle of *Lysaght v Edwards* (1876) Ch D 499. See also *Serunjogi v Katabira* CS No 547 of 1987 (unreported); (1988-90) HCB 148. The purchaser could apply for a vesting order under s 175 of the *RTA*, see *In re Mutaka* [1980] HCB 27.
4. It should be noted that at common law if the intended lessee enters into possession under an unregistered lease, a tenancy at will is created and once he or she pays rent it becomes a yearly, monthly, or weekly tenancy depending on the manner rent is paid (see Chapter Ten).

******

INDEFEASIBILITY OF TITLE

The Registration of Titles Act confers upon a registered proprietor 'indefeasibility of title'. The term 'indefeasibility' although widely used by judges and writers, is not used anywhere in the *RTA*. But its meaning and effect is gathered from a number of sections scattered in the Act: sections 56, 61, 184 and 189. Sections 56 and 61 state the effect of the certificate of title and sections 184 and 185 provide for the protection of the registered proprietor against claims and proceedings. These sections are extracted below.

Section 56. Certificate to be conclusive evidence of title

No certificate of title issued upon an application to bring land under this Act shall be impeached or defeasible by reason or on account of any informality or irregularity in the application or in the proceedings previous to the registration of the certificate, and every certificate of title issued under any of the provisions herein contained shall be received in all courts as evidence of the particulars therein set forth and of the entry thereof in the Register Book, and shall be conclusive evidence that the person named in such certificate as the proprietor of or having any estate or interest in or power to appoint or dispose of the land therein described is seized or possessed of such estate or interest or has such power.

Section 61. Estate of Registered proprietor paramount

Notwithstanding the existence in any other person of any estate or interest, whether derived by grant or otherwise which but for this Act might be held to be paramount or to have priority, the proprietor of land or of any estate or interest in land under the operation of this Act

shall, except in case of fraud, hold the same subject to such incumbrances as are notified on the folium of the Register Book constituted by the certificate of title; but absolutely free from all other incumbrances whatsoever, except the estate or interest of a proprietor claiming the same land under a prior registered certificate of title, and except as regards any portion of land that by wrong description of parcels or boundaries is included in the certificate of title or instrument evidencing the title of such proprietor not being a purchaser for valuable consideration or derived from or through such a purchaser.
Provided that the land which is included in any certificate of title or registered instrument shall be deemed to be subject to the reservations, exceptions, covenants, conditions and powers, if any, contained in the grant thereof, and to any rights subsisting under any adverse possession of such land, and to any public rights of way and to any easements acquired by enjoyment or user or subsisting over or upon or affecting such land, and to any unpaid rates and other moneys which without reference to registration under this Act are by or under the provisions of any written law declared to be a charge upon land in favour of any Government department or officer or any public authority, and to any leases, licences or other authorities granted by the Minister or any Government department or officer or any public authority, and also, where the possession is not adverse, to the interest of any tenant of the land, notwithstanding the same respectively are not specifically notified as incumbrances on such certificate or instrument.

Section 184. Registered proprietor protected against ejectment except in certain cases
No action of ejectment or other action for the recovery of any land shall lie or be sustained against the person registered as proprietor under the provisions of this Act, except in any of the following cases:

(a) the case of a mortgagee as against a mortgagor in default;
(b) the case of a lessor as against a lessee in default;
(c) the case of a person deprived of any land by fraud as against the person registered as proprietor of such land through fraud or as against a person deriving otherwise than as a transferee *bona fide* for value from or through a person so registered through fraud;
(d) the case of a person deprived of or claiming any land included in any certificate of title of other land by misdescription of such other land or of its boundaries as against the registered proprietor of such other land not being a transferee thereof *bona fide* for value;
(e) the case of a registered proprietor claiming under a certificate of title prior in date of registration under the provisions of this Act in any case in which two or more certificates of title may be registered under the provisions of this Act in respect of the same land,

and in any case other than as aforesaid the production of the registered certificate of title or lease shall be held in every court to be an absolute bar and estoppel to any such action against the person named in such document as the grantee, owner, proprietor or lessee of the land therein described, any rule of law or equity to the contrary notwithstanding.

Section 189. Purchasers protected
Nothing in this Act contained shall be so interpreted as to leave subject to an action of ejectment or to an action for recovery of damages as aforesaid or for deprivation of the estate or interest in respect to which he is registered as proprietor any purchaser *bona fide* for valuable consideration of land under the operation of this Act, on the ground that the proprietor through or under whom he claims was registered through fraud or error or has derived from or through fraud a person registered as proprietor through fraud or error; and this whether such fraud or error consists in wrong description of the boundaries or of the parcels of any land or otherwise howsoever.

In the New Zealand case of *Fraser v Walker and others* [1967] 1 AC 569, at p 580, Lord Wilberforce in his speech in the Privy Council, said with reference to similar provisions that:

> It is these sections which ... confer upon the registered proprietor ... 'indefeasibility of title'. The expression, not used in the Act itself, is a convenient description of the immunity from attack by adverse claim to the land or interest in respect of which he is registered, which a registered proprietor enjoys. This conception is central of registration. It does not involve that the registered proprietor is protected against any claim whatsoever; ... there are provisions by which the entry on which he relies may be cancelled or corrected, or he may be exposed to claims in *personam*. These are matters not to be overlooked when a total description of his rights is required. But as a registered proprietor, and while he remains such, no adverse claim ... may be brought against him.

The conclusiveness of a certificate of title is illustrated by the cases of *Re an Application by G. N. M. Mallo*.

****

Except as stated in the Registration of Titles Act, production of a certificate of title is conclusive evidence of proprietorship.

Re: an Application by G. N. M. Mallo
[1964] EA 31

[BMZ was the original registered proprietor of the subject land. Before BMZ died, his son, CMZ, allegedly purchased the land from him and became registered as proprietor. CMZ bequeathed the land to GJ who sold it to FN, the current registered proprietor. The applicant, heir of BMZ, alleged that CMZ, FN and GJ conspired to forge the transfer to CMZ. He brought proceedings against them for damages. Meanwhile, FN mortgaged the land to the respondent and the mortgage was registered. When FN defaulted in payment of the debt, the respondent advertised the land for sale. Upon hearing of the sale, the applicant lodged a caveat against the land. By notice of motion, under s. 149 of the *Registration of Titles Act*, the applicant sought an order for the continuation of the caveat pending determination of his suit for damages. The respondent opposed the application claiming that since his mortgage was registered it was indefeasible.]

Sheridan J: The respondent relies squarely on the protection which his registered claim is given by Section 145 of the *[Registration of Titles] Ordinance* ...

The definition of 'proprietor' in Section 2 includes the owner of a mortgage whose name is entered as the proprietor thereof in the Register. Further, in the absence of fraud and with none of the five specified exceptions applying, s.184 makes the production of the registered certificate of title, and it has been produced, an absolute bar to any claim. Nor does it make any difference that there may have been intervening fraud, and that there might be infirmities in the mortgagor's title. This would be so even if Florence Nasuna had executed the mortgage, in the knowledge of George Jagwe's fraud; it would still constitute a valid incumbrance in favour of a bona fide mortgagee. See *Gibbs v Messrs. McIntyres & Creswell* [1891] AC 248.

The application for the extension is dismissed with costs.

****

Forged instrument of transfer

Lwanga v Registrar of Titles
Misc C No 7A of 1977 (unreported); [1980] HCB 24

[This case deals with an application to recover land under s.190 of the *Registration of Titles Act*, transferred to the registered proprietor by forgery of a third party. The facts of the case are set out in the judgement.][17]

[17] The facts and holding are based on the High Court Bulletin digest.

Odoki AG J:... This was an application by notice of motion brought [under s. 190 of the *Registration of Titles Act*], calling upon the Registrar to appear and substantiate his grounds for refusing to register 320 acres of land situate at Kigalama in the names of Yusufu Galiwango who died in 1939. The application was supported by an affidavit of the applicant, the son of late Yusufu Galiwango.

Yusufu Galiwango had bought the same land from one Mukasa in 1920, but Galiwango died before registering the land into his name. By a forged agreement dated 30/9/1952, one Katamba purported to have obtained the suit land as a gift from Galiwango. On 5/2/1953, Katamba forged a transfer of the said land into his name and he was duly registered as proprietor thereof. Katemba sold the land to *Salongo* who thereby became the registered, proprietor of the said land.

In 1958, the applicant found out Katemba's fraud whereupon he prosecuted Katemba in criminal case before the Principal Court of Buganda. Katemba was convicted of forgery and sentenced to imprisonment, and an order was made that 'the land comprised in the 320 acres at Kigalama be transferred into the names of Yusufu Galiwango by the Assistant Registrar of Titles'. Katemba's appeal against this decision was dismissed and the decision of the Principal Court confirmed.

The applicant tried to enforce the said court order but the Assistant Registrar, refused, advising that the applicant should first obtain a consequential order before the land could be registered in Galiwango's names. He also advised the applicant to search the register since the register showed Salongo as the present proprietor.

Salongo, the present proprietor testified that he never knew about Katemba having been prosecuted for fraud in respect of the land but admitted learning of Katemba's imprisonment, and his being sued by the applicant in a civil case in the Principal Court of Buganda. However, the proceedings in this civil case were stayed as the criminal case against Katemba was still pending. When the criminal case ended in his favour, the applicant decided to abandon the civil case.

The respondent attacked this application on the ground that the applicant had no right to invoke the provisions of s.190 *R.T.A* since he was neither an owner nor a proprietor or an executor. In reply, counsel for the applicant contended that the application was brought under s 34 r. 1 Civil Procedure Rule according to which any person interested in the land could apply to the court for the determination of his claims

Held:

1. Whereas the owner and proprietor could invoke the provisions of s.190 *R.T.A*, it was not clear who an owner was since only 'proprietor' was defined in s 2. *R.T.A.* to include any person who possessed a registrable interest in land whether that interest was legal or equitable. Accordingly, if the applicant in the instant was the heir, he had a right to make the application under s 190 *R.T.A.*
2. The proper procedure for bringing an application under s 190 *R.T.A.* was by originating summons under Order 34 *C.P.R* and not by notice of motion as was done in the instant case. Although the procedure followed in bringing the instant application was therefore wrong, the court would ignore the procedural defects and consider the application on its merits.
3. Before a person who has obtained judgement for the recovery of land against a registered proprietor could be registered as proprietor, he first had to apply to the court to make an order under s 185 *R.T.A.* Such order was referred to as a consequential order since it was made consequent upon the recovery land. This was the only method prescribed by the *R.T.A.* for executing orders of decrees relating to registered land. Accordingly, the Registrar of Titles was justified in refusing to transfer the land into the names of Yusufu Galiwango before the applicant had obtained a consequential order.
4. According to s 189 *R.T.A.* the title of a bona fide purchaser for value could not be impeached since a person who was registered through fraud could pass a good title to a bona fide purchaser for value unless the purchaser was not a bona fide purchaser or was privy or party

to the fraud. This was one of the paradoxes of registered conveyance, that the registration obtained by fraud was void and yet capable of becoming a good root of title to a bona fide purchaser for value – *Gibbs v Messer* [1891] AC 248.

5. In the instant case, Salongo was a bona fide purchaser for value and his title could not therefore be impeached or cancelled notwithstanding that he got his title from one registered through fraud, unless it was proved, which was not, that he was not a bona fide purchaser for value or that he was privy or party to the fraud perpetuated by Katemba. Accordingly, Salongo's title was protected by s 189 *R.T.A*.

****

Registration that derives from a void instrument is effective to vest or divest title.

Breskvar and another v Wall and others
(1971) 126 CLR 376 (High Court of Australia)

[Mr and Mrs Breskvar (appellants) borrowed money from Petrie on security of their land. They handed Petrie their certificate of title and a memorandum of transfer of the property signed in blank (space for the name of the transferee was left blank). Under the Queensland Stamp Act 1894, a blank instrument of transfer was 'absolutely void and inoperative' both at law and in equity. Petrie without authority of the appellants inserted in the memorandum of transfer the name of Wall, first respondent, as the transferee and had the land registered in Wall's name. Wall then sold the land to A Pty Ltd, which bought in good faith and without notice of earlier transactions. Before A Pty Ltd could be registered as proprietor of the land, the Breskvars lodged a caveat to prevent registration of any dealing affecting the land and commenced these proceedings to have Wall's registration cancelled and the Register rectified to restore their names as proprietors. They based their action on two main arguments. Firstly, that since the memorandum of transfer was executed by way of security only it was ineffective to transfer the fee simple estate to Wall. Secondly, that in any event the memorandum of transfer was void because of the Stamp Act. Though the Supreme Court found that both Wall and Petrie acted fraudulently, it dismissed the application. On appeal to the High Court of Australia.]

Barwick, CJ: ... [E]xcept in and for the purposes of such excepted proceedings the conclusiveness of the certificate of title is definitive of the title of the registered proprietor. That is to say, in the jargon which has had currency, there is immediate indefeasibility of title by the registration of the proprietor named in the register. The stated exceptions to the prohibition on actions for recovery of land against a registered proprietor do not mean that 'indefeasibility' is not effective. It is really no impairment of the conclusiveness of the register that the proprietor remains liable to one of the excepted actions any more than his liability for 'personal equities' derogates from that conclusiveness. So long as the certificate is unamended, it is conclusive and of course when amended it is conclusive of the new particulars it contains.

The Torrens system of registered title of which the Act is a form is not a system of registration of title but a system of title by registration. That which the certificate of title describes is not the title which the registered proprietor formerly had, or which but for registration would have had. The title it certifies is not historical or derivative. It is the title which registration itself has vested in the proprietor. Consequently, a registration which results from a void instrument is effective according to the terms of the registration. It matters not what the cause or reason for which the instrument is void. ... Thus the effect of the Stamp Act upon the memorandum of transfer in this case is irrelevant to the question whether the certificate of title is conclusive of its particulars....

******

Note

For further illustration and discussion of the principle of indefeasibility see the cases extracted below under the heading 'Exceptions to indefeasibility', especially, *Kampala Brothers Ltd v Damanico (U) Ltd* CA No 22 0f 1992; and *Sajjaka Nalima v Rebecca Musoke* CA No 12 of 1985.

Questions

1. 'It is in fact the registration and not its antecedents that vests and divests title' (per Lord Wilberforce in *Fraser v Walker and others* [1967] 1 AC 569, at 579). Discuss this statement with reference to relevant provisions of the *RTA* and decided cases.
2. 'The Torrens system of registered title ... is not a system of registration of title but a system of title by registration' (per Barwick CJ, in *Breskvar and another v Wall and others* (1971) 126 CLR 376, at 385). Discuss with illustrations.
3. Omara entrusts his certificate of title with his lawyer for safe custody. Muyaye, a cleaner at the lawyer's office, steals the certificate of title and using forged instruments of transfer sells the land to Rubanga, who buys in good faith without notice of the forgery. Rubanga is subsequently registered as the proprietor of the subject land. Advise Omara.
4. A writer commenting on the case of *Fraser v Walker*, said that '[T]he case has taken the protection of the purchaser to such an extreme that the ownership of property is entirely at the mercy of a small sheet of paper (the certificate of title). This title has now become as vulnerable as an uncrossed cheque or other negotiable instrument.' (Taylor, Scotching *Fraser v Walker* (1970) 44 *ALJ* 248, pp 251.) Do you agree with the writer's criticism? Does the decision like *Fraser v Walker* make the Torrens System unsuitable to Uganda's circumstances? What remedy is available under the Act for people in Mr Fraser's position?

****

Exceptions to indefeasibility

The principle of indefeasibility is not absolute. It is subject to a number of exceptions mentioned in sections 61 and 184 of the *Registration of Titles Act* as well as exceptions to indefeasibility created by judges and other legislation. These exceptions are discussed in the following materials.

Fraud

Under the *RTA*, the most important and common exception to indefeasibility of title is fraud. The expressions 'fraud' or 'registered through fraud' are not defined in the Act. However, the scope of these expressions has been limited by judicial decisions to actual fraud as the cases below illustrate. Its scope and meaning is found in case law.

****

Fraud means actual fraud by the registered proprietor whose title it is sought to impugn.

Hotel International Ltd v The Administrator of the Estate of Robert Kavuma
CA No 3 of 1995 (unreported, Supreme Court of Uganda)

[Namwandu Mugalasi owned two plots of land: plot 2361 and 2825. She sold plot 2361 to Sebagereka and the latter was registered as proprietor of the land. Later Sebagereka sold the plot to Mulindwa, but the transfer was not registered because Sebagereka was forced into exile. In his absence, Mulindwa and Namwandu Mugalasi exchanged plots so that Mulindwa became the owner of plot 2825 and Namwandu Mugalasi owner of 2361. Nevertheless, plot 2361 remained registered in Sebagereka's name. Mulindwa commenced constructing a building on plot 2825. Before the building was completed, Mulindwa died. Meanwhile, the appellant acting through one Richardson embarked on a plan to purchase plot 2361, which was still registered in Sebagereka's name. Richardson noticed that Mulindwa's widow had lodged a caveat against the land claiming it on behalf of her late husband's estate. Richardson negotiated with Mrs Mulindwa and purchased the land. The forms of transfer were sent to Sebagereka in Nairobi where he signed them. The appellant was registered as the proprietor of plot 2361. The respondent, on behalf of the estate of Namwandu Mugalasi, instituted proceedings in the High Court to set aside the transfer and registration of the appellant as proprietor of plot 2361, allegedly, because it was registered through fraud. The trial judge found that the appellant was registered through fraud because at the time of purchase it had notice of Namwandu Mugalasi's interest in plot 2361. Accordingly, His Honour ordered the Registrar to cancel its registration. The appellants appealed.]

Karokora JSC: On the question of whether or not Richardson [agent] of the appellant was aware of the respondent's interest in the suit property, there was evidence that when appellant started building a boundary wall between Plot 2825 and 2361, PW1, son of Namwandu Mugalasi stopped them, alleging that they were encroaching on his mother's land, Plot 2361. In order to establish respondent's claim, the appellant requested Atlas Surveys Ltd through their lawyer to carry out survey and establish the ownership of the land in question. On surveying the land, it was found out that Plot 2361 belonged to Samwiri Sebagereka, but there was Kasiita Mulindwa's Caveat on that title. Even the small triangular piece of land, which PW1 had claimed as being burial ground owned by the Plaintiff, was part of Plot 2361, which belonged to Samwiri Sebagereka. The widow of Kasiita Mulindwa told Richardson that her late husband had purchased the land from Sebagereka before he died. That was how he came to commission a gentleman of Atlas Surveys to travel to Nairobi and get in touch with Sebagereka and ask him to sign transfer forms transferring Plot 2361 to Kasiita Mulindwa, which Sebagereka did. After the transfer from Sebagereka, the appellant bought from the administrator of the estate of Kasiita Mulindwa through the Administrator General.

Richardson, DW1 stated in his evidence that he had no reason to believe that the administrators of the estate of Kasiita Mulindwa were selling the land to them (appellant) which Kasiita Mulindwa had already sold to respondent. Although the affidavit of late Lubowa reveals that Kasiita Mulindwa had given his plot 2361 with all the building thereon to Namwandu Mugalasi in exchange for empty land on Plot 2825 which Kasiita very much wanted for constructing on a modern hotel, this evidence appears to have come to the attention of Richardson at the time of the trial long after the purchases and transfers had been completed.

I must observe that as a first appellate Court I am under a duty to subject the entire evidence to that fresh and exhaustive scrutiny and re-evaluate evidence and make my own conclusion, taking into consideration the fact that I did not have opportunity of observing the witnesses and testing their veracity. See *Sell v Associated Motor Board* (1968) EA 123 and *Pandya v R* (1957) EA 336.

It must be noted that there was no evidence led to prove that when the appellant bought the suit land from the administrators of the estate of Kasiita Mulindwa, they knew or were aware of the swapping of the Plots as averred in Late Lubowa's affidavit, Exhibit P12. From DW1's evidence, it is clear that when PW1 claimed that the land belonged to his mother DW1 carried out investigation and established that the suit land was in Samwiri Sebagereka's names with Kasiita Mulindwa's Caveat. They discovered that the mother of PW1 did not own the suit land.

He thereafter proceeded to buy the suit land and got registered as the proprietor when there was no evidence that he had knowledge of the respondent's unregistered interest in the suit land. His title would in view of the above be conclusive evidence of his ownership under Section 56 of *RTA*. If it is true that the respondent had unregistered interest in the suit land as alleged by PW1, in his evidence and averred to by Late Lubowa in his affidavit that interest would be of no effect to the registered interest of appellant in view of Section 51 of *RTA*, which provides:

> No instrument until registered in the manner herein provided shall be effectual to pass any estate or interest in any land under operation of this Act or to render such land liable to any mortgage; but upon

> such registration the estate or interest comprised in the instrument shall pass or, as the case may be, the land shall become liable in manner and subject to the covenants and conditions set forth and specified in the instrument or by this Act declared to be in instrument of ...

The Supreme Court had occasion to deal with a similar matter in the case of *Kazzora v Rukuba*, Civil Appeal No.1 13/1992 whereby Rukuba who bought later and got registered before Kazzora who had bought long before but had not registered, acquired better title. The Supreme Court cited with approval the decision in *Kristofa Zimbe v Tokana Kamanza* 7 ULR 68 that in the absence of fraud on the part of the first person to be registered, he takes better title than a person to whom the land was first sold but failed to register it under *Registration of Titles Act* (*RTA*).

I would respectfully agree with the above principle and would state that in the instant case since no fraud has been proved as attributable to the appellant in the purchase and registration of the suit land, the unregistered interest of the respondent would not prevail over the appellant's registered interest though the respondent had bought long before the appellant purchased.

On the question of whether or not the appellant's title could be impeached under Section 76 of *RTA*, the Learned Trial Judge had held that the title would be impeached on the ground that it was obtained by fraud.... [H]e held as follows:

> I have no alternative but to say that with this notice on the Register of Titles, for someone to take a blank form to Sam Sebagereka in exile and obtain transfer to the Administrator of the estate of Kasiita Mulindwa with intention of transferring to the appellant not to respondent, was a fraudulent act.

With due respect to the Learned Principal Judge, it must be observed that when the witness travelled to Nairobi to take the blank form, the appellant was setting in motion the transfer of land from Sebagereka to the estate of Kasiita Mulindwa, because the caveat of Kasiita Mulindwa was on Sebagereka's title. There was no caveat of the respondent on the register, which was brought to the notice of the appellant. The caveat on the register had been filed by Kasiita Mulindwa against Sam Sebagereka's title. So when Sebagereka signed the transfer form in favour of Kasiita Mulindwa, the appellant bought a clean title from the Administrator General. There was no evidence adduced by respondent to prove that they bought from the Administrators of the estate of Kasiita Mulindwa fully knowing of the facts deposed to by late Lubowa in his affidavit Exh. P12. If the administrators of the estate of Kasiita Mulindwa knew of the respondents' unregistered interest in the said suit land, went ahead and sold to the appellant who had no prior knowledge of the respondent's unregistered interest, the purchase by appellant would not impute fraud on them, because fraud by persons from whom a purchaser acquired land does not affect the purchaser, see *Assets Company Ltd v Mere Roihi & Others* 1905 AC 176; *Waimiha Sawmiling Co Ltd v Waione Timber Co Ltd* (1962) AC 756, through the Administrator General, see also *Sejjaka Nalima v Rebecca Musoke* CA No. 12/1985 (SC) unreported, unless there is evidence that he was made aware of the respondent's unregistered interest but that he refrained from investigating for fear of learning the truth. On the contrary, in this case, after PW1 had told him that the suit land, in which appellant had shown interest, belonged to his mother, Ronnie Richardson for appellant, through their lawyers investigated and eventually found out that the suit land belonged and was registered in the names of Samuwiri Kato Sebagereka. It had a caveat of Kasiita Mulindwa. So when the Administrator of the Estate of Kasiita Mulindwa sold to appellant through the Administrator General, after the title had been transferred from Sebagereka to Kasiita Mulindwa (deceased) no fraud would be attributable to them (appellant).

Therefore, in the circumstances, ground 1 of this appeal succeeds.

(Wambuzi CJ and Oder JSC, also upheld the appeal.).

****

Note

For further discussion of the definition of fraud see *Sejjaka Nalima v Rebecca Musoke* CA No 12 of 1985 (see extract below).

****

Fraud committed by other persons cannot be used to impeach title of a proprietor unless he or she was a party to such fraud or was aware of the fraud.

Kampala Bottlers Ltd v Damanico (U) Ltd

CA No. 22 of 1992 (Unreported, Supreme Court of Uganda)

[The appellant was the registered proprietor of certain land in Kampala. The appellant alleged that the respondent trespassed on their land by clearing and grading it. The respondent admitted entry upon the land in question but denied that such entry was wrongful as it had a lease of five years over the suit property granted by Kampala City Council. The respondent alleged that the certificate of title held by the appellant was obtained by fraud. At the trial the sole issue was whether or not the appellant obtained its title of the suit property by fraud. The trial Judge found that there was fraud and gave judgement in favour of the respondent. The appellant appealed on the ground, *inter alia*, that the trial Judge erred in holding that the certificate of title was obtained by fraud.]

Wambuzi CJ: In arguing the first ground, Dr. Byamugisha for the appellant submitted that by a letter dated 13th October 1988, exhibit P.2, the appellant who had initially obtained a lease in respect of the suit property was granted an extension of two years with effect from 1st May, 1988. The Commission of Lands was accordingly notified by letter, exhibit P.3. Apparently, it was necessary to re-survey the plot, which was done. The City Council of Kampala demanded ground rent by letter dated 28th August, 1991 which was paid as per exhibit P.7. Exhibit P 1 which is the certificate of title was accordingly prepared and was executed on 26th September, 1991. Learned Counsel submitted that by the time the respondent was granted a lease of the same plot, the appellant had already been registered as proprietor. Learned Counsel submitted that the City Council dealt with the appellant as if it was not necessary to apply for extension of the lease as the lease offer had not been utilised because of the re-survey which had not been completed until 1991. Learned Counsel referred us to sections 184, 42 (4) and 56 of the Registration of Titles Act to the effect that the title of a registered proprietor cannot be impeached because of irregularities, that fraud must be proved. No particulars of fraud were pleaded and there is no evidence to support the learned trial Judge's finding of fraud.

For the respondent, Mr Kateera submitted in effect that a certificate of title is evidence of a grant without which the certificate is meaningless. Learned Counsel argued in effect that the grant made to the appellant expired in 1990 and was not renewed. Accordingly, the lease subsequently prepared by the Land Office was without authority.

It is not in dispute that the appellant was initially granted a lease over the suit property. The dispute is whether or not this lease was extended as claimed by the appellant. It is also not disputed that the appellant is the registered proprietor but it is claimed for the respondent that the registration was obtained by fraud.

In so far as is relevant, section 56 of the Registration of Titles Act provides as follows:

> ... [E]very certificate of title issued under any of the provisions herein contained shall be received in all courts as evidence of the particulars therein set forth and the entry thereof in the Register Book, and shall be conclusive evidence that the person named in such certificate as the proprietor of or having any estate or interest in or power to appoint or dispose of the land therein described is seized or possessed of such estate or interest or has such power.

According to these provisions, it would appear to me that production of the certificate of title in the names of the appellant is sufficient proof of the ownership of the land in question unless the case fall within the provisions of section 184 of the *Registration of Titles Act*... .

In the first place and needless to say, lack of grant is not one of the grounds for impeaching the title of a registered proprietor on the wording of this section and also of section 56 to which I referred earlier in this judgement. I must, therefore, reject Mr Kateera's argument that a certificate of title is meaningless unless a grant has been shown to have been made in respect of the land in question.

Secondly, on the wording of section 184 it would appear that an action for recovery of land can lie or be sustained only by 'a person deprived of any land' against the person registered as proprietor of such land through fraud.

In the case before us it must be shown that the appellant was registered as proprietor of the land through fraud. In its written statement of defence, the respondent pleaded in paragraph 6 as follows:

> It is submitted that the certificate of title annexed to the plaint was obtained by fraud as since 1990 the City Council of Kampala never sat to give a further extension of the lease to the plaintiff.

Normally, where fraud is pleaded, particulars of the fraud must be given. It was submitted before us that the particulars of the fraud in the case were the fact that the City Council did not sit since 1990 to give further extension of the lease to the plaintiff. I must confess I am a little at a loss as to who was being alleged to have been fraudulent.

Be that as it may, on the question of fraud which in a way was the sole issue in the lower Court, the learned trial Judge had this to say,

> The spring board of the 1st issue is to get the meaning of 'fraud'. It is well established law that fraud means actual fraud or some act of dishonesty. In *Waimiha Saw Milling Co. Ltd vs Waione Timber Co. Ltd.* (1926) AC 101 at p.106. Lord Buchmaster said 'Now fraud implies some act of dishonesty'. Lord Lindley in *Assets Co vs Mere Roihi* (1905) AC 176 states, 'Fraud in these actions (i.e. Actions, seeking to effect (sic) a registered title) means actual fraud, dishonesty of some sort not what is called constructive fraud an unfortunate expression and one very apt to mislead, but often used, for want of a better term, to denote transactions having consequences in equity similar to those which flow from fraud' . . .

The way the 1st issue has been framed does not compel me to determine who committed the fraud. The facts disclosed an irregularity surrounding the grant so grave as to amount to a dishonest dealing with the grant. Both the Land Office and Council Chairman and Town Clerk share responsibility for this by their refraining from carrying out basic inquiry. ...

In my considered view, there is no sound reason disclosed why the Land Office and that of the Council Chairman and Town Clerk could not peruse the minute under which the Plaintiff's certificate was processed. That was the basic pre-requisite. They refrained from doing so and the result was fraud. I therefore find that fraud was committed.

Dr Byamugisha submitted that even if there had been any fraud on the part of the Council, that fraud could not be used to impeach the Plaintiff's title.

In support of his argument, he referred to me ss 56 and 184 of the Registration of Titles Act.

I wish to answer Dr Byamugisha's argument by the following quote from the case of *Lusweswe v Kasule & a*nor HCCS No. 1010 of 1983, where Odoki J. as he then was said,

> Therefore while the cardinal rule of registration of titles under the Act is that the Register is everything, the court can go behind the fact of registration in cases of actual fraud on the part of the transferee.

Taking the last point first and with respect to the learned trial Judge, I do not think that Dr Byamugisha's point was answered by the authority cited. If anything, the authority supports Dr Byamugisha's point and as already indicated in this judgement, fraud must be attributable to the transferee. I must add here that it must be attributable either directly or by necessary implication. By this I mean the transferee must be guilty of some fraudulent act or must have known of such act by somebody else and taken advantage of such act.

Returning to the judgement of the learned trial Judge, he seems to have held that there was fraud because he could not otherwise understand how all those concerned would fail to notice the duration of the lease which was indicated in the minute of the City Council Meeting. He went on to find fraud committed by someone in the Land Office by the Chairman of the Council and by the Town Clerk. The latter two apparently for failure to notice the error.

With respect, this verges on constructive fraud if there was any fraud rather than actual fraud as required by the authorities referred to in the lower court. Besides, it was not shown nor did the learned trial Judge find that the appellant was guilty of any fraud or that he knew of it.

Further, I think it is generally accepted that fraud must be proved strictly, the burden being heavier than on a balance of probabilities generally applied in civil matters. The learned trial Judge did not indicate the standard at which fraud had been proved. There may have been negligence on the evidence before the learned trial Judge but equally all those concerned may have thought that the appellant was entitled to a term after the re-survey as the offer had not been utilised. With respect I am unable to say that fraud was proved against the appellant or anybody for that matter.

I would allow the appeal, set aside the judgement and Decree of the High Court and substitute therefore judgement for the appellant with costs here and in the Court below.

Platt JSC: . . . I strongly deprecate the manner in which the Respondent alleged fraud in his written statement of defence. Fraud is very serious allegation to make; and it is, as always, wise to abide by the *Civil Procedure Rules Order* VI Rule 2 and plead fraud properly giving particulars of the fraud alleged. Had that been done, and the Appellant had been implicated, then on the Judge's finding that would have been the end of the defence. If, on the other hand, the officials had been implicated, then on the usual interpretation of section 184(c) of the *Registration of Titles Act*, that would have been found to be insufficient. It is generally held that fraud must reside in the transferee. Whether the learned Judge's wide interpretation of the words of s 184(c) '... as against the person registered as proprietor of such land through fraud...' can mean that the fraud of third parties quite apart from the transferee, is sufficient to set aside registered title, is a matter which may possibly need further elucidation. But it is not open for consideration in this case, because of another procedural lapse. Had that been the Respondent's case, he should have brought the Land Office officials and Town Council officials before the Court. It is important that before someone's reputation is besmirched, he has had an opportunity to defend himself. The officials here might have explained the confusion in their action. Even incompetence might not be fraudulent. ...

Before I leave the matter, I should perhaps add one or two words on the place in proceedings such as this, the preliminary steps leading to registration of title of land.

Registered title cannot be set aside for mere irregularity in the preliminary stages. (See Sec. 56 of the *Registration of Titles Act*). It is fraud that has to be proved where section 184 (c) of the *Registration of Titles* Act is involved. It may be that the various steps taken illustrate fraud. Such a case was *Sewanyana v Martin Aliker* No. 4 of 1990 (SC.). The authority had no right to grant the land. The allocatees had put in false papers, which had been wrongly passed by the Council's officer. Altogether there was collusion and fraud in the transferee.

Oder JSC, agreed with the Chief Justice's judgement.

****

Note

See also the Supreme Court judgement in *Rurangaranga v Mbarara Municipal Council et al* CA No 10 of 1996 (unreported). In that case, Wambuzi CJ held that, 'an application for registration which to the knowledge of the applicant is based on an unauthorised grant is in itself fraudulent in so far as it is a false representation to the Registrar of Titles that the lease had been granted by the Council,' (see excerpt of the case below).

****

Notice of fraud acquired by the advocate employed by the proprietor is imputed upon the proprietor.

Sejjaka Nalima v Rebecca Musoke

CA No. 12 of 1985(Supreme Court of Uganda); [1992] 5 KALR 132.

[The respondent is the widow of the late Professor Musoke who was the registered owner of the disputed land. She and one Kazoora were the executors of the deceased's will. The High Court granted the executors probate of the will, but the respondent found it prudent not to administer the estate because Kazoora and the deceased's elder children were overseas. Meanwhile, unknown to the respondent, one Semanda fraudulently applied to the Chief Magistrate's Court for letters of administration of the deceased's estate. Having obtained the letters of administration, he was registered as the proprietor of the disputed property. Three months later he sold the land to Sendaula, an accomplice. Sendaula was registered as proprietor of the land. Six months later Sendaula sold the land to the appellant at about three times the price he paid for it, and the appellant was registered as proprietor. The respondent instituted proceedings in the High Court for an order to cancel the appellant's registration and reinstate the name of Professor Musoke as proprietor of the land. The High Court held that under the *Succession Act* the letters of administration granted to Semanda were null and void. Accordingly, the purported transfer of title to Semanda, Sendaula and the appellant had no legal effect. The trial Judge ordered the appellant's name to be cancelled and replaced by that of Professor Musoke. On appeal to the Supreme Court, the appellant's counsel argued that the relevant provisions of the *RTA* prevailed over the *Succession Act*. Moreover, he submitted that in any case, as a registered proprietor, his client's title was indefeasible. The respondent claimed that the appellant was registered through fraud.]

Odoki JA: ...I respectfully agree with the principles of construction as stated by the learned trial Judge. But with respect, I think he misdirected himself when he held that the *Succession Act* was a latter enactment to the *Registration of Titles Act.* The learned trial Judge held that the *Succession Act* was enacted in 1965 but according to the data appearing at the beginning of the *Succession Act* (Cap.139) the date of commencement is indicated as 15th February, 1906. There is nothing in the Act to show that S.223 was amended or added to the Act in 1963. On the other hand the *Registration of Titles Act* (Cap.205) was enacted in 1922 by Ordinance No. 22 of 1922 and appears to have commenced on 1st May 1924. But the learned trial Judge surprisingly held that the Act was made in 1965. Again there is nothing in the Act to indicate that S. 189 was added to the Act in 1965. It is not clear therefore how the trial Judge arrived at the find that the *Registration of Titles Act* was made in 1965.

It seems plain to me that the *Succession Act* was made in 1906 and is therefore an earlier Act to the *Registration of Titles Act* which was made in 1922. The decision of the Court of Appeal in *Barclays Bank v. Gulu Miller* (1959) E.A. 541 supports my view that the *Registration of Titles Act* was made in 1922. In that case Sir Kenneth O'Connor P. said at page 549

> In 1922 the *Registration of Titles Ordinance* (Cap. 102 of the 1923 Revised Edition of the laws and now Cap. 123 of the 1951 Revised Edition) was enacted which introduced Torrens System of *Registration of Titles.* This repealed the *Registration of Titles Ordinance* 1908 and the *Equitable Mortgages Ordinance* 1912 and by S.3 provided that except so far as was expressly enacted to the contrary, no Ordinance or rule so far as was enacted to the contrary, no Ordinance or rule so far as inconsistent with the Ordinance should apply to land whether freehold or leasehold which was under the operation of the Ordinance.

It follows, therefore, that the *Succession Act* being an earlier Act could not amend or repeal by implication the *Registration of Titles* Act which is a later act. Moreover, the two Acts do not deal with the same subject matter. The *Succession Act* is a general Act dealing with the law of Succession to both movable and immovable property, whereas the *Registration of Titles* is a special Act dealing with registered land. Since the *Registration of Titles Act* is both a later and special Act its provisions which are inconsistent with those of the *Succession Act* which is earlier and general, must prevail over those of the latter Act.

In my view, Section 3 of the *Registration of Titles Act* makes this point clear when it provides:

> Except so far as is expressly enacted to the contrary, no Act or Rule so far as inconsistent with this Act shall apply or be deemed to apply to land whether freehold or leasehold which is under the operation of this Act. This Act shall not be construed as limiting or a bridging the provisions of any law for the time being in force in Uganda relating especially to the property of married women.

I therefore think that Mr Kiingi [Counsel for the appellant] is correct in saying that this section makes the Act a special enactment whose provisions prevail over the provisions of another inconsistent law dealing with registered land. ...

In *Figueiredo v. Talbot* [1962] EA 167] the Court of Appeal held that the general provisions of Section 274 of the *Succession Ordinance* must be read subject to the specific provisions of s.143 of the *Registration of Titles Ordinance* which was also a later enactment. Sir Alastair Forbes V-P who wrote the judgement with which the other members of the court concurred, said, at page 171,

> Where more persons than one are registered as proprietors, 'the registered proprietor' must mean all such persons; and the definition of proprietor in S.2 of the Ordinance supports this view. The Section does not indicate that one of several registered proprietors may make a deposit of certificate of titles. Here 'registered proprietor' of the property is Mrs Talbot and Mr G. B. Talbot. There is no evidence whatever that Mr G. B. Talbot joined with Mrs. Talbot in depositing the duplicate certificate of title with the appellant with intent to create a security thereon. In my opinion, unless both executors joined in such deposit, the deposit would be ineffective to create an equitable mortgage. Reference was made to S.274 of the *Succession Ordinance* (Cap.34) which reads (omitting the illustrations):
>
> ... When there are several executors or administrators, the powers of all may in the absence of any direction to the contrary be exercised by any of them who has proved the will or taken out administration.

That general provision must, however, be read subject to the specific provisions of the Ordinance which is also a later enactment. Section 143 of the Ordinance provides, inter alia:

> If in any case probate or administration is granted to more persons than one all of them for the time being shall join and concur in every instrumental surrender or discharge relating to the land, lease or mortgage.

While this does not specifically refer to the creating of an equitable mortgage by deposit of the title deeds, it is the obvious intention of the legislature that in relation to registered land all executors must concur in transactions affecting the land. In these circumstances I think the term: 'registered proprietor' in S.138 of the Ordinance is to be construed as I have indicated which is the ordinary meaning of the words, and is not to be read subject to S.274 of the *Succession Ordinance*.

Since the provisions of the *Registration of Titles Act* prevail over the provisions of the *Succession Act* in the event of any inconsistency, the provisions of S.233 of the *Succession Act* must be read subject to the provisions of S. 189 of the *Registration of Titles Act*. ...

[The next question is whether the appellant acquired an indefeasible title.]

Mr Kiingi for the appellant submitted that the learned trial Judge ought to have looked at the *Registration of Titles Act* only in deciding the case. He submitted further that the first issue was wrongly framed. The issue he argued was not whether the letters of administration were capable of passing a good title but whether appellant could obtain a good title from a person who purportedly transferred land to him, that is whether the appellant having been registered as proprietor was protected by law. Counsel contended that the deceased's interest in the property did not pass when Dick Semanda obtained letters of administration, but when he was registered as proprietor. He contended further that Semanda having subsequently transferred the property to Sendaula, the latter obtained a good title so long as he did not know of the former's fraud. Mr Kiingi then submitted, that even if the Magistrate lacked jurisdiction or that Semanda obtained registration by fraud, the annulment of the letter of administration could not affect the titles of bona fide purchasers. It was his submission that there is nothing in Section 233 of the *Succession Act* to show that once the letters of administration are annulled the subsequent purchaser loses his title.

Mr Mulira, for the respondent conceded that the learned trial Judge's statutory interpretation was baffling and could not be of much use. He also conceded that the issue was whether the appellant was protected as a bona fide purchaser. He pointed out that S.189 of the *Registration of Titles Act* protects only bona fide purchasers registered without fraud or error, and does not protect every registered proprietor. He submitted that if the registration is visited with some infirmity, the purchaser is not protected. Learned Counsel also contended that nothing legal could flow from illegal proceedings. He cited the case of *Mawji v Arusha General Stores* [1970] E.A. 137 in support of this proposition. ...

In deciding the issues before him the learned trial Judge had to consider the evidence relating to the manner in which the name of Prof. Musoke had been removed from the register. This evidence included the circumstances under which the letters of administration had been obtained by Semanda, how he registered himself on the register, how he transferred the title to Sendaula, and how the title was transferred to the appellant. All this evidence was relevant to the issue before the court.

In my opinion, the question of interpretation of the various statutes in relation to each other was not strictly necessary to determine those issues. I agree with both Counsels that the learned trial Judge's interpretation was rather baffling for the reasons already given. What was called for was the application of the relevant provisions of the law to the issues before him. Nor do I think that it was necessary to make an order annulling the letters of administration since that order was not prayed for nor essential to the decision of the case as Semanda was not a party to this suit. An order directing the Registrar of Titles to cancel the appellant's name from the register and reinstate the name of Prof. Musoke was all that was required. I agree with the submission of Counsel for the appellant that annulment of letter of administration obtained by Semanda could not automatically affect the title of a subsequent bona fide purchaser who was not a party to Semanda's fraud. Therefore I do not see the relevancy of the argument of Counsel for the respondent that nothing legal could flow from an illegal order.

The substantial issue which arose for consideration at the trial and in this appeal was whether the appellant was a bona fide purchaser for value without notice. In the fourth ground of appeal the appellant complains that the learned trial Judge erred in law in failing to hold that the appellant's title as a bona fide purchaser for value of the suit property without notice of any fraud or of the respondent's interest enjoyed the protection afforded by the provisions of the *Registration of Titles* Act and the relevant case law.

Mr Kiingi submitted that since the trial Judge found that Semanda and Sendaula were guilty of fraud but did not so find in case of the appellant, he ought to have decided the case in favour of the appellant. Counsel submitted further that the appellant was not guilty of fraud because he had no notice of it. He contended that the appellant had no duty to make inquiries as to how previous owners had acquired their titles, nor was mere knowledge of unregistered interest sufficient to clothe him with fraud. It was his contention that fraud means actual dishonest dealing but does not include constructive fraud. Learned Counsel then submitted that since the appellant was a bona fide purchaser without notice of any fraud he was protected by the provisions of Section 145, 184 and 189 of the *Registration of Titles Act.*

In reply Mr Mulira submitted that the issue whether the appellant was a bona fide purchaser was specifically framed, and that there was sufficient circumstantial evidence to connect the appellant with acts of fraud. Learned Counsel contended that the cheque the appellant issued for payment of the suit property was a forgery as it was signed by him in the name of his infant son. He submitted further that M/s Musoke & Co. Advocates acted for the appellant in transferring the suit property and since the advocates knew of the respondent's interest in the property the appellant must be presumed to have had constructive notice of the interest. Counsel also contended that the advertisement in the newspaper regarding respondent's intention to apply for probate was notice to the appellant of the respondent's interest. ...

On the evidence before him I am of the opinion that the learned trial Judge was justified in finding that both Semanda and Sendaula obtained title to the suit property through fraud. Indeed both of these findings were not seriously challenged in this appeal.

However, the learned trial Judge appears not to have adequately dealt with the issue whether the appellant was a bona fide purchaser for value without notice of the fraud of Semanda or Sendaula. In his judgement the trial judge referred to the appellant's defence when he said,

> It is the claim of the defendant in this case that he bought the house from Lameka Nteyafa Sendaula as a bona fide purchaser for valuable consideration.

After holding that the determination of this issue depended on statutory interpretation of the relevant statutes he concluded that the appellant could not be protected after the letters of administration had been annulled for just cause.

While, therefore, the learned trial Judge appears to have had this issue in mind, he did not make a specific finding whether the appellant was guilty of fraud and was therefore not a bona fide purchaser for value whose title could not be protected by law. He may have found it unnecessary to deal with the issue in detail since he based his decision on the reasoning that the annulled letters of administration could not become a good root of title to a bona fide purchaser for value even without notice.

This being a first appeal this court has power under rule 29(1)(a) of the Rules of the court to reappraise the evidence and draw its own inferences of fact. It is well settled that an appeal to this court from a trial in the High Court is by way of retrial, and this court has the duty to reconsider the evidence, evaluate it itself and draw its own conclusions while bearing in mind that it has neither seen nor heard the witnesses and making due allowance for this. See *Sele v Associated Boat Company* [1968] E.A. 123 at page 126.

Before I examine the evidence which was adduced on the issue whether the appellant was a bona fide purchaser, it is necessary, in my view, to consider the doctrine of bona fide purchaser under our law. This common law doctrine is provided for under S.189 of the *Registration of Titles Act*. The Section however does not define who is a bona fide purchaser, but merely provides for his protection.

There is a lot of Uganda or East African authorities on this section. However, in the case of *Luswere v G. W. Kasule and another*, Civil Suit No. 1010 of 1983 (unreported) I had occasion to consider this section and said,

> The effect of this section is that once a registered proprietor has purchased the property in good faith his title cannot be impeached on account of the fraud of the previous registered proprietor. A bona fide purchaser therefore obtains a good title even if he purchases from a proprietor who previously obtained by fraud.
>
> However, before a purchaser can claim the protection of s. 189 of the *Registration of Titles Act*, he must act in good faith. If he is guilty of fraud or sharp practice, he will cease to be innocent and therefore lose the protection. An action for ejectment lies against him under section 184 (c) of the Act which provides in relevant parts as follows:
>
> ...No action of ejectment or other action for the recovery of any land shall lie or be sustained against the person registered as proprietor under the provisions of this Act except in any of the following cases, ...

> (c) the case of a person deprived of any land by fraud as against a person deriving otherwise than as a transferee bona fide for value from or through a person registered through fraud; ...
> and in any case other than as aforesaid the production of the registered certificate of title or lease shall be held in every court to be an absolute bar and estoppel to any such action against the person named in such document as the grantee, owner, proprietor or lessee of the land therein described any law or equity to the contrary notwithstanding.

As regards the sanctity of the register, I said,

> Therefore while the cardinal rule of registration of titles under the Act is that the register is everything the court can go behind the fact of registration in cases of actual fraud on the part of the transferee: See *Olinda De Souze Figueredo v. Kassamamli Nanji* [1962] E.A. 757 *Harshad Ltd. v. Globe Cinema Ltd & Others* [1960] E.A. 1046, Re Malo [1964] E.A. 731, *Wainiha Saw Milling Co. Ltd v. Wainone Timber Co. Ltd.* [1926] A.C. 101, *Gibbs v. Messer* [1891]A.C. 248 64 T.L. Rep. 237 *Assets Co. Ltd. v. Mere Roihi & Others* [1905] A.C. 176, 92 T.L. Rep. 397.

The next question to consider is the meaning of fraud as used in the Act. It is I think well settled that fraud means actual fraud or some act of dishonesty. Where there are a series of subsequent transfers, for the title of the incumbent registered proprietor to be impeachable, the fraud of the previous proprietors must be brought home to him. In *Assets Co. Ltd.v. Mere Roihi & others* (supra) Lord Lindly said,

> Further it appears to their Lordships that the fraud which must be proved in order to invalidate the title of a registered proprietor for value whether he buys from a prior registered owner or from a person claiming under a title certified under the *Native Lands Act* must be brought home to the persons whose registered title is impeached or to his agents. Fraud by persons from whom he claims does not affect him unless knowledge of it is brought home to him or his agents. The mere fact that he might have found out fraud if he had been more vigilant and had made further inquiries which he omitted to make does not itself prove fraud on his part. But if it be shown that his suspicious were aroused and that he abstained from making inquiries for fear of learning the truth, the case is very different and fraud may be properly ascribed to him.

The respondent maintains that there was adequate circumstantial evidence to saddle the appellant with fraud. It was submitted that the appellant knew of the respondent's unregistered interest through the advertisement in the newspaper of her intention to apply for probate, and secondly, through M/s Musoke and Co. Advocates who were acting for both appellant and Sendaula. But the appellant contended that mere knowledge of unregistered interest was insufficient to clothe him with fraud. He relied on Section 145 of the Registration of Titles Act. ...

I agree that the object of this section and indeed the entire Act is to save persons dealing with registered proprietors from the trouble and expense of going behind the register in order to satisfy themselves of its validity, and thus simplify and expedite the process of transfer of title. But the section cannot be called in aid in cases of fraud.

The section stipulates that mere knowledge of unregistered interest cannot of itself be imputed as fraud. Therefore, in my view, where this knowledge is supported by other circumstances it may amount to fraud.

In *Katarikawe v.Katwireme & another* Civil Suit No. 2 of 1973 (unreported) the High Court, while dealing with S 145 of the Act said,

> although mere knowledge of unregistered interest cannot be imputed as fraud under the Act, it is my view that where such knowledge is accompanied by a wrongful intention to defeat such existing interest, that would amount to fraud. In the absence of a Statutory definition of fraud I would adopt the definition in a similar Kenyan Statute which defines fraud as 'fraud shall on the part of a person obtaining registration include a proved knowledge of the existence of an unregistered interest on the part of some other person, whose interest be knowingly and wrongfully defeats by such registration'.

> I take this view because I doubt whether the framers of the Act ever intended to encourage dishonest dealings in land such as manifest in this case.

This decision was approved by the court in the Case of *Marko Matovu & others v. Muhamed Sseviri and another* Civil Appeal No. 7 of 1978 (unreported). The brief facts of that case were that the appellants applied for a lease on 17/10/75 and after inspection of the land by the local land committee on 21/11/75, they were offered a lease on 27/7/76, which they accepted on 10/20/76, and paid the prescribed fees. When they went to survey the land, they found that the first respondent had already surveyed it for himself and had started fencing. The first respondent obtained title on 2/9/76. The appellants instituted the suit for cancellation of that title on the ground that it was obtained by fraud and in breach of the rules of natural justice. The trial Judge held that there was something fishy about the respondent's application but he refused to find that the irregularities amount to fraud, and gave judgement for the respondent.

On appeal, the appellants contended, inter alia, that the learned Judge erred in law and in fact in holding that fraud had not been proved. The Court of appeal found that the evidence showed that the respondent's application was deliberately backdated to support the view that the inspection of this land was carried on 21/11/75. It also found that there was an attempt to falsify the dates on the respondent's application and other documents were destroyed and replaced by others obtained by underhand means. Further, there was evidence to show that the respondent was assisted by some agents of the Land Commission to defeat the appellant's right to title of which the respondent was fully aware. The court also observed that the Commission had entertained another application on the same land on which the appellants were the customary tenants without giving them a hearing. In allowing the appeal, the court said,

> Not only was there unfair play but also fraud. It is fraud if, as it was held in *Katarikawe v Katwiremu and another*, Civil Suit No. 2 of 1973, a person procures registration to defeat an unregistered interest on the part of another person of which he is proved to have had knowledge.

In the present case it was not disputed that the respondent was the widow of late Prof. Musoke who was the registered proprietor of the suit property, and that she obtained probate in respect of this property from the High Court before the appellant became the registered proprietor of the property. The notice in the newspaper about her intention to apply for probate was notice to the whole world and therefore the appellant may be said to have had knowledge of it. On being granted probate, the respondent acquired a registrable interest in the property and could have lodged a caveat to protect her interest. However, I do not think that notice in the newspaper was sufficient by itself to give the appellant actual notice of her interest in the property at the time he purchased it, unless it was supported by other evidence.

It was contended for the respondent that M/s Musoke & Co. Advocates were acting on behalf of Sendaula and the appellant, and that since the advocates knew of the unregistered interest of the respondent and the fraud of Sendaula that knowledge must be imputed on the appellant. It is common ground that M/s Musoke & Co. Advocates were acting on behalf of Sendaula for clearing off the mortgage on the title. The advocates also witnessed the signature of Sendaula and the appellant on the transfer. In his evidence the appellant did not deny or admit that the advocates were acting for him but he admitted that they witnessed the Memorandum of Agreement. On this evidence it seems to me that the advocates were acting for both parties to this transaction.

If the advocates were acting for the appellant as well, could notice of the respondent's unregistered interest and of the fraud of Sendaula be imputed on the appellant? It seems to me that where a purchaser employs an agent, such as an advocate, to act on his behalf the notice he receives, actual or constructive, is imputed on the purchaser. And similarly where the advocate acts for both parties any notice he acquires is ordinarily imputed on both parties. There is an exception to this principle where the agent deliberately defrauds the purchaser. ...

There was other evidence from which appellant's notice of fraud could be inferred In his own evidence, the appellant stated,

> Sendaula's brother approached me and told me about the land and the house. I told the brother to tell Sendaula to come to my office. I asked Sendaula to go to the house. It was a Saturday. We met a Mr Ochiti. He asked if I was a lawyer. I told him I wanted to buy the land. I asked him to allow me to inspect the house. I inspected the house. I also asked him in what capacity he was there. He told me that he was a tenant and that their lease would expire at the end of December, 1983... The following day I went to make a search. I looked at the register. I found that the registered owner was Sendaula.

It may be that the appellant had no duty to inquire as to whose tenant Mr Ochiti was, but the fact that he asked the tenant in what capacity he was occupying the house when the purported landlord, Sendaula, was with him was very strange. In view of the fact that Sendaula had obtained the title to the land by fraud, it is possible that Sendaula and Ochiti did not know each other. It should also be noted that the appellant did not go further to ask Ochiti who was his landlord. Instead he went to investigate the title at the Land Office. It is reasonable to infer from the appellant's conduct that his suspicions were aroused but that he feared to learn the truth from the tenant, by inquiring from him who was his landlord. Had he done so he would have definitely found out that Ochiti's landlord had been Prof. Latimer Musoke. As Lord Lindley said in *Assets Co. Ltd. v. Mere Roihi* (supra) where the purchaser's suspicions were aroused but he abstains from making inquiries for fear of learning the truth, fraud may be properly ascribed to him.

In the case of *Luswere v. Kasule* (supra) the plaintiff was the registered proprietor of two plots of land, Plot 120 and Plot 121 (Mailo Register Kyadondo Block 249 at Gaba). He built a residential house on Plot 120 with a drive-in-passing through Plot 121, and both plots were enclosed in one compound. The first defendant forged a transfer to himself and got registered as the proprietor of Plot 121. He then transferred to the second defendant who took possession of both plots and leased the house on Plot 120, still registered in the name of the plaintiff, to an Embassy. The plaintiff sued the defendants for an order cancelling their certificates and reinstating his name on the register, on grounds of fraud. The second defendant pleaded that he was a bona fide purchaser for value. It was held that the circumstantial evidence adduced was incompatible with the second defendant being a bona fide purchaser and was only consistent with fraud. The court took into account the occupation of Plot 120 by the second defendant when he had purchased only Plot 121, his apparent failure to inquire from the neighbours the ownership of the two plots and his failure to open up the boundaries of the two plots.

The last piece of evidence relied on by the respondent to prove fraud on the part of the appellant was the cheque issued by the appellant to pay the balance of the purchase price. ....

Counsel for the respondent argued that the cheque was a forgery. Although it may not be possible on the evidence to find whether the cheque was a forgery or not, I am of the view that it was extremely strange that the appellant signed on the name of his minor son, instead of signing for him or in his own right as a signatory. If his son could not sign any cheque, then the appellant must have been the signatory. This unexplained strange conduct may be seen as an attempt by the appellant to conceal the fraud.

While the burden of proving the case lies on the plaintiff, it is well settled that the onus of establishing the plea of a bona fide purchaser lies on the person who sets it up. It is a single plea and is not sufficiently made out by proving purchase for value and leaving it to the plaintiff to prove notice if he can.

In view of the evidence I have considered regarding the conduct of the appellant, I am unable to find that he succeeded in establishing that he was a bona fide purchaser for value without notice of the fraud of the previous registered proprietors through whom he derived title. On the contrary there was, in my view, sufficient circumstantial evidence to saddle him with fraud. That being so, the appellant cannot claim the protection of s. 189 of the *Registration of Titles Act*.

Wambuzi CJ ... I also agree that the learned trial Judge misdirected himself firstly, on the chronological order of the statutes. According to him the *Registration of Titles Act* was enacted in 1963 and the *Succession Act* in 1965. The correct dates are however that the *Registration of Titles Act* was enacted in 1922 and the *Succession Act* in 1906. This makes the *Succession Act* the earlier of the two enactments.

Secondly on the subject matter of Statutes. ... S.189 of the *Registration of Titles Act* provides:

> Nothing in this Act contained shall be so interpreted as to leave subject to an action of ejectment or to an action for recovery of damages as aforesaid or for deprivation of the estate or interest in respect of which he is registered as proprietor any purchaser for valuable consideration of land under the operation of this Act, on the ground that the proprietor through or under whom he claims was registered as proprietor through fraud or error. ...

The purpose of this Section is to protect a bona fide purchaser for valuable consideration whose name is entered on the register.

S.233 (1) of the *Succession Act* provides:

> The grant of probate or letters of administration may be revoked or annulled for just cause.

S.1(4) of the *Administration of Estates (Small Estates) (Special Provisions) Decree*, 1972 in somewhat similar terms provides as follows:

> The grant of probate or letters of administration may be revoked, altered or annulled for just cause and any errors appearing therein may be rectified by the court.

With respect, I see nothing in either of the last two sections contradictory to or inconsistent with the provisions of s.189 of the *Registration of Titles Act*. Both Sections provide for annulment of probate or letters of administration for just cause, a totally different subject from protection of a bona fide purchaser in s.189 of the *Registration of Titles Act*. Even in the passage relied on by the learned trial Judge, Griffith C.J. said, in *Goodwin v. Phillips* [1908] 7 CLR:

> Where the provisions of a particular Act of Parliament dealing with ***a particular subject*** are wholly inconsistent with the provisions of an earlier Act dealing with the ***same subject matter*** ...

Emphasis is supplied, the subject matter must be the same in both enactments.

And thirdly on the effect of the Statutes, s.233 of the *Succession Act* and s.1 of the *Administration of Estates (Small Estates) (Special Provisions) Decree*, 1972 are both silent as to what happens if the executor or administrator has transferred property to third parties before annulment of probate or letter of administration as the case may be. The learned trial Judge appears to have held the view that upon annulment of the letters of administration in this case all transacting relating to the letters of administration were annulled including any transfers of property. The learned trial Judge concluded therefore that s.233 of the *Succession Act* and s.1(4) of the *Administration of Estates 9 Small Estates)(Special Provisions) Decree*, 1972 impliedly repealed s. 189 of the *Registration of Titles Act*. As earlier pointed out in this judgement, the *Succession Act* was earlier than the *Registration of Titles Act* and could not therefore be said to have impliedly repealed the provisions of a later Act. Secondly, both the *Succession Act* and the *Administration of Estates (Small Estates) (Special Provisions) Decree* are general Acts dealing with administration of estates and land is dealt with as one of the subject matters of an estate. On the other hand, the *Registration of Titles Act* is a specific Act dealing with registered land. Neither Act could be said to repeal impliedly the provision of s.189 of the *Registration of Titles Act*. A general provision must be read subject to the specific provision, see *Souza Figueredo v. George Blacquire, Talbot and another* [1962] E.A. 167.

The second, third and fourth grounds of appeal were argued together. They were to the effect that s.189 of the *Registration of Titles Act* gives absolute protection to a bona fide purchaser for valuable consideration without notice of fraud who becomes the registered proprietor of the lands in question. The section does not contain the words 'without notice' but otherwise I am in complete agreement with the arguments in this respect. The only question here being whether the appellant was a bona fide purchaser for valuable consideration.

As already remarked in his judgement the third issue at the trial whether the defendant, now the appellant, was a bona fide purchaser for value of the lands in question was not answered. Be that as it may, it is the duty of this court to re-appraise the evidence and come to its own decision, see *Selle and another v. Associated Motor Boat Company Ltd and others* [1968] EA. 123. The learned trial Judge found in effect that the letters of administration were fraudulently obtained and were accordingly declared null and void. The registration of Dick Sangomwami Ssemanda as proprietor of the property in question was equally fraudulent. Sendaula who allegedly purchased the property from Dick Sangomwami Ssemanda was found not to be bona fide purchaser and that he too was fraudulent in his dealings with the property. There is ample evidence to support those findings and in any case there is no appeal on any of those matters.

There is no evidence nor was the matter argued in the lower court or before us, whether or not Dick Sangomwami Ssemanda was a real or a fictitious person. Unlike in *Gibbs v Messer* ... and, for that matter, the parties in the case before us accepted that Ssemanda and, for that matter, Sendaula were real persons who fraudulently had themselves registered as proprietors of the land in question at different times.

As to the bona fides of the appellant I wish to examine the evidence in a little detail [His Honour discussed the evidence, and continued.]

Section 145 of the *Registration of Titles Act* provides, in so far as is relevant to this case:

> Except in the case of fraud, no person contracting or dealing with or taking or proposing to take a transfer from the proprietor of any registered land, lease or mortgage shall be required or in any manner concerned to inquire or ascertain the circumstances in or the consideration for which such proprietor or any previous proprietor thereof was registered . . .

In my view a purchaser is, under this Section, entitled to rely on the fact that the vendor is a registered proprietor in all cases except in the case of fraud. Accordingly, it is my view that the appellant is not protected by this section. Since the allegation is that Sendaula acquired the property fraudulently, the appellant was not absolved from investigating the title. ...

There is not much in the way of authorities in Uganda directly in point as to the bona fides of a purchaser. The position appears to be, however, that in the absence of fraud a court will not go behind the fact of registration. In *Olinda De Souza Figureiredo v. Kassamali Nanji* [1962] EA 757 [at 758] Sheridan J quoted with approval the Privy Council in *Waimiha Saw Milling Co Ltd v Waione Timber Co Ltd* [1926] AC 101, as follows:

> The Cardinal Principle of the Statute is that the register is everything, and that except in case of actual fraud on the part of the person dealing with the registered proprietor such person upon the registration of title under which he takes from the registered proprietor has an indefeasible title against all the world.

What does this cardinal principle of the Statute mean in practical terms? Among the authorities referred to us by Mr Kulumba Kiyingi I find the New Zealand case of *Assets Company Ltd. v. Mere Roihi and others* [1905] AC 176 almost on all fours with the case before us. [His Honour cited with approval a passage from Lord Atkin's judgement (which was also cited by Odoki JA) and continued]. I am persuaded that this is a sound and practical interpretation of the law. In the case before us, therefore, can the appellant be regarded as a bona fide purchaser? I think no, for the following reasons. As already pointed out in this judgement Musoke and Company must have known about the alleged fraud. The same advocates acted for, and accordingly were the agents of the appellant as already pointed out. The information contained in Exh.8 is that the property in question was registered in the names of the late Professor Latimer Musoke and that the probate of his estate was granted by the High Court of Uganda to his widow, Mrs Rebecca Musoke. The title deed indicates that Lameck Nteyaffa Sendaula was registered as proprietor on 29th April 1982 and that the previous registered proprietor was Dick Sangomwami Ssemanda of P. O. Box 170, Kampala the administrator of the estate of Latimer Kamya Musoke (deceased). The deed must have been examined by Musoke & Co. Advocates for both parties as well as the parties themselves. These facts were more than enough to arouse the suspicion of any bona fide purchaser or his agent and a little inquiry would have established the respondent's interest in the property. Either the purchaser or his agent knew of the respondent's interest or they refrained from investigating for fear of learning the truth.

The term 'bona fide purchaser' is not defined in the Act. However, in *Ali Abdul Kader Salehbhai Assabwalla v. Khadija Bring Gafoor & others* [1962] E.A. 571 the Court of Appeal considered the expression 'bona fide' in relation to s.8 of the *English Trade Marks Act*, 1938 applicable to Aden. The section provides in so far as is relevant:

> No registration of a trade mark shall interfere with:
>
> (a) any bona fide use by a person of his own name or of the name of his place of business, or of the name, or of the name of the place of business, of any of his predecessor in business.

In this connection and after considering a number of authorities, Sir Alastair Forbes, V.P. said at page 578,

> In the light of these comments I do not think that it is to be accepted that a person will lose the protection of s.8 merely because confusion may result from the use by that person of his own name. The term 'bona fide' intent, and if the name is used honestly in the belief that confusion will not arise and without the intention of wrongfully diverting business, it seems to me that the use is 'bona fide' within the meaning of the section.

Applying this reasoning to the case before us, can it be said that the appellant honestly intended to purchase the property in question and did not intend to acquire the property wrongfully? I think the appellant knew of the respondent's interest but ignored it relying on the appellant's vendor being registered proprietor. This way he was knowingly perpetuating a fraud and I cannot say that he was a bona fide purchaser.

Lubogo Ag. JA agreed with the judgement of Odoki JA.

Appeal dismissed.

****

Notes

1. In *Sekabanja v Sajjabi* (CS No 6 of 1976; [1983] HCB 54) it was held that a registered proprietor who acquires title by way of gift (volunteer) is not a bona fide purchaser for *value,* therefore his or her title is not protected under s 184(c) of the *Registration of Titles Act.* In that case, the plaintiff and the deceased together purchased two plots of land but, for some technical reasons, the land was registered only in the deceased's name. The deceased donated to the defendant the plaintiff's plot, which was subsequently registered in the defendant's name. The Court ordered the Registrar to cancel the deceased's name and substitute it with that of the plaintiff.
2. In Australia, there are conflicting authorities as to whether a volunteer acquires an indefeasible title. For example, in *King v Smail* [1958] VR 273, the Supreme Court of Victoria held that a volunteer takes land subject to defects that affected his or her immediate transferor. This was also the position at common law. The court reasoned that if the Torrens Acts intended to override this long established general rule, they would have expressly stated so. (See also *Rasmussen v Rasmussen* (1995) 1 VR 613). In contrast, in *Bogdanavic v Koteff* (1988) 12 NSWLR 472, the Supreme Court of New South Wales held that upon registration

a volunteer acquires an indefeasible title just like a proprietor who gave consideration. In the latter case, the respondent inherited the disputed land and was registered as proprietor. The appellant had unregistered claims over the land, which the respondent was not aware of until after his title was registered. The court held that the principle of indefeasibility was the essence of the Torrens system and under this doctrine the registered proprietor has a legal title subject only to interests preserved by registration.

****

Notice of unregistered claims

Under the general law, a purchaser of a legal interest takes the land subject to any equitable interest of which he or she had notice prior to acquisition (see *Uganda Post and Telecommunications v AKM Lutaaya* CA No 36 of 1996). In contrast, Section 145 of the *Registration of Titles* Act provides that:

> Except in the case of fraud, no person contracting or dealing with or taking or proposing to take a transfer from the proprietor of any registered land, lease or mortgage shall be required or in any manner concerned to inquire or ascertain the circumstances in or in consideration for which such a proprietor or any previous proprietor thereof was registered, or to see to the application of purchase or consideration money, or shall be affected by notice actual or constructive or any trust or unregistered interest, any rule of law or equity to the contrary notwithstanding, and knowledge that any such trust or unregistered interest is in existence shall not of itself be imputed as fraud.

The meaning and effect of this provision is illustrated by the following case.

****

Except in case of fraud a registered proprietor is not bound by unregistered claims even if he or she had notice of such claims.

Shah v Modern Sweet Mart Ltd
(1956-57) 8 ULR 99

[In 1954, the plaintiff purchased certain premises from one Alvares, now deceased, and was subsequently registered as proprietor. At the time of purchase, the defendant was in possession of part of the premises under a tenancy agreement entered into with Alvares. Under this agreement, the defendant became a tenant for a period of 7 years effective from 1 October 1952. The agreement was not registered as required by s 9(3) of the Registration of Titles Ordinance. The plaintiff sought possession of the part of the premises occupied by the defendant.]

Keatinge J: The plaintiff, H.K.Shah, says in evidence that he entered into possession in October 1954, but he says he did not become aware of the agreement till February or March 1956. When negotiating the purchase he was not informed and did not inquire on what terms any tenants were in occupation. But J.A.C. Alvares, states that his father was ill at the time and that he and also Mr Dholakia, the advocate who seems to have acted for both parties, were present when the terms of the sale were fixed. He says that at the time the plaintiff was informed of the agreement and that a few days later he handed a copy of the agreement to Mr Dholakia in the presence of the plaintiff.

The plaintiff does admit that before the purchase he inspected the premises and saw Prabhudas, managing director of the defendant company, there. He denies that Prabhudas informed him of the tenancy for seven years. Prabhudas said he did so inform the plaintiff and also told him that the rent had been paid in advance till the end of December 1954. The plaintiff has had to concede that it is correct that the defendant had paid in advance and that he (the plaintiff) received the rent from Alvares. But in spite of this peculiar arrangement he says he did not inquire as to the terms of the defendant's tenancy.

In February 1955, the defendant gave up the rooms on the first floor. The plaintiff agrees that that arrangement was come to verbally and was confirmed in the letter dated February 13th, 1955 (Exhibit 3). The plaintiff says he does not know the contents of the letter as he does not understand English. Prabhudas does not understand English and he says this letter was drafted by Mr Dholakia in the presence of both of them. The letter is written in English, and the last sentence reads: 'This letter will form part and parcel of the original tenancy agreement.' In my opinion, it is also clear from the plaintiff's advocate's letters of September 7th, 1955 and November 2nd, 1955 (Exhibits 6 and 8) that the advocates were aware of the agreement.

It is argued for the defendant that the plaintiff being aware of the agreement he is bound by it in equity. Assuming for the moment that the doctrines of equity do apply to this Protectorate then notwithstanding in fact that the agreement has not been registered I am of opinion, on the authority of *Walsh v. Lonsdale* (1882), 21 Ch.D.9, *Abdulali Jivanji & Co. v. Dawood Haji Nasser Bros. (1918), 7 E.A.L.R. 167* and *Pardhan Jivraj v. Whelpadale* (1926), 3 U.L.R. 193, that as between the parties to it the agreement would be an equitable lease. I am also of opinion that as the plaintiff had notice of the agreement he would be bound by it.

The doctrines of equity are applied to this Protectorate by cl. 15 (2) of the Uganda Order-in-Council, 1902 and their application is limited, *inter alia,* by any modifications, amendment or replacement by any Ordinance. Section 145 of the *Registration of Titles Ordinance* reads:

> Except in the case of fraud no person contracting or dealing with or taking or proposing to take a transfer from the proprietor of any registered land, lease or mortgage shall be required or in any manner concerned to inquire or ascertain the circumstances in or the consideration for which such proprietor or any previous proprietor thereof was registered, or to see to the application of any purchase or consideration money, or *shall be affected by notice actual or constructive of any trust or unregistered interest, any rule of law or equity to the contrary notwithstanding,* and knowledge that any such trust or unregistered interest is in existence shall not of itself be imputed as fraud. [Emphasis supplied.]

It is submitted that in view of the above section the doctrines of equity cannot be applied to this matter. In my opinion, the defendant holds an 'unregistered interest' and although the plaintiff had notice of such interest in my judgement this section specifically prohibits the application of the rules of equity. In the circumstances, this court must hold that the plaintiff is not bound by the tenancy agreement made between the defendant and Alvares.

****

Notes

1. It is respectfully submitted that Keatinge J in *Shah v Modern Sweet Mart Ltd,* rightly applied s 145 of the *Registration of Titles Ordinance.* (Compare with the judgement of Karokora JSC in *Uganda Posts and Telecommunications v Lutaaya* CA No 36 of 1995, extracted below. See also *Sempa Mbababali v W K Kidza and others* CS No 615 of 1969; [1985] HCB 46; and *Njuki v Musisi Nyanzi* HCCS No 0434 of 1996. Both cases are extracted below.
2. It is suggested that *Shah v Modern Sweet Mart Ltd, supra,* could have been decided in the defendant's favour under s 61 of the *Registration of Titles Act,* which was not cited in the judgement. That section provides that title of a registered proprietor is indefeasible except, inter alia, as against the interest of any tenant, notwithstanding that such interest is not registered. Since the defendant was in possession as an equitable tenant, his interest should have prevailed over that of the plaintiff. See also *Uganda Posts and Telecommunications v Lutaaya, supra.*

3. In Australia, the effect of the provision corresponding with s 145 *RTA* on the definition of fraud has been considered in several cases. A good illustration is that of the case of *RM Hosking Properties Ltd v Barnes* [1971] SASR 100. In that case, the landowner leased its premises to the defendants for a period of two years with an option to renew for a further two years. The lease was not registered. Before the lease expired, the landowner sold the premises to the plaintiffs. At the time of purchase, the plaintiffs were aware of the defendants' unregistered lease and, indeed, purchased the land subject to the occupancy of the defendants. When the defendants purported to exercise their option to renew the plaintiffs declined and served them with notice to vacate the premises. The plaintiffs brought proceedings in the Supreme Court of South Australia for possession. The issue was whether the plaintiffs were registered through fraud. Walters J held that the plaintiffs, despite their knowledge of the unregistered lease, were not guilty of fraud. His Honour found that there was no evidence of actual dishonesty and to hold that 'mere notice' of an unregistered interest amounted to fraud would stultify the notice provision.

   Similarly, in the case of the *Bank of South Australia v Ferguson* (1998) 151 ALR 729 at 732, the High Court of Australia in a joint judgement (per Brennan CJ, Gaudron, McHugh, Gummow and Kirby JJ) observed:

   > Not all species of fraud which attract equitable remedies will amount to fraud in the statutory sense. The distinction may be illustrated as follows. In some circumstances, equity subjects the interest of a purchaser of an unregistered land to an antecedent interest of which the purchaser has notice. However, in respect of land ...[under the Torrens system], registration of a transfer is not fraudulent in the statutory sense required to qualify the operation of the doctrine of indefeasibility, merely because the transferee knows that the registration will defeat an antecedent unregistered interest of which the transferee has notice.

4. Note that *notice of fraud* constitutes fraud. See *Kampala Bottlers Ltd v Damanico*; and *Sajjaka Nalima v Rebecca Musoke,* extracted above.

****

A proprietor takes the land subject to the interest of any tenant of the land in possession, even if he or she had no actual notice of such tenant.

Uganda Posts and Telecommunications v Lutaaya
CA No. 36 of 1995 (unreported, Supreme Court of Uganda)

> [DW3, Nansikombi, was the registered proprietor of the suit land measuring 300 acres. In 1977, the appellant entered into possession of part of the land without DW3's consent. Thereafter, the appellant constructed on the land a satellite power station and several buildings. Allegedly, the appellant and DW3 subsequently came to some understanding and DW3 acquiesced in the appellant's occupation of her land. In 1987, DW3 leased the suit land to Lutaaya, the respondent, and the lease was registered. According to the respondent, he only became aware that the land occupied by the appellant was part of the land leased to him after registration of the lease, when he surveyed the land. The trial Judge found the appellant liable for trespass and awarded damages to the respondent. The appellant appealed to the Supreme Court.]

Karokora JSC: ... Mr Kasule [Counsel for the appellant], submitted that the respondent had admitted in evidence that when he acquired the suit land in 1987, the Earth Satellite Power Station at Mpoma was on the land he was going to buy. However, the respondent stated that he did not know at the time that the land he was going to buy included the land on which the Earth Satellite Power Station was situated. Mr Kasule submitted that if what the Respondent said was true, then it must have been a gross negligence on his part and [he] must suffer the consequence, if on surveying the land he had purchased, he discovered that the Earth Satellite Power Station was on the land he had bought.

Against the above submission, Mr. Ssekandi [Counsel for the respondent] submitted, relying on the case of *Nakabili v Masaka District Growers* (1985) HCB 38 that the only interest that can affect registered proprietor would be the registered encumbrances. Since the appellant's land on which the Earth Satellite Power Station is situated was not registered as an incumbrance upon the respondent's Title, the appellant's claim of interest on the land would not be sustained.

I have gone through the entire evidence on record and submissions of both Counsel on the appeal and must observe that the law is very clear that if a person purchases an estate which he knows to be in occupation of another than the vendor, he is bound by all the equities which the parties in such occupation may have in the land. The above proposition was stated in one old English case of *Jones v Smith* (1841) 1 Hore 43 at page 60. But earlier on in *Taylor v Stibbert* (1803–13) All ER 432, Loughborough L.C. held that if a vendor is not in possession of the land he is selling, the purchaser must make inquiries of the person in possession or otherwise the property purchased will be subject to that person's right. Then in *Barnhart v Greenshields* (1853) 0 Moo PCC 18 Lord Kingsdown stated:

> If there is a tenant in possession of land a purchaser is bound by all the equities which the tenant could enforce against the vendor.

Then in *National Provincial Bank Ltd v Hastings Car Mart Ltd & others* (1964) 1 All ER 688 Lord Denning held inter alia at page 698:

> The charge of the bank upon the matrimonial house was a valid charge, but they took it subject to the deserted wife's equity to remain in occupation.

In *Hodgon v Marks* (1970) 3 ALL ER 513 the occupation of the land constituted constructive notice to a purchaser of the rights of the occupier. The occupation of the suit land by appellant put the would be purchaser upon notice of claim adverse to the registered owner. See also *William & Glyn's Bank v Boland* 1981 AC 487 where, although the bank had a charge on the matrimonial home where both the husband and wife lived together, it would not succeed to obtain an order for possession after the husband had defaulted to pay, because the bank's charge upon the house was subject to the wife's overriding interest of being in actual possession. So likewise, I think on this appeal, although the respondent is the registered leaseholder of the land, on which the suit land is situated, in my view, the respondent must have acquired the leasehold title subject to appellant's interest of being in actual occupation.

In view of the above, I would accept Mr Kasule's submission that although the respondent is the registered proprietor of the leasehold estate on which the portion in dispute is situated, it must be noted that this paramouncy of interest in his estate is subject to appellant's existing adverse possession at the time of respondent's acquisition of the leasehold. The above finding is reinforced by Section 61 of the *Registration of Titles Act* (*RTA*). ...

It must be observed that since the vendor, the Uganda Mixed Farm Ltd, was not in actual occupation of the suit land, the purchaser, respondent, ought to have made inquiries of the person in possession otherwise the property purchased would be subject to appellant's rights on that land. In fact, the respondent conceded in evidence that he saw the Mpoma Earth Satellite Power Station but did not know that the land he was buying included the land on which the Earth Satellite Power Station is.

Clearly, if this is true, then the respondent must be guilty of gross negligence for having deliberately omitted to make discovery inquiries. Consequently, and in all fairness, I think the respondent would be estopped by both the doctrine of equitable estoppel and the overriding interest of appellant's actual occupation of the land as provided in the proviso to Section 61 of *RTA*, since the appellant was in adverse possession of the suit land with the knowledge of the respondent by the time the respondent acquired the leasehold.

Furthermore, although the initial entry on this land was not authorised, after DW3 had discovered their presence, she first acquiesced in their occupation and later consented to their occupation and was compensated for some sugar cane which were growing there. Mr Kasule, Counsel for the appellant submitted that the appellant were on the land as Kibanja Owner with the consent of DW3. Therefore any other person who acquired the same land in leasehold had to respect the Kibanja Owner.

Against the above submission, Mr Ssekandi, Counsel for respondent, submitted that a Government could not own land in the capacity of Kibanja Owner.

I must observe that whereas I have not come across an authority which states that a Government can own land in the capacity of Kibanja Owner, I must add that I am not aware of any authority which excludes Government from owning land in that capacity. In my view, if Customary tenure is a system of land ownership in Uganda for any person, I can see no justification for denying the Government to benefit or own land under that system, and especially if the owner of that land recognised its existence on that land. In any case, since the appellant had been on this land since 1977, and had established all the installation thereon, if the respondent wanted to take over the suit land, then he ought to have taken all the necessary steps to compensate him for the development carried out on the land as prescribed by the law – Article 19 of the 1967 Constitution, then in existence.

Therefore, considering all the circumstances of the acquisition of respective interest of each of the parties, it would be hard and far-fetched in my view, to say that appellant trespassed on respondent leasehold, which he acquired when it (appellant) had already been in occupation of part of the same land for 10 years with the knowledge of respondent and consent of DW3. In the circumstances, therefore, this ground, would succeed.

Oder JSC and Tsekooko JSC agreed

****

Notes

With due respect, it is submitted that Karokora JSC misdirected himself when he held that where at the time of purchase a buyer knows that another person is in occupation of the land he or she is bound by all the equities such a person might have in the subject land. The authorities he cited state the legal position at common law, which is different from the Torrens System. Section 145 of the *Registration of Titles Act,* which His Honour did not cite, states that except in the case of fraud a potential purchaser or lessee, 'shall [not] be affected by notice actual or constructive of any …unregistered interest, *any rule of law or equity to the contrary notwithstanding.*' The section specifically states that 'mere notice' is not fraud. In the instant case, the appellant did not allege let alone prove that the respondent was involved in any fraud. If anything, the respondent was a victim of the landowner's fraud. (Compare with *Shah v Modern Sweet Mart Uganda Ltd* (1956-57) 8 ULR 99). It is submitted that the case should have been decided on the basis that under s 61 of the *Registration of Titles Act*, where possession is not adverse, a proprietor takes title subject to the interest of 'any tenant of the land' notwithstanding that the interest is not notified on the certificate. On the facts of the case, though the appellant corporation entered the land as a trespasser, by the time the land was leased to the respondent the landowner had accepted it as her tenant or *kibanja* holder.

****

A purchaser with knowledge of unregistered claims over the land is not a bona fide purchaser.

Sempa Mbabali v W K Kidza and others
CS No 615 of 1969; [1985] HCB 46

[The plaintiff's father was the registered proprietor of the suit land. In his will, he devised the land to his children to be divided amongst them in certain portions except for 35 acres he had set aside as burial land. The land for burial was to be surveyed first and the remainder to be distributed to the beneficiaries in accordance with the will. Before the land was surveyed, Danze, one of the beneficiaries, sold his share of the land to the defendants. The latter surveyed the portion of the land they purportedly purchased from Danze and had the land registered in their name. Later it transpired that the land registered in the defendants' name included part of the land reserved for burial. The plaintiff brought this action on behalf of the deceased's estate for the registration to be cancelled on ground of fraud. The defendants claimed to be a bona fide purchasers for value without notice, and that their title was protected by s. 184(c) of the *Registration of Titles Act.*][18]

Odoki J:... A bona fide purchaser of legal estate for value without notice has an absolute unqualified and unanswerable defence against the claims of any prior equitable owner. The onus of proof lies on the person setting it up. It is a single plea, and is not sufficiently made out by proving purchase for value and leaving it to the plaintiff to prove notice if he can. In the present case, the defendants merely raised the plea in their pleading but they adduced no evidence to establish it. The defendants knew all along that part of the land they had purchased was for burial grounds and that Danze had sold them land before his share had been ascertained. The fact that they went ahead and surveyed the land they had purportedly bought from Danze before his portion was ascertained in accordance with the will, shows they were not bona fide purchasers without notice of the plaintiff's interest in the land reserved for burial grounds. They even removed boundary marks stones. The plea of bona fide purchaser therefore failed and the defendants were guilty of fraud and were not therefore protected by s 184 of the *Registration of Titles Act.*

****

Question

Are the facts of *Sempa Mbabali v W K Kidza* and others, *supra*, materially distinguishable from those of *Shah v Modern Sweet Mart Ltd*, *supra*? If so, in what way are they distinguishable? If not, which decision do you prefer and why?

****

Registration of title with knowledge that another person has filed a suit over the land does not necessarily constitute fraud.

Njuki v Musisi Nyanzi
HCCS No 0434 of 1996

[The plaintiff alleged that he purchased the disputed land in the 1940s from one Kintu, then the registered owner of the land. Kintu died sometime in the 1960s before executing transfer of the land to the plaintiff. The plaintiff did not personally occupy the land, but rather he appointed various caretakers to cultivate it. In 1995, the defendant claiming to have purchased the land from the executor of Kintu's estate, entered the land and started excavating the soil. The plaintiff lodged a caveat to protect his alleged equitable interest in the land pending the transfer of title in his name. In response, the defendant did likewise. Subsequently, the plaintiff applied for the removal of the defendant's caveat under s 149 of the *Registration of Titles Act.* The defendant's caveat lapsed and was removed. Meanwhile, the plaintiff instituted this action against the defendant claiming, inter alia, damages for trespass and injunction. Pending the disposal of the suit, the Registrar of Titles issued an order under s 175 of the *RTA* vesting the land in the plaintiff and registered him as proprietor. On the basis of his registration, the plaintiff pleaded that his title was unimpeachable. The defendant in response argued that the plaintiff was registered through fraud.]

Sebutinde J: ...In order for the Defendant to successfully impeach the Plaintiff's title on grounds of fraud, not only must he have clearly and distinctively pleaded the allegations of fraud against

[18] The facts and holding are based on the High Court Bulletin digest.

the Plaintiff but in addition he must strictly prove beyond a mere balance of probabilities, that in securing his title, the Plaintiff was guilty of dishonest or fraudulent act alleged or knew of such act by someone else and took advantage of it. The Defendant pleaded, '[T]he order of the Registrar of Titles vesting the suit property in the plaintiff ...was null and void on grounds of fraud'. The particulars of fraud are contained in sub-paragraphs (i) to (iii) of paragraph 14, and I shall examine each one.

Firstly, the Defendant alleged that, 'the Plaintiff obtained the vesting order knowing that the suit property had issues of contention and that the matter was before court'. Defendant's counsel argued that since the Plaintiff's suit ... was still pending, the Plaintiff should have waited for the outcome of the suit instead of dishonestly obtaining a vesting order and a certificate of title during the pendency of the suit in order to defeat the Defendant's equitable interest therein. It is a fact that the Plaintiff filed this suit on 07/05/96. It is also not in dispute that the vesting order was issued by the Registrar of Titles on 23/12/96 and that the registration of the Plaintiff as proprietor of the suit property occurred on the same day. Furthermore, [the Registrar of Titles] testified that in exercise of his powers ... under section 175 of the *RTA*, he examined the Plaintiff's application for a vesting order dated 12/09/96 and after satisfying himself that the suit property had been sold by the registered proprietor, the late JOSEPH DAUDI KINTU, to the Plaintiff on 01/08/47; that the purchase price due under the sale agreement ... had been fully paid and that there was no caveat on the Register or court injunction preventing the registration of the transfer, he issued the vesting order ...on 23/12/96 and on the same day registered the Plaintiff as proprietor of the suit property. In his testimony, the Defendant conceded that as at 23/12/96, he did not have a caveat on the Register in respect of the suit property (his earlier caveat having been vacated in April 1996); nor did he take out a temporary injunction restraining the registration of transfers or other dealings on the suit property pending the disposal of this suit. The above unchallenged evidence establishes that the plaintiff's vesting order and registration of title were indeed obtained during the pendency of this suit and that at that time, there was no legal impediment restraining the registration of dealings on the suit property. The Supreme Court has held that the English Law doctrine of *Lis pendens* (whereby a pending suit or proceedings affecting land and registered in the Register of pending actions, acts as a bar to the registration of transfers or other dealings on that land until such suit or proceeding has been disposed of), does not apply in Uganda and that instead the purchaser of land in Uganda protects himself either by a caveat or court injunction: J.W.KAZZORA vs. M.L.S.RUKUBA [CA No 13 of 1992]. In view of the evidence ...outlined above and in line with the above decision, I agree with the submissions of the Plaintiff's Counsel that on the 23/12/96, there existed no legal impediment preventing the Registrar of Titles from making the vesting order... or registering the suit property in the Plaintiff's names. Consequently, I find that there was no fraud or act of dishonesty or illegality on the part of the Registrar of Titles or of the plaintiff in the manner in which the vesting order or registration of title to the suit property was obtained.

[Her Honour dismissed the defendant's other arguments, and entered judgement for the plaintiff's favour.]

****

Notes

1. Butagira J held *In the Matter of Ruzhwengyibwa and in re Ruzigana* (see extract), that a proprietor is registered through fraud if he or she obtains title with knowledge that X, a rival claimant to the land, had already filed an action in a Magistrate's court asserting title. In that case, as it transpired, the Magistrate held that X was the owner of the subject land. It is arguable whether Butagira J would have held that the proprietor was registered th rough fraud had the Magistrate not held that X was the owner of the disputed land. In other words,

was the outcome in *re: Ruzhwengyibwa* influenced by the fact that the Magistrate had earlier held that X was the owner of the land in question? It suggested that it was.

2. In *Nakabiri and others v Masaka District Growers Co-operative* (CS No 835 of 1983; [1985] HCB 38), the plaintiffs sued for cancellation of the defendant's registration on ground of fraud. The plaintiffs' late father was originally the registered proprietor of the subject land. They alleged that a certain woman ('TP') tricked their late father into transferring and registering the land in her name. On realising this, the deceased lodged a caveat. TP sold the land to the defendant and it was registered as proprietor. The Registrar did not explain how the caveat was removed to facilitate the defendant's registration. The issue was whether the defendant was a bona fide purchaser. Manyindo J held that: 'The defendant union was not a bona fide purchaser for value as at the time of purchase the title was encumbered with caveats. The presumption must be that the defendant bought the land well knowing that its ownership was in dispute.'
3. Compare the above cases with the following case of the Supreme Court of Western Australian: *Milne Feeds Pty Ltd v Bride and others* (1993) 10 WAR 542. In the latter case, the defendant mortgaged his land to a bank. When he defaulted the bank sold the land to S Ltd, and it was registered as proprietor. The defendant sued the bank and S Ltd claiming that the sale by the bank was fraudulent and that S Ltd was either a party to the bank's fraud or had notice of it. Before the dispute was resolved, S Ltd sold the land to the plaintiff who proceeded to register the land in its name. It was not disputed that prior to purchase the plaintiff was aware of the defendant's claim over the land. In an action against the defendant to remove the caveat he lodged against the land, one of the issues was whether the plaintiff was registered through fraud. Malcolm CJ held that fraud is established by showing that the registered proprietor participated with knowledge of a dishonest and fraudulent design to deprive the other of their land. Knowledge here means actual knowledge or calculated abstention from inquiry. His Honour said that in this case the defendant had to prove that the transaction by which the bank sold to S Ltd was fraudulent, and that the transaction by which S Ltd sold to the plaintiff was fraudulent or that the plaintiff participated with knowledge that it was fraudulent. Malcolm CJ was emphatic that mere knowledge by the plaintiff that the defendant claimed to be a victim of fraud by the bank and S Ltd, was not proof of fraud against the plaintiff.

Questions

1. In view of the foregoing cases, would you say that registration with notice that ownership of the land is in dispute necessarily constitutes fraud? Why?
2. Assume that Lule is the registered proprietor of certain land. Patel disputes Lule's title and threatens to sue him for fraud. Meanwhile, Lule sells the land to Kabenge, who is aware of Patel's claim over the land. Kabenge is registered as proprietor. Does the fact that Kabenge was aware of Patel's claim mean that he was registered through fraud? If not, what sort of evidence does Patel need to adduce to establish that Kabenge was registered through fraud?

****

Judicial inroads on the concept of indefeasibility

Although section 61 of the RTA states that title of a registered proprietor is indefeasible except for the exceptions stated in the section, this has not prevented the courts from making further inroads to the concept of indefeasibility. In *Fraser v Walker and others* [1967] 1 AC 569 at p 585, Lord Wilberforce said:

> [T]heir Lordships have accepted the general principle that registration under the [Torrens System] confers upon a registered proprietor a title to the interest in respect of which he is registered which

> is ... immune from adverse claims, other than those specifically excepted. In doing so they wish to make it clear that this principle in no way denies the right of a plaintiff to bring against a registered proprietor a claim in personam, founded in law or in equity, for such relief as a court acting in personam may grant.

A claim *in personam* is a personal obligation assumed by the registered proprietor either before or after registration of title. For example, in the Australian case of *Bahr and another v Nicolay and others* (1988) 164 CLR 604, the proprietors prior to registration promised the former owner that they would re-transfer the land to them if they repaid the purchase price within a certain period. It was held that the promise was an *in personam* obligation, which in equity was binding on the proprietors. In the following case, the High Court justifies its right to enforce personal obligations against a proprietor on the basis of its power to make a vesting order under s 174 of the *RTA*.

****

The title of a trustee is not indefeasible against claims of the beneficiary.

Adonia v Mutekanga
[1970] E A 429

> In 1948, Mutekanga (respondent) was appointed as the heir and guardian of the estate of a deceased person, which included the disputed land. In 1950, he was registered as proprietor of the land. In 1955, the High Court ruled that Adonia, appellant, was the owner of the subject land. However, the respondent remained as the registered owner. In 1965 the High Court acting under s. 174 of the *Registration of Titles Act*, ruled that the respondent held the land as a trustee for the appellant and issued an order vesting the land in the appellant. Following that order the appellant was registered as proprietor of the subject land. The appellant sub-divided the land and sold part of it to another person. Subsequently, the respondent brought proceedings in the High Court claiming that he was the beneficiary of the residue of the land retained by the appellant. The trial Judge upheld the respondent's claim and set aside the vesting order with regard to the land retained by the respondent. The appellant contended, *inter alia*, that as a registered proprietor his title over the subject land was indefeasible.

Spry JA:... Mr. Kiwanuka (for the appellant) argued that ... the application for a vesting order could not have been competent, because the matter did not fall within the provisions of s.184 of the *Registration of Titles Act*....

I must with respect, disagree. The *Registration of Titles Act* is not a very satisfactory statute and some of its provisions appear to be in conflict with others. The Act must therefore be read as a whole if the intention of the legislature is to be ascertained. It is quite true, as Mr Kiwanuka says, that s.56 provides that a certificate of title 'shall be conclusive evidence that the person named in such certificate as the proprietor of or having any estate or interest in ... the land therein described is seized or possessed of such estate or interest'... [W]hile s.184 provides that 'No action of ejectment or other action for the recovery of any land shall lie or be sustained against the person registered as proprietor', except in certain specific cases none of which is here relevant. Section 174, however, enables the making of a vesting order, 'Whenever any person interested in land under the operation of the Act or any estate or interest therein appears to the High Court to be a trustee of such land, estate or interest within the intent and meaning of any law for the time being in force relating to trust and trustees.' ... In my view, the latter section cannot possibly be governed by s.184, as this would virtually deprive it of all meaning. Although the conception of the sanctity of the register runs through the Act, it is clear that the legislature intended to reserve to the High Court the power to enforce fiduciary obligations and it was expressly under this power that the Acting Chief Justice made his order of 5 May 1965.

Appeal dismissed in part. Sir Charles Newbold P and Duffus VP, agreed.

****

Overriding statutes

The principle of indefeasibility of title may be overridden by other legislation, as the following case illustrates.

****

The provisions of the Expropriated Property Act, 1982, override the principle of indefeasibility

Tanna v SR Munyinza and another

CA No 12 of 1992 (Supreme Court of Uganda); (1992) KALR 125

[The facts of the case are stated in the judgement of Oder JSC.]

Oder JSC: Briefly, the facts were that the suit property was originally owned by one Vipinchandra Dharatal Desai. On 21st December, 1965, Desai executed a legal mortgage in favour of Uganda Commercial Bank to secure repayment of shillings 43,000/= lent to him by the Bank. The mortgage was duly registered as an incumbrance on the suit property. In 1972, Desai left the country as a 'Departed Asian'. Consequently, the property was expropriated by the Uganda Government and, from August 1972, was vested in the 2nd respondent as the legal owner by virtue of the provisions of the *Assets of Departed Asians Decree*, 1973 (Decree No. 27 of 1973). Due to default in repayment the suit property was sold by public auction on 22nd February, 1982 on instructions of the bank as the mortgagee to recover the loan. The bank had express powers of sale in case of default under the mortgage. It was the appellant who bought the suit property at the auction. Attempts were subsequently made to register the transfer of the suit property to the appellant but the Registrar of Titles rejected the transfer. ... Pursuant to the Court Order of 27th March 1986, the appellant was registered as the proprietor.

Mr Sekandi, Counsel for the respondents submitted that as the Suit Property was an expropriated property, it was vested in the Government. This meant, therefore, that it was affected by the provisions of Section 1 of the *Expropriated Properties Act.*

Consequently, the registration of the transfer of the Suit Property to the appellant having been carried out after the Act had come into force; it meant that the sale and transfer was nullified by the Act. Regarding Section 56 of the *Registration of Titles Act*, Mr Sekandi submitted that that Section did not apply due to the operation of the 1982 Act.

As I have said elsewhere in this judgement the main point for decision in this appeal, in my view, is the effect of Section 1 of the *Expropriated Properties Act*, 1982. What is the validity of the sale of the Suit Property to the appellant in relation to the provisions of the Act? The relevant provisions of Section 1 of the Act state as follows:

1. Any property or business which was,

   Vested in the Government and transferred to the Departed Asians Property Custodian Board under *The Assets of Departed Asians Decree*, 1973. ...
   shall from the commencement of this Act, remain vested in the Government and be managed by the Ministry of Finance.

2. For the avoidance of doubt, and notwithstanding the provisions of any written law governing the conferring of title to land, property or business and the passing or transfer of such title it is hereby declared that,

(a) any purchases, transfers and grants of, or any dealings of whatever kind in, such property or business are hereby nullified; and

(b) where any property affected by this Section was at the time of its expropriation held under a lease or an agreement for a lease, or any other specified tenancy of whatever description, and where such lease, terminated, the same shall be deemed to have continued, and to continue in force until such property has been dealt with in accordance with this Act: and for such further period as the Minister may by regulations made under this Act prescribe.

This Act, in my view, *was the culmination of various statutes which had previously applied to what is commonly known as the property or business of "Departed Asians"*. Its purpose, as stated in the preamble, was

> To provide for the transfer of the properties and businesses acquired or otherwise expropriated during the Military regime to the Ministry of Finance, to provide for the return to the former owners or disposal of the same by Government and to provide for other matters connected with or incidental thereto.

Section 1(1)(a) provides that any property or business which was vested in the Government and transferred to the Departed Asians Property Custodian Board under the *Assets of Departed Asians Decree*, 1973 shall, from commencement of the Act, remain vested in the Government and managed by the Ministry of Finance. The properties or businesses which Section 1 of the Act declared as remaining vested in the Government had been earlier vested in the Government by Section 4, and transferred to the Departed Property Custodian Board by Section 13, of the *Assets of Departed Asians Decree*, 1973. In the circumstances, all that Section 1 (1) of the Act seems to have done is to have vested such properties or businesses back in the Government. In addition, Section 1 (2) (a) of the Act also nullified certain transactions with regard to such properties or businesses. As I understand it, the meaning of Section 1 (2) (a) of the Act appears to be this:

(i) It nullified any:
   (a) purchases,
   (b) transfers and grants of or
   (c) dealings of whatever kind in
(ii) properties now vested in the Government.
(iii) Such transactions were nullified notwithstanding the provisions of any written law governing the conferring of title and the passing or transfer of such title to
   (a) land,
   (b) property or
   (c) business.

The Suit Property in the instant case had been owned by a departed Asian prior to 1972. As the agreed facts at the trial indicate, the Suit Property was expropriated by the Government and put under the control of the Departed Asians Property Custodian Board ... In the circumstances there would be no doubt that the Suit Property was one of those to which the Expropriated Properties Act, 1982 applied. Section 1 (a) of the Act vested it back in the Government and brought it under the management of the Ministry of Finance. Consequently, in my view, if any of the transactions listed in Section 1(2)(a) above was carried out in respect of the Suit Property, such transaction was nullified by that Section, if the transaction was effected between the time when the Suit Property was first vested in Government by the *Assets of Departed Asians Decree*, 1973 and the time when the Act of 1983 came into force, namely on 21st February, 1983.

Further, according to the agreed facts the Suit Property was sold to and purchased by the appellant on 22nd February, 1982 in the process of enforcement by U.C.B. of its rights of sale as a mortgagee. Consequent to the sale and purchase U.C.B. transferred the title of the Suit Property to the appellant. The purchase and transfer in question were, in my view, nullified by Section 1 (2)(a) of the Act notwithstanding any written law under which U.C.B. was entitled to sell and transfer the Suit Property as the mortgagee to the appellant.

The sale to and purchase by the appellant having been nullified by the Act of 1982, I do not think that it is necessary to consider in this appeal whether or not the procedure of sale was carried out in accordance with the provisions of the *Mortgage Decree*, 1974, or whether or not notice was given to the mortgagor before the sale. For the same reasons, I also think that it is not necessary to consider the effect on the transactions in question of the provisions of Section 56 of the *Registration of Titles Act* (cap. 205).

In the result, I would dismiss this appeal with costs.
(Wambuzi CJ and Platt JSC agreed)

****

Notes

1. The above case was followed in *Makerere Properties Ltd v Attorney General* (CA No 36 of 1996,unreported, Court of Appeal of Uganda). In that case, Makerere Properties Ltd (appellant) was the registered proprietor of the suit property. In 1972, all its directors were expelled from Uganda subsequent to which the property fell under the management of the Departed Asians Property Custodian Board (DAPCB). In 1981 the DAPCB acting under s 17(3) of Decree 27 of 1973, purported to return the property not to the appellant company but to S A Pirani, one of its directors. The latter sold the land to Karia who had the land registered in his name. In subsequent proceedings the High Court found that the purported return of the land to S.A Pirani was fraudulent. The Divestiture Committee dealing with expropriated property advised the Minister to issue to the appellant a certificate of repossession for the property. However, the Minister declined to issue the certificate on the ground that the property had already been returned to the owner. The High Court upheld the Minister's decision. Moreover, it held that the land was already registered in Karia's name. On appeal, Twinomujuni JA held: 'In my judgement the principles which were applied in [*Tanna v SR Rosemary Muniyinza and Another*] fully apply to the instant case. Any purported return of the suit property to S.A.Pirani in 1981 and the subsequent registration of the property into the names of M.R.Karia were both nullified by Act 9 of 1982 as they were both affected between 1973 and 21st February 1983.' (Egwau JA and Manyindo DCJ, concurred).
2. Section 3 of the *Registration of Titles Act* (cap 205), provides that unless enacted to the contrary, 'no Act or rule so far as is inconsistent with this Act shall apply or be deemed to apply to land ... which is under the operation of this Act.' Clearly, the *Expropriated Properties Act* is one of the legislations that expressly overrides the *Registration of Titles Act.* Also under the *Land Act*, 1998, s. 4(c) renders mailo land subject to customary and statutory rights of lawful and bona fide occupants, and s. 32 renders title of a registered proprietor subject to the interest of a tenant by occupancy.
3. Notwithstanding s. 3 of the *RTA,* its provisions may be overridden impliedly by subsequent inconsistent legislation in accordance with statutory rules of interpretation. These principles are discussed in the case of *Sejjaka Nalima v Rebecca Musoke* CA No 12 of 1985; [1992] 5 KALR 132 (see excerpt below). Thus, for example, though the *Land Act*, 1998, does not expressly say so, it is suggested that its provisions supersede conflicting provisions of the *Registration of Titles Act.* For example, where a landowner sells 'family' land contrary to s. 40 of the *Land Act*, the transaction is void notwithstanding that the purchaser was a bona fide purchaser for value without notice and his or her title is registered under the *Registration of Titles Act.*

Question

Kyeyo, a Ugandan business person residing in London, enters into negotiations to purchase certain customary land from members of a certain clan who own the land. Gava, a trespasser on the land, forges the clan leader's signature on a document offering to sell the land to Kyeyo. The latter, unaware of the forgery, buys the land and pays the money to Gava. Subsequently Kyeyo is registered as proprietor of the land under the *Registration of Titles Act.* Gava absconds with the money and his whereabouts are unknown. The clan members seek your legal advice as to their claim over the subject land. (It is suggested that your advice should take into account the possible effect of the *Land Act* upon the provisions of the *Registration of Titles Act.*)

****

REMEDIES

Registrar's powers to cancel a certificate

Under s.69 of the RTA, the Registrar of Titles has the power to recall a certificate in certain cases, including where a certificate has been issued in error or through fraud. Section 92 of the *Land Act,* 1998, gives the Registrar similar powers. Under the latter provision, the Registrar of Titles has the power to call, cancel, and issue a fresh certificate in circumstances mentioned in the section. These include where a certificate is issued in error, contains a misdescription, is wrongly or illegally obtained or retained. Before exercising his or her powers, the Registrar is required to give a fair hearing to the parties concerned and there is a right of appeal to the District Land Tribunal.

****

Power of the registrar to cancel a certificate obtained by fraud

Rurangaranga v Mbarara Municipal Council
CA No 10 of 1996 (unreported)

[In 1974, Mbarara Town Council granted a 2-year lease to the second and third respondents and a certificate of title was issued to them. There was a tacit understanding that they would be granted a longer term if they developed the land within that period. The respondents proceeded to develop the land, which included construction of a building. When the lease expired, they were given a 1-year extension to allow them to complete the building. No certificate was issued for the extension but the Council gave the respondents permission for temporary occupation of the land. During the civil war that led to the toppling of the Amin regime, the respondents left Mbarara and authorised a third party to manage the land. Shortly thereafter, the appellant applied to the Council for a lease over the subject land. The Council's 'Technical Committee' purportedly terminated the respondent's lease and granted a 49-year lease to the appellant. The latter had the lease registered in his name. Three years later when the respondents returned to Mbarara, the Council 'returned' the land to them. The appellants sued the Council and the two respondents to recover the land claiming that their title was indefeasible. In their defence, the respondents alleged that the appellant obtained the lease by connivance with some Council officials. The respondents counter-claimed for an order to the Registrar to cancel registration of the appellant's lease on the ground of fraud. The trial Judge granted the order, hence the appeal.]

Wambuzi CJ: … …What is the effect if a title to land is issued without authority as in this case? The matter was not argued nor did the learned trial judge allude to it. He appears to have assumed that nothing could be done unless fraud was proved. In his own words:

> This does not, however, dispose of this case because the plaintiff is the registered title holder of Plot 13 Mahkan Singh Street, and the registration can only be challenged - S. (1) (C) (sic) in case of a person deprived of any land by fraud as against the person registered as proprietor of such land through fraud.

I am not so sure that this is entirely correct. In so far as is relevant S.69 of the *Registration of Titles Act* provides:

> In case it appears to the satisfaction of the Registrar that any certificate of title or instrument has been issued in error.... or that any entry or endorsement has been made in error on any certificate of title or instrument, or that any certificate of title, instrument, entry or endorsement has been fraudulently or wrongfully obtained, or that.... any certificate of title or instrument is fraudulently or wrongfully retained, he may by writing require the person to whom such document has been so issued or by

> whom it has been so obtained or is retained to deliver up the same for the purpose of being cancelled or corrected or given to the proper party, as the case requires...

On the face of it, it would appear that the Registrar of Titles has power to cancel a certificate fraudulently or wrongfully obtained or retained. In my view, it was open to the court in the case before us to declare that the certificate of title was wrongfully obtained. This would open the way for the second and third respondents to pursue their rights before the first respondent and the Registrar of Titles. I am aware of the provisions of Sections 56 and 184 of the *Registration of Titles Act*, but in this case the action was brought by the appellant and not by the respondents and I see no valid reason in law to prevent the second and the third respondents who were in possession of the property in question from pursuing any rights they may have had under S.69 of Registration of Titles Act.

I am also aware that these matters were not pleaded but the case appears to have been conducted and evidence adduced around the general theme as to whether or not the lease to the appellant was properly granted. On the pleadings, the first respondent denied it legally granted any lease to the appellant.

Be that as it may, the court went on to consider whether fraud had been established. On the evidence before him, the learned trial Judge found that Bainomugisha, the land agent, orchestrated the appropriation of the suit property with the assistance of the then Town Clerk, Banyu and thus defrauded the second and third defendants.

Quite rightly in my view the learned trial judge posed the question,

> Whether the plaintiff was part of the fraud himself or was aware of the fraud on the part of somebody else, in this case on the part of Bainomugisha and Banyu.

He then made the curious finding that,

> The plaintiff obtained registration of his title under the *Registration of Titles Act* by applying to the Registrar of Titles and producing those supporting documents that he was required to produce. Hence, the act of registration was not in itself fraudulent but presumably tainted with fraud.

The question to ask is what were the supporting documents that were required to be produced? If those documents included or were based on the grant of the lease by the Council, the learned trial Judge found the relevant minute was false as the Council did not grant nor authorise the granting of the said lease. The purported offer of the lease to the appellant the learned trial Judge found on the evidence to have been the work of Bainomugisha purporting to be authorised by the Council. What evidence did the appellant put before the Registrar of Titles that he had been granted the lease by the Council for the issuance of the certificate of Title?

It would appear to me that an application for registration which to the knowledge of the applicant is based on an unauthorised grant is in itself fraudulent in so far as it is a false representation to the Registrar of Titles that the lease had been granted by the Council. ...

For my own part I am satisfied on the evidence that:

(1) The appellant knew that the property he had applied for had been developed or substantially developed by another person and he lied about it in his evidence.

(2) Through his lawyers, the appellant was assured that the property had been withdrawn from the first developer. Exh. ER 7 is a detailed letter by the Town Clerk giving details of the lease offer to the third party, the expiry of the lease, a copy of the letter of the Land Agent suggesting appropriate action, a copy of the minute of the General Purpose Committee and resolution not to extend the lease of the third party. One would have expected the same letter which gave such details regarding withdrawal of the first offer to provide similar details regarding the grant of the lease to the appellant, such as date of the meeting of the Council, the minute regarding the decision of the Council, etc. On the contrary this important issue is dealt with in one sentence:

> The whole matter is in order and you can advise your client to go ahead with payment for the property.

This lends support to the inference that those details were not there. In other words, that there was no meeting of the Council and no decision to grant the lease to the appellant by the Council.

(3) It is admitted by the appellant that there was no Council at the material time but there was no indication in the Court below or before us of under what authority the officials acted for the Council.

On the evidence I am unable to fault the learned trial Judge's conclusion that the appellant was aware that his application had not been considered or granted by the Council and he knew of the fraud on the Land Office by the Council officials and he took advantage of it by applying and obtaining a lease in respect of the property in question.

I would dismiss the appeal against the decision of the lower court on the issue of fraud and related orders.

(Karokora JSC, delivered a similar judgement. Tsekooko JSC dissented.)

****

Questions

1. Do the Registrar's powers under the *RTA* and the *Land Act* to recall and or cancel a certificate of title constitute an exception to indefeasibility of title? Give reasons.
2. On what basis did the Court find that the appellant in *Rurangaranga v Mbarara Municipal Council*, was registered through fraud? Was it on the basis that he participated in fraud of the Council officers or on the ground, that he had notice of the fraud?

****

Judicial remedies

Cancellation of certificate

Under s. 185 of the *Registration of Titles Act*, the High Court has the power to direct cancellation of a certificate of title in circumstances mentioned in the section:

> Upon the recovery of any land, estate or interest by any proceeding from the person registered as proprietor thereof, it shall be lawful for the High Court in any case in which such proceeding is not herein expressly barred, to direct the Registrar to cancel any certificate of title or instrument, or any entry or memorial in the Register Book relating to such land, estate or interest, and to substitute such certificate of title or entry as the circumstances of the case require and the Registrar shall give effect to such order.

In the case of *Lwanga v Registrar of Titles* [1980] HCB 24 (see extract above), Odoki J held:

> Before a person who has obtained judgement for the recovery of land against a registered proprietor could be registered as proprietor, he first had to apply to the court to make an order under s 185 *RTA*. Such order was referred to as a consequential order since it was made consequent upon the recovery land. This was the only method prescribed by the *RTA* for executing orders of decrees relating to registered land

****

The High Court may issue an order for cancellation of a certificate of title under s 185 RTA, consequent upon proceedings in lower courts.

In the Matter of Ruzhwengyibwa and In the Matter of Ruzigana
Misc C No 48 of 1976 (unreported)

[The applicant and the respondent asserted rival claims over the subject land. While the dispute was going on, the respondent applied for a certificate of title in respect of his land, including the disputed land. The applicant complained to the District surveyor but in vain. He then instituted a suit in the Magistrates court seeking an order that he was the rightful owner of the land. Before the court determined the matter the respondent went ahead and obtained a certificate of title, which included the disputed land. The suit in the Magistrate's court continued. Subsequently, the Magistrate held that the applicant was the owner of the disputed land. This is an application by way of Notice of Motion for an order under s 185 of the *Registration of Titles Act*, directing the Registrar to cancel or alter the certificate of title of the suit land on the ground that the respondent was registered through fraud and/or wrong description of the land.]

Butagira J: ...[His Honour found that a Magistrate's court has jurisdiction to entertain a suit concerning registered land.] What a Magistrate's court cannot do is to order cancellation of Title. This power is reserved to the High Court under section 185 of the *Registration of Titles Act*... It is my considered opinion that though a Magistrate's court cannot order a cancellation of Title, its decision declaring the land or part of it affected by the Title to belong to one of the parties to the dispute, can be relied on to support an action in the High Court for cancellation of Title on the ground of fraud or misdescription. This of course presupposes that the judgement of the Magistrate's court has concluded the matter i.e. it has not been upset either on appeal or otherwise or no appeal has been made. As matters stand now, in my opinion the judgement of the trial court has finally determined the matter in dispute between the parties.

...The judgement of the trial court though delivered after the respondent had obtained Title, deals with a suit which was filed before the title was applied for. The title was therefore, applied for by the respondent fully knowing well that part of the land applied for was subject to dispute between him and the applicant. Knowledge of other persons' rights or claims and the deliberate acquisition of a registered title in the face of such knowledge has been held to be a fraud in a number of cases from Australia, see *Davis v Wekey* (1872) 3 U,L,R.D, *Bell v Beckman* (1889) 10 NSW Esq. 251... I respectfully agree that in such circumstances fraud has been committed. In my opinion, what the respondent did in this case amounted to fraud, and I so hold. The applicant is therefore entitled to come to this court pursuant to section 184 and 185 of the *Registration of Titles Act* to have the title cancelled or altered. I make this order pursuant to section 185 of the *Registration of Titles Act*, directing the Registrar of Titles to alter the certificate of Title... by cancelling from it the portion of the land which belongs to the applicant....

****

Notes

1. In *re: Lubwama* (Misc C No 4 of 1990 (unreported); [1991] HCB 74, a Magistrate Grade II, convicted the registered proprietor of the offence of obtaining registration of the subject land by false pretence contrary to s. 296 of the *Penal Code Act*. The Magistrate ordered that the land be restored to its proper owner. The issue was whether the Magistrate had the power to make such order. Karokora J held that the trial magistrate had the jurisdiction to try the said offence and to declare, on the basis of the evidence before him, that the transfer was void under s. 76 of the *Registration of Titles Act*. Further, that an order stemming from a criminal case such as the instant one can form a basis for a consequential order under s. 185 of the *RTA*. However, His Honour held that:

> [W]hereas a Magistrate could declare a transaction or transfer null and void, and whereas he can order restoration of the land to the rightful owner, the effect of the consequential order under section 185 of the *RTA* was within the exclusive jurisdiction of the High Court. It was only the High Court which had the exclusive jurisdiction to make an order directing the Chief Registrar of Titles... to cancel the name of the guilty party from the register of titles and substitute it with the name of the rightful owner.

2. Under s. 77(1)(d) of the *Land Act*, the District Land Tribunal has the jurisdiction to make consequential orders relating to cancellation of entries on certificates of title or cancellation of title and vesting of title in cases handled by lower land tribunals. Except during the transitional period (s 98 of the *Land Act*), Magistrates' courts no longer have jurisdiction to deal with any disputes involving land. Such jurisdiction is vested with the Land Tribunals and the High Court. However, it is arguable that in cases similar to *In re: Lubwama, supra*, which strictly are not cases of land disputes but rather criminal offences, the Magistrate's courts retain their jurisdiction to determine whether the registered proprietor committed a criminal offence. It is submitted that on the basis of a Magistrate's judgement, the true owner of the land could apply to the District Land Tribunal or the High Court for a consequential order for cancellation of the certificate under s 185 of the *Registration of Titles Act.* See also *In the Matter of Ruzhwengyibwa and in re: Ruzigana, supra.*
3. In *Kazzora v Rukuba* CA No 13 of 1992, unreported, it was held that doctrine of *lis pendens* (whereby a pending suit affecting land registered in the Register of pending actions, acts as a bar to the registration of dealings affecting that land until action is disposed of) does not apply in Uganda. Accordingly, the only way to protect an unregistered claim is by lodging a caveat or by injunction. See also *Njuki v Musisi Nyanzi* HCCS No 0434 of 1996.
4. The issue whether notice of rival claims to land constitutes fraud, is dealt with in a number of cases extracted above.

Question

If you were counsel for the applicant in *re Ruzhwengyibwa and Ruzigana, supra*, and heard that the respondent had made an application for a certificate of title over the disputed land, what legal steps would you have taken to protect your client's interests? See s 17 of the *Registration of Titles Act.* See also *Acar and others v Acar-Aliro* (CA No 30 of 1982 (unreported); [1982] HCB 60.

****

A donee of land may apply for a vesting order as proprietor under s 185 of the RTA.

In Re Mutaka

MISC C. No. 81 of 1976; [1980] HCB 27

> [P B was the registered proprietor of the subject land. He donated the land to the applicant, but died before title was transferred to the applicant. The applicant sues for a vesting order as proprietor of the land.][19]

Odoki AG: This was an application under s.185 *Registration of Titles Act* and 0.34 r. 7 Civil Procedure Rules for an order directing the Registrar of Titles... to remove caveats lodged on [certain] ...mailo land then registered in the name of one Paulo Bakunga (deceased), and register the same in the names of the applicant, Ivan Mutaka. The general ground of the application was that the applicant was the son of the late Paulo Bakunga and by way of a gift *inter vivos* evidenced in writing and dated December 13th 1933, the deceased gave the said land to the applicant.

In the affidavit supporting the application, the applicant swore that he was the son of the late Paul Bakunga Nsubuga, who died without having effected a transfer thereof; that in 1934, and

[19] The facts of the case and the holding are based on the High Court Bulletin digest

1936, the Registrar of Titles lodged caveats on the deceased's land and that the caveats had never been removed; that it was decided in the Principal Court Civil Suit No. 327 of 1958 and upheld in Uganda High Court Civil Appeal No. 149 of 1561 that the applicant was entitled to the land his father had given him; that after the overthrow of the Buganda government he unsuccessfully sought from the Administrator General, a grant of a certificate of succession so that the Registrar could transfer the land into his names; and that, he was the lawful successor to the land in question...

The Assistant Registrar of Titles Mityana testified that the land comprised in Block 425 (c) was already registered in the name of the applicant subject to the caveats lodged by the Registrar of Titles. With regard the land comprised in Blocks 161 and 82, the applicant lodged his caveat in 1934, claiming an interest therein by gift inter vivos, and that the Registrar of Titles had also lodged caveats thereon on behalf of other beneficiaries. The witness further said that if the applicant wanted to have the land registered in his name, he should first obtain a certificate of succession or letters of administration.

Held

1. In order to rely on the provisions of s.185 *RTA* and have the Registrar book rectified by cancellation, an applicant who invokes it has to satisfy the court that he had recovered the land, estate or any interest in question by any proceeding from the person already registered as proprietor thereof.
2. For purposes of the condition stated above, a 'proprietor' means the owner where in possession, remainder, reversion or otherwise of land or of lease or mortgage whose name appears or is entered as the proprietor thereof in the Register book and includes the donee of a power to appoint or dispose of the same (*RTA* s.2).
3. The Principal Court of Mengo declared, in Civil Suit no.327/58 (*Paulo Kamya v. Samusoni Mukasa & others*), that the land which the applicant sought to be transferred into his names was granted to him *inter vivos* by the late Paulo Babunga but also noted that the deceased died before executing a transfer in favour of the applicant.
4. Although the plaintiff in that suit was the 'head heir' of the deceased land, the 100 acres of land in dispute in the Principal Court were already registered in the names of the second defendant. And the land granted by one Paulo Gabunga deceased to the applicant was also found, by the court, to be still registered in the deceased's names. Accordingly, the plaintiff, whose name did not appear on the Register book and who was not a donee of power to dispose of the land, was not the registered proprietor of the land in dispute but merely a claimant thereof.
5. Accordingly, even if the applicant obtained judgement against the plaintiff in the suit before the Principal Court, he did not thereby obtain judgement against the registered proprietor of the land in a way that would enable him to maintain on application under s.185 *RTA*.
6. The proper course for the applicant would, in the circumstances, have been to proceed under s.175 *RTA* which empowers the Registrar of Titles to make a vesting order in cases of completed purchase or alternatively to proceed under s.143 *RTA* which deals with registration of title following succession on death.
7. In order to invoke and rely on the provisions of s.175, *RTA*, and before the court can make a vesting order, the following circumstances must provide:
   (a) that there has been a sale of land the title of which is registered under the Act;
   (b) that the whole of the purchase price has been paid;
   (c) that the purchaser (or those claiming under him) has taken possession of the land;
   (d) that the entry into possession by the purchaser has been acquiesced in by the vendor or his representatives;
   (e) that a transfer had not been executed and cannot be obtained because,

(i) the vendor is dead or
(ii) the vendor is residing out of the jurisdiction or
(iii) the vendor cannot be found (*Re: Trustee of Lugave Clan* [1960] E.A.322).

8. The word 'purchaser', in the technical sense does not denote a person who buys land but one to whom land is expressly transferred by act of the parties as for instance by conveyance on sale, by gift or by valuable consideration and includes a person who, for valuable consideration, acquires an interest in property.
9. A sale, imports the idea of a transfer of a right of property in consideration of a sum of money but there may be instances where there is a conveyance or sale when the transaction is not properly a sale in the ordinary understanding of the word because it is not for money (*Coats_J & Pty Ltd. v. Inland Revenue Commissioners* (1897) 1 Q.B.)
10. As the rights of a purchaser under a sale for money and those of a donee of the gift against the vendor or donor should be identical under the *Registration of Titles Act*, a gift of land inter vivos can properly be described as or equated to a sale on purchase of land for the purposes of s.175 *RTA*. Accordingly, a transferee by gift inter vivos could apply for a vesting order under s.175 *RTA* if he fulfils the conditions laid thereunder and since the applicant did, he was entitled to apply for such an order.
11. Although s.143 *RTA* deals with registration of titles upon succession on death the applicant could obtain registration of the land gifted to him thereunder after obtaining a certificate of succession or letters of administration from the Administrator General.

****

Notes

The case of *In Re: Mutaka*, raises an interesting proposition in relation to the rights of a donee *inter vivos* of land. At common law, a gift of land (or any other property), *inter vivos*, is not effective unless effected by transfer of a complete legal title to the donee. In the context of the *Registration of Titles Act,* title is transferred by registration under the Act (s. 51). In the instant case since the deceased died before the transfer was registered, the gift to the applicant was incomplete at law. The rule of equity is that the court will not assist a volunteer to perfect an incomplete gift. In other words, as far as equity is concerned property in a gift does not pass to the donee until the donor has done all that needs to be done to effect a transfer of a legal title. If the donor has not done so, the court of equity cannot assist the donee to complete the transaction (*Milroy v Lord* [1861-73] AA ER Rep 783). The issue is, what is the minimum requirement under the Torrens system, for the court of equity to be satisfied that the donor had done all that needs to be done to complete the transfer of title? This issue did not arise in *re Mutaka.* In Australia, the High Court in *Corin v Patton* ([1990] 92 ALR 1) held, *obiter dictum*, that the donor must have done all that which needs to be done to enable the legal transfer to be effected without further action on the donor's part. That stage is only reached where the donor has signed an instrument of transfer in a registrable form and handed it over to the donee together with a certificate of title (or authority to procure the certificate from whoever has it) to enable registration. From the brief facts in *re: Mutaka* it is not clear as to whether the deceased had signed all the necessary documents and whether the Court had in mind the common law rule in relation to incomplete gifts.

****

Compensation for deprivation of land

Under s. 186 *RTA,* a person deprived of land may seek compensation from whoever wrongfully deprived him or her of the land. In certain circumstances he or she is entitled to seek compensation from the Government.

> *Section 186.* Any person deprived of land or of any estate or interest in land in consequence of fraud or through the bringing of such land under the operation of this Act or by the registration of any other person as proprietor of such land, estate or interest or in consequence of any error or misdescription in any registered certificate of title or in any entry or memorial in the Register Book may bring and prosecute an action for the recovery of damages against the person upon whose application such land was brought under the operation of this Act, or such erroneous registration was made, or who acquired title to the estate or interest through such fraud, error or misdescription:

Provided that:

(a) except in the case of fraud or of error occasioned by any omission, misrepresentation or misdescription in the application of such person to bring such land under the operation of this Act or to be registered as proprietor of such land, estate or interest or in any instrument signed by him such person shall upon a transfer of such land *bona fide* for value cease to be liable for the payment of any damage which but for such transfer might have been recovered from him under the provisions herein contained; and in such last-mentioned case, and also in case the person against whom such action for damages is directed to be brought as aforesaid is dead or has been adjudged bankrupt or cannot be found within the jurisdiction of the High Court, then and in any such case such damages with costs of action may be recovered from the Government; and

(b) in estimating such damages the value of all buildings and other improvements erected or made subsequently to the deprivation shall be excluded.

See also sections 187-194. The limitation period for bringing action under the Act is six years from the date of deprivation, see s 196.

10
Leases

STATUTORY DEFINITION OF LEASEHOLD

Section 4(5) of the *Land Act,* 1998, defines leasehold as a form of tenure:

(a) created either by contract or by operation of law;

(b) the terms and conditions of which may be regulated by law to the exclusion of any contractual agreement reached between the parties;

(c) under which one person namely, the landlord or lessor, grants or is deemed to have granted another person namely the tenant or lessee exclusive possession of land usually but not necessarily for a period defined, directly or indirectly, by reference to a specific date of commencement and a specific date of ending;

(d) usually but not necessarily in return for a rent which may be for a capital sum known as a premium or for both a rent and a premium but may be in return for services or may be free of any required return;

(e) under which both the landlord and the tenant may, subject to the terms and conditions of the lease and having due regard for the interests of the other, exercise such of the powers of a freehold owner as are appropriate and possible given the specific nature of a leasehold tenure.

****

ESSENTIAL FEATURES OF A LEASE

At common law there are two essential features of a lease:

1. Exclusive possession and
2. Certainty of duration.

Both features are illustrated below. Although virtually in all leases the tenant pays rent, the requirement for rent payment is not an essential feature of a lease either at common law or under s 4(5) of the *Land Act.*

****

Exclusive possession

The main distinction between a lease and a licence is that a lessee has a right to exclusive possession of the land.

****

If a person is granted exclusive possession for a term, in law he or she is a lessee regardless of the subjective intention of the parties.

Street v Mountford
[1985] 2 ALL ER 289

[The respondent, Street, granted the appellant, Mrs Mountford, the right to occupy certain furnished rooms, subject to termination by 14 days' written notice and subject to other terms stipulated in the agreement. The question raised by this appeal is whether the agreement created a tenancy or a licence.]

Lord Templeman: ... Counsel for Mrs Mountford seeks to reaffirm and re-establish the traditional view that an occupier of land for a term at a rent is a tenant providing the occupier is granted exclusive possession. It is conceded on behalf of Mr Street that the agreement dated 7 March 1983 granted exclusive possession to Mrs Mountford. The traditional view that the grant of exclusive possession for a term at a rent creates a tenancy is consistent with the elevation of a tenancy into an estate in land. The tenant possessing exclusive possession is able to exercise the rights of an owner of land, which is in the real sense his land albeit temporarily and subject to certain restrictions. A tenant armed with exclusive possession can keep out strangers and keep out the landlord unless the landlord is exercising limited rights reserved to him by the tenancy agreement to enter and view and repair. A licensee lacking exclusive possession can in no sense call the land his own and cannot be said to own any estate in the land. The licence does not create an estate in the land to which it relates but only makes an act lawful which would otherwise be unlawful.

Counsel for Mr Street relies on recent authorities which, he submits, demonstrate that an occupier granted exclusive possession for a term at a rent may nevertheless be a licensee if, in the words of Slade LJ in the present case, 'there is manifested the clear intentions of both parties that the rights granted are to be merely those of a personal right of occupation and not those of a tenant'. In the present case, it is submitted, the provisions of the agreement ... manifest the clear intention of both parties that the rights granted are to be those of a personal nature and not those of a tenant....

There can be no tenancy unless the occupier enjoys exclusive possession; but an occupier who enjoys exclusive possession is not necessarily a tenant. He may be owner in fee simple, a trespasser, a mortgagee in possession, an object of charity or a service occupier. To constitute a tenancy the occupier must be granted exclusive possession for a fixed or periodic term certain in consideration of a premium or periodical payments. The grant may be express, or may be inferred where the owner accepts weekly or other periodic payments from the occupier

Occupation by service occupier may be eliminated. A service occupier is a servant who occupies his master's premises in order to perform his duties as a servant. In those circumstances the possession and occupation of the servant is treated as the possession and occupation of the master and the relationship of landlord and tenant is not created: see *Mayhew v Suttle* (1854) 4 E & B 347, 119 ER 137. The test is whether the servant requires the premises he occupies in order the better to perform his duties as a servant. ...

In the present case the ... agreement ...professed an intention by both parties to create a licence and their belief that they had in fact created a licence. It was submitted on behalf of Mr Street that the court cannot in these circumstances decide that the agreement created a tenancy without interfering with the freedom of contract enjoyed by both parties. My Lords, Mr Street enjoyed freedom to offer Mrs Mountford the right to occupy the rooms comprised in the agreement on such lawful terms as Mr Street pleased. Mrs Mountford enjoyed freedom to negotiate with Mr Street to obtain different terms. Both parties enjoyed freedom to contract or not to contract and both parties exercised that freedom by contracting on the terms set forth in the written agreement and on no other terms. But the consequences in law of the agreement, once concluded, can only be determined by consideration of the effect of the agreement. If the agreement satisfied all the requirements of a tenancy, then the agreement produced a tenancy and the parties cannot alter the effect of the agreement by insisting that they only created a licence. The manufacture of a five-pronged implement for manual digging results in a fork even if the manufacturer, unfamiliar with the English language, insists that he intended to make and has made a spade....

Errington v Errington [1952] 1 All ER 149, [1952] 1 KB 290 concerned a contract by a father to allow his son to buy the father's house on payment of the instalments of the father's building society loan. Denning L J referred (see [1952] 1 All ER 149 at 154, [1952] 1 KB 290 at 297) to the judgement of Lord Greene MR in *Booker v Palmer* where, however, the circumstances and the conduct of the parties negatived any intention to enter into legal relationships. Denning LJ continued ([1952] a All ER 149 at 154-155, [1952] 1 KB 290 at 297-298):

> We have had many instances lately of occupiers in exclusive possession who have been held to be not tenants, but only licensees – when a requisitioning authority allowed people into possession at a weekly rent ... when a landlord told a tenant on his retirement that he could live in a cottage rent free for the rest of his days ... when a landlord, on the death of the widow of a statutory tenant, allowed her daughter to remain in possession, paying rent for six months: *Marcroft Wagons, Ltd v Smith*; when the owner of a shop allowed the manager to live in a flat above the shop, but did not require him to do so, and the value of the flat was taken into account at £1 a week in fixing his wages ... In each of those cases the occupier was held to be a licensee and not a tenant ... The result of all these cases is that, although a person who is let into exclusive possession is, prima facie, to be considered a tenant, nevertheless he will not be held to be so if the circumstances negative any intention to create a tenancy. Words alone may not suffice. Parties cannot turn a tenancy into a licence merely by calling it one. But if the circumstances and the conduct of the parties show that all that was intended was that the occupier should be granted a personal privilege with no interest in the land, he will be held only to be a licensee.

In *Errington v Errington* and in the cases cited by Denning L J there were exceptional circumstances which negatived the prima facie intention to create a tenancy, notwithstanding that the occupier enjoyed exclusive occupation. The intention to create a tenancy was negatived if the parties did not intend to enter into legal relationships at all, or where the relationship between the parties was that of vendor and purchaser, master and service occupier, or where the owner, a requisitioning authority, had no power to grant a tenancy. These exceptional circumstances are not to be found in the present case, where there has been the lawful, independent and voluntary grant of exclusive possession for a term at a rent.

If the observations of Denning LJ are applied to the facts of the present case it may fairly be said that the circumstances negative any intention to create a mere licence. Words alone do not suffice. Parties cannot turn a tenancy into a licence merely by calling it one. The circumstances and the conduct of the parties show that what was intended was that the occupier should be granted exclusive possession at a rent for a term with a corresponding interest in the land which created a tenancy. ...

My Lords, the only intention which is relevant is the intention demonstrated by the agreement to grant exclusive possession for a term at a rent. Sometimes it may be difficult to discover whether, on the true construction of an agreement, exclusive possession is conferred. Sometimes it may appear from the surrounding circumstances that there was no intention to create legal relationships. Sometimes it may appear from the surrounding circumstances that the right to exclusive possession is referable to a legal relationship other than a tenancy. Legal relationships to which the grant of exclusive possession might be referable and which would or might negative the grant of an estate or interest in the land include occupancy under a contract for the sale of the land, occupancy pursuant to a contract of employment or occupancy referable to the holding of an office. But where as in the present case the only circumstances are that residential accommodation is offered and accepted with exclusive possession for a term at a rent, the result is a tenancy. ...

[The other Law Lords agreed with Lord Templeman's reasoning.]

****

Questions

1. What does the term 'exclusive possession' mean? Is an occupier with exclusive *occupation* necessarily a tenant?

2. How does the court determine whether or not an occupier is granted the legal right to the exclusive possession of the premises? See also *City Council of Kampala v Mukubira* [1968] EA 497 and *City Council of Kampala v Mukiibi* [1967] EA 368 (excerpts of both cases appear below).
3. Give practical examples of circumstances where it might be legally important to determine whether or not a person in occupation of another's land has exclusive possession.
4. Lord Templeman identifies certain special circumstances where an occupier who had exclusive possession might not be a tenant. What are they?
5. Is exclusive possession an essential feature of a lease under s. 4(5) of the *Land Act*? If so, is it a determinant of a lease?

****

Certainty of duration

A grant of an uncertain term does not create a lease. At common law, the duration of a lease must be certain or ascertainable before the lease takes effect otherwise it is void at law (*Lace v Chantler* [1944] 1 All ER 305, see extract below).

****

A lease for the duration of the war is void for uncertainty

Lace v Chantler
[1944] 1 ALL ER 305

[The plaintiff sub-let a dwelling house to the defendant for the 'duration of the war'. The issue raised was whether letting 'for the duration of the war' creates a valid lease.]

Lord Greene MR: ... The question immediately arises whether a tenancy for the duration of the war creates a good leasehold interest. In my opinion it does not. A term created by a leasehold tenancy agreement must be expressed either with certainty and specifically or by reference to something which can, at the time when the lease takes effect, be looked to as a certain ascertainment of what the term is meant to be. In the present case, when this tenancy agreement took effect, the term was completely uncertain. It was impossible to say how long the tenancy would last. Mr Sturge in his argument has maintained that such a lease would be valid, and that, even if the term is uncertain at its beginning when the lease takes effect, the fact that at some future time it will be rendered certain is sufficient to make it a good lease. In my opinion, that argument is not to be sustained.

I do not propose to go into the authorities on the matter, but in Foa's *Landlord and Tenant*, 6th ed, p.115, the law is stated in this way, and, in my view, correctly: 'The habendum in a lease must point out the period during which the enjoyment of the premises is to be had; so that the duration, as well as the commencement of the term, must be stated. The certainty of a lease as to its continuance must be ascertainable either by the express limitation of the parties at the time the lease is made, or by reference to some collateral act which may, with equal certainty, measure the continuance of it, otherwise it is void. If the term be fixed by reference to some collateral matter, such matter must either be itself certain ... or capable before the lease takes effect of being rendered so ...' The important words to observe in that last phrase are the words 'before the lease takes effect'. Then it goes on: 'Consequently, a lease to endure for "as many years as A shall live," or "as the coverture between B and C shall continue" would not be good as lease for years, although the same results may be achieved in another way by making the demise for a fixed number (ninety-nine for instance) of years determinable upon A's death, or the dissolution of the coverture between B and C.' In the present case, in my opinion, this agreement cannot take effect as a good tenancy for the duration of the war.

******

Notes

1. In England, the House of Lords in *Prudential Assurance Co Ltd v London Residuary* and others [1992] 3 All ER 504, re-affirmed the rule that the maximum duration of the term must be certain (or capable of being rendered certain) before the lease takes effect. In that case, the House of Lords held that a lease granted until the landlord requires the land for purposes of widening a certain road, was void for uncertainty. Lord Templeman (at p. 510) said: 'My Lords, I consider that the principle in *Lace v Chantler* ... reaffirming 500 years of judicial acceptance of the requirement that a term must be certain applies to all leases and tenancy agreements. A tenancy from year to year is saved from being uncertain because each party has power by notice to determine at the end of any year.' The term continues until determined as if both parties made a new agreement at the end of each year for a new term for the ensuing year. In the same case, (at p. 512) Lord Browne-Wilkinson while agreeing with his brethren's exposition of the common law was critical of the rule. His Lordship said: 'No one has produced any satisfactory rationale for the genesis of this rule. No one has been able to point to any useful purpose that it serves at the present day.'
2. Section 4(5)(c) of the *Land Act*, states that a lease entails a grant of exclusive possession of land 'usually *but not necessarily* for a period defined, directly or indirectly, by reference to a specific date of commencement and a specific date of ending'[20]. It is arguable that unlike the common law, under the Act the maximum duration of a lease need not be ascertainable from the outset.

******

Distinction between leases and licences

A landowner may give permission to another to occupy his or her land as a lessee or a licensee. In the following case some of the legal significances of the distinction between a lease and a licence are illustrated.

******

A licence is personal to the licensee

Runda Coffee Estate Ltd v Jagar Singh
(1966) E.A. 564

[In 1950 St. Benoist Plantation Ltd ('the company'), which at the material time was the owner of the subject farm, allowed the defendant's father ('the father') to build a combined shop and house on a plot of land within the farm. The permission was subject to a condition that the licence to live and trade on the farm could be revoked by the company or a subsequent purchaser, if compensation was paid on termination. In 1956, the farm was sold to Cheleta Ltd, which had actual notice of the obligation for the payment of compensation. In the same year the father expended money to install electricity and water in the building. In 1963, the father died without leaving a will. As eldest son, the defendant occupied his father's premises continuously before and after his death. In 1963 Cheleta Ltd sold the farm to Cheleta Coffee Plantation Ltd. The following year the latter sold the farm to Runda Coffee Estates Ltd, the plaintiffs/appellants. The trial Judge found that Cheleta Coffee Plantation Ltd and the appellants had actual and constructive notice of the company's undertaking to pay compensation to the father upon termination of the licence to occupy the land. The appellants sued the defendant (respondent) on the ground that he was unlawfully occupying a building on its

---

[20] This provision seems to be at variance with s 2 (interpretation provision) of the Act, where 'leasehold land tenure' is defined as the holding of land 'for a given period from a *specified date of commencement*...'.

farm. The appellants sought an order for possession and mesne profits. In his defence, the respondent claimed that he was in possession pursuant to a contractual licence granted to his father in 1951. He claimed that the appellants were estopped from evicting him without payment of compensation. The trial Judge awarded possession of the building to the appellants subject to payment of compensation to the respondent. The appellants appealed against the order for payment of compensation.]

Newbold P: A considerable number of points were argued on the appeal. These included whether the plaintiffs, by reason of the transfer of the farm being under the *Registration of Titles Act*, took the farm free of any encumbrance to pay any compensation: whether the claim for compensation was time-barred; whether compensation could properly be ordered to be paid to a person who was not a party to the proceedings and who was not in existence at the time of judgement; whether the contractual licence given to the father was terminated by each of the sales of the farm and if compensation was payable who was liable therefor; whether the amount of compensation for the building was correctly assessed; and whether the order for costs was correct. All of these points, however, only arise for consideration if the defendant as successor to his father (and for this purpose I shall assume that the defendant is a lawful successor to his father and that no difficulty arises by reason of the fact that the defendant was not, at the time of the proceedings, the administrator of his father's estate) is entitled to compensation under the terms of contractual licence either, first by reason of s.40 of the *Transfer of Property Act*, or, secondly, by reason of the estoppel which he pleaded. If he is not, then the question of mesne profits arises; if he is, then the points I have referred to above arise.

Before I consider these two basic issues it would be convenient to deal with the claim for compensation in respect of the expenditure for laying on light and water. I am unable to see any basis on which these amounts could be recovered by the defendant. These amounts appear to be claimed in the defence on the basis that the expenditure was incurred 'in the expectation of being allowed to stay' on the terms of contractual licence given to the father in 1950. The judge made no finding that anyone had agreed to reimburse the father these amounts, nor does he set out any reason for holding that the defendant was entitled to recover these amounts. I am satisfied from the evidence that the father was told at the time that he incurred such expenditure that it was on his own account. There was thus no contractual obligation to reimburse the expenditure with the result that s.40 does not apply. Nor does expenditure of money by a person on another's land of itself give rise to any equity. The oft-quoted dictum of LORD KINGSDOWN in *Ramsden v Dyson*, ((1866) L.R. I H.L. at p.170), which is the foundation for the doctrine that in certain circumstances the expenditure of money on another's land gives rise to certain equities, is followed by a passage at p.171 which is of equal importance. It is as follows:-

> If, on the other hand, a tenant being in possession of land, and knowing the nature and extent of his interest, lays out money upon it in the hope or expectation, then, if such hope or expectation has not been created or encouraged by the landlord the tenant has no claim which any court of law or equity can enforce.

Whatever may be the position in relation to the expenditure on the building consequent upon the licence given to the father in 1950, the father would have had no claim to be reimbursed the cost of installing light and water, as this was an expenditure he incurred for his own purpose and after being informed that the installation must be at his own cost. As the father would not have been entitled to be reimbursed the expenditure, clearly the defendant is not so entitled....

The second basic issue is whether the plaintiffs, by reason of the licence given by the plaintiff's predecessor in title to the father, are estopped from recovering possession of the building from the defendant without payment of compensation. In order to decide this question it is necessary to consider the nature of an estoppel. An estoppel is a rule of evidence which may enable a cause of action to succeed but which can never of itself found a cause of action (see *Nurdin v Lombank* ([1963] EA 304 (CA)). The right to plead an estoppel does not give any title to the thing which is the subject matter of the estoppel (see *Balwaant v Kipkoech* ([1963] EA 651 (CA)). Before an equitable estoppel, which may consist of the representation of a legal relationship, can arise there must be clear and unequivocal representation (see *Century Automobile Ltd v Hutching Biemer Ltd* ([1965] EA 304 (CA). *Inwards v Baker* ([1965] 1 All E R 446) is perhaps the clearest example of a case where the expenditure of money by a person on another's land, by reason of expectation made by the owner of the land, of being allowed to occupy that land, gives rise to an estoppel precluding the owner from giving any evidence of an act which would terminate that occupation except in accordance with the representation. This right to continue in occupation, however, creates no title in the land and the right is co-extensive with, and dependent upon, a clear and unequivocal representation. ...

Bearing elements of estoppel in mind, I turn to consider whether on the facts of this case the defendant, who is the successor (as I have assumed) of the father can by reason of a licence granted to the father on the terms as found by the judge and which I have set out, resist the termination by the plaintiffs, who are the successors in title to the St. Benoist Plantations Ltd., of the defendant's occupation of the building unless compensation is paid. The right of the father to plead an estoppel gave him no title in the building which he could pass on to the defendant or which passed to the defendant by operation of law. The defendant, therefore, must rest his right to plead an estoppel upon a clear occupation until compensation is paid. But the representation found by the judge is merely a licence to the father to occupy the building until termination of the licence and payment of compensation. Even if this means that the payment of compensation is a condition precedent to the termination of the licence there is nothing in the representation which suggests that this licence to the father is anything other than a personal licence to him.

In *Errington v Errington* ([1952] 1 All E R 149 at p 155) Denning, LJ said of persons who by permission were occupying a building in respect of which they had expended a sum of money:

> They were not tenants at will, but licensees. They had a mere personal privilege to remain there, with no right to assign or sub-let. They were, however, not bare licensees they were licensees with a contractual right to remain. As such they have no right at law to remain, but only in equity, and equitable rights now prevail.

This must be the position. Can it seriously be suggested that this licence given to the father to remain on another's land conferred some sort of right on the father which he could assign to another, or which he could dispose of to another by will, or which devolved upon another by the operation of law? If the father went bankrupt could the trustee in bankruptcy go into occupation and demand compensation or dispose of this licence as if it were an asset of the bankruptcy? These questions have only to be posed for them to be answered by an emphatic negative. All of this shows clearly the personal nature of the licence given to the father and this in turn shows that no clear and unequivocal representation was made which entitles the defendant to plead that the plaintiffs are estopped from terminating the defendant's occupation of the building, except on payment of compensation to him. I am satisfied, therefore, that the plaintiffs were not estopped from terminating the occupation of the defendant unless they paid compensation either to him or to any other person.

As the plaintiffs were entitled to terminate the occupation of the building by the defendant without payment of compensation, and as they did terminate such occupation from March 1, 1965, and as the defendant continued wrongfully to occupy the building until May 31, 1966, the plaintiffs are clearly entitled to mesne profits. ... For these reasons I would allow the appeal.

(Duffus Ag VP and Law JA, agreed with the order.]

****

Note

For further discussion of the distinction between a lease and licence see *Street v Mountford* [1985] 2 ALL ER 289 (see extract above).

****

DISTINCTION BETWEEN A LEASE AND A *KIBANJA*

A *kibanja* holder is a customary tenant on mailo land. In some cases it may not be clear whether a person in occupation of another's land is a *kibanja* holder or an ordinary tenant. The following case illustrates this point.

****

Determining whether the occupier is a lessee or kibanja holder

Lukwago v Bawa Singh and another
[1959] EA 282

[The plaintiff inherited a *kibanja* from his father, but since he was a minor, his guardian paid the rent for him. The second defendant, mailo owner, sent a circular to all tenants including the plaintiff's guardian to the effect that their rent would be 400 shillings as opposed to the 10 shillings prescribed under the *Busuulu and Envujjo Law* 1928 (repealed by the *Land Reform Decree*). In the meantime, the second defendant leased the land, including the land occupied by the plaintiff, to the first defendant for a period of 33 years. The lease was registered under the *Registration of Titles Act*. When the plaintiff refused to pay the increased rent, the first defendant served him with an eviction notice and later demolished his house. The plaintiff sued for damages for trespass to land. The defendants claimed that there was a contractual tenancy, which they terminated when the plaintiff failed to pay the increased rent.]

Bennet J: The main issue in this case is whether or not at the time the house was demolished the plaintiff was in lawful possession of the plot. If he was, then both defendants, by their servants or agents, committed an act of trespass in entering upon the plot and demolishing the house....

On behalf of defendant, it is contended that the fact that during the years 1950, 1951 and 1952 rent was being paid by Erisa Lukwago at the rate of shs. 60/- per annum and not at the rate of shs. 10/- as provided for in s 2 of the *Busulu and Envujjo Law*, leads to an inference that there was a contractual tenancy between the plaintiff and the second defendant, that the plaintiff was not a 'mukopi' within meaning of the *Busulu and Envujjo Law*. It is not clear to me why it should have been necessary for the second defendant to have relied upon inference, when he could well have gone into the witness box and give evidence on the matter. Ernisti, his treasurer and rent collector, did not given evidence of any contractual tenancy. His explanation of how Erisa Lukwago came to pay rent of shs 60/- per annum was that the rent was increased when the estate of second defendant was carved up into plots. He ventured the opinion that a mailo owner can circumvent the provisions of the *Busulu and Envujjo Law* by carving his land up into plots, a doctrine which is, no doubt, very convenient to landlords but disastrous to tenants.

Erisa Lukwago denied, when giving evidence, that there was any tenancy agreement between himself and the second defendant. He alleged that he had agreed to pay rent at the rate of Shs.60/- per annum because he had sub-let part of the plot. Erisa's evidence denying the existence of any special tenancy agreement is quite uncontradicted by any other evidence, and I accept it.

It is of the essence of the relationship between a mailo owner and the holder of a kibanja that the latter's right of occupation inures for an indeterminate period and is heritable by his successor. It may well be that Africans in Buganda can enter into a relationship of landlord and tenant which is not governed by the *Busulu and Envujo Law*, as for instance where land is demised by one African to another for a fixed term of years. In the instant case, however, there is no evidence that the land in suit was leased to the plaintiff for any fixed term, nor is there any sufficient evidence of a tenancy agreement.

I accordingly, find that the plaintiff was at the time when the house was demolished a 'mukopi' within the meaning of the *Busulu and Envujo Law*, and as such his rights over the land could only be terminated in accordance with the provisions of that law. ....

In these circumstances, I find that the plaintiff's rights over the plot had never been extinguished at the time when the house was demolished, and that he was in lawful possession thereof.

It is true that the first defendant had a valid lease over the plot, but under the proviso to s.61 of the *Registration of Titles Ordinance* (Cap. 123) his title was subject to the interest of any tenant on the land, and in my judgement, the plaintiff was a 'tenant' within the meaning of the proviso.

It follows that both defendants committed an act of trespass when they, by their servants or agents, entered upon the plaintiff's land and demolished the housing standing thereon.

Questions

1. On what basis did the Court in *Lukwago v Bawa Singh,* hold that the defendant was a kibanja holder under the *Busulu and Envujjo Law*, 1928, as opposed to a tenant at common law?
2. How do you determine whether a person in occupation of another's land is a trespasser, tenant, or *kibanja* holder?
3. With reference to the *Land Act,* discuss the legal significance of the distinction between a 'tenant', a 'trespasser' and a '*kibanja* holder'. (See s 30, *Land Act*).

CREATION OF A LEASE

Formal requirements

Section 100 of the *Registration of Titles Act*, provides that a 'proprietor of any freehold or mailo land under the operation of this Act may, subject to the provisions of any law or agreement for the time being in force, lease the same for any term exceeding three years by signing a lease thereof in the form of the Eighth Schedule to this Act ....' Under s 51 of the Act, a lease is not effective until it is registered under the Act.[21] There are no formal requirements for the creation of a lease that is less than three years, including periodic tenancies.

Effect of failure to follow formal requirements

At law

An unregistered lease agreement operates as a contract, which is enforceable as between the parties (*Souza Figueiredo and Co Ltd v Moorings Hotel Co Ltd* [1960] EA 926, see excerpt in Chapter nine). Where the intended lessee enters into possession pursuant to the agreement, a tenancy at will is created. Such tenancy becomes a periodic tenancy once rent is paid and accepted on a periodic basis.

****

A tenancy at will becomes a periodic tenancy upon payment of rent

Bweya Steel Works Ltd. v. National Insurance Corporation[22]
CS No. 63 of 1985; [1985] HCB 58

[The defendant entered into a written tenancy agreement with a certain company. The name of the company was subsequently changed to Bweya Steel Works Ltd., the present plaintiff. The plaintiff

[21] See chapter nine.

[22] The facts and holding in this case are extracted from the High Court Bulletin digest of cases.

was successor in title to the said company and therefore became the tenant of the defendant by virtue of that tenancy agreement. This tenancy expired after 3 years and was not renewed, but the plaintiff continued in occupation of the premises with the knowledge and consent of the defendant. The plaintiff claimed that it remained in possession pursuant to a tenancy agreement entered into with the defendant for a term of 15 years. The plaintiff brought this action against the defendant for specific performance of this agreement.]

Odoki J : ... The offer of the alleged 15 year tenancy was made by the then General Manager in 1977. There was no written evidence to support this promise. In 1984, the defendant wrote to the plaintiff informing it of the termination of the tenancy and giving it fourteen days to vacate the premises.

The plaintiff contended first that the offer was accepted when the plaintiff paid the required rent. It was also submitted for the plaintiff that he was entitled to an order to specific performance against the defendant because the plaintiff performed part of its contract by paying a big consideration for the contract. By this he meant the large sum of money paid as rent.

Counsel for the defendant submitted first that the plaintiff had not entered into any written contract with the defendant. It was further submitted that even if the promise was made it was not supported by sufficient consideration.

Thirdly, it was argued for the defendant that the tenancy held by the plaintiff was a tenancy at will and further that the nature of the tenancy could be determined by the mode of payment of rent. He contended that since the plaintiff was paying rent quarterly the plaintiff had a quarterly tenancy with the defendant.

Lastly, Counsel submitted that sections 51 and 108 of the *Registration of Titles Act* (cap.205) required any tenancy or sublease for a period of three years or more to be in writing and not oral. He submitted that the only tenancy the plaintiff had was a tenancy at will.

Held

1. The plaintiff had failed to prove that a promise was made. Even if the promise was made, there was no contract between the defendant and the plaintiff, as the terms of the contract were not spelt out. Parties must make their own contract and agree to its terms with sufficient certainty. If the terms are unsettled or indefinite, there will be no contract.
2. If the promise was ever made it was a bare promise not supported by any sufficient consideration and was therefore not binding.
3. Where a plaintiff has wholly or in part executed his part of an oral agreement in the confidence that the defendant would do the same, the court often orders specific performance on the ground that it would be a fraud on the defendant's part not to carry out the contract. However, for any acts to suffice as part-performance they must be unequivocally and in their own nature referable to some such agreement as that alleged. The acts must be such as to prove the existence of some contract and consistent with the contract alleged. The plaintiff's act of payment of the reserved rent cannot be held to be unequivocally and in its own nature referable to the alleged contract nor does it prove the existence of such a contract nor is it necessarily consistent with it. The plaintiff was therefore not entitled to an order for specific performance of the alleged tenancy agreement for 15 years.
4. A tenancy at will is implied when a person is in possession by the consent of the owner. A tenant, who with the consent of the landlord remains in possession after his lease has expired, is a tenant at will until some other interest is created. In the present case, the plaintiff remained in occupation after the expiration of the three year tenancy with the consent of the landlord, the defendant. Prima facie, the plaintiff was a tenant at will unless some other interest was created. It was agreed that the plaintiff might rent quarterly for an indefinite period. In the absence of any agreement between the parties as to the period of the tenancy or proof of any custom or practice applicable, it was reasonable to infer from the mode of

payment of rent that the tenancy between the defendant and the plaintiff was a quarterly tenancy. The plaintiff therefore held a quarterly tenancy with the defendant.

5. The landlord has a right to terminate a periodic tenancy upon giving the tenant proper notice. The general principle is that a weekly or other periodic tenancy is determinable by notice to quit which in the absence of special stipulation should be given so as to expire at the end of the complete period of the tenancy, and should be equal in length to the period. Notice to quit is a unilateral act determining a tenancy without the consent of the opposite party and as such must be strictly construed. A notice is therefore bad if it does not expire at the proper time. Since the plaintiff had a quarterly tenancy, it was entitled to three months notice to quit expiring at the end of the current period during which the notice was given. The 14 days' notice was therefore invalid and ineffectual to terminate the tenancy.

****

Notes

1. In *Bains v Chogley* (1949) 16 EACA 27, the respondent granted a lease to Sidi Bilal for a period of five years at a monthly rent. The lease was unregistered and the magistrate held that Sidi Bilal was a tenant at will. On appeal to the Kenya Supreme Court, it was held that Sidi Bilal was a yearly tenant by virtue of s. 106 of the Indian *Transfer of Property Act*. On further appeal, the East Africa Court of Appeal upheld the Supreme Court decision. In delivering his judgement Sir Barclay Nihill CJ cited with approval the following passage from De Lestang J's judgement: '[I]n order to create a tenancy there must be a consensus, which in a proper case may be inferred from payment and acceptance of rent between the parties giving rise to the relation of landlord and tenant. ...In the present case, the respondent always intended that Sidi Bilal should be his tenant and he accepted rent from him in that capacity. It is true that the parties intended a particular kind of tenancy but it is equally clear that they were ad idem that Sidi Bilal should occupy as a tenant distinguished from a mere licensee at will.' See also *Souza Figueiredo and Co v Moorings Hotel Co Ltd* [1960] EA 926 (see extract in Chapter nine), and *Rukandema Kamuru v Kabale Town Council* CA No MKA 10 of 1085 (see extract below).

2. Note that because the agreement is a contract either party can sue the other for damages for breach of contract or for specific performance (see *Souza Figueiredo and Co v Moorings Hotel Co Ltd, supra*).

****

Equity

In equity, an agreement to grant a lease, which does not comply with the legal formalities, may nonetheless create a lease recognised in equity ('equitable lease'). This rule is commonly referred to as the principle of *Walsh v Lonsdale*.

****

The principle of Walsh v Lonsdale

Walsh v Lonsdale
(1881) 21 CH D 9

[The defendant entered into a contract to lease certain premises to the plaintiff for a term of 7 years at an annual rental payable in advance. Although the agreement did not comply with the legal formalities for the creation of a lease in excess of three years, the plaintiff entered into possession. When the defendant defaulted in payment of rent in advance, the defendant distrained the plaintiff's goods. The plaintiff commenced proceedings claiming illegal distress. The plaintiff argued that since the lease was not executed by deed as was required by law, there was only a tenancy at will which by virtue of possession and payment of rent became a legal tenancy from year to year. And since payment of rent in advance is inconsistent with a yearly tenancy, it followed that the distress was unlawful.]

Jessel MM: ... There is an agreement for a lease under which possession has been given. Now since the *Judicature Act* the possession is held under the agreement. There are not two estates as there were formerly, one estate at common law by reason of the payment of the rent from year to year, and an estate in equity under the agreement. There is only one Court, and the equity rules prevail in it. The tenant holds under an agreement for a lease. He holds, therefore, under the same terms in equity as if a lease had been granted, it being a case in which both parties admit that relief is capable of being given by specific performance. That being so, he cannot complain of the exercise by the landlord of the same rights as the landlord would have had if a lease had been granted. On the other hand, he is protected in the same way as if a lease had been granted; he cannot be turned out by six months' notice as a tenant from year to year. He has a right to say, 'I have a lease in equity, and you can only re-enter if I have committed such a breach of covenant as would if a lease had been granted have entitled you to re-enter according to the terms of a proper proviso for re-entry.' That being so, it appears to me that being a lessee in equity he cannot complain of the exercise of the right of distress merely because the actual parchment has not been signed and sealed...

****

Does the principle of Walsh v Lonsdale apply to lease of land subject to the Registration of Titles Act?[23]

Souza Figueiredo and Co v Moorings Hotel Co Ltd
[1960] EA 926

[See Chapter nine for the facts and detail holding of this case.]
Sir Kenneth O'Connor P.: [After quoting extracts from several Australian cases, which held that the doctrine of *Walsh v Lonsdale* applied under the Torrens System, concluded]: In my opinion, all the above quoted extracts would be applicable in Uganda except the statement that an unregistered lease operates to create an equitable term of years. I would not agree that in Uganda any estate or interest in land is created by an unregistered lease. Such a document may, however, give a right to require a registrable lease and its terms may be enforceable as a contract. ...

Note

See the notes on this case in Chapter nine.

****

COVENANTS IN A LEASE

Covenants in a lease may be express or implied by statute or common law. One of the commonest covenants in leases is a covenant against a lessee not to sublet or part with possession without the landowner's consent. The cases of *City Council of Kampala v Mukiibi* [1967] EA 368, and *City Council of Kampala v Mukubira* [1967] EA 497, both extracted below, provide a contrasting

[23] Section 51 of the *Registration of Titles Act*, provides that no estate or interest in land can be created unless the transaction is registered under the Act. See discussion of this provision in Chapter nine.

illustration of what constitutes parting with possession. As against the landlord, the common law implies two main covenants: of quiet enjoyment and covenant not to derogate from the grant. The operation of these covenants is illustrated by the case of *Shah Champshi and others v The Attorney General of Kenya* [1959] EA 630, and *Aldin v Latimer Clark Muirhead & Co Ltd* [1894] 2 Ch 437, respectively (see extracts below).

****

Covenant not to sub-let or part with possession

A tenant breaches a covenant not to sublet or part with possession only if he or she grants 'exclusive possession' to another.

City Council of Kampala v Mukiibi
[1967] E.A. 368 (U)

[The City Council, plaintiffs, let the suit property to the defendant subject to certain covenants, inter alia, that the defendant shall not sublet or part with possession of the premises. The Council reserved to itself a right of re-entry in the event of breach of any covenant. The Council sought to terminate the lease on the ground that the defendant in breach of the tenancy agreement parted with possession by subletting the premises to other people for their business. The defendant denied the allegation. The issue was whether the defendant had sublet or parted with possession.]

Sir Udo Udoma CJ: The case of the plaintiff is that the defendant has committed a breach of the covenant contained in clause 2 (14) of the agreement by assigning and subletting part of the premises to various persons as sub-tenants; and that by reason of that breach the plaintiff is entitled to re-enter and recover vacant possession of the premises. The defendant has denied having committed any breach of any of the covenants. He has maintained that he is still in possession of the premises; and that he has neither let nor assigned nor parted with the possession of the same to anyone else.

...The complaint against the defendant in particular was specific. He was charged with having committed a breach of the covenant contained in clause 2(14) of the agreement in that he had sublet the premises of which he is tenant to sub-tenants.

On the strength of that complaint, a letter dated January 3, 1966, was addressed to the defendant. Therein he was notified of the allegations against him, and vacant possession of the premises was demanded, failing which action was to be instituted for its recovery.

As a follow-up to that letter and acting on the authority and the terms of their appointment, the committee set out to accomplish its task. It visited, among other shops, the premises of the defendant. ... On arrival at the premises the [committee] found on the premises six male hairdressers, one of whom was Stephen Kayondo, in occupation of the front shop of the premises; and two hairdressers. ... The defendant informed the committee that all of them were his employees; that he had engaged each of them to work for him at a daily rate of pay; and that each of them was paid daily by him personally at the close of business every evening. [But] the barbers ... told the committee that each of them was self-employed; that ...each of them was paying rent to the defendant for use and occupation of the premises at the daily rate of Shs.3/50. ...

Counsel for the plaintiff submitted that the evidence of the plaintiff and its witnesses should be accepted and that the evidence clearly establishes that the defendant did sublet and part with the possession of the premises by putting the hairdressers into possession of the same and charging each of them rent daily thereby; that the hairdressers were therefore his tenants although there was no written agreement between them. Counsel further urged the court to find that the so-called employment agreements were not genuine....

In his submissions counsel referred the court to *Stening v. Abrahams* [[1931] 1 Ch D 470]; *Abraham v. MacFisheries Ltd.* [[1925] 2 KB 18]; *Roe d Dingley v Sales* (1813); E & E. Digest;

and *Chaplin v. Smith* [1926] 1 KB 198 and contended that the defendant should be ordered to give up vacant possession of the premises and to pay to the plaintiff the mesne profits claimed.

Counsel for the defendant on the other hand submitted that, even if the court should come to the conclusion that the hairdressers were permitted the use and occupation of the premises at a daily rent payable to the defendant, such hairdressers were licensees. They had neither interest nor estate in the premises because the defendant was all the time in full possession of the premises and kept the key of the said premises himself; that that being so the defendant has not committed any breach of the covenant contained in the agreement. ...

The real question for decision by the court is whether by permitting the hairdressers the use and occupation of the premises of which the defendant is tenant, those hairdressers, who were paying rent daily for such occupation to the defendant, could be properly described as tenants. Counsel for the plaintiff has urged the court to find that they were tenants properly so-called even though there were no written agreements and the rents fixed were paid to the defendants daily, and that the court should hold that the defendant had committed a breach of the tenancy agreement.

In *Abraham v. MacFisheries Ltd,* a lease of two adjoining messuages and shops contained a covenant by the lessees that they would not assign, transfer, underlet, or part with the possession of the said premises or any part thereof other than an underletting for residential purposes only without the consent of the lessor, not unreasonably withheld. The lessees agreed with a company of wine merchants to grant them an underlease of one of the messuages and shops subject to the consent of the lessor. A draft underlease was being prepared; the lessees allowed the wine merchants to occupy the premises and therein to execute repairs and to install and carry on their business. The lessor later refused consent to the underlease when applied for. It was held that the lessees had committed a breach of the covenant not to part with the possession of any part of the premises.

In *Stening v. Abrahams* it was held that a lessee's covenant not to 'part with the possession of the demised premises or any part thereof' was broken only if the lessee entirely excludes himself from the legal possession of part of the premises; and that on the particular facts and documents in the particular case a seven years exclusive licence to erect an advertisement hoarding against the front walls of the lessee's house followed by its erection was not a breach of the covenant.

In *Roe d. Dingley v. Sales* where a lease contained a proviso for re-entry in case the tenant should demise, lease, grant or let the demised premises, or any part or parcel thereof, or convey, etc. to any person whomsoever, for all or any part of the term, without the licence of the lessor in writing; and the defendant, without such licence, agreed with a person to enter into partnership with him, and that he should have the use of the back-chamber and some other parts of the premises exclusively and of the rest jointly with the defendant, and accordingly let him into possession of the said premises. It was held that the lessor was entitled to re-enter.

In *Chaplin v. Smith* a lessee had covenanted with his lessor that he would not assign or underlet or part with possession of the demised premises or any part thereof. He assigned his business, that of a motor garage proprietor, to a company of which he was the managing director and in which he held a controlling interest. He carried on the business of the company on the premises which were stated to be its registered address and on which the name of the company was exposed. He kept the key of the premises in his possession. The company agreed to indemnify him in respect of the rates and taxes. The company appeared in the valuation lists for the parish as the occupier of the premises for the purpose of poor rate. Subsequently a second company was formed of which the lessee was the managing director and which took over the business, assets, and liabilities of the first company. In negotiating for this transfer, the lessee stipulated that he should remain in possession as actual tenant of the demised premises. It was held that no interest in the demised premises had passed to the companies or either of them and that there had been no breach of the lessee's covenant not to part with possession of the premises or any part thereof.

The decision in *Chaplin v. Smith* was based on the statement of the law which was affirmed by the Court of Appeal in *Peebles v. Crosthwaite* [(1896) 13 TLR 37] to the effect that a lessee who retains the legal possession of premises does not commit a breach of covenant against parting with possession by allowing other people to use the said premises.

This principle was brought out quite clearly in his judgement in the case by BANKES, L.J., when he said at p.207:

> In the present case there was no agreement to sell the demised premises. In that respect it is more favourable to the tenant. And if the true facts are, as I think they are, that the appellant and the successive companies came to terms on the basis that he neither could nor would part with possession, but would at all costs remain in possession himself and allow the company's business to be conducted on the premises while he remained in possession of them, then in my view of the authorities there was no parting with possession. The lessee of a double-fronted shop with a door in the middle and a counter on either side, who has covenanted not to part with possession of the demised premises or any part thereof, may surely agree to allow a licensee to carry on a business in one part while the lessee himself remains in possession of the whole premises and carries on his own business in the other part. In that case there is no parting with possession, and I see no distinction between that case and this.

It is noteworthy that in the course of arguments in that case SCRUTTON, L.J. at p. 204 asked the question: 'But was the occupation exclusive?' and continued, 'Generally an occupation or use which is not exclusive is not evidence of the de facto possession' (quoting PULLOCK AND WRIGHT ON POSSESSION, p. 35.)

It seems to me that of the cases cited and relied upon by the counsels for the plaintiff only the decision in *Abraham v. MacFisheries Ltd*, and *Roe d. Dingley v. Sales* would appear to support the case of the plaintiff on the issue of a breach of the covenant contained in the agreement. It is also clear that the decisions in *Stening v. Abrahams* and *Chaplin v. Smith* are in my view more in favour of the defendant. Be that as it may it seems quite plain that the facts found in the cases other than *Chaplin v. Smith* and *Roe d. Dingley v. Sales* are quite different and distinguishable from the facts and circumstances of the instant case.

In *Abraham v. MacFisheries Ltd*, the lessee had in fact divested itself of the possession of the said messuages by actually getting a sublease drafted and permitting the wine merchants to enter into possession of the messuage and therein to effect repairs and alterations suitable for the purpose of their business, on the assumption that the lessor would not withhold his consent. Furthermore, the key of the second messuage was handed over to the wine merchants, which is a strong evidence that the lessee had parted with the possession of that part of the premises. On the evidence in that case it was found by the court that the wine merchants refused to give up possession when demanded and had to be ejected therefrom by force.

In *Roe d. Dingley v. Sales* the lessee concerned had actually parted with a part of the premises and the prospective tenant had exclusive use of that part of the premises.

In view of these facts and circumstances, I am not satisfied that these authorities are applicable to the case of the plaintiff under consideration. And, as already pointed out, rather than support the case of the plaintiff *Chaplin v. Smith* in my view fully supports the case of the defendant.

On the facts of the instant case, I am rather inclined to the view that the hairdressers were mere licensees. They were not tenants in the proper legal sense of the term. They were not in exclusive possession of the premises and I so hold. A point of great importance which supports the case of the defendant that he never at any time parted with the possession of the premises is the fact that he was always in charge of the key. It was his practice always to open the premises in the morning and to admit the hairdressers and at the close of business in the evening after collecting his own dues to lock up the premises and retain the key with him.

It is clear from the evidence that the hairdressers could only make use and occupy the premises with the leave and licence of the defendant, who could turn them out at any time. By the use and occupation of the premises the hairdressers did not in any way acquire any estate or interest in the premises. ...

In *Russell v. Beecham and Another* by a covenant in a lease for thirty years, the lessee undertook that he would not 'assign or part with the lease or the premises hereby demised or any part thereof' without the licence and consent in writing of the lessor or his trustees.

The lease contained a proviso for re-entry for breach of covenant by the lessee. In November, 1921, the lessee, without the consent of the original lessor or his trustees, sublet part of the demised premises for a term of three years without giving the lessee notice under s.14(1) of the Conveyance and Law of Property Act, 1881.

The trustees of the original lessor brought an action against the lessee to recover the demised premises on the ground that the lessee had committed a breach of the covenant not to part with the premises or any part thereof.

It was held inter alia that in the construction of the covenant the words 'Part with' mean 'part with entirely or completely' and do not apply to parting with possession of only a part of the lessee's interest in the premises which was what the lessee had done, and where, as here, a covenant which entailed a forfeiture was in ambiguous language it would be construed strictly.

On the principle established in *Russell v. Beecham and Another* as regards the strict interpretation of the covenants in a lease which entails a forfeiture, it is to be noted that the covenant contained in cl. 2 (14) of the agreement is not in the usual terms. It is practically prohibitive in form. There is no provision that the consent of the lessor may be given, if sought by the lessee and such consent not to be unreasonably withheld to either sublet or assign the premises to a third party. Therefore it must be very strictly construed as against the plaintiff, and the background that to the knowledge of the plaintiff the defendant was not a hairdresser or barber by trade at the time when the premises were demised to him.

On the principles enunciated above and on my findings that the defendant did not at all material times in fact and in law divest himself of the possession of the premises or any part thereof, I have come to the conclusion that the order for vacant possession must be refused. There will be therefore judgement for the defendant in respect of the recovery of vacant possession with costs. ...

****

Notes

Compare the foregoing case with that of *City Council of Kampala v Mukubira*, extracted below.

Questions

1. Udo Udoma CJ said that a tenant could not be in breach of covenant not to part with possession unless he or she parts with 'legal possession'. What does the expression 'legal possession' mean?
2. Assume that after losing the case, the City Council employs you to close the 'loopholes' in its tenancy agreements. Suggest possible legal terminologies you would include in the agreement and their significance.

****

A tenant parts with possession if he or she retains no control over the premises

City Council of Kampala v Mukubira
[1968] EA 497

[The City Council (the plaintiffs) leased certain premises to the first defendant. One of the covenants of the lease prohibited the lessee to assign, underlet, or part with possession of the premises or any part thereof. Since the commencement of the lease, the first defendant allowed the second defendant to carry on business in the premises. The Council instituted proceeding for vacant possession claiming that the first defendant was in breach of the lease agreement. After filing this suit, the Council wrote to the first defendant demanding rent, which was in arrears. The issue was whether the first defendant had parted with possession. Secondly, if so, whether by demanding rent after filing the action the plaintiff impliedly waived the breach.]

Goudie J: ... It is undisputed that at least since the commencement of the tenancy the second defendant has been carrying on some form of business in the suit premises and that he has been in physical occupation thereof by reason of some relationship between himself and the first defendant. It is the Council's case that at the least the first defendant parted with possession to the second defendant in breach of his agreement. The first defendant, on the other hand, says he has always held one key to the premises, he has visited these from time to time, and the second defendant is running a business in the suit premises in conjunction with the first defendant as his partner. ...

[First] Mr Shah [for the first defendant] argued that the Council's letter of February 22, 1967 demanding rent for January and February 1967, after the Council had exercised their option of forfeiture of the tenancy operates as a waiver in law. However, the suit was filed on May 27, 1966. The filing of a suit is an 'irrevocable election to determine the lease' and no subsequent action can operate as a waiver of this option whilst the suit is pending (*Evans v Enever* [1902] 2 KB 315, per LORD COLERIDGE). ...

[Next] Mr Shah argued that the second defendant was at most a licensee and pointed to the evidence that the first defendant held one key to the premises throughout. He referred me to Civil Suit No. 456 of 1966 – *City Council of Kampala v. Mukibi* (1967) E.A. 368. It is true that in that suit the learned Chief Justice held that although the occupying partners were paying 'rent' to the tenant, he had not infringed the covenant 'not to assign, underlet or part with the possession of the premises or any part thereof'. He also referred to possession of the key by the tenant as 'a point of great importance.' I am not, of course, bound by the decision but, naturally, it is given persuasive weight. The facts in that case were, however, utterly different from those in the instant case. In the barber's case the evidence was that the tenant locked and unlocked the door each day, that not being a barber himself he nevertheless furnished the premises for use as a barber's shop, and that he kept a great deal of personal control over the premises. In the present case I am satisfied that the first defendant on his own admissions only paid very infrequent visits, and took no personal part in the business even supervisory or for checking purposes.

I find unhesitatingly that the first defendant has failed to show in this case any partnership arrangement between himself and the second defendant and that the agreements suggesting a partnership were deliberately designed to deceive the landlords. I find that there was a breach of the agreement in that the first defendant parted with possession of the premises to the second defendant. I further find the rent and mesne profits due is claimed.

There will be judgement for the plaintiff as prayed with costs.

****

Covenant of quiet enjoyment

At common law, there is an implied covenant against the landlord that he or she and persons claiming under him or her, shall not interfere with the tenant's use and enjoyment of the demised premises. The case below illustrates the meaning of this covenant.

****

A common lessor is not liable for breach of covenant of quiet enjoyment for unlawful interference with a tenant's possession caused by another tenant unless he or she permitted the act.

Shah Champshi Tejshi and others v The Attorney General of Kenya
[1959] EA 630

[The Government/respondent granted a lease to the plaintiffs/appellants. The plaintiffs claimed that under the lease they had an implied right of access to a certain road. Later, the Government leased the adjoining land to another person (Dominion Properties Ltd). The latter blocked the plaintiffs' alleged access road. The plaintiffs sued the Government for breach of covenant of quiet enjoyment.]

Sir Kenneth O'Connor P: ...Mr Slade [for the appellants] said that the appellants' case rested on the covenant for quiet enjoyment which is implied in every Crown Grant by s. 76 (b) of the *Crown Lands Ordinance*. He said that there had been a lawful interruption of the appellants' quiet enjoyment of their premises by Dominion Properties Ltd., a person claiming under the Crown.

The difficulty in Mr Slade's way was that it had not been shown in the court below that the interruption of the quiet enjoyment of the appellants' premises was a lawful interruption; or that, if it was unlawful, the Crown had caused or permitted it. There was nothing to show that the Crown had authorised Dominion Properties Ltd. to interfere with light or access to or from the appellants' premises. The case of *Sanderson v Berwick on Tweed* (1884), 13 QB.D. 547 shows that a lessor is not liable under a covenant for quiet enjoyment for unlawful user by its lessee of land leased to him which causes damage to the premises of another lessee from the lessor, unless the lessor has caused or permitted the damage. So also a lessor is not liable to his lessee, under a covenant for quiet enjoyment for damages for a nuisance caused by another of his lessees merely because the lessor knows of it and does not himself take any steps to prevent what is being done. There must be active participation on his part to make him responsible for the nuisance: *Malzy v Eichholz* [1916] 2 K.B. 308. That was a case of nuisance; but I think that the principle applies to infringement of a quasi-easement of light or access. Obstruction of light is regarded as a particular form of nuisance: *Colls v Home and Colonial Stores Ltd.* [1904] A.C. 179 per LORD LINDLEY at p. 208; and so, in certain circumstances, may be the blocking of a lane giving access to one's premises. Though the foundations of the rights of action for nuisance and for disturbance of an easement are distinct, similar principles as to the nature of the remedies for them apply to both: (*GALE ON EASEMENTS* 11th Edn. p. 514). In *Harris v James* (5) (1876), 45 L.J.Q.B. 545, BLACKBURN, J (as he then was) said:

> I do not think when a person demises property he is to be taken to authorise all that the occupier may do. If land were let on an agricultural lease, and there were a requirement that the tenant should cultivate the soil as well as possible, and the tenant brought a large quantity of inodorous manure on the land and placed it so as to be a nuisance, I do not think that his landlord would be liable, for he could not be said in any sense to have authorised the creation of this nuisance; nor would he in the case put by Mr Crompton, of letting ground on a building lease where the lessee created a nuisance by obstructing light and air by means of the buildings he erected; there the lessor would not be liable, because he had not authorised his tenant to build so as to obstruct the light and air of others.

This dictum is obiter; but it is entitled to very great respect. ...

The appellants, in the court below, chose not to join Dominion Properties Ltd. as a party and not to obtain and produce the grant from the Crown to that company or any evidence of its contents, and failed to adduce any evidence whether the Commissioner of Lands had approved building plans for plot 4990 including the erection of a building on part of the lane. In the result, there is nothing but a statement in an advocate's letter (which is not evidence of the fact stated) to show that the grant to Dominion Properties Ltd. did not reserve rights of access from and to, and light from, the lane for the building on plot 940. And there is no evidence that the Crown permitted Dominion Properties Ltd. to build on portion of the lane. A mere admission in the defence that the Governor granted adjoining land to Dominion Properties Ltd. coupled with a denial that he did so wrongfully or in breach of any covenant for quiet enjoyment is not enough. I think that, as the Lands Office approved the appellants' building plans, it is highly probable that it also approved the building plans of the Crown's other lessee Dominion Properties Ltd. and that the building was constructed in accordance with those plans. But there is no evidence of this and it is not the function of this court to make assumptions in favour of appellants who do not take steps to prove their case in the court below. I regret having to decide the case on this argument which may be devoid of merit; but I think it is clear that the appellants have not shown that they have a cause of action against the Crown for a breach of the covenant for quiet enjoyment. As their case rests upon that covenant, it must fail in-limine.

****

Note

Failure by the landlord to deliver possession of part of the leased premises may constitute breach of an implied covenant of quiet enjoyment, which could entitle the tenant to sue for damages, see *A M Dharas & Sons v Elys Ltd* [1963] EA 573 (see extract below).

Questions

1. Lumi leases a building to Kikuubo for purposes of retail trading. A month later, builders contracted by Lumi erect scaffolding in front of the windows and door of the shop in order to carry out repairs to the upper part of the building leased to other tenants. The poles interfere with access to Kikuubo's shop and result in loss of business. Advise Kikuubo whether he has a cause of action against Lumi for breach of covenant for quiet enjoyment and or derogation from the grant. (See eg *Owen v Gadd* [1956] 2 QB 99).
2. Mrs Osile leased certain premises from Patel on a weekly basis. Disputes arose between the two whereupon Patel served on Osile a notice purporting to terminate the lease. When she refused to quit Patel sent her a series of letters threatening to evict her from the rooms and to put her property on the street. On several occasions, Patel made calls at the premises knocking on her door demanding to have the rooms and yelling obscenities at her. Advise Mrs Osile whether she has any cause of action for breach of covenant of quiet enjoyment. (See eg *Kenny v Preen* [1963] 1 QB 501; and *Rukandema Kamuru v Kabale Town Council* CA No MKA 10 of 1985, see extract below)..

****

No Derogation from grant

At common, it is implied that when a person leases their land they undertake not to do anything in relation to the leased premises that defeats the main purpose for which the land was leased. The case below illustrates this point.

****

Aldin v Latimer Clark Muirhead & Co Ltd
[1894] 2 CH 437

[Munro leased part of his land to the defendant for a term of 21 years for carrying on timber trade. At the date of the lease the greater part of the adjacent land retained by Munro was open space. After Munro's death, both portions of land were sold to the defendants. The latter proceeded to erect buildings on the adjacent land in such a manner that they affected the free flow of air to the plaintiff's timber drying sheds. The plaintiff contended that the defendant's acts constituted either 'derogation from the grant' or a violation of the covenant of 'quiet enjoyment'.]

Stirling J: ...The legal principle invoked on behalf of the plaintiff appears to be recognised in several modern cases ... The result of these judgements appears to me to be that where a landlord demises part of his property for carrying on a particular business, he is bound to abstain from doing anything on the remaining portion which would render the demised premises unfit for carrying on such business in the way in which it is ordinarily carried on, but that this obligation does not extend to special branches of the business which call for extraordinary protection. ...

In the present case, the lease of the... was not merely granted for the purpose that the land demised might be used by the Plaintiff for the purpose of carrying on his business as a timber merchant, but it contains an express covenant binding him to carry on that business. In my opinion, Munro became subject to the obligation to abstain from doing anything on his adjoining property which would substantially interfere with the carrying on of that business in the ordinary course; and that obligation binds the present defendants, as assigns from him, subject to the existing lease. ...

I think that the plaintiff is entitled to an inquiry what sum of money will compensate him for the damage done to him by reason of the defendants' buildings rendering the sheds of the plaintiff less fit for use by him in the ordinary course of his business as a timber merchant. ...

****

Notes

The covenant not to derogate from the grant does not apply where the tenant uses the land for a 'special purpose' or a purpose that was not in the contemplation of both parties at the time of the lease. The reason is that the tenant cannot extend the landlord's obligation beyond what was contemplated by both parties (*Robinson v Kilvett* (1888) 41 Ch. D 88).

Questions

1. What is the difference between a covenant not to derogate from grant and a covenant of quiet enjoyment?
2. Odongo leases part of his building to Odonkara for ten years for purposes of carrying on a business of motorcycle retail and repair shop. Two years later, Odongo leases the remainder of the premises to Boda-Boda, for the same purpose. Odonkara loses more than half of his regular customers to Boda-Boda. Advise Odonkara of possible cause of action, if any, against Odongo.

****

Termination of leases

A lease for a fixed period terminates when the period agreed upon expires. However, the lease may be terminated earlier by either party by notice where the power to do so is expressly provided in the lease agreement. A lease may also be terminated by forfeiture for breach of terms of the agreement, subject to the court's power to grant relief from forfeiture. With respect to periodic tenancies, either party can terminate the tenancy by service of an appropriate notice. These principles are illustrated in the following cases.

****

Termination by notice

A lease for a fixed period cannot be terminated by notice unless the power to do so is expressly reserved in the lease agreement or in the case of forfeiture. In contrast, a periodic tenancy is terminable by either party by serving an appropriate notice, as the following case illustrates.

****

A yearly tenancy is terminable by notice of at least six months expiring at the end of a full period.

Rukandema Kamuru v Kabale Town Council
CA No MKA 10 of 1985 (unreported High Court of Uganda)

[The respondent, Kabale Town Council, allowed the appellant to occupy the subject premises without a tenancy agreement. Between 1980 and 1983 the appellant paid to the respondent (and the respondent accepted) rent on a yearly basis. After receiving rent for 1983, the respondent wrote to the appellant giving him one month to quit the premises. The notice stated that the Council wanted to use the premises for its own purposes. Thereafter the respondent evicted the appellant. The appellant unsuccessfully sued the respondent in the Magistrate's Court for wrongful eviction. This is an appeal against the Magistrate's decision.]

Karokora JSC:...I am satisfied that from the conduct of the respondent through their agent ...the Town Clerk, that the respondent became the landlord of [the] appellant from 1980 up to ...1983 when the respondent ... terminated the tenancy... I accept [the] appellant's evidence to the effect that he was paying his rent to [the] respondent annually. This relationship of tenant/ landlord continued to exist until it was terminated by [the respondent]. Otherwise, what business had the Town Clerk to do with the appellant/plaintiff if he was not acting on behalf of the respondent when he wrote to [the] appellant directing him to start paying rent for Plot III if the respondent was not his landlord? Why did the Town Clerk write Exhibit P3 terminating the tenancy? ...Why was [the] defendant receiving rent for Plot III from [the] plaintiff for four years if they were not the landlord[s]? I must state that from the conduct of the defendant, there was tenancy relationship between the appellant and respondent. Since payment of rent was on a yearly basis, a yearly tenancy was implied in the absence of any other explanation. That is the law as spelt out by Megarry QC and Wade in *The Law of Real Property*" 3rd ed. Page 640.

Now having determined that there was a yearly tenancy between the appellant and respondent, question is whether or not the eviction by [the] respondent ...after the appellant had paid for the whole year of 1983 was lawful.

The law governing determination of yearly tenancy is spelt out by R E Megarry QC & Wade in *The Law of Real Property* 3rd ed. At page 641:

> A yearly tenancy may be determined by such notice and at such time as the parties agree. See *Allison v Scorgall* (1920) 3 KB 443. In default of such agreement, it can be determined by at least half a year's notice expiring at the end of a completed year of the tenancy.

Now therefore considering the facts of this case, since there was a tenancy, it is my view that the respondent could lawfully have determined their tenancy by giving half a year's notice commencing at the end of 1983 which wasn't the case here. See *Masumba v Kasaka* (1971) ULR 222. In the circumstances therefore, the tenancy was wrongfully terminated. In the circumstances therefore [the] respondent is ordered to refund the appellant the amount of rent for which he never used the [premises].

As regards damages for wrongful eviction I think regard must be had to the loss of profit between 1st March when the tenancy was terminated and June 1984 when it should lawfully have occurred bearing in mind half year's notice after 1983 December. See *Masumba v Kasaka*

(1971) ULR 222. I must state that the respondent's conduct was high-handed and unlawful, bearing in mind that they had already received rent for the whole of 1983 from the appellant. In the circumstances the appellant was entitled to aggravated damages. In the case of *Masumba v Kasaka* the High Court awarded aggravated damages ... to the plaintiff whose tenancy had been illegally determined almost 1½ months prior to when it could have been determined. In this case, the tenancy could have been determined in 1984 June i.e about 16 months prior to the time when it ought to have lawfully been determined.

[His Honour ordered the respondent to refund to the appellant the money he paid for rent in advance, general damages for loss of trade and aggravated damages for the illegal eviction.]

****

Note

See also *Bweya Steel Works Ltd v National Insurance Corporation* CS No 63 of 1985 (see extract above).

Question

On 1 January of a certain year, Olinga enters into a contract to lease his house to Aliker on a year-by-year basis. In July of the following year, Mafuta offers Olinga to pay twice the rent Aliker is paying for the house. Olinga finds the offer irresistible. Advise Olinga of the earliest date he can terminate Aliker's lease by notice.

****

Forfeiture

Forfeiture is the re-entry by the landlord for breach of covenant that entitles the landlord to terminate the lease. The following case illustrate the manner of termination of a lease by forfeiture.

****

Forfeiture can only be manifested by actual physical re-entry or by the commencement of an action for possession.

Kasaja v Registrar of Titles

Misc. Appn. No 51 of 1993; [1992] 4 KALR

> [The applicant was the registered proprietor of the suit property. In 1956, he leased the property to one TM for a period of 49 years and the lease was registered under the *Registration of Titles Act*. The lessor reserved a right of re-entry in the event of breach of any covenant including non-payment of rent. In 1992, the applicant purported to enforce forfeiture on the ground that rent was in arrears for a period of twenty years and for failure to maintain the buildings in tenantable repair. At the time, soldiers and their families occupied the premises. As it was not possible for the applicant to take physical possession of the premises without a court order, the applicant served notice of re-entry upon the occupants and the Director of Army Barracks, and sent a copy to the local RC executives. In addition, he put notices on all buildings and in newspapers. Later the applicant applied to the Registrar for the re-entry to be noted under s. 113 of the *RTA*. The Registrar rejected the application on the grounds that he was not satisfied that the applicant had re-entered as required under sections 102(b) and 113 of the Act. This is an application under s. 190 for the Registrar to substantiate his grounds for refusal.]

Ongom J: ...In an affidavit ...deponed by Jonathan N. Tibisaasa, Ag. Chief Registrar of Titles, ...the respondent avers that physical re-entry upon and possession of the suit land is required by the terms of [the lease] and the provisions of the *RTA* and that since the applicant admits he has never physically done both, the application for noting of the re-entry was misconceived and justifiably rejected by the respondent. He further avers that the present application is premature and an abuse of court process as the applicant has never requested him to furnish grounds for the rejection of the application for noting the re-entry as required by the provisions of the *RTA*.

At the hearing, Ms Mulyagonja reiterated the averments in the two affidavits deponed in support of the application. She submitted that the applicant's application for his re-entry to be noted by the respondent was wrongly rejected, as it was not necessary for him to take physical possession of the leased premises in order to constitute a re-entry. She cited the case of *Lugogo Coffee Co Ltd v Combined Growers Ltd* HCCS NO.5543 of 1973 in support of her contention. That case differs from the instant case in that the lessor took possession of the building and closed all doors and put her lock on them and that the lessee did tender prior to the lessor's re-entry after default to pay rent for 10 years but the lessor refused to receive the rent. In the instant case, no physical possession was possible or attempted owing to the old age of the applicant and the fact that some of the tenants are soldiers.

Ms Mulyagonja further contended that the applicant's unequivocal demand to determine the leases did have that effect in law. She cited the case *Moore v Ull Mining Co Ltd* [1908] Ch D 575 in support of her contention, she submitted that the applicant's re-entry and application to have it noted were lawful. She prayed for grant of the orders sought.

Mr Peter Walubiri contended for the respondent that the only issue for this court to determine is whether or not the applicant did re-enter the suit premises in accordance with the requirements of sections 102 (b) and 113 of the *RTA* and the terms of the leases. He submitted that the notional re-entry purportedly made by the applicant did not amount to a re-entry under the provisions of the *RTA* and that the respondent justifiably rejected the application to have it noted in the Register Book of Titles. He submitted that both the *RTA* and the leases required the lessor to make physical possession of the leased premises to determine the leases and that this was not done. He contended that the law does not provide for mere declarations, notices, or adverts in the press. He invited court to reject cases cited by Ms Mulyagonja on the ground that they either differ from the instant case or stated what is contrary to the provisions of Sections 102(b) and 113 of the *RTA*. That was the pleadings and position of the parties to this application.

As I stated earlier, both leases empowered the lessor to enter upon the [land and] resume possession of the demised premised upon default of payment of rent. This is one of the powers statutorily implied under the provisions of section 102(b) of the *RTA*. It is not denied by the respondent that the lessees breached the covenants to pay rent and keep the leased premises in good and tenantable repair and that the applicant made some kind of re-entry pursuant to the covenant in consequence thereof.

A decision on whether the mode of re-entry adopted by the applicant determined the leases and thus justified the respondent to make an entry of such re-entry in the Register Book and necessitated this application depends on the construction of section 102(b) and 113 of the *RTA* and the leases themselves.

Section 102(b) provides that in every lease made under the provisions of the *RTA* there shall be implied in the lessor and his transferee that in case of default of payment of rent for a space of 30 days or in case of any breach or non-observance of any of the covenants expressed in the lease or implied by law on the part of the lessee or of his transferee:

> It shall be lawful for the lessor or his transferee to re-enter upon and take possession of the leased property.

Section 113 provides in effect that if it is proved to the satisfaction of the Registrar that the lessor or sub-lessor or his transferee has re-entered upon the premises under the power of section 102 of the *RTA* or in conformity with the provisions for re-entry contained in the lease or that the lessee or sub-lessees has abandoned the leased promises and that the lessor or sub-lessor or his transferee has thereupon re-entered and occupied the said premises by himself or by his tenants undisturbed by the lessee or sub-lessee, the Registrar may make an entry of such re-entry and the term for which the land was leased shall, upon the entry being made, determine. The leases themselves empower the lessor to enter upon and resume possession of the demised premises.

From the above it seems abundantly clear that re-entry without undisturbed occupation of the demised premises by the lessor is not sufficient to determine the lease. The case of *Moore v. Ull Coats Mining Co Ltd* cited by Mr Walubiri clearly lays down the principle that where the term in the lease is that the landlord may re-enter upon breach of a covenant he must actually re-enter upon breach of a covenant or he must do that which in law is equivalent to re-entry, viz. commence an action for the purpose of obtaining possession. It was stated clearly in that case that the mere giving of notice of intention by the lessor to re-enter coupled with a statement that the lease has determined which had not in fact happened, is not sufficient to constitute re-entry in law. I take that to be a correct statement of the law. I found no authority for the proposition that anything less than the issue of a suit demanding possession can suffice to constitute legal re-entry.

Applying this principle to the instant case, I find that the purported service notices and adverts thereof did not amount to re-entry in law. The respondent was, therefore, right in rejecting the application for noting the re-entry-as there was no re-entry to speak of.

****

Note

In *Naluswa v Luswabi* (Misc. C No 5 of 1974, unreported), the applicant by Notice of Motion sought an order directing the Registrar of Titles to record determination of a lease and re-entry in the Register Book under ss. 105 and 113 of the *Registration of Titles Act.* The application was based on a judgement in a Magistrate's Court, held in the applicant's favour for the respondent to pay the applicant all outstanding rent. Allen Ag J held that the application was misconceived because under s. 105, the applicant had to satisfy the Registrar that he had recovered possession. Moreover, under s. 113 the applicant had to approach the Registrar in order to apply for an entry to be made. The applicant could only approach the court for an order of mandamus if the Registrar refused to make an entry. Until then, the courts had no jurisdiction under either section to order the Registrar to make an entry.

****

As between the parties a lease is effectively terminated when the lessor makes a lawful re-entry even if the re-entry is not endorsed in the Register Book.

Lugogo Coffee Co (U) Ltd v Singo Combined Coffee Growers Ltd
CS No 554 Of 1973

[Namiro was the registered owner of the suit property. In 1957, she leased the property to the defendant company for 49 years. In 1972, Namiro purported to re-enter on the ground that the defendant had defaulted in payment of rent for ten years. Later she applied to the Registrar of Titles to record the re-entry in the Register Book. But the Registrar declined claiming that he was powerless to do so under s.113 of the *Registration of Titles Act.* Meanwhile, Namiro sold the land to the plaintiff. The plaintiff instituted proceedings against the defendant for vacant possession. The defendant claimed to be in legal occupation pursuant to the 1957 lease agreement with Namiro.]

Nyamchoncho J: At the trial both counsel agreed to have two preliminary issues determined. These are: (1) Whether the Registrar's refusal to make an entry of the re-entry in the Register Book negatives the determination of the lease which would, otherwise take place if the re-entry by the lessor was a valid re-entry. (2) Whether the defendant is entitled to a relief against forfeiture for non-payment of rent.

Counsel for the plaintiff company argued that the power of the Registrar of Titles under s.113 (Cap 205) to make an entry of a re-entry by the lessor in the Register Book are not mandatory. He agreed that if an entry of the re-entry is made in the Register Book, the lease is determined. But if he refuses to make such entry because of a mistaken view of the law, the lease is determined as well because a lease is a contract and a breach of its covenants entitles the lessor to avoid the contract. He urged the court so to hold.

Counsel for the defendant company contended that although a lease is a contract it is governed by statute and can be determined only in accordance with the provisions of s.113. He said that the Registrar of Titles acted properly to refuse the application, as the applicant had not physically entered upon the land. In reply, counsel for the plaintiff company submitted that Byatisi Namiro did re-enter upon the land. He did not think that re-entry on the land requires physical entry. He referred me to *Moore v. Allocoats Mining Co. Ltd.* [1908] Ch. D. 575, *Aglionby v. Cohen* [1957] 1 QB 558. [Rent]... payment was delayed for 10 years. The lady refused it. He repeated that the relief should be refused because there was an unreasonable delay by the defendant to go to court to ask for such relief. The powers of the Registrar of Titles under s.113 of the Act are not mandatory. He should be satisfied that the lessor has re-entered upon the premises in strict conformity with the provisions for re-entry. If he is so satisfied he makes an entry of such re-entry in the Register Book. If he is not satisfied, he refuses to make such entry. In the instant case the Registrar of Titles in his letter dated 29th June, 1972, refused to make the entry on the grounds that the provisions of s.113 of the Act have not been complied with. The Registrar of Titles was in error to refuse to make an entry on this ground. There is nothing in s.113 which should be complied with by the lessor. The lessor has only to comply with the provisions for re-entry contained in the lease. Clause 2 of the lease states:

> If the lessee shall fail to pay the rent hereby reserved on its due date... the lessor may forthwith enter upon or resume possession of the demised premises...

There is overwhelming evidence that the lessee was in arrears with his rent for 10 years. In pursuance of this clause, the lessor resumed possession of the premises. The letter of 19th April, 1972 by counsel confirms this. There the lessor applied to the Registrar of Titles under 2.113 of the Act. There is an affidavit sworn by the lessor, para.3 thereof, show that the arrears of rent were from 1967–1971 and 1972. Paragraph 6 also shows that on 26th April, 1972, at 4.15 p.m. the lessor re-entered upon the premises in the company of Mr. P. Ejiet, an Inspector of Police, Mr Wasswa and Mr N. K. Ladia her advocate. She took possession of the building and closed all doors, put her locks on the doors. With this evidence before the Registrar of Titles, I fail to see why he thought the lessor had failed to prove her case. The Registrar of Titles amended his decision in February, 1973 by his letter to Mr Mayanja-Nkangi counsel for the plaintiff. This time he correctly cited the provisions which had to be complied with. He then referred the parties to settle the matter by court action. Again, the Registrar in rejecting the application ignored the lessor's affidavit and the lessor's letter dated 28th April, 1972, which set out the reasons for re-entry. He said he could not make an entry because the lessee was still in possession. This decision, I think is based on a wrong view of the law.

Now the question is whether by the refusal of the Registrar of Titles to make an entry of such re-entry in the Register Book the lease is still subsisting. I have not seen any judicial decision in Uganda or East Africa on this question although I do not think this is the first case to come before the court. There is, however, a similar provision in Australia which has been so judicially considered. In AUSTRALIA TORRENS SYSTEM, the Author at p.939 says:

> As between the lessor and the lessee, the lease is determined by the lessor's lawful re-entry, but until the proper entry is made in the Register the lessee is able to confer a good title on a person who becomes duly registered without notice of the lessor's re-entry.

He refers to *Baker's Creek Co. v Hack* [1894] 15 N.S.W. Eq. 207. I have not been able to see this case.

I agree with the comment. The agreement between the lessor and the lessee is contained in a lease. It is a contract. A breach of a condition in the contract entitles either party to avoid the contract. By the lessor's re-entry upon the premises the contract was rescinded. By section 113, it had to be perfected by the Registrar of Titles by making an entry of such re-entry in the Register Book. Before the entry is made in the Register Book, the lessee would appear to have an equitable title only. The entry on the Register Book terminates it. In my opinion the refusal by the Registrar of Titles to make an entry of such re-entry does not have the effect of keeping the lease subsisting. As the author says above that until the entry is made in the register, the lessee can confer a good title on a person who becomes duly registered without notice of the lessor's re-entry, it follows that he cannot confer any title to a person who has knowledge of the lessor's re-entry. This inability to confer any title shows that the lease is terminated by the lessor's re-entry for all intents and purposes as between the lessor and the lessee although the law has not recognised that re-entry.

I would, therefore, answer the first issue in the negative.

The second issue is whether the defendant is entitled to relief against forfeiture for non-payment of rent. Mr Mayanja-Nkangi for the plaintiff company argued that the defendant company acted improperly by refusing to pay rent for 10 years and thereafter up to the present day, and moreover it slept over its rights to apply for the relief, it is guilty of laches. As this is an equitable remedy, the court should exercise its discretion and refuse the relief.

Mr Balikuddembe for the defendant company argued that it was not true that the defendant company did not pay rent for the 10 years i.e. between 1967–1972. He said there is evidence to show that the rent was paid in one lump for the 10 years and that since 1972 rent has been tendered but refused. The defendant company is still willing to pay. He referred me to paragraph 1409 and 1400 *Halsbury's Laws of England* Vol. 23, 3rd Ed. He asked the court to grant this relief sought.

I have some difficulty to decide this issue without proper evidence before me. One thing is however clear that the defendant company did not tender the rent due from 1967 to 1972 until after the lessor had resumed possession of the demised premises on 26th April, 1972…but it was promptly rejected that day in a letter dated 29th April 1972 by counsel for the plaintiff. The defendant did not apply for the relief promptly. The lessor didn't institute an action against the defendant company. On 31/5/73 it filed claiming possession of the demised premises etc. In the original written statement of defence of 3rd July, 1973 no relief was prayed. On 20th December, 1973 the defendant company applied for and was allowed to file an amendment praying for the relief. Relief from forfeiture for non-payment of rent has been recognised by courts. This relief can be applied for before or after judgement. In this case it has been applied for, no judgement has yet been given. The lessee did tender the rent in full, on 29th April 1972 which was refused. If the lessee then had applied for relief, it may be it could have obtained it.

Re-entry on non-payment of rent is regarded in equity merely as a security for the rent and provided the lessor and other persons interested can be put in the same position as before the lessee is entitled to be relieved against the forfeiture on payment of the rent and any expenses to which the lessor has been put. (See para. 1409 *Halsbury's Laws* 3rd Ed.)

The defendant company may have acted improperly by not tendering the rent when it was due (the defendant company alleges that the lessor's whereabouts were not known). I think the lessor too is to blame, why did she wait for 10 years without taking any action? It may be true that the defendant company could not trace her whereabouts. In any case the fact that the defendant company is a bad payer of rent does not amount to a ground for refusing relief – see *Gill v. Lewis* [1956] 1 All E.R. 844 in which at p. 854 E, Lord Hodson L.J. so held. Moreover she allowed the defendant to continue using the premises up-to now. I think I would answer the second issue in the affirmative too.

(Action dismissed).

****

Notes

1. It is submitted that the learned Judge's statement that 'Before the entry is made in the Register Book, the lessee would appear to have an equitable title only' is incorrect. Under the *Registration of Titles Act* (s 51), title is vested and divested by registration. Registration is equivalent to a legal title under the general law. Therefore, as long as the lease is not cancelled in the Register Book it continues to be a 'legal' title. It is for this reason, as His Honour rightly pointed out, that, so long as the re-entry is not entered in the Register, the lessee could confer a good title to an innocent third party.
2. The courts' power to grant relief from forfeiture is discussed in several other cases. These include: *Kiwanuka-Musisi v Seggane* [1973] 561 (U); *Haji Musa v Ondowa* HCCC 360 of 1971 (unreported); and *Butagira v Namukasa* CA No 69 of 1989 (unreported). See extracts below.
3. The equitable power to grant relief from forfeiture is enacted in s 24 of the *Judicature Statute*, 1996.

****

Relief from forfeiture

Under s. 27 of the *Judicature Statute*, 1996, a lessee may apply to court or District Land Tribunal[24] for relief from forfeiture of a lease for breach of covenant. Section 27 of the *Judicature Statute* provides as follows:

> 27. (1) Where a lessor is proceeding, by action or otherwise to enforce a right of re-entry or forfeiture for non-payment of rent the lessee, his or her executors, administrators or assigns may in the lessor's action or in an action brought by himself or herself apply to the High Court for relief.
>
> (2) The High Court, under subsection (1) of this section, may
>
> (a) grant any relief it considers fit on such terms as to costs, expenses, damages, compensation, penalty or otherwise including the granting of an injunction to restrain any future non-payment of rent as it thinks fit; or
>
> (b) refuse the relief sought as it thinks fit.
>
> (3) Where relief is granted under the provisions of this section the lessee, his or her executors, administrators or assigns shall hold the demised property according to the terms of the lease without necessity of a new lease.
>
> (4) The High Court may, after judgement in any action for a right of re-entry or forfeiture, grant relief from forfeiture on application made in that behalf within six months from the date of the execution of judgement by the lessee, his or her executor, administrator or assign on such terms and conditions as to payment of rent and costs or otherwise as it may impose.

It is submitted that s. 27 of the *Judicature Statute* only applies to ordinary leases and not to tenancies by occupancy created by virtue of s. 32 of the *Land Act*. This is because the power to grant relief from forfeiture of a tenancy by occupancy is specifically dealt with under the *Land Act*. Section 33 of the Act provides that the Land Tribunals may grant a tenant by occupancy relief from forfeiture for non-payment of rent subject to terms stipulated in the section.

Section 27 of the *Judicature Statute* is identical with s 24 of the *Judicature Act*, 1967, which was repealed by the former. Accordingly, although the cases below were decided under the 1967 Act, it is submitted that the principles they express would still be the same under the current law.

****

[24] See 77(2) of the *Land Act*.

The court will not grant relief from forfeiture where the land has already been re-let to another tenant

Kiwanuka-Musisi v Segane
[1973] EA 561

[The respondent leased the suit land to the applicant/lessee subject to a right to re-enter and terminate the leases on breach of any covenant in the lease. Upon alleged breach of certain covenants including non-payment of rent, the respondent served the applicant notice warning him of the breach. After expiration of the notice the respondent re-entered. The re-entry was recorded in the Register Book. Then the respondent, to the applicant's knowledge, leased the land to one Serugunda. The latter proceeded to demolish old buildings on the land to replace them with new ones. Five months after the land was leased to Serugunda, the applicant instituted these proceedings for relief from forfeiture.]

Nyamuchoncho J: ... The applicant does not admit breach of the covenants or default in payment of rent, while the respondent asserts that the applicant was in breach of the covenants and failed to tender the rent on the due date. S. 102(b) of the *Registration of Titles Act* (cap 205) permits the lessor to re-enter in case of any breach or non-observance continues for the space of thirty days. S. 113 of the said Act permits the Registrar of Titles to make an entry in his Register of such re-entry if he is satisfied that the re-entry was in conformity with the provisions of s. 102 (b) of the said Act. I have heard no evidence to suggest that ss. 102 (b) and 113 were not complied with, and so I make no finding on that. I am unable to decide which party is in breach.

Turning to the application itself, I note that the relief the applicant is seeking is an equitable relief. The provision for re-entry on non-payment of rent is regarded in equity as merely a security for rent, and accordingly, provided that the landlord can be put in the same position as before, the tenant is entitled to be relieved against the forfeiture on payment of the rent and any expenses to which the landlord has been put: *Haji Musa v Martin Ondowa*, H.C.C.C 360 of 1971 (unreported). The court has a discretion to grant or refuse the relief, and it will not grant the relief if it would entail an injustice to the landlord, eg where the landlord has re-let the premises.... In this case, the piece of land in question was re-let on 1 July 1971 to Serugunda, whether rightly or wrongly, I cannot say. The effect of this application, if granted, would therefore entail injustice to the landlord. I agree with the submission of counsel for the respondent that applicant came too late to apply for the relief. For these reasons the application is dismissed with costs.

Note

See also *Gomba Marines and Contractors (Ltd) v Kiwana* (Misc. Appn. No 131B/93, unreported), extracted below.

******

Courts have no jurisdiction to grant relief from forfeiture under s. 27(4) of the Judicature Statute where the application is made more than 6 months after delivery of judgement for re-entry

Gomba Marines and Contractors (Ltd) v Kiwana
(Misc. Appn. No 131B/93, unreported, High Court of Uganda)

The respondent is the registered proprietor of the suit property. In 1969, the respondent leased the property to a third party for a period of 49 years, who in turn assigned the lease to the applicant company. The assignment was noted in the Register Book in May 1970. Two years later, following the expulsion of Asians from Uganda, the MD of the appellant company left Uganda leaving no adequate arrangements for the payment of ground rent. The property was vested in the Departed Asians Custodian Board and remained so until 9 April 1991, when the respondent re-entered on the ground of non-payment of rent. The re-entry was noted on the Register Book. Subsequently, the Registrar purported to reinstate the lease, but was stopped by court order dated 24/6/92. With the permission of the Ministry of Lands, the respondent sub-divided the suit property. Allegedly by the time of this action she had already sold one of the plots. The company filed this application to restore the lease. It sought relief from forfeiture under s 24(4) of the *Judicature Act*, 1967.[25]

Byamugisha J: ... Counsel [for the applicant] submitted that this Court has power to grant relief in suitable cases where third party interests are not involved. He referred to a number of authorities where court declined to grant relief against forfeiture where the suit property had already passed to a third party. The authorities are: *Butagira v Namukasa* (CA No 6 of 89); *Kiwanuka Musisi v Segane* (1974) EA 561; *Bidandi Ssali v Attorney General* (CS No 831 of 1989).

Turning to the affidavit of the respondent in which she claimed that she has carried out substantial developments on the land and has transferred part of it to a third party; counsel pointed out that there was no evidence of this. He also claimed that the applicant company has made substantial investments worth millions of shillings in the property and stands to lose it. He prayed that relief be granted.

While responding to the above submissions, counsel for the respondent stated that the application is brought under the wrong provisions of the law. He pointed out that under section 24(4) of the *Judicature Act*, there is no statutory power conferred on the Court where the re-entry was peaceful and not by Court order. ... He claimed that section 24 is inapplicable. In case the Court is inclined to grant the application, counsel pointed out that the application was brought after the expiry of six months from the date of re-entry, which was completed on 9 April 1991. No order for extension of time was sought and even it was, no power is conferred on this court to extend the time fixed in the *Judicature Act*.

On the merits of the application itself, counsel pointed out that the subject matter of the lease is non-existent. It was his submission that the purpose of relief against forfeiture is to restore parties to their former positions before the default complained of was committed. He pointed out that subsequent to the re-entry, Plot 5 was subdivided and it became plot 432 and 433 and one of them has since been sold to a third party.

Counsel concluded his submission by stating that the principle by which relief is being sought in this case is rooted in equity and there has been delay in seeking the regularisation of the lease. He pointed out that delay defeats equity and helps those who are vigilant. He referred to the case of *Lugogo Coffee Ltd v Singo Combined Growers* Ltd (1976) HCB 92 where relief was refused to an applicant who brought the application 10 years after default. ...

Turning to the application itself, I shall first determine whether it was brought under the right provisions of the law. It was filed under the provisions of section 24(4) of the *Judicature Act*, which states as follows:

> The High Court may, after judgement in any action of re-entry or forfeiture, grant relief from forfeiture on application made in that behalf within six months from the date of the execution of judgement by the lessee, his executor, administrator, or assign on such terms and conditions as to payment of rent and costs or otherwise as it may impose.

The counsel who appeared in this matter did not cite any authority which has judicially interpreted the provisions of the above section. Essentially, it gives the High Court discretion to grant relief against forfeiture on an application made by the lessee within a period of six months after judgement in any action for re-entry. This means as I understand it that there should be a judgement in existence in an action brought by a lessor or lessee for forfeiture of the lease where the lessee has defaulted. In order for the provisions of the section to apply the application has to be brought [within a period of] six months after the date of judgement. To this extent, I am inclined to agree

---

25 The *Judicature Act* was repealed and replaced by the *Judicature Statute*, 1996. Section 24(4) of the former Act is identical with s. 27(4) of the latter.

with the submissions of counsel for the respondent that the instant application was brought under the wrong provisions of the law. The respondent re-entered the suit property peacefully without any order from court. The ruling of this court dated 24/6/92 was directed against the Registrar of Titles to stop him from reinstating the lease, which had been effectively removed in 1991. Even if it could be said that the ruling in question is a judgement within the meaning of the section, the instant application was filed well over six months after the ruling was delivered and no extension of time was sought. This application is therefore barred by the statute.

In case it is found that this finding is wrong, is the applicant company entitled to the relief it is seeking? I agree with the statement of the law and the authorities cited by counsel for the applicant that relief against forfeiture is equitable in nature and a lessee will irretrievably lose his right to relief unless he makes an application before the lessor has actually re-entered. In particular, relief cannot be granted where parties have altered their position and some new interests have been created. In other words, relief will be refused if it is likely to cause injustice to the lessor. In the instant case, the respondent averred that part of the land was subdivided to create two plots. One of the plots has already been transferred to ... a third party and she has carried out substantial developments on the second plot ...On the other hand the affidavit of the [applicant] does not state what developments are on the land, if any. It has not been shown by affidavit that the land has been put to the use for which it was leased. The suit land was leased for purposes of erecting recreational facilities, residential accommodation, and many others. The lessee or its Managing Director left this country barely two years after the lease had been concluded and I do not think the company had time to carry out the developments stated in the lease. Another reason, which I feel militates against the grant, is the delay in bringing the application. The repossession certificate was first issued on 20/04/84 and no steps were taken to regularise the lease. There has been inordinate delay in bringing the application in my view. On the whole I am not satisfied that the applicant has made out a case sufficient to entitle it to the relief it is seeking. The parties have changed their positions and new interests have been created. I therefore decline to grant the relief sought and dismiss the application with costs to the respondent.

****

Notes

1. The possible grounds upon which a court may grant or refuse to grant relief from forfeiture have been stated in several cases, see for example: *Butagira v Namukasa* CA No 6 of 1989; *Lugogo Coffee Co (U) Ltd v Combined Coffee Growers Ltd* CS No 554 of 1973 (see extract); *Haji Musa Magala v Ondowa* CS No 360 of 1971.
2. In *Shiloh Spinners Ltd v Harding* [1973] AC 691 at 725, Lord Wilberforce said, with reference to equitable jurisdiction to relieve from forfeiture, that to obtain relief a person seeking it must show that relief is 'appropriate' and that it 'involves consideration of the conduct of the applicant for relief, in particular whether his default was wilful, of the gravity of the breaches, and of the disparity of the value of the property of which forfeiture is claimed as compared with the damage caused by the breach'. However, in reading these cases, readers should be mindful of the following observations of Lord Loreburn LC in *Hyman v Rose* [1912] AC 632 at 631:

   I desire in the first instance to point out that the discretion given by the section is very wide. The Court is to consider all the circumstances and the conduct of the parties. Now it seems to me that when the Act is so express to provide a wide discretion, meaning, no doubt, to prevent one man from forfeiting what in fair dealing belongs to some one else, by taking advantage of a breach from which he is not commensurately and irreparably damaged, it is not advisable to lay down any rigid rules for guiding that discretion. ... It is not safe, I think, to say that the Court must and will always insist upon certain things when the Act does not require them, and the facts of some unforeseen case may make the Court wish it had kept a free hand.

Loreburn LC was speaking with reference to the statutory jurisdiction to grant relief from forfeiture similar to that conferred to the High Court by s. 27 of the *Judicature Statute*.

3. The statutory power to grant relief from forfeiture can only be exercised where the breach is for non-payment of rent and not for breach of other covenants (*Butagira v Namukasa* CA No 6 of 1989).
4. Historically, the courts of equity have asserted the right to relieve against forfeiture of property for breach 'of covenant or condition where the primary object of the bargain is to secure a stated result which can effectively be attained when the matter comes before the court, and where the forfeiture provision is added by way of security for the production of that result' (per Lord Wilberforce in *Shiloh Spinners Ltd v Harding* [1973] AC 691 at 722, 723.) This includes relief from forfeiture for breach of covenant to pay rent, to insure premises, to repair, covenant not to commit waste and not to assign without consent (at pp. 722-724). The courts in Uganda have the jurisdiction to apply the doctrines of equity and would probably assert the same powers. However, it is a moot point whether, in view of the power to grant relief from forfeiture under s. 27 of the *Judicature Statute*, the courts retain their inherent equitable jurisdiction to do the same. In *Shiloh Spinners Ltd v Harding*, Lord Wilberforce expressed a view that the fact that under various statutory provisions the courts had power to grant relief from forfeiture did not necessarily mean that the legislature intended to override the courts' inherent equitable jurisdiction to do the same. At p. 725, His Lordship said: 'In my opinion where the courts have established a general principle of law or equity, and the legislature steps in with particular legislation in a particular area, it must, unless showing a contrary intention, be taken to have left cases outside that area where they were under the influence of the general law.' In that case, the various statutory provisions that gave the courts power to grant relief from forfeiture for breach of specified covenants in a lease did not mention breach of covenant not to assign without consent. The House of Lords held that in an appropriate case a court of equity could grant relief against forfeiture for breach of such covenant 'if it was fair and just to do so' (per Lord Wilberforce at p. 725). It is suggested that a possible argument could be made with respect to the power of the courts in Uganda.

Question

In *Shiloh Spinners Ltd v Harding* [1973] AC 691 at 723, Lord Wilberforce said that it was not the purpose of the equitable jurisdiction to 'relieve against men's bargains'. On the contrary, the general rule is that 'contractual promises should be observed and contractual rights respected'.(per Lord Simon at p. 727). How do you reconcile these statements with the courts' power to grant relief from forfeiture? What are the possible policy considerations?

****

Application for relief after peaceable re-entry

Section 27(1) of the *Judicature Statute*, provides that a lessee may seek judicial relief from forfeiture where the lessor is '*proceeding*, by action or *otherwise* to enforce re-entry or forfeiture for non-payment of rent'. This raises a question whether under this provision the court has the jurisdiction to grant relief to a lessee where the lessor re-enters without resort to court. There is no Ugandan case interpreting the provision. The following English case deals with this issue with respect to s. 146(2) of the English *Law of Property Act*, 1925, which is identical with s. 27(1).

****

The courts may grant the lessee relief from forfeiture even where the lessor has lawfully re-entered without resort to court

Billson v Residential Apartments
[1992] 2 All ER 141

[The plaintiffs/respondents were the proprietors of the subject premises, which they leased to the defendants/appellants. The lease contained a covenant against carrying out alterations without the respondents' consent. The appellants started a major renovation of the premises without the respondents' consent. The latter sent them a notice under s. 146 of the *Law of Property Act* 1925 (UK) requiring them to remedy the breach within a reasonable time. The appellants however continued with the renovation. One day at 6 am, the respondents peaceably re-entered the vacant premises and changed the locks. At 10 am on the same day, the appellants regained possession. The respondents successfully sued for re-possession. The lower court rejected the appellant's application for relief from forfeiture under s. 146(2) of the LPA, on the ground that once the landlord re-entered the court had no jurisdiction to grant relief under that provision.. This is an appeal to the House of Lords.]

Lord Templeman: ...Section 146(1) prevents the landlord from enforcing a right of re-entry or forfeiture by action or otherwise so that the landlord cannot determine the lease by issuing and serving a writ or by re-entering the premises until the tenant has failed within a reasonable time to remedy the breach and make reasonable compensation. Section 146(2) enables the tenant to apply to the court for relief where the landlord is proceeding 'by action or otherwise' to enforce his right of re-entry or forfeiture. If the landlord 'is proceeding' to determine the lease by issuing and serving a writ, the tenant may apply for relief after the writ has been served. If the landlord 'is proceeding' to determine the lease by re-entering into possession, the tenant may apply for relief after the landlord has re-entered.

Mr Reid [for the respondents] submitted and referred to authority for the proposition that on the true construction of 5 146(2) a tenant cannot apply for relief against forfeiture after the landlord has re-entered without obtaining a court order. Thereafter the landlord is no longer 'proceeding' to enforce his rights; he has succeeded in enforcing them. The proposition is in my opinion historically unsound because the effect of issuing and serving a writ is precisely the same as the effect of re-entry; in each case the lease is determined. The landlord is entitled to remain in possession if he has re-entered and he is entitled to possession if he has issued and served a writ because the lease no longer exists. In each case the tenant seeks relief because the lease has been forfeited. The proposition is also inconsistent with the language of s 146(2). The tenant may apply for relief where the landlord is 'proceeding, by action or otherwise' to enforce his rights. The tenant may apply for relief where the landlord is 'proceeding' by action and also where the landlord is proceeding 'otherwise' than by action. This can only mean that the tenant may apply for relief where the landlord is proceeding to forfeit by re-entry after the expiry of a s 146 notice. If re-entry bars relief, the right of the tenant to apply for relief where the landlord is proceeding otherwise than by action is substantially inoperative and the words 'or otherwise' in s 146(2) have no application. In my opinion those words must have been included because Parliament intended that a tenant should be able to obtain relief against a landlord whether the landlord has asserted his rights by a writ or by re-entering. It is said that a tenant served with a s 146 notice could during and after the expiration of the notice apply for relief under s 146(2) but if he fails to do so he is at the mercy of the landlord who decides to re-enter and whose rights are therefore, it is said, quite unaffected by the provisions of s 146(2) designed to relieve tenants from the consequences of breach of covenant. In my opinion the ambiguous words 'is proceeding' can mean 'proceeds' and should not be construed so as to produce the result that a tenant served with a s 146 notice can only ensure that he will be able to apply for relief if he does so before he knows whether or not the landlord intends to proceed at all or whether, if the landlord decides to proceed, he will issue and serve a writ or will attempt to re-enter. ...

The right conferred by s 146(2) on a tenant to apply for relief against forfeiture may, without violence to the language, be construed as a right to apply 'where a lessor *proceeds*, by action or otherwise' to enforce a right of re-entry, so construed, s 146(2) enables the tenant to apply for relief whenever and however the landlord claims that the lease has been determined for breach of covenant. I have no doubt that this was the object and intention and is the effect of s 146. ...

My Lords, I accept the conclusion that a landlord who serves a notice under s 146(1) can be said, for the purposes of s 146(2), to be proceeding to enforce his rights under the lease. A tenant authorised by s 146(2) to apply to the court for relief against forfeiture if he fails to comply with a s 146 notice may make that application after service of the notice for the purpose of elucidating the issues raised by the notice, ascertaining the intentions of the landlord, and setting in train the machinery by which the dispute between the landlord and the tenant can be determined by negotiation or by the court. But the fact that the tenant may apply to the court for relief after service of the s 146 notice does not mean that if he does not do so he loses the right conferred on him by s 146(2) to apply for relief if and when the landlord proceeds, not by action but 'otherwise' by exercising a right of re-entry. No absurdity follows from a construction which allows the tenant to apply for relief before and after a landlord re-enters without first obtaining a court order.

In the words of Laskin JA in *Re Rexdale Investment Ltd and Gibson* [1967] 1OR 251 at 259, dealing with provisions in the Ontario legislation indistinguishable from s 146(2), the argument that a tenant cannot apply for relief after a landlord has determined the lease by re-entry:

> depends on a detached grammatical reading of the phrase 'is proceeding' ... which makes nonsense of the phrase 'or otherwise' (as covering physical re-entry) by making ineffective, in any practical sense, the provision for relief from forfeiture applicable to such re-entry. We do not construe statutes, especially when they are remedial ... to the point of self-contradiction. In my opinion, the phrase 'is proceeding' is more properly read in the sense of 'has proceeded', and I am fortified in this view by the fact that the exercise of the power of termination is manifested effectively by the mere taking of proceedings as well as by physical re-entry. What [s 146(2)] means, therefore, is that when the landlord has terminated the lease by action or by actual re-entry without action, the tenant may seek relief from forfeiture in the pending action, if any, or, if none, by proceedings initiated by him, in the latter case, one would expect prompt reaction by the tenant ... The English cases relied on ... [*Rogers v Rice* [1892] 2 Ch 170]; *Locke v Pearce* [1893] 2 Ch 271 and *Quilter v Mapleson* (1882) 9 QBD 672] are distinguishable, if need be ... by the fact ... that they relate to re-entry in pursuance of a judgement for possession.

These observations by a distinguished Canadian Judge, who subsequently became Chief Justice of the Supreme Court of Canada, support the views which I have formed concerning the construction of s. 146 and the ambit and effect of the earlier decisions.

[Other members of the Court agreed.]

****

Repudiation of a lease

Under the general law of contract, breach of a fundamental term of the agreement entitles the innocent party to repudiate or rescind the contract. This principle applies to lease agreements (*Shevill v Builders Licensing Board* (1982) 149 CLR 620 (High Court of Australia). But in this context the remedy is more important for the tenant than the landlord since the latter more often than not reserves a right to terminate the lease for breach of any term. The following case illustrates the tenant's power to repudiate a lease.

****

A tenant may repudiate the lease where the landlord delivers possession of only part of the leased premises.

A.M. Dharas & Sons v Elys Ltd
(1963) E.A. 573

[The plaintiffs let a shop and a basement store to the defendants for a period of ten months commencing on 1 March 1961. The tenancy agreement was subject to a term that the plaintiffs would continue to occupy and use the store until 31 March. The defendants duly took possession of the basement. When April came the plaintiffs refused to give up vacant possession of the store and the defendants vacated the premises on 31 July. The plaintiffs sued the defendants claiming damages for breach of the tenancy agreement. In the plaint, the damages were expressed as rent for the unexpired period of the tenancy. The defendants submitted that the plaintiffs had breached the tenancy agreement by failing to give vacant possession of the whole demised premises and, that consequently, they were entitled to repudiate the agreement and vacate the premises as they did. The defendant counter claimed a refund of a proportion of the rent they paid attributed to the part occupied by the plaintiff.]

Udo Udoma CJ: ...I accept the evidence of the defendants and their witness and find as a fact that throughout the period they were in occupation of the shop, the only communicating door between the shop and the store was kept locked up by the plaintiffs; that the defendants, being deliberately kept out of it by the plaintiffs, had no access to the said store; and that after April 1, 1961, when possession of the store ought to have been given, the plaintiffs had wilfully refused to give vacant possession of the said store to the defendants but had themselves continued in possession thereof to the detriment of the defendants. Such conduct on the part of the plaintiffs, I am of opinion was completely incompatible with the due and diligent performance of their obligations under the terms of the tenancy agreement. I hold that it was in breach thereof.

I also find that despite that default, the plaintiffs had proceeded to levy and had in fact successfully levied distress for, and had recovered from the defendants rent in arrear for the months of June and July 1961. It was in consequences of the levy of distress, and because the plaintiffs still deliberately refused to give vacant possession of the store to the defendants that the defendants had to vacate the premises on July 31, 1961, that is to say, before the expiration of the time fixed by the tenancy agreement. ...

Counsel for the defendants has submitted that this action is not maintainable on the ground that since it was the plaintiffs who had committed a breach of the tenancy agreement by failing to deliver vacant possession of the whole premises demised, the defendants were entitled to repudiate, and to treat the contract as at an end, and to vacate the premises as they did. They were not under obligation any more to perform their part of the contract.

On the other hand, it was contended for the plaintiffs that, if even the court should find that the plaintiffs had failed to deliver vacant possession of the store to the defendants, since the defendants had been given vacant possession of a part of the demised premises, they were not entitled to repudiate the contract of tenancy. They were still bound to pay the rent agreed, and could only sue for damages for breach of contract, because failure on the part of the plaintiffs to deliver vacant possession of only part of the demised premises could only mount to a breach of the covenant for quiet enjoyment. ...

I ...agree that failure by the plaintiffs to deliver possession of a part of the demised premises, that is, the store to the defendants may be regarded as a breach of the implied covenant for quiet enjoyment, which would entitle the defendants to sue for damages. On the authority of *Markham v Paget* ([1908] 1 Ch 697), in the absence of express covenant as in the instant case, the mere relation of landlord and tenant implies in law a covenant of quiet enjoyment. In the old English case of *Coe v Clay* ((1829) 11 Ex. 775; 156 ER 1045) it was laid down that he who lets agrees to give possession, and if he fails to do so, the lessee may recover damages against him, and he is not driven to bring an action for ejectment.

In that case the defendant had agreed … to let the plaintiff certain premises, and the plaintiff, being unable to get possession because a preceding occupier wrongfully refused to quit, had sued the defendant for damages. At the trial …it was argued on behalf of the defendant that the plaintiff had committed no breach of the contract as the agreement amounted to an actual demise of the premises; that the plaintiff had an interest upon which he might have brought an action for ejectment; and that it was no fault of the defendant if a person not claiming under him committed a wrong for which the plaintiff had a distinct remedy by ejectment. Judgement was however entered for the plaintiff, the court holding that he who lets agrees to give possession and not merely to give a chance of a law suit. …

On the evidence in this case, and finding as I do that the conduct of the plaintiffs in refusing to deliver possession of the store to the defendants was inconsistent with the terms of the tenancy agreement and wholly incompatible with the due performance thereof the irresistible inference to be drawn from the conduct of the plaintiffs is that they never had any intention of putting the defendants into vacant possession of the store. That being so, and as the rent reserved under the agreement was of the whole of the premises purported to be demised, that is to say, the shop and the store and to be issuing therefrom, and as the defendants were deliberately kept out of the enjoyment of the whole premises, I am of the opinion on the authorities above cited, that this action to recover the rent reserved by the tenancy agreement is not maintainable in law. At best, as the demise in question is not by deed, the rent reserved could be regarded as suspended during the duration all the time that the defendants are kept out of store. The defendants are not liable to pay such rent and no action can successfully be brought to enforce payment of such rent. In the result this action must fail.

I turn now to the counterclaim by the defendants which is, as already observed, for a refund of a proportion of the rent already paid in respect of the store, the possession of which was never delivered to the defendants. I do not propose to deal at length with this aspect of the case as there was no evidence before me as to what part of the rent fixed under the tenancy agreement was apportionable to either the shop or the store. There was also no evidence that the shop and the store were each of equal value.

It is quite clear that this is not a claim founded on a breach of contract as such for which damages may be awarded, but rather an action to recover rent paid in respect of a part of premises, the possession of which was not delivered to the defendants. In other words, it is an action to recover over payment in respect of the premises.

In my view it was the duty of the defendants to prove to my satisfaction the apportioned value of the store, the possession of which had been denied them ascertained at the date when they ought to have been in possession of the said store, that is to say, the date at which the store was withdrawn from the letting. For in law it is the duty of a tenant claiming apportionment to prove the apportioned value of the land withdrawn from the demise, ascertained at the date of such withdrawal.

In the circumstances of this, it is doubtful whether an action to recover a proportion of the rent paid to the plaintiffs is the proper action which should have been brought. The rent having been agreed in respect of the whole of the premises let, that is to say, shop and store, and the plaintiffs having failed to perform their contract in that they deliberately refused to deliver vacant possession of a part of other demised premises to the defendants, it is doubtful whether the plaintiffs are entitled to keep any portion at all of the rent paid. It seems to me that their refusal of vacant possession to the defendants ought to disentitle them to retain any part of the rent received by them. …

Be that as it may, I am of the opinion that the defendants have failed to satisfy me as to what portion of the rent should be refunded to them. This counterclaim therefore fails.

****

Note

Readers should note the Chief Justice's statement in the last paragraph. Not only were the defendants entitled to repudiate the lease agreement but also to recover *all* the rent they paid to the plaintiff and damages for breach of contract. Unfortunately for the defendants, their counsel did not properly plead their case .

****

11

Mortgages

A mortgage is a transaction whereby a landowner uses his or her land or interest in land as security for a loan.

Creation of a mortgage

Legal mortgage

Section 114 of the *Registration of Titles Act* (cap 205), provides that a proprietor of any land registered under the Act may mortgage the land by signing a mortgage thereof in the eleventh schedule to the Act. Section 51 of the Act provides that the mortgage is not effective until registered under the Act.

Nature of a registered mortgage

Section 115 states that when a mortgage created under the Act is registered it shall 'have effect as a security, but shall not operate as a transfer of the land thereby mortgaged'. The nature of a mortgage under the Torrens System legislation has been considered in a number of Australian cases. For example, in *Partridge v McIntosh & Sons Ltd* (1933) 49 CLR 453, at 466, Dixon J said (with reference to corresponding New South Wales legislation):

> The statutory mortgage does not upon registration effect a transfer to the mortgagee of an estate in the land, or confer on him an immediate right to possession or to perception of the profits of the land. He has, of course, an interest in the land at law, but it is in the nature of a charge.

Similarly, in *The English Scottish and Australian Bank Limited v Phillips* (1937) 57 CLR 302, at pp 321 to 324, Dixon, Evatt and McTiernan JJ, made the following observation with regard to the South Australian legislation:

> Under the system of registration governing the present case, the statutory charge described as a mortgage is a distinct interest. It involves no ownership of the land the subject of the security. Like a lease, it is a separate interest in land which may be dealt with apart altogether from the fee simple or other estate or interest mortgaged. ... In relation to the present case, the most important consideration arising in this plan is the failure to limit the persons who may deal in the interest created by a mortgage or a lease. ... A mortgage under the system is the creature of statute and its incidents depend upon the provisions of the statute and so much of the general law as is availed of by or under those provisions.... It appears to us that the plan of the legislation is to treat mortgages as distinct and persisting interests capable of the same ready transfer by registration as estates in fee simple and without any discrimination or concern as to the relation of the transferee or transferor thereof to any other estate or interest

Equitable mortgage

An equitable mortgage is a mortgage of land enforceable in a court of equity. Equitable mortgages are recognised under the *Registration of Titles Act*. Section 138 of the Act provides that notwithstanding anything in the Act contained, an equitable mortgage of land may be made by deposit by the registered proprietor of a certificate of title with intent to create a security thereon whether accompanied or not by a note or memorandum of the deposit, subject to the provisions thereinafter contained. It is thereinafter provided that every equitable mortgage as aforesaid shall be deemed to create an interest in land and that every equitable mortgagee shall cause a caveat to be entered. The operation of this provision and effect of an equitable mortgage is illustrated by the following case.

****

Barclays Bank DCO v Gulu Millers Ltd
[1959] E.A 540

[The respondent (the company) was the registered proprietor of a lease. It deposited its certificate of title with the appellant (the bank) and at the same time executed a memorandum in which it stated that it had deposited the title deeds with the intent to create an equitable mortgage upon the property comprised therein as security for moneys due to the appellant payable on demand. When the respondent defaulted, the appellant sued for a declaration, inter alia, that it had a right to sell the mortgaged property. The trial Judge dismissed the action on the ground that the appellant being an equitable mortgagee could not in the first instance seek an order for sale. His Honour held that before an equitable mortgagee could seek an order for sale, it must in the first place ask the court to order the equitable mortgagor to execute a legal mortgage. The bank appealed against the decision.]

Sir Kenneth O'Connor P: ...Under the doctrines of equity, a deposit of deeds by way of security was taken to be equivalent to an agreement to execute a legal mortgage ...and to carry with it all the remedies incident to a legal mortgage: *Carver v. Wake* (1877) 4 Ch.D.605. The primary remedy was foreclosure, not sale: ... *James v James* (1873), L.R. 16 Eq. 153, but the court had power in a proper case to order a sale *Russel v Russel* 28 ER 1121 ... subject to the mortgagor being given six months in which to redeem: *Thorpe v. Gartside* 160 ER 587.... Probably the clearest statement in the earlier cases of the way in which courts of equity regarded equitable mortgages by deposit of title deeds, and of the remedies open to an equitable mortgagee before the enactment of s. 48 of the Chancery Procedure Act, 1852 (the fore-runner of s. 25 of the Conveyancing Act, 1881), is contained in the judgement of PEPYS, M.R., in *Parker v. Housefield* (39 ER 1004). The immediate contest in that case was whether the plaintiff, an equitable mortgagee by deposit of title deeds, was entitled to an immediate sale of the property, or whether the mortgagor should be given six months in which to redeem. But the case contains a useful statement of the principles upon which equity proceeds. The Master of the Rolls said at p.1004:

> The question was, whether, in the case of an equitable mortgage by a deposit of title deeds, the decree ought to give to the mortgagor six months to redeem, as in cases of legal mortgages. ... To determine this, it is material, in the first place, to consider in what light courts of equity view such equitable mortgages; and it appears that a deposit of title deeds has always been considered an imperfect mortgage, which the mortgagee is entitled to have perfected, or rather as a contract for a mortgage, which, according to the well-known doctrine of courts of equity, would give to the party claiming the benefit to such contract all such rights as he would be entitled to if the contract had been completed. Accordingly, in the very commencement of the doctrine of equitable mortgages, viz., in the cases of *Featherstone v. Fenwick,* in the year 1784 and *Harford v. Carpenter,* in the year 1785, both cited in *Russell* (Bro. C.C. 269) we find LORD THURLOW saying, that a deposit of deeds entitled the holder to have a mortgage, and to have his lien effectuated. In *Birch v Ellames* (2 Anst. 428) the Chief Baron of the Exchequer says: 'A deposit of title deeds as security for a debt is now settled to be evidence of an agreement to make a mortgage, and such agreement is to be carried into execution by the court.' The decree in that case was that the defendant should pay, or stand foreclosed and convey. In *Ex parte Wright* (19 Ves. 255) LORD ELDON says, that a deposit of title deeds was evidence of an agreement for a mortgage, and that an equitable title to a mortgage was, in equity, as good as a legal mortgage. Such being the light in which courts of equity view equitable mortgages by deposit of title deeds, it would seem to follow that the remedy to be afforded to such mortgagees should, as nearly as possible, correspond with that to which legal mortgages are entitled; and, accordingly, from the search which I have directed to be made as to the form of decrees upon such subjects, I find that such has been the principle adopted...

In *Perry v. Keane* [(1836) 6 LJ Ch 67] the plaintiffs filed a bill praying for foreclosure or sale. Deeds had been deposited as security and the mortgagors had undertaken that they would (if necessary) execute a mortgage to the plaintiffs, such mortgage to contain a power of sale. The Master of the Rolls (LORD LANGDALE) said that there could be no doubt that the plaintiffs were entitled to a decree to have a mortgage executed to them; but, as they had asked for foreclosure, they were entitled to it. They were not given an order for sale, though they would have preferred to have a sale.

In *Lister v. Turner* [(67 ER 991] there was an equitable mortgage by deposit of title deeds with an agreement in writing by the depositor, upon the request of the mortgagee, to execute a formal mortgage to the mortgagee. It was decreed inter alia that, in default of payment, the mortgaged property should be sold. WIGRAM, V-C., said at p.922 that the claim of the plaintiff for what was due and to have the same raised in the ordinary manner upon the property comprised in the security was clear. Having decided certain issues not relevant to this case, the learned Vice-Chancellor continued:

> The next question is as to the form of the remedy to which the plaintiff is entitled: whether the decree is to give the plaintiff the benefit of a legal mortgage or to direct a sale. The decisions with regard to the right of an equitable mortgagee are uniform: but in this case the express terms of the contract are that Slater shall convey the premises by way of legal mortgage, and that such mortgage shall contain a full and absolute power of sale; and to make the suit available for its objects it is necessary that there should be a decree for sale. There is no reason, therefore, why such decree should not be made.

Perry v. Keane and *Lister v. Turner* were both decided before the entry into force of the Chancery Procedure Act, 1852 and were, accordingly, decided under the doctrines of equity irrespective of s.48 of that Act or s.25 of the Conveyancing Act, 1881.

I am satisfied on the authority of *Perry v. Keane* and *Lister v. Turner*, that, under the doctrines of equity and irrespective of s.25 of the Conveyancing Act, 1881, where there is an equitable mortgage by deposit of documents of title accompanied by a memorandum by the depositor agreeing, at the request or demand of the mortgagee, to execute a legal mortgage with an unqualified power of sale, the court would have power, at the instance of the mortgagee, to order a sale of the property. It would also have power to make a foreclosure order.

It remains to be considered whether the remedies available in England in 1902 under the doctrines of equity for enforcement of equitable mortgages made by deposit of title deeds were before 1902, or have since been 'modified, amended or replaced' by any local Ordinance within s.15 (2) of the Uganda Order in Council, 1902. They have not, so far as I know been modified by any subsequent Order in Council neither, in my opinion, is their application prevented or qualified by the proviso to s 15(2).

In 1922 the *Registration of Titles Ordinance* (Cap.102 of the 1923 Revised Edition of the Laws and now Cap. 123 of the 1951 Revised Edition) was enacted which introduced a complete Torrens System of registration of title. This repealed the *Registration of Titles Ordinance*, 1908, and the *Equitable Mortgages Ordinance*, 1912, and by s.3, provided that, except so far as was expressly enacted to the contrary, no Ordinance or rule so far as inconsistent with the Ordinance should apply to land whether freehold or leasehold which was under the operation of the Ordinance. Part III provided for the bringing of land under the Ordinance and by s. 9(3) it was enacted that no dealing with any land however held prior to that Ordinance should, after its commencement, operate to pass any estate or interest whatever until such dealing was registered as therein provided. Section 113 and subsequent sections dealt with mortgages. Mortgages were to be created by the signature by the proprietor of a mortgage in a scheduled form. There was no provision permitting a mortgage to be made by another means. Again, having regard to s.9(3), it would appear that at this date, equitable mortgages merely by deposit of documents of title could not be created so as to pass any estate or interest in land. Once more this was reversed and, by Ordinance 9 of 1931, provisions on the lines of s.138 of the present *Registration of Titles Ordinance* were enacted. No copy is available here of Ordinance 9 of 1931; but it appears from the marginal note to s.138 of the present Ordinance that the provisions of that section derive from s.2, s.3 and s.4 of Ordinance 9 of 1931. Section 138 provides that notwithstanding anything in the *Registration of Titles Ordinance* contained, an equitable mortgage of land may be made by deposit by the registered proprietor of a certificate of title with intent to create a security thereon whether accompanied or not by a note or memorandum of the deposit, subject to the provisions thereinafter contained. It is thereinafter provided that every equitable mortgage as aforesaid shall be deemed to create an interest in land and that every equitable mortgagee shall cause a caveat to be entered. It was conceded, and the learned judge has found, that a caveat was entered in the present case.

It cannot have been the intention of the legislature in enacting s.138 and its predecessors enabling equitable mortgages by deposit to be created, that an equitable mortgagee should be unable to enforce his security. As no method of enforcement was enacted, it must have been the intention that an equitable mortgagee should have any remedies open to him under the general law, so far as these were not inconsistent with the *Registration of Titles Ordinance* or other local enactment. HOGG in his work on REGISTRATION OF LAND TITLE THROUGHOUT THE EMPIRE at p.284 says:

> In most jurisdictions the proper remedy of the equitable mortgagee by deposit of certificate of title appears to be foreclosure, effected by an order of the court for the land to be transferred by the debtor to the creditor free from any right of redemption; if a proper transfer cannot be had, a vesting order may be made.

and he adds, at p.285:

> There seems to be no reason why an equitable mortgagee by deposit should not have the ordinary remedies of an equitable mortgagee under the general law; for instance, he would probably be entitled to have a receiver appointed.

and at p.205:

> It has, however, been said that the old procedure of foreclosure is still applicable to equitable or non-statutory mortgages.

The doctrines of equity are, by virtue of s. 15 of the Order in Council, part of the general law of Uganda and I think that when equitable mortgages were permitted to be created, the doctrines of equity would regulate the enforcement of such mortgages in the absence of express provision for their enforcement in any enactment which applies locally.

As has already been said, the primary remedy of an equitable mortgagee is foreclosure under order of the court; and in a proper case, the court might, as an alternative, make an order for sale. Section 130, however, which is the only express provision in the *Registration of Titles Ordinance* dealing with foreclosure, makes it clear that an attempt by a mortgagee to exercise his power of sale by public auction must already have been made before a foreclosure order can be applied for. It would seem that that section was primarily intended to apply to mortgages made under s. 114 (which I will call registered mortgages) and not to equitable mortgages under s.138; but it is nevertheless an indication that in enforcing mortgages under the *Registration of Titles Ordinance*, sale, and not foreclosure, is intended to be the first remedy to be tried. Section 131 seems to support that inference. It would be anomalous if it were to be held that the reverse order of remedies to equitable, as compared with registered mortgages. Perhaps, at some time, the legislature will intervene and give some express remedies applies to equitable mortgagees and state how they should be exercised. In the meantime I incline to the view that an order that the property be put up for sale should precede an order for foreclosure. Since the principle upon which the court acts in enforcing an equitable mortgage is that it is as good as a legal mortgage and carries similar remedies (*Parker v. Housefield* [39 ER 1004]; *Carver v. Wake* [(1877) 4 Ch D 605] I think that the remedies of an equitable mortgagee under the Uganda *Registration of Titles Ordinance* should be assimilated by the court as closely as may be to the remedies provided by that Ordinance for a registered mortgagee, and that this principle would apply to the period which should be allowed for an equitable mortgagor to redeem, no less than to the order of remedies available to him. Accordingly, I think that the court should not make an order for sale until it is satisfied that steps have been taken and periods of default have elapsed which would make a registered mortgagee's power of sale applicable (see s.115, s.116 and s.117) and should not make a foreclosure order until conditions obtain which would justify the making of a foreclosure order under s.130 if the mortgage were a registered mortgage. The issue of a plaint in a suit to enforce an equitable mortgage would be sufficient notice to satisfy the requirements of s.115, s.116 and s.30 of the *Registration of Titles Ordinance*. Provided that these conditions have been complied with, I do think it essential that a foreclosure order in respect of an equitable mortgage of registered land in Uganda should as in England give the mortgagor six months from the date of the order in which to redeem. A reasonable time should be allowed having regard to the periods of default which have already occurred.

I was not impressed by Mr. James's argument that the company had been 'dragged through the courts unnecessarily' and that the court, even if it had power to order a sale, should, in the first instance, order a legal mortgage to be executed. It was the duty of this debtor to pay his creditor on demand. Failure to pay on demand is admitted. The company should have paid what was due, whether by arranging a transfer to a new mortgagee or otherwise, and, if it did not do so, cannot complain if the bank seeks to realise its security in any way open to it. The ordinary way of enforcing an equitable mortgage is by foreclosure or sale under order of the court, and I see nothing which should deter the court from making such an order in this case.

[Forbes VP and Windham JA, agreed.]

****

Notes

1. The creation of an equitable mortgage by way deposit of title deeds in also illustrated by the Tanzanian case of *Guaranty Discount Co Ltd v Credit Finance Corporation Ltd and another* [1963] EA 347, on appeal to the East Africa Court of Appeal. In that case, the mortgagor deposited her title deeds with the mortgagee upon advance of a further 'substantial' sum not covered by the existing mortgage. The deposit was not accompanied with a memorandum. The issue was whether the title deeds were deposited with a view to create a new charge to secure the sum advanced. In delivering his judgement, Newbold JA said (at p. 362) that: 'Where title deeds are handed over by a debtor to a creditor against the payment of money a very strong presumption arises that the deposit has been made with the view to the creation of an equitable mortgage over the entire interest of the debtor in the properties concerned and for the entire amount then due by the debtor to the creditor and which the facts show was advanced against the security of the properties.' Similarly, at p 362, Sir Ronald Sinclair P said: 'A deposit of title deeds with intent to create a security gives an equitable charge. What was the intent in the present case? As between the debtor and his creditor the mere fact of possession of title deeds raises a presumption that they were deposited with him as security for his whole debt. Here the title deeds were deposited, not with the mortgages, but some months later and upon a further advance of a very substantial sum not covered by the mortgage. ...In my view, the inference is that the title deeds were deposited with intent to create a security – a new charge – and not merely in pursuance of the mortgages or the prior agreement.'

2. It is important to remember that under s. 138 of the *Registration of Titles Act,* an equitable mortgage must be protected by a caveat (see *Barclays Bank D.C.O v Gulu Millers, supra*; *Jakana v Senkaali* CS No 491 of 1984; [1988-90] HCB 150).
3. Under the general law, an equitable mortgage could arise in a number of other ways (apart from title deposit). For example, it could arise from a contract to grant a mortgage or an attempt to create a legal mortgage, which does not comply with legal formalities. However, it would seem that the Act only recognises an equitable mortgage if created by way of title deposit and protected by a caveat, see *Buganda Timber Co Ltd v Mulji K Metha* [1961] EA 477, at 481, per Sir Kenneth O'Connor P.
4. It should be noted that the case of *Barclays Bank DCO v Gulu Millers Ltd,* was decided before the *Mortgage Decree* 1974 was enacted. The Decree repealed sections 117-121, 129-133 of the *Registration of Titles Act,* which prescribed the mortgagees' remedies. The Decree makes provision for similar remedies (except the equitable remedy of foreclosure) and stipulates the procedure for enforcing these remedies (see ss 2, 5, 8, and 9). Nevertheless, the case is still good authority for its general exposition of the law of mortgages. In addition, it was held in *Barclays Bank (U) Ltd v Northcote* CS No 1467 of 1974, that the precedent established by *Gulu Millers,* that an equitable mortgagee is entitled to identical remedies as a legal mortgagee extends to remedies under the Decree.

****

MORTGAGE OF CUSTOMARY LAND

Under the *Land Act,* 1998, s 9(2)(c), a holder of a customary certificate of ownership is entitled to mortgage the land where his or her certificate does not preclude it. The Act does not prescribe any particular formalities for the creation of a mortgage over customary land. However, s. 9(3) provides that where 'a holder of a certificate of ownership ... undertakes any transaction in respect of the land to which the certificate relates [he/she] shall provide the Recorder with the copy or other accurate record of the transaction and the Recorder shall keep all such records in the prescribed manner'. Section 9(4) provides that no transaction purporting to create a mortgage 'shall have the effect of passing any interest in the land to which the transaction relates unless it is registered by the Recorder'.

Questions

1. What are the policy reasons for s. 9(4) of the *Land Act*?
2. Ofono lends Omondi one million shillings, which is secured by a mortgage over the latter's customary land. Under the agreement, Ofono has a right to sell the land or become the owner of the land if Omondi fails to pay back the money within twelve months. The mortgage agreement is in writing and witnessed by a local elder. Both parties being ignorant of s. 9(3), of the *Land Act,* the transaction is not recorded. Omondi defaults in payment of the debt as agreed by the parties. Ofono sues Omondi in the District Land Tribunal. Suppose you are the Chairperson of the Tribunal, discuss the issues that are likely to arise and how you would deal with them. Would you, for example, interpret the effect of failure to comply with s. 9(3) of the *Land Act* in a similar way as the courts treat unregistered transactions under s. 51 of the *Registration of Titles Act*? (See *Souza Figuiredo and Co Ltd v Moorings Hotel Co Ltd* [1960] EA 926, see excerpt in Chapter nine). Why or why not? See also below cases dealing with the mortgagees' remedies. (You are required to assume that the land is not subject to s. 40 of the *Land Act*).

****

Legal mortgagee

The *Mortgage Decree*, 1974, provides for the remedies of a mortgagee and the procedure to be followed to enforce the remedies. The remedies are:

(a) action for breach of covenant (s. 1);
(b) sale of the land (s. 2);
(c) appointment of a receiver (s. 3); and
(d) possession (s. 6).

For purposes of the Decree, s 18 defines the term 'mortgage' as 'any mortgage, charge…whether legal or equitable which constitutes a charge over an estate or interest in land in Uganda...and which is registered under the [*Registration of Titles*] *Act*'.

The following cases illustrate the exercise of the mortgagees' remedies under the Decree.

****

Mortgagee may exercise the power of sale without resort to court

Barclays Bank of (U) Ltd v Livingstone Katende Lutu
CA No 22 of 1993 (unreported, Supreme Court of Uganda)

[The respondent mortgaged his land to the appellant bank to secure a loan advanced to a third party, and guaranteed by the respondent. When the third party defaulted, the appellant, after service of notice to the third party, advertised the land for sale by public auction. The respondent successfully applied for a temporary injunction to restrain the sale. The trial Judge held that even though there was an express provision in the agreement giving the mortgagee a right to sell the land if the mortgagor defaulted, the power of sale could not be exercised without a court order. The bank appealed against the judgement.]

Manyindo DJC, Odoki JSC and Platt JSC: The reasons given by the learned Judge have caused the Bank to be aggrieved and it would seem for good reason. He concluded:

> As regards the first condition the legal mortgage stipulated that the first defendant would proceed to sale by public auction the property in question without resort to Court. In a way, the jurisdiction of this Court would be ousted and the applicant would be condemned unheard. That would, in my opinion, violate the principle of natural justice. For this particular condition the applicant had shown a prima facie case with a probability of success.

The learned Judge went on to consider that in the case of land, a temporary injunction is usually granted.

Thirdly, the learned Judge was impressed by the discrepancy between the greater value of the subject matter than the loan; the outstanding loan would indeed be ascertained. Altogether, he would suffer irreparable loss.

It is one of those cases perhaps where it can be said that hard cases make bad law. The learned Judge must have sympathised with the Plaintiff who had tried to help a friend and now would lose a great deal. The law firmly provides that business expediency is to be preferred, and if the mortgage documents so provides, the mortgagee may sell without recourse of the Court. That agreement provides:

> B) At any time after payment of the monies hereby secured has been demanded and the mortgagor or the Principal Debtor has made default in paying the same, the Bank may, in addition to any other powers enjoyed by it hereunder or under the Registration of Titles Act and the Mortgage Decree (No. 17 of 1974) or under the general law and without any previous notice or concurrence on the part of the Mortgagor:

> Sell or concur with any other person in selling the mortgaged Property or any part or parts thereof in one or more lots by Public auction or private treaty and subject to such terms and Conditions as the Bank shall in its absolute discretion think fit ... and the mortgagor hereby irrevocably consents to the carrying out of any such sale or resale by private treaty.

It follows that once demand has been made and the Mortgagor/principal debtor had made default in paying the debt, the Bank may exercise its power of sale without recourse to the Court. This power conforms to Section 9 of the *Mortgage Decree* No. 17 of 1974. Section 9 provides:

> Where the mortgage gives power expressly to the mortgagee to sell without applying to Court, such sale shall be by public auction unless the mortgagor and encumbrancers subsequent to the mortgagee, if any, onsent to a sale by private treaty.

The Plaintiff seems to have laboured under the misconception that in all cases the mortgagee should apply to the Court for foreclosure (See Section 7 of the Decree No. 17 of 1974). The mortgagor's right to redeem the land is confined to repayment of the loan, if the mortgagee has the power of sale without the Court ordering foreclosure.

The learned Judge thought that Section 9 of the Decree of 1974 must involve the ouster of the jurisdiction of the Courts, and would therefore violate the principle of natural justice. It seems that perhaps the learned Judge has not expressed himself well, because there can hardly be a principle of natural justice which outshines a legislative provision. Sale without recourse to the Court having been agreed by the parties themselves, is sanctioned by Section 9 of Decree 17 of 1974.

The learned Judge directed himself carefully, basing his approach to ordering a temporary injunction on *Giella v Casman Brown* [1973] EA 358 and other cases. On the ground chosen by the learned Judge there could be no possibility of success.

What the learned Judge might have explored is whether the Plaintiff had received any demand to pay ... the guarantee, as he claimed. But the Judge did not do so and there is neither a cross appeal nor a notice to confirm judgement on different grounds. What is before the Court is the appeal and that question (*sic*) the learned Judge's approach to the mortgage agreement. No question of natural justice arises on the basis of this agreement. It was not possible on that ground to say that there was a probability of the Plaintiff succeeding on his suit. The terms of the agreement had to be upheld and as a sale by public auction [or] private treaty had been agreed by the Plaintiff that by itself could not be an irreparable loss.

The Plaintiff has of course been let down. The interest is extremely high at 41%. But there is no ground on which the Court can intervene to grant the Plaintiff the right to pay by instalments [except where the Bank] so agrees. It is immaterial whether the property mortgaged is of greater value than the loan.

The result is that the appeal is allowed, and the orders of the High Court set aside. The Bank may wish to exercise its powers of sale, and if so, no doubt, it will make demand and do all such things that are required of it. The Plaintiff should perhaps study paragraph 2 (viii) of the mortgage agreement as to how service is effected by post or service at the last known place of business or abode of the Plaintiff. The Plaintiff has had from October 1992 until the present date to get this matter settled. The interest is mounting all the time, and prejudicing the balance payable to him. It is in his interests that he comes to terms with the agreement that he made as quickly as possible, and chooses the best beneficial course open to him.

*****

Notes

1. The preceding case deals with a mortgagee's power of sale where the mortgage is registered under the *Registration of Titles Act*. For discussion of a mortgagee's powers of sale under an unregistered mortgage, see *Barclays Bank of (U) Ltd v Northcote* CS No 1467 of 1974, extracted above.
2. In *Barclays Bank of (U) Ltd v Livingstone Katende Lutu*, the Court declined to grant an injunction to stop the mortgage sale. Discuss circumstances in which a court might intervene and grant an injunction to prevent a mortgage sale. (Some of the possible circumstances are mentioned in the case, see also eg *Sajabi v Amreliwalla and Wamala* [1955] 22 EACA 71; *Mubiru v Uganda Credit & Savings Bank* (1978) HCB 109; *Cuckmere Brick Co Ltd v Mutual Finance Ltd* [1971] Ch 948).

****

Where a mortgage sale is unlawful, the selling mortgagee and the purchaser may be held liable in damages to the mortgagor

Sajabi v Amreliwalla and Wamala
(1956) 22 EACA 71

[The appellant mortgaged his land to Pioneer Assurance Society Ltd and the mortgage was registered under the *Registration of Titles Act*. Later, Pioneer Motors assigned the mortgage to the first respondent. When the appellant defaulted, the first respondent, purporting to act under s 117 of the *RTA*,[26] sold the land to the second respondent by private treaty and without notice to the appellant. The circumstances indicated that the second respondent knew that no notice under s 115 of the *RTA* had been given and that another purchaser was willing to pay a substantially higher price. The appellant sued both respondents alleging that the sale was unlawful, fraudulent and collusive and claimed damages. The trial Judge dismissed the claims against the purchaser holding that no fraud or collusion had been established. However, he held that the first respondent had sold unlawfully in that no notice of sale had been given and awarded damages. The appellant appealed against the whole decision claiming that the damages were inadequate. The first respondent appealed against the award of damages claiming that the sale was lawful]

Briggs Ag VP: ... The provisions of section 117 of the *Registration of Titles Ordinance* which allow a mortgagee to sell the mortgaged premises by private treaty and protect a purchaser against the consequences of previous irregularities seem to me to be singularly inappropriate to the needs of this country. If the power to sell were only by public auction, it might be reasonable to dispense with an order of Court, since the sale would normally be advertised and in ordinary cases the mortgagor would have sufficient notice of it to enable him to obtain an injunction if there had been any impropriety. But the law as it stands apparently makes it possible for a mortgagee who has given notice of sale, the validity of which is to his knowledge in dispute, to complete the sale and effect registration in favour of the purchaser in secret, and without the mortgagor having any knowledge of what is being done. If there is collusion in the purchase, his own title will of course be impeachable, but in any such case the rights of the mortgagor may be defeated by a further transaction in favour of an innocent third party. We are told by the chief clerk of a prominent firm of local practitioners that in over thirty years' experience he has known only one or two cases of mortgagees having sold by private treaty, and he could not give particulars of even one such sale from memory. This seems to me to indicate that local practitioners themselves recognise that the practice is eminently undesirable and may lead to subsequent difficulties. This attitude would in my view be no more than one would expect of prudent and fair-minded members of the Bar. But the extreme rarity of these transactions in practice does

[26] Section 117 of the *RTA*, has since been repealed by s. 16(b) of the *Mortgage Decree, 1974*.

not in my view diminish, indeed it emphasises, the urgent need for amendment of the law. There may well be an occasional case where a sale by private treaty would best serve the legitimate interests of the mortgagee without unfairly prejudicing the mortgagor. I would suggest that to meet such a case the amended section might permit sale by private treaty with leave of the Court to be obtained on application with notice to the mortgagor. I leave open the wider question whether in a country such as this it may not be desirable that every mortgagee's sale should be conducted under the Court's supervision.

The English rule, that, although a mortgagee in selling is not a trustee for the mortgagor, he must sell in good faith and at a reasonable price, applies in Uganda. It obviously requires that a mortgagee must not take a lower price than he knows to be obtainable. It also, I think, leads to the conclusion that, if the mortgagee acts in secret and conceals what he is doing from the mortgagor, he may expose himself to some suspicion of not having acted in good faith. This suspicion must at least be increased if the mortgagee sells in secret with knowledge that the validity of his notice of sale is challenged on grounds that are prima facie unreasonable. I have dealt first with those considerations because they affect and largely determine the view which I take of this appeal.

I deal next with the question whether lawful notice of intention to sell was given in this case by or on behalf of the mortgagee. [His Honour found that Pioneer Assurance Society gave a notice when it was still registered as proprietor of the mortgage. However, he held that the first respondent could not take advantage of that notice because the point was not pleaded in the High Court. After observing that the first respondent also gave the appellant notice of intention to sell after the mortgage was assigned to them, his Honour continued.] As regard the first respondent's own notice of 22nd September 1952, he was not the registered mortgagee when it was given, so prima facie he could have no right to give it and it was invalid. His counsel sought to argue that the words 'the mortgagee or his transferee' in section 115 of the *Registration of Titles Ordinance* mean that the original mortgagee can always give a valid notice of sale, even if he has ceased to be entitled to the benefit of the mortgage and a transferee is entitled thereto. Such a construction is quite impossible. The words 'or his transferee' are inserted to make it clear that the rights to give notice of intention to sell, and thereafter to sell in case of default, are not merely rights personal to the original mortgagor, but pass with the general benefit of the mortgage to a transferee on a registered transfer thereof. I am satisfied that the notice of 22nd September, 1952, was invalid, and I am also satisfied that, if the solicitors for the second respondent had examined the register at the time of the negotiations for the sale to him, they must have observed that between October, 1950, and 17th November. 1952, the first respondent was not registered as mortgagee. The contract under which the first respondent as mortgagee sold to the second respondent was concluded on 25th October, 1952... though the transfer was not executed until 21st November. It may be true to say that an intending purchaser from a mortgagee is excused by the provisions of section 117 from inquiring into the validity of the notice of sale: but were not the facts here apparent on the face of the register such as to shout to an honest purchaser, 'beware of irregularities'? And does section 117 entitle a purchaser to ignore the probability visible on the register that no lawful notice could have been given? Perhaps it does: but unless the second respondent and his solicitors were prepared to be wilfully blind, one would have expected an inquiry to be made. An honest man acting without collusion does not wish to invite a lawsuit by deliberately accepting title from a mortgagee who is to put it at the lowest, probably acting unlawfully. In view of the fact that neither respondent sought at the trial or on the pleadings to rely on the notice given by the Pioneer Company, it seems fair to say that, not only did the first respondent sell without lawful notice, but the second respondent, unless he was wilfully blind, must have known that that was the position. This might not alone support a finding of collusion, but at least it makes it much easier to infer collusion from other evidence pointing thereto.

The sale being unlawful, the right to damages against the first respondent is established apart from any question of fraud or collusion, but it remains to consider these questions as determining the position of the second respondent. There is a considerable body of evidence, which leads to an inference of dishonest conduct in the first respondent, but most of this does not affect the second respondent. There is, however, one series of events, the evidence of which in my opinion conclusively implicates him. [His Honour, discussed the evidence and continued]…I find that the two respondents were acting together collusively, the sale was not a bona fide transaction, and the second respondent has rendered himself liable in damages equally with the first…

I pause at this point to remark that a finding of collusion against the second respondent would ordinarily justify rectification of the register by retransferring the land to the appellant subject to the mortgage: but in this case that is impracticable, since registered interests have been created in innocent third parties whose titles are unimpeachable. The appellant's remedy is only in damages….

The measure of damages is the value of the land at the time of the unlawful sale, less the amount of money due on the mortgage at that date. The latter figure was stated by the first respondent to be sh 65,700 and I am prepared to accept that as correct.

Bacon J.A:…The case for the respondents is briefly as follows. They rely on sections 115 to 117 of the *Registration of Titles Ordinance* (Cap. 123 of the Laws of Uganda, 1951). Harping on his punctilious compliance with the statutory requirement as to giving notice of an intended sale, and on the letter of the law whereby a mortgagee who has duly given such a notice is empowered to sell the mortgaged land, the first respondent contends that in effect the appellant stood by and acquiesced in the sale by private treaty of his land and that consequently his inaction on that occasion has put beyond his reach any remedy which he might otherwise have had for the allegedly disastrous result of the sale. The first respondent concedes that the letter of the law differs from the spirit in which it is applied, to the extent that in Uganda it is only very rarely indeed that a mortgagee sells his mortgagor's land by private treaty, but says that, although it may be the almost invariably accepted custom to sell such property by public auction, nevertheless section 117 expressly provides for the possibility of the mortgagee electing to sell and selling privately, and that accordingly it is but vain pleading when the appellant now complains that the respondents resorted to fast practice for personal gain at the appellant's expense.

The second respondent adopts the first respondent's contention and asserts that he (the second respondent) is innocent of fraud, collusion or dishonesty in any form and was a bona fide purchaser of the land in question.

Both respondents assert that not only was the sale irreproachable as a transaction but that it was effected at a reasonable and proper price.

In my opinion, the law on this matter is clear. On the one hand, strict compliance with the terms of section 115 followed after the requisite time by a private sale of the land concerned cannot be said to be illegal per se, or of itself to entitle the mortgagor to any remedy either at law or in equity. On the other hand choice of a sale by private treaty which that section gives to a mortgagee in no way abrogates from his obligation, if he chooses to enforce his rights, to enforce them at every stage in all good faith and in particular to sell at a fair price, although he is not a trustee for a mortgagor. If the sale is by public auction duly advertised and to all appearances properly conducted there is a strong prima facie case of fulfilment of that dual obligation. But where the sale is by private treaty the practical safeguard afforded by the publicity attending the usual procedure is of course denied to the mortgagor and it is incumbent on them to make particularly sure that the mortgagor's interests are amply protected.

The first respondent's contentions fail at the outset. He did not duly give the statutory notice under section 115 of the *Registration of Titles Ordinance* because at the date of his notice, he was not the registered mortgagee and the mortgage accordingly was ineffectual for the purpose of entitling him to give any such notice. It was not until nearly two months after the first respondent issued his notice that the mortgage was retransferred to him and the retransfer registered. Accordingly, he had no legal right to sell the land at all.

I now turn to the second respondent's position. He testified at the trial that he had acted throughout with the assistance of his legal adviser. Having seen an advertisement of an intended sale of the land by public auction he discovered that the auction would not take place. Thus warned and advised, he proceeded to negotiate the sale by private treaty. An examination of the register at that time would disclose to any intending purchaser that the proposed vendor had no right to sell. By proceeding with the purchase in those circumstances, the second respondent invited the inference of collusion with the first respondent in an unlawful dealing with the land behind the back of the registered owner who was the appellant.

(His Honour concurred with the order made by Briggs Ag VP and Worley P agreed).

****

Notes

1. Section 117 of the *Registration of Titles Act*, which Briggs Ag VP criticised, was eventually repealed by s. 16(b) of the *Mortgage Decree*, 1974 – almost twenty years later. Under the Decree, a mortgagee may sell by private treaty only if the mortgagor and secondary mortgagees, if any, consent to a sale by private treaty (see ss. 8(1) and 9, of the Decree).
2. It should be noted that s 115 of the *Registration of Titles Act,* which also featured in the case, is still applicable. The provision should not be confused with s 8(2) of the *Decree*. It is suggested that s 115 of the Act deals with the time when a *right to sell arises,* whereas s 8(2) of the Decree deals with the time when the mortgagee can *actually proceed to sell* the land.

Questions

1. Discuss possible circumstances where it might be advisable for the mortgagee to sell by private treaty rather than by public auction. If you were advising a mortgagee wishing to sell the land by private treaty, what precautions would you advise him or her to take to avoid suspicion of collusion or fraud?
2. Section 8(4) of the Decree provides that failure to give notice of the date and place of the sale required under the section shall not affect the validity of the sale, though the mortgagee might be held liable for any resulting loss. In addition, s 8(7) states that title of the purchaser under that section shall not be impeached on the ground that the order for sale was improperly made. Would the court have found the purchaser liable if the case of *Sajabi v Amreliwalla* were decided under the Decree?

****

Equitable mortgagee

An equitable mortgagee is entitled to all the remedies available to a legal mortgagee under the *Mortgage Decree*, except that such a mortgagee cannot sell the land without resort to court.

****

Barclays Bank of (U) Ltd v Northcote and another
CS NO. 1467 OF 1974 (unreported, High Court of Uganda)

[This case discusses remedies available to an equitable mortgagee under the *Mortgage Decree* and the appropriate procedure such a mortgagee must follow to exercise the remedies. The facts of the case are summarised in the judgement.]

Ssekandi AG J: ... This is an action to recover money loaned to the defendants by the plaintiff bank by way of overdraft. The debt was secured by deposit of title deed accompanied by a memorandum of deposit of deeds in which among other things the 1st defendant agreed to create an equitable mortgage in favour of the plaintiff and undertook on demand to execute a legal mortgage with an unqualified power of sale. The case proceeded ex parte as the defendants could not be served personally and substituted service was instead effected by order of the court.

The plaintiff bank adduced evidence to show that on 23rd July1970, the first defendant deposited with the plaintiff bank the duplicate certificate of title for leasehold land, more properly described as Plot 14, Buziga Hill, Kampala, registered under Vol.249 Folio 11. The first defendant further executed a memorandum in writing for the deposit of title deeds in which he expressed an intention to create a legal mortgage with powers of sale in favour of the plaintiff on demand. On completion of these transactions, the plaintiff bank advanced the defendants, on their current account, a sum of money by way of a floating overdraft, which at the time of filing this suit amounted to shs.125,424/15 ...

The plaintiff's bank has demanded payment of this money but there has been no response from the defendants.

On the basis of the available evidence, therefore, I am satisfied that the plaintiff bank has established that the sum of shs.125,424/15 is due and payable by the defendants. In my view, the interest rate of 12% is rather excessive. It is, therefore, my order that the interest payable should be calculated at 6% on the gross amount payable commencing from the date of this judgement until payment in full. Since both defendants were operating a joint account, the debt owing to the plaintiff's bank is due and payable by the defendants jointly and severally in the principal sum plus interest as mentioned above.

The plaintiff has asked for other orders from the court which I shall now address myself to. It is prayed that this court make an order against the first defendant for foreclosure or sale of the property. It is also further prayed that a receiver be appointed for the sale of the property.

In order to determine the appropriate remedy available to the plaintiff, I wish to refer briefly to the nature of the transaction between the plaintiff and the first defendant as evidenced by memorandum of deposit of title deeds. The plaintiff bank tendered in evidence Exhibit p.2, which is an executed memorandum of deposit of title deeds duly signed by the first defendant. This is a standard form containing familiar provisions in the bank business whereby a borrower secures a loan from the bank by deposit of title deeds and execution of a memorandum of deposit of title deeds.

The memorandum dated 23rd July, 1970 expresses the intention of the first defendant to create an equitable mortgage upon all the property described in the schedule and the first defendant further undertook on demand to execute a valid legal mortgage with powers of sale and appointment of a receiver as may be required. The bank duly registered a caveat on the title of the first defendant on 17th December 1970.

The *Registration of Titles Act* (CAP.205) provides for the creation of equitable mortgages by deposit of title deeds as a security (see: Section 138 of the Act). However, neither the Act nor the *Mortgage Decree* (No. 17 of 1974) makes any provision for the remedies available to an equitable mortgagee. It would, therefore, appear that one has to look elsewhere for such remedies. This very point fell for judicial determination in *Barclays Bank D.C.O v. Gulu Millers Limited* (1959) E.A.540. In a most thorough and historical review of the relevant authorities on the issue, Sir Kenneth O'Connor, P. ruled in his judgement that the law applicable to equitable mortgages is to be found in the doctrines of equity which are statutorily applicable in Uganda. Sir Kenneth further held that under the doctrines of equity a deposit of title deeds by way of security accompanied by an undertaking to create a legal mortgage on demand is equivalent to an agreement to execute a legal mortgage and carried with it all the remedies incidental to a legal mortgage. A mortgagee, in whose favour an equitable mortgage is created, by deposit of title deeds accompanied by a memorandum agreeing to execute a legal mortgage with an unqualified power of sale on demand, is entitled to apply to the court to exercise the powers available to a legal mortgage.

He need not seek execution of the legal mortgage before applying to the court for the remedies provided.

It would appear that the difference between an equitable mortgage and a legal mortgage as regards remedies is that whereas a legal mortgagee may realise his security under a mortgage by exercising most of the statutory powers conferred upon him without recourse to the courts, an equitable mortgagee must of necessity apply to the courts for exercise of any of these powers. In accordance with the principles laid down in *Barclays Bank vs. Gulu Millers Ltd.*, (supra), the court may avail to an equitable mortgagee all the remedies available to a legal mortgagee. The remedies available to a legal mortgagee are now set out in The *Mortgage Decree*, 1974 and these are in my view equally available to an equitable mortgagee subject to certain considerations set out later in this judgement.

The remedies provided for by the Decree are twofold: Firstly, a mortgagee may sue the mortgagor on the covenant in the mortgage or secondly, realise his security under the mortgage in any manner provided in the Decree. A mortgagee may realise his security under the mortgage:
(a) by appointing a receiver,
(b) by taking possession of the Mortgaged land; and
(c) by foreclosure.

A Mortgagee is free to pursue any one or all the remedies provided for by the Decree because such remedies are cumulative: Subject to his not recovering more than is due to him, he may employ any or all of the remedies to enforce payment: (see: Megarry and Wade, *The Law of Real Property* 3rd Edition p.915).

In the instant case, the plaintiff bank has applied for all the available remedies without giving an indication as to which of the remedies the bank would prefer the court to make available to it. I would personally consider that in cases of equitable mortgages the mortgagee should in the first instance sue the Mortgagor and obtain an order for an account to determine what is due by the mortgagor to the mortgagee, for principal and interest secured by the memorandum of deposit. Then, the mortgagee should seek a declaration that the bank is entitled to a charge on the land comprised in the certificate of title referred to in the memorandum of deposit to secure the amount found due and payable on the taking of such account plus accruing interest till payment together with costs of the suit. This should be followed by a prayer for an order that if payment is not made within the time stipulated, the mortgagee may realise his security by pursuing any or all of the remedies provided for in the *Mortgage Decree*, 1974. (See generally, *Barclays Bank D.C.O. v. Gulu Millers* (supra).

In considering which of the remedies provided for by the Decree is most appropriate, it is, I think pertinent to have regard to the traditional remedies granted by the courts of equity, with regard to equitable mortgages. It would appear to me that the primary remedy of an equitable mortgagee is foreclosure. An equitable mortgagee has no legal estate and the court's order absolute where this remedy is considered appropriate is to convey the land to the mortgagee unconditionally, i.e., free from any right to redeem. Foreclosure, however, puts an end to other remedies, since if the mortgagee takes the whole security he cannot also claim payment.

I should think, therefore, that before foreclosure is ordered there ought to be evidence of the value of the property so that it can be ascertained whether the mortgagee cannot obtain full payment by recourse to other available remedies such as appointment of a Receiver or taking possession. (See generally Megarry and Wade, *The Law of Real Property*, 3rd Edition p. 915).

The plaintiff bank in this case has also applied for appointment of a Receiver. In view of absence of evidence regarding the state and value of the property, I am inclined to grant this as the initial remedy.

I therefore appoint the Official Receiver as from today to act as a Receiver in respect of the mortgaged property and to act as agent of the Mortgagor; to account for any moneys received as stipulated in s. 5(3) of the *Mortgage Decree*, 1974, particularly, to apply to any accruing income from the property for the payment of the principal debt and interest owed by the defendants to the plaintiff bank.

In addition, I declare that the plaintiff bank is entitled to a charge on the land described in the memorandum of deposit of title deeds (Exhibit. P.2) dated 23rd July, 1970 in the amount of Shs.125,424/15 plus interest at 6% until payment in full. The defendants are ordered to pay into court the principal amount due plus interest within six months from the date of this judgement. Once the full amount due from the defendants is paid into court within the said six months, the plaintiff bank shall deliver all documents of titles to the first defendant. However, should the defendants default in payment of the full amount and interest as aforesaid ordered within the six months stipulated, the plaintiff shall be entitled to foreclosure to obtain full payment of the due debt from the mortgaged property.

The plaintiff is awarded costs of this suit.

****

Customary mortgagee

Although s. 9(5) of the *Land Act* suggests that a mortgage of customary land may be created under the *Mortgage Decree*, it is submitted that the Decree, as presently worded, only applies to land registered under the *Registration of Titles Act* (see definition of 'mortgage' and 'Act' in s 18 of the Decree). Accordingly, the remedies of the mortgagee provided by the Decree do not apply to a mortgagee of customary land. On the authority of *Barclays Bank of (U) Ltd v Northcote and another, supra*, it is thought that the courts could by similar reasoning apply as far as possible the provisions of the Decree in determining the mortgagees' remedies and the procedure for enforcing those remedies. The following case, which was decided before the Decree, applies the common law principles to a customary mortgage.

****

The common law and the doctrines of equity apply to a mortgage of customary land

Waswa v Asumani Kikungwe
(1952-6) 7 ULR 1

[M.W borrowed a sum of money from A. K. He signed two written documents to the effect that if he failed to pay the money back by a certain date then A.K could immediately take his house situated at the village of Amusi in Teso. Default having taken place A.K took possession of the house. M.W unsuccessfully applied to the lower courts to allow him more time within which to pay. This is an application to the High Court for revision of the lower court's decision.]

Edwards CJ: ... I am ... concerned at the order for A. K. immediately to take possession of M. W.'s house. The two documents comprise what, in English law, would be called a 'mortgage'. Were such transactions known to native law and custom in Teso, say, fifty years ago? I doubt it. ... But, if people like A. K. bring such matters before a Court ...and, if people like himself and the petitioner create a mortgage, which is so eminently a concept of English law, they cannot complain if the English law of equity comes in to alleviate the harshness of the terms of the written agreement. Under English law a mortgagor is usually allowed a period of six months from date of default to redeem. I, accordingly, confirm the amounts as found by the [lower Court] and I direct that this sum be paid in full [within a period of six months from the date of the lower Court's judgement]... In default of payment in full ... the mortgage property will be sold by public auction ...

I shall grant A. K. leave to bid at the auction. If the sale proceeds exceed the debt, with interest and expenses of sale, the balance will be held by the District Commissioner for a period of three months from date of sale to enable any person other than the parties to this suit to establish his claim to ownership of the house in question; so that, if successful, he can participate in any surplus; if no claim is made within three months from the date of the sale the surplus will be paid over to M.W. If the sale proceeds do not reach the amount of the debt plus interests and costs, A.K. will be at liberty to take out execution for the balance against any other property of M.W.

****

Note

See also *Matambulire v Yozefu Kimera* CA No 37 of 1972; [1975] HCB 150 (see extract below).

****

EQUITY'S PROTECTION OF A MORTGAGOR

The courts have inherent equitable jurisdiction to intervene in a mortgage agreement to protect the mortgagor against excesses of the mortgagee. The judicial protection of the mortgagor is usually summed up by the maximum that 'once a mortgage always a mortgage'. This maxim applies in two broad ways: (i) the test for a mortgage is substance and not form; and (ii) there must not be clogs or fetters on the equity of redemption.[27] Situations where the courts may intervene are illustrated in the following cases. When reading the cases, readers should bear in mind the underlying policy for judicial intervention in mortgage agreements and whether in Uganda's circumstances such intervention is justifiable.

****

Once a mortgage, always a mortgage

****

Test for a mortgage is substance not form

Matambulire v Kimera
CA No 37 of 1972 (High Court of Uganda); [1975] HCB 150.

[The case raises the issue whether or not a transaction entered into by the parties was a mortgage or a contract of sale and the legal consequences thereof. The facts of the case are summarised in the judgement.]

Ssekandi AG. J: The question to be decided, in this case, is whether the transaction between the plaintiff/respondent and the defendant/appellant, of which the agreement is evidence, was a contract for the sale of the 'Kibanja' or something else. I have no doubt that the parties never contemplated an outright sale. The agreement, properly construed, was for a loan. The plaintiff/respondent borrowed shs.3,800/- from the defendant/appellant with an undertaking that he would repay the loan in a year's time. In the event of failing to pay the whole amount on the due date the defendant/appellant would be free to take possession of the 'Kibanja' including the house, in satisfaction of the debt. It was the intention of the parties all along that the Kibanja would act as security for the loan. The plaintiff/respondent so testified and his evidence was not challenged on that point.

If the transaction was not a contract of sale of the 'Kibanja', what then was it? This question has to be answered in order to determine the law applicable to this case. It is my opinion that the

[27] Megarry and Thompson, *Megarry's Manual of the Law of Real Property* (7th ed, London, Sweet and Maxwell, 1993), p 466.

transaction in this case was a mortgage and it is to the law regulating mortgages that I shall turn for guidance.

All the characteristics of a mortgage are satisfied here.

A mortgage is defined in *Stround's Judicial Dictionary* (Fourth Ed.), at page 1706, as a conveyance of land or an assignment of chattels as a security for the payment of a debt. Megarry and Wade, in their book, *The Law of Real Property* (2nd Ed.) at p.840 state that the essential nature of a mortgage is that it is a conveyance of a legal or equitable interest in property, with a provision for redemption.

The provision for redemption is no longer essential as equity has always regarded the security of an interest in land as a mortgage and the right to redeem the land by payment of the debt and interest as an inviolable right of the mortgagor which cannot be taken away by any provision, to the contrary in the contract. A mortgage is distinguished from a pledge on the ground that in a mortgage the borrower retains possession of his property and the lender only acquires the title to ownership in the property. In the case of a pledge, the lender acquires possession whereas the borrower retains ownership in the property.

Once it is determined that the nature of the transaction in this case is a mortgage, the next question is to determine whether the defendant/appellant was right in taking possession of the land on the expiration of the re-payment date. If not, what remedy is open to the plaintiff/ respondent?

In Uganda, the law applicable to mortgages is twofold. If the land mortgaged is regulated by the *Registration of Titles Act*, that Act applies. In the case of unregistered interests in land, the applicable law is the common law and the doctrines of Equity, See s.3 of the *Judicature Act*, 1967. It is my view that the *Registration of Titles Act* is not applicable in this case as the plaintiff's interest in the land was not registered under that Act.

The correct position of the law was, in my view, properly stated by this court, per Gurthrie Smith. J., in *Erieza Wamala vs. Musa Musoke* (supra.) It was said there, at p.120:

> It is an old established rule that if money is lent on the security of land, the lender will get security and nothing more. He will not be allowed to take advantage of the necessities of the borrower so as to get the land for himself. Therefore, if the borrower wishes to redeem the land within a reasonable time he will always be allowed to do so, even though the due date is past. This rule is so strict that not even an express agreement will be allowed to exclude the borrower's right to redeem. If the lender wishes to do so his remedy is to sue the borrower and get an order from the court that unless the borrower pays up in full within six months his right of redemption is to be barred.

The statement just quoted expresses, in clear terms, the complicated rules which have been devised by the courts to regulate mortgages and protect a borrower from losing his land. The rules are so well established that the aphorism 'Once a Mortgage always a Mortgage' has been coined to emphasise the essential nature of the right to redeem in a mortgage. See: *Samuel vs Jarrah Timber Corporation* (1904) A.C. 323.

The essential nature of a mortgage is that the mortgagor has two distinct interests in the land. Firstly, he has the legal right to redeem on the due date, neither before nor after. Secondly, equity had always recognised the right of the mortgagor to redeem his land at any time after the date set for repayment of the debt. The equity of redemption, as it is generally known, is inviolable and any agreement purporting to deprive the mortgagor of this equitable right to redeem would be struck down by the courts as a clog on the equity of redemption and, therefore rendered void.

In the instant case, the defendant/appellant evicted the plaintiff/respondent in strict compliance with the contract. However, in contracts of this nature a lot is read into the specific terms of the contract and it is always necessary to seek the assistance of the courts before enforcing the literal meaning of the contract. The defendant/appellant was entitled to enter into possession but, if he chose to do this, he held the Kibanja as a trustee of the borrower who always retains the right to redeem his 'Kibanja' on payment in full of the outstanding debt.

On repayment of the debt, the lender must make a true account of the use of the property and any benefits must be set off from the debt due. The plaintiff/respondent brought this action barely a month after the defendant/appellant took possession of the 'Kibanja'. He has all this time wished to pay the full amount of the debt so as to redeem this 'Kibanja. It cannot be said that he has unreasonably delayed in exercising his equitable rights.

The other remedy and probably the most appropriate, is for the lender to apply to the court for an order of foreclosure. The order of foreclosure if made would declare that the equitable right to redeem would come to an end at the expiration of six months if the debt is not repaid in full with interest within that time. At the expiration of the six months, on default of payment, the lender would take possession of the land and the borrower's rights in the property would come to an end. See generally, Megarry and Wade, 'The *Law of Real Property*' p.840-846 (3rd). The appellant did not make any application to the court for an order of foreclosure in this case, just moved in, evicting the respondent in the process. In doing this, he was clearly in breach of the terms of the mortgage.

The only question remaining is to consider whether the evidence of Sessanga (DWs), that the plaintiff/respondent offered his Kibanja in repayment of the debt amounted to a distinct and fresh offer of sale of the Kibanja as submitted by Mr Njuba. I agree that a fresh offer of sale does not amount to a clog on the equity of redemption. But, there was no such offer here. The plaintiff/respondent denied having made such offer and in fact he alleged that the defendant/appellant forcibly evicted him from the Kibanja on 3/2/1969. I believe the story of the plaintiff/respondent on this matter. Had he voluntarily surrendered the 'Kibanja' in re-payment of the debt he could not have instituted this action so soon after the eviction with an offer to repay the whole amount so as to redeem his 'Kibanja'. Besides, it appears the defendant/appellant was not interested in the money but the Kibanja and he said so in so many words in court. He said he lent the money to the plaintiff/respondent knowing he would fail to repay so that he would take the Kibanja. That would not be permissible at all and equity has always intervened to protect helpless debtors in danger of losing their property to unscrupulous creditors.

In the circumstances, I agree with the trial magistrate that the respondent had only secured his Kibanja as a mortgage. He was, therefore, entitled to redeem it on payment of the debt in full plus interest, at any time, even after the expiration of the repayment date. The equity of redemption is inviolable.

****

Notes

1. The definition of a 'mortgage' in *Stround's Judicial Dictionary, supra*, quoted in the judgement, refers to a mortgage created at common law. Under the Torrens System, a mortgage does not involve conveyance of title to the creditor rather it constitutes a charge over the land (see s 115, *Registration of Titles Act*, cap 205).

2. The case of *Matambulire v Kimera* was decided before the *Mortgage Decree*, 1974 came into effect. It is thought that the remedy of foreclosure is no longer available where the mortgage is registered under the *RTA* (see s 130, *Mortgage Decree*).

****

NO CLOGS ON THE EQUITY OF REDEMPTION

The court of equity will not allow any term in a mortgage agreement, which constitutes a clog or fetter on the mortgagor's right to redeem. As the cases below illustrate, there are conflicting decisions as to what amounts to a clog on the equity of redemption. This is partly due to the fact that modern courts are more reluctant to intervene in mortgage agreements than their predecesors.

****

Illusory right

A right to redeem that is 'illusory' amounts to a clog on the equity of redepmtion

Fairclough v Swan Brewery Company Limited
[1912] AC 565 (PC)

[The defendant had a lease for seventeen years over certain hotel premises. He mortgaged the lease to the plaintiff, a brewing company, as security for a loan. The terms of the mortgage included (a) that the defendant must not redeem earlier than six weeks before his leasehold expired, and (b) that during the continuance of the mortgage the defendant must only serve beer purchased from the mortgagee. The defendant sought an early redemption so that he could be released from the obligation under the second clause. The issue was whether the clause was a 'clog' on the equity of redemption.]

Lord Macnaghten: ... [I]t is now firmly established by the House of Lords that ... equity will not permit any device or contrivance being part of the mortgage transaction or contemporaneous with it to prevent or impede redemption. The learned counsel on behalf of the respondents admitted, as he was bound to admit, that a mortgage cannot be made irredeemable. That is plainly forbidden. Is there any difference between forbidding redemption and permitting it, if the permission be a mere pretence? Here the provision for redemption is nugatory. The incumbrance on the lease the subject of the mortgage according to the letter of the bargain falls to be discharged before the lease terminates, but at a time when it is on the very point of expiring, when redemption can be of no advantage to the mortgagor even if he should be so fortunate as to get his deeds back before the actual termination of the lease. For all practical purposes this mortgage is irredeemable. It was obviously meant to be irredeemable. It was made irredeemable in and by the mortgage itself.

Appeal allowed.

****

Question

Why did Lord Macnaghten hold that the right to redeem was 'illusory'?

****

Postponement of redemption

Postponement of the date of redemption is not necessarily a clog on redemption

Knightsbridge Estates Trust, Limited v Byrne and others
[1939] Ch 441

[The appellants (Knightsbridge) mortgaged their freehold estate to the respondents (Byrne) to secure a loan. By deed, the appellants covenanted to repay the debt over a period of forty years paying half-yearly equal instalments. A few years later, the appellants, wishing to take advantage of falling interest rates, sought to repay and discharge the mortgage before the date for payment so that they could get a loan elsewhere on better terms. The appellants instituted proceedings for a declaration that the clause postponing redemption for forty years was a clog on the equity of redemption and, therefore, void. The trial judge dismissed the application. On Appeal.]

Greene MR: ... It was not contended that a provision in a mortgage deed making the mortgage irredeemable for a period of years is necessarily void. The argument was that such a period must be a 'reasonable' one, and it was said that the period in the present case was an unreasonable one by reason merely of its length ...

Now an argument such as this requires the closest scrutiny, for, if it is correct, it means that an agreement made between two competent parties, acting under expert advice and presumably knowing their own business best, is one which the law forbids them to make upon the ground that it is not 'reasonable'. If we were satisfied that the rule of equity was what it is said to be, we should be bound to give effect to it. But in the absence of compelling authority we are not prepared to say that such an agreement cannot lawfully be made. A decision to that effect would, in our view, involve an unjustified interference with the freedom of business men to enter into agreements best suited to their interests and would impose upon them a test of 'reasonableness' laid down by the Courts without reference to the business realities of the case ...

Assuming ..., without in any way deciding, that the period during which the contractual right of redemption is postponed must be a 'reasonable' one (a question which we will now proceed to examine), we are of opinion that the respondents have failed to establish (and the burden is on them) that there is anything unreasonable in the mere extension of the period for forty years in the circumstances of the present case.

But in our opinion the proposition that a postponement of the contractual right of redemption is only permissible for a 'reasonable' time is not well founded. Such a postponement is not properly described as a clog on the equity of redemption, since it is concerned with the contractual right to redeem. It is indisputable that any provision which hampers redemption after the contractual date for redemption was passed will not be permitted. Further, it is undoubtedly true to say that a right of redemption is a necessary element in a mortgage transaction, and consequently that, where the contractual right of redemption is illusory, equity will grant relief by allowing redemption. This was the point in the case of *Fairclough v Swan Brewery Co.* [[1912] AC 565]...

Moreover, equity may give relief against contractual terms in a mortgage transaction if they are oppressive or unconscionable, and in deciding whether or not a particular transaction falls within this category the length of time for which the contractual right to redeem is postponed may well be an important consideration. In the present case no question of this kind was or could have been raised.

But equity does not reform mortgage transactions because they are unreasonable. It is concerned to see two things – one that the essential requirements of a mortgage transaction are observed, and the other that oppressive or unconscionable terms are not enforced. Subject to this, it does not, in our opinion, interfere. The question therefore arises whether, in a case where the right of redemption is real and not illusory and there is nothing oppressive or unconscionable in the transaction, there is something in a postponement of the contractual right to redeem, such as we have in the present case, that is inconsistent with the essential requirements of a mortgage transaction? Apart from authority the answer to this question would, in our opinion, be clearly in the negative. Any other answer would place an unfortunate restriction on the liberty of contract of competent parties who are at arm's length – in the present case it would have operated to prevent the respondents obtaining financial terms which for obvious reasons they themselves considered to be most desirable. It would, moreover, lead to highly inequitable results. The remedy sought by the respondents and the only remedy which is said to be open to them is the establishment of a right to redeem at any time on the ground that the postponement of the contractual right to redeem is void. They do not and could not suggest that the contract as a contract is affected, and the result would accordingly be that whereas the respondents would have had from the first the right to redeem at any time, the appellants would have had no right to require payment otherwise than by the specified instalments. Such an outcome to a bargain entered into by business people negotiating at arm's length would indeed be unfortunate, and we should require clear authority before coming to such a conclusion. ....

[The trial judge] ... does not express the opinion that the postponement in the present case is to be regarded as void by reason merely of its length. He holds that the period is 'having regard to all the provisions of the deed, unreasonable' .... We find ourselves unable to take the view that the Court is entitled in such a case as the present to treat as unreasonable provisions in a mortgage deed entered into by two parties such as we have here with the assistance of competent advisers. For all the Court can know, provisions which may appear to it to be disadvantageous to the mortgagor may have been regarded by him, and correctly regarded, as of no practical consequence from a business point of view...

(A further appeal to the House of Lords was dismissed, but on different grounds ([1940] AC 613).

****

Collateral advantages

Sometimes terms are inserted in a mortgage agreement, which seek to give the mortgagee other advantages in addition to the repayment of the principal sum and interest. The question is whether a collateral advantage is a clog on the equity of redemption.

****

Collateral advantages expiring with the repayment of the mortgage debt, are not a clog on the equity of redemption.

Biggs v Hoddinott
[1895-9] All ER 625

> [A covenant contained in a mortgage of a hotel to a brewer provided that during the continuance of the mortgage (which was expressed to be irredeemable for five years) the mortgagor would only sell on the premises beer brewed by the mortgagee. The mortgagor sought an earlier redemption and a release from the trade agreement. His application was unsuccessful. On appeal.]

Sir Nathaniel Lindley MR: We have listened to a very ingenious and learned argument with a view to induce us to lay down a proposition of law which would be very unfortunate for business men. The proposition is, that while two people are engaged in a mortgage transaction they cannot enter into any other transaction with each other, and that any such transaction must be entered into before or after the mortgage, so that it cannot be said that the mortgagee gets any collateral advantage out of the mortgage.

Counsel for the defendants did not attempt to uphold this on any rational principle, but relied on authority. Of course we must follow the authorities whether we like them or not, but do they support that proposition? *Jennings v Ward* [(1705) 2 Vern 520; 23 ER 935]... was the first case relied on. That was a redemption suit, and the stipulation which was in question seriously interfered with the right of redemption of the mortgaged property on payment of principal, interest, and costs, and SIR JOHN TREVOR, M.R., ordered redemption without regard to that stipulation. He said (2 Vern. at p.520):

> A man shall not have interest for his money and a collateral advantage besides for the loan of it, or clog the redemption with any by-agreement.

That language has found its way into the books, and it has been understood as if he meant exactly what he said without regard to the circumstances of that case, and it has been said that a mortgagee cannot have principal, interest, and costs, and also some collateral advantage. But when the authorities are considered, it is found that the general proposition has been departed from again and again .... The proposition as stated in *Jennings v Ward* is too wide. If properly limited it is good law and good sense, and when one looks at the cases where it has been applied and those where it has not, one sees what it means.

The principle is this: A mortgage is regarded in equity as a security for the money advanced, and a mortgagor may always redeem on payment of principal, interest, and costs; and no bargain which prevents such redemption is valid. There is another principle which is not peculiar to mortgages, and that is that an unconscionable bargain will not be enforced; and there is no case of any bargain being set aside which does not come under one of these two heads.

I think the decision of Romer, J., was right; and to say, as we are asked to do, that a covenant like this one is a collateral advantage and must be disregarded as unconscionable would be to lay down a proposition which would shock any business man, and we are not driven to do it by authority and are not going to say that.

Chitty LJ: This is a mortgage for a term of years effected in the usual way, and it contains a covenant by the mortgagors during the continuance of the security to take all their beer from the mortgagee, and a covenant by the mortgagee to supply it. It is contended that the covenant by the mortgagors is void in equity.

The first observation I desire to make is that it in no way affects the equity of redemption, as redemption can take place just as if the covenant was not in the deed. There is no stipulation that damages for breach of the covenant shall be covered by the security, so this is not a case where the equity of redemption is affected. In equity a mortgage has always been looked upon as only a security for money, and here the right of the mortgagors to redeem on payment of principal, interest, and costs is maintained. It is said that a general principle has been established that a mortgagee shall not stipulate for any collateral advantage to himself, and that there are authorities which show that. That has not been made out. I think the real principle is that the mortgagee shall not impose on the mortgagor any unconscionable or oppressive bargain. There is nothing of that kind in this case. The arrangement is for the common benefit of both parties. Though the mortgagee does by the operation of the covenant get an opportunity for the sale of his beer, the mortgagors get presumably good beer supplied upon the usual terms. It would be contrary to good sense to say that this trade contract entered into by two business men with their eyes open, should be set aside on the ground of its being contrary to some fanciful doctrine of equity.

... In this case, the covenant does not fall within any such supposed rule of equity as the defendants have contended for.

****

Note

The editor of the All England Replacement Report, notes (at 625): 'The dictum of Sir Nathaniel Lindley, M.R., "that a mortgagor may always redeem on payment of principal, interest, and costs and no bargain which prevents such redemption is valid" must be read subject to the qualification that the right to redeem may be postponed, so long as this will not be unreasonable or oppressive.' See also *G and C Kreglinger v New Patagonia Meat Cold Storage Co Ltd* [1914] AC 25, extracted below.

****

A collateral advantage continuing after redemption

Noakes & Co Limited v Rice
[1902] AC 24

[The respondent mortgaged his leasehold public house to the appellant brewing company as security for a loan. Under the mortgage agreement the respondent covenanted that during the continuance of the term, and whether any money should or should not owe on the security of the mortgage, he will not use or sell any liquors except such as should be purchased from the appellants (mortgagees). The respondent being desirous to pay off all money due on the security sought a declaration to the effect that upon payment to the appellant of all moneys due, the respondent was entitled to a reconveyance of the property together with a release of all covenants contained in the mortgage; and that the appellant was not entitled thereafter to the benefit of the covenant in question. The order was granted by the trial judge and affirmed by the Court of Appeal. Further appeal to the House of Lords.]

Lord Davey: My Lords, there are three doctrines of the Courts of Equity in this country which have been referred to in the course of the argument in this case. The first doctrine to which I refer is expressed in the maxim, 'Once a mortgage always a mortgage.' The second is that the mortgagee shall not reserve to himself any collateral advantage outside the mortgage contract; and the third is that a provision or stipulation which will have the effect of clogging or fettering the equity of redemption is void.

My Lords, the first maxim presents no difficulty: it is only another way of saying that a mortgage cannot be made irredeemable, and that a provision to that effect is void. ...

My Lords, the second doctrine to which I refer, namely, that the mortgagee shall not reserve to himself any collateral advantage outside the mortgage contract, was established long ago when the usury laws were in force. The Court of Equity went beyond the usury laws, and set its face against every transaction which tended to usury. It therefore declared void every stipulation by a mortgagee for a collateral advantage which made his total remuneration for the loan indirectly exceed the legal interest. I think it will be found that every case under this head of equity was decided either on this ground, or on the ground that the bargain was oppressive and unconscionable. The abolition of the usury laws has made an alteration in the view the Court should take on this subject, and I agree that a collateral advantage may now be stipulated for by a mortgagee, provided that no unfair advantage be taken by the mortgagee which would render it void or voidable, according to the general principles of equity, and provided that it does not offend against the third doctrine. On these grounds I think the case of *Biggs v Hoddinott* [[1898] 2 Ch 307]... in the Court of Appeal was rightly decided.

The third doctrine to which I have referred is really a corollary from the first, and might be expressed in this form: Once a mortgage always a mortgage and nothing but a mortgage. The meaning of that is that the mortgage shall not make any stipulation which will prevent a mortgagor, who has paid principal, interest, and costs, from getting back his mortgaged property in the condition in which he parted with it. I do not dissent from the opinion expressed by my noble and learned friend opposite (Lord Lindley), when Master of the Rolls, in the case of *Santley v Wilde* [[1899] 2 Ch 474]... He says: 'A clog or fetter is something which is inconsistent with the idea of security; a clog or fetter is in the nature of a repugnant condition'. But I ask, 'security' for what? I think it must be security for the principal, interest, and costs, and, I will add, for any advantages in the nature of increased interest or remuneration for the loan which the mortgagee has validly stipulated for during the continuance of the mortgage. There are two elements in the conception of a mortgage: first, security for the money advanced; and, secondly, remuneration for the use of the money. When the mortgage is paid off the security is at an end, and, as the mortgagee is no longer kept out of his money, the remuneration to him for the use of his money is also at an end. I confess I should have decided the case of *Santley v Wilde* ... differently from the way in which it was dealt with in the Court of Appeal. After the payment of principal and interest, and everything which had become payable up to the date of redemption, the property in that case remained charged with the payment to the mortgagee of one-third share of the profits, and the stipulation to that effect should, I think, have been held to be a clog or fetter on the right to redeem. The principle is this – that a mortgage must not be converted into something else; and when once you come to the conclusion that a stipulation for the benefit of the mortgagee is part of the mortgage transaction, it is but part of his security, and necessarily comes to an end on the payment off of the loan. In my opinion, every yearly or other recurring payment stipulated for by the mortgagee should be held to be in the nature of interest, and no more payable after the principal is paid off than interest would be. I apprehend a man could not stipulate for the continuance of payment of interest after the principal is paid, and I do not think he can stipulate for any other recurring payment such as a share of profits. Any stipulation to that effect would, in my opinion, be void as a clog or fetter on the equity of redemption ...

Now, applying what I have said to the present case, the decision becomes easy. In the first place, I do not think that the respondent's covenant to deal exclusively with the brewers continued after the payment off of the loan and the redemption; and secondly, if it did, it was an attempt to charge it on the property, and that constituted a clog or fetter which, according to well-established principles, was void.

Halsbury L.C.: ... [M]y Lords, taking this case, it appears to me that undoubtedly this was a mortgage, and that the equity of redemption is clogged and fettered here by the continuance of an obligation which would render this house less available in the hands of its owner during the whole period and beyond the whole period of the term, apart from the realisation of the security. Under those circumstances, as a matter of the merest and simplest reasoning, I am wholly unable to come to any other conclusion than that there is a clog and fetter here which the law will not permit.

That seems to me, my Lords, to be the whole of this case...

Lord Macnaghten L.J.: ... Redemption is of the very nature and essence of a mortgage, as mortgages are regarded in equity. It is inherent in the thing itself. And it is, I think, as firmly settled now as it ever was in former times that equity will not permit any device or contrivance designed or calculated to prevent or impede redemption. It follows as a necessary consequence that, when the money secured by a mortgage of land is paid off, the land itself and the owner of the land in the use and enjoyment of it must be as free and unfettered to all intents and purposes as if the land had never been made the subject of the security.

In the present case it is hardly necessary to appeal to this principle. The mortgage deed under consideration expressly and in terms provides that on repayment of the money advanced the mortgagees are to reconvey the mortgaged premises to the mortgagor, or as he shall direct. That, of course, means that the land is to be reconveyed freed and discharged from all burden and liability in respect of or arising out of the contract under which the advance was made ...

Appeal dismissed

****

Neither a collateral advantage nor postponement of the redemption date necessarily amounts to a clog on the equity of redemption.

G and C Kreglinger v New Patagonia Meat Cold Storage Co. Ltd
[1914] AC 25

[The respondents (New Patagonia) were a company carrying on the business of preserving and canning meat. In the course of this business they had at their disposal a large number of sheepskins. The appellants (Kreglinger) were a firm of wool-brokers. By an agreement dated August 24, 1910, the appellants lent the respondents a sum of money secured by a floating charge over all the respondents' property. In their agreement the appellants promised that provided the respondents punctually paid the interest due they would not demand repayment of the principal sum until September 30, 1915. However, the respondents were free at any time to pay off the loan subject to giving one calendar month's notice. The agreement further provided that for a period of five years from the date thereof the respondents should not sell sheepskins to any person other than the appellants so long as the latter were willing to buy at the best price offered by any other person and that the respondents should pay to the appellants a commission on all sheepskins sold by them to any other person. The respondents paid off the loan in a space of only two and a half years (as they were entitled to do under the agreement), but the appellants claimed that their right to purchase the sheepskin continued for the full five years regardless. It was submitted for the respondents that the right claimed by the appellants restricted their freedom of trade and was therefore in the nature of a clog. Moreover, that whether this right clogged the right to redeem or was in the nature of a collateral advantage, it was not intended and it could not endure after redemption. The trial judge held that the provision giving the mortgagee a right to purchase the sheepskin was a clog on the equity of redemption and, therefore, it was void. The Court of Appeal affirmed the decision. On further appeal.]

Viscount Haldane L.C.: ... My Lords, the question in the present case is whether the right to redeem has been interfered with. And this must, for the reasons to which I have adverted in considering the history of the doctrine of equity, depend on the answer to a question which is primarily one of fact. What was the true character of the transaction? Did the appellants make a bargain such that the right to redeem was cut down, or did they simply stipulate for a collateral undertaking, outside and clear of the mortgage, which would give them an exclusive option of purchase of the sheepskins of the respondents? The question is in my opinion not whether the two contracts were made at the same moment and evidenced by the same instrument, but whether they were in substance a single and undivided contract or two distinct contracts ... The question is one not of form but of substance, and it can be answered in each case only by looking at all the circumstances, and not by mere reliance on some abstract principle, or upon the dicta which have fallen obiter from judges in other and different cases. ... In applying a principle the ambit and validity of which depend on confining it steadily to the end for which it was established, the analogies of previous instances where it has been applied are apt to be misleading. For each case forms a real precedent only in so far as it affirms a principle, the relevancy of which in other cases turns on the true character of the particular transaction, and to that extent on circumstances.

My Lords, if in the case before the House your Lordships arrive at the conclusion that the agreement for an option to purchase the respondents' sheepskins was not in substance a fetter on the exercise of their right to redeem, but was in the nature of a collateral bargain the entering into which was a preliminary and separable condition of the loan, the decided cases cease to present any great difficulty. In questions of this kind the binding force of previous decisions, unless the facts are indistinguishable, depends on whether they establish a principle. ... What is vital in the appeal now under consideration is to classify accurately the transaction between the parties.... We are considering the simple question of what is the effect on the right to redeem of having inserted into the formal instrument signed when the money was borrowed an ordinary commercial contract for the sale of skins extending over a period. It appears that it was the intention of the parties that the grant of the security should not affect the power to enter into such a contract, either with strangers or with the appellants, and if so I am unable to see how the equity of redemption is affected. No doubt it is the fact that on redemption the respondents will not get back their business as free from obligation as it was before the date of the security. But that may well be because outside the security and consistently with its terms there was a contemporaneous but collateral contract, contained in the same document as constituted the security, but in substance independent of it. If it was the intention of the parties, as I think it was, to enter into this contract as a condition of the respondents getting their advance, I know no reason either in morals or in equity which ought to prevent this intention from being left to have its effect. What was to be capable of redemption was an undertaking which was deliberately left to be freely changed in its details by ordinary business transactions with which the mortgage was not to interfere. ... I think that the tendency of recent decisions has been to lay undue stress on the letter of the principle which limits the jurisdiction of equity in setting aside contracts. The origin and reason of the principle ought, as I have already said, to be kept steadily in view in applying it to fresh cases. There appears to me to have grown up a tendency to look to the letter rather than to the spirit of the doctrine. The true view is, I think, that judges ought in this kind of jurisdiction to proceed cautiously, and to bear in mind the real reasons which have led Courts of Equity to insist on the free right to redeem and the limits within which the purpose of the rule ought to confine its scope. ... I will add that, if I am right in the view which I take of the authorities, there is no reason for thinking that they establish another rule suggested by the learned counsel for the respondents, that even a mere collateral advantage stipulated for in the same instrument as constitutes the mortgage cannot endure after redemption. ...

Lord Parker of Waddington:.... My Lords, after the most careful consideration of the authorities I think it is open to the House to hold, and I invite your Lordships to hold, that there is now no rule in equity which precludes a mortgagee, whether the mortgage be made upon the occasion of a loan or otherwise, from stipulating for any collateral advantage, provided such collateral advantage is not either (1) unfair and unconscionable, or (2) in the nature of a penalty clogging the equity of redemption, or (3) inconsistent with or repugnant to the contractual and equitable right to redeem.

[After outlining the terms of the parties' agreement Parker LJ, continued.] I doubt whether, even before the repeal of the usury laws, this perfectly fair and businesslike transaction would have been considered a mortgage within any equitable rule or maxim relating to mortgages. The only possible way of deciding whether a transaction is a mortgage within any such rule or maxim is by reference to the intention of the parties. It never was intended by the parties that if the defendant company exercised their right to pay off the loan they should get rid of the option. The option was not in the nature of a penalty, nor was it nor could it ever become inconsistent with or repugnant to any other part of the real bargain within any such rule or maxim. The same is true of the commission payable on the sale of skins as to which the option was not exercised. Under these circumstances it seems to me that the bargain must stand and that the plaintiffs are entitled to the relief they claim.

****

Notes

1. Readers interested in the historical origins and reasons for equity's protection of mortgagors are referred to Viscount Haldane VC's full judgement in *G and C Kreglinger v New Patagonia Meat Cold Storage Co Ltd.*
2. Cheshire and Burns, *Modern Law of Real Property*, (14th ed, London, Butterworth, 1988), p 646, comment that:

> The *Kreglinger* case ... reveals a judicial appreciation of a mortgage as a transaction freely concluded by businessmen without colour of oppression, which should therefore form no exception to the maxim *pacta sunt servanta*. This is a more realistic and reasonable approach, and more compatible with the business conditions of the twentieth century.

Questions

1. Obviously none of the preceding English cases is of binding authority in Uganda. However, in your view, should the courts play a greater or lesser role in policing mortgage agreements? Consider your answer from the perspective of the mortgagees and mortgagors.
2. Should the law ban all collateral advantages? Give reasons for and against collateral advantages.

****

Oppressive or unconscionable interest rate

In Uganda, there is no law that limits the rate of interest that a lender can charge. Nevertheless, the court may intervene where the interest rate charged by the mortgagee is oppressive or unconscionable. The following Tanzanian case illustrates this point.

Juma v Habibu
[1975] EA 103 (T)

> [The appellant borrowed money from the respondent secured by a mortgage over the respondent's land, at an interest rate of 60% per annum. The trial magistrate ordered the appellant to pay the loan and the contractual interest. On appeal, the issue was whether the agreed rate of interest was 'unconscionable' and unlawful.]

Mapigano, AG J: ... Mr Mangat, who appeared for the appellant, submitted in this court that the rate of interest was harsh and unconscionable, and he referred me to the decision of this court in *Simion Kashumali v Leornard Mutajwaha* (1968), HCB 135. ... The digest [of the judgement] shows that there was an action to recover money lent plus interest at 25% p.a. the interest demanded being part of the loan agreement. The judge seems to have stated *obiter* that the interest at 25% p.a. was excessive. The judge... stated, again *obiter*, that the respondent would not be allowed more than 9% interest on the loan until the date when the first judgement was pronounced, and 6% interest on the decretal amount, if any. The report is silent on why the judge arrived at the opinion that interest until judgement at first instance should be 9% p.a. I therefore find hardly any guidance in that decision as reported in the digest.

I feel however that the trial Magistrate did not pause to consider whether the interest contracted was excessive. It was not beyond his powers to do so. The court has a discretion to award interest at less than the contractual rate, when that rate is manifestly excessive or unconscionable. This is within the letter and spirit of s. 29 of the Civil Procedure Code, which says:

> The Chief Justice may make rules prescribing the rate of interest which shall be carried by judgement debts, and, without prejudice to the power of the court to order interest to be paid up to the date of judgement at such rates as it may deem reasonable, every judgement debt shall carry interest at the rate prescribed from the date of the delivery of the judgement until the same shall be satisfied.

While the rate of interest on the decretal amount from the date of judgement until satisfaction of the decree is prescribed in 0. 20, r. 21 as 7% p.a. or such rate not exceeding 12% p.a. as the parties may expressly agree in writing, and this has not been varied by the Chief Justice, the rate of interest up to the date of judgement is a matter of judicial discretion of the trial court, and by construction, this discretion can be exercised to the prejudice of any contractual stipulation.

In the instant case, as I have indicated above, the trial court awarded, uncritically, the contractual rate even though the appellant had pleaded in effect, that the interest was harsh. In *Mohamed Mohamedi v Athman Shamte* [1960] EA 1062, Mosdell J, appeared to say that when the rate of interest exceeds 48% per annum, the court may assume, unless the contrary is proved, that the rate is excessive. The criterion of 48% appears to have a history whose roots are thousands of kilometres away from this country. It appears to have been borrowed from English cases decided under the English Money Lenders Acts 1909 and 1911. It does not appear to me to be a proper standard for this country, though to be fair to the judge, he did eventually hold that the trial court had exercised its discretion judicially when it reduced the interest from 84% p.a. to 60%. I feel however that having regard to the social, political and economic climate of present-day Tanzania where the eradication of exploitation is declared policy and where unfair play is frowned at, it is not only interest above 48% which may be regarded as exploitive. Without pretending to lay down any standard, I would venture to say that anything above 20% p.a. should appear prima facie harsh and irreconcilable to public morality as obtaining today. This means that anything above that point could perfectly cause the court to raise its eyebrows and to require the party who claims it to prove that it is proper and fair in the circumstances of the case as a whole.

I am of the strong view that the interest at 60% per annum which the trial Court allowed without demur, was apparently unreasonable and extortionate, and there being no evidence to prove that it was not extortionate, I consider that in allowing it the trial court exercised its discretion unjudicially [sic]. I am therefore constrained to reduce it to 12% p. a.

****

Note

Though the High Court in the foregoing case based its authority to intervene on s. 29 of the Civil Procedure Code (T), it is submitted that the court could also have intervened on the basis of its inherent equitable jurisdiction to grant relief against 'contractual terms in a mortgage transaction if they are oppressive or unconscionable"' (see Greene MR in *Knightsbridge Estates Trust, Limited v Byrne and others* [1939] Ch 441, at 457, see extract above).

Questions

1. Mapigano Ag J stated: 'Without pretending to lay down any standard ... an interest rate above 20% ... could perfectly cause the court to raise its eyebrows and to require the party who claims it to prove that it is proper and fair in the circumstances of the case as a whole.' In the context of Uganda's prevailing social and economic circumstances, would you apply the same standard? If not, what is the maximum interest rate above which a court in Uganda justifiably 'raise its eyebrows'?

2. Should the courts retain the power to intervene in mortgage agreements on the ground that the interest rate is excessive? What about the notion of freedom of contract? Discuss these questions from the viewpoint of the mortgagor and mortgagee.

3. In the foregoing judgement, it is clear that in determining whether the interest rate is harsh the court will not simply look at the interest rate, but will take into account all circumstances of the case. Discuss the sort of factors that a court might consider and why those factors should have an impact on its decision.

****

12
Co-ownership of Land

TYPES OF CO-OWNERSHIP

Co-ownership is where two or more persons are entitled to the simultaneous use or enjoyment of land each claiming not a separate portion but a mutual right in the whole. There are two types of co-ownerships:

1. Tenancy in common, and
2. Joint tenancy.

****

Tenancy in common

'Tenants in common hold in undivided shares, but the tenants have quite separate interests and the only fact which brings them into co-ownership is that they both have shares in a single property which has not yet been divided among them' (per Ntabgoba Ag J in *East Africa General Insurance v Ntende* CS No 1387 of 1975; [1979] HCB 227). Because tenants in common have distinct shares in the property, upon death of a co-owner his or her share devolves upon his or her successor (*Kitiiza v Registrar of Titles* Misc Appn No 82 of 1977).

Joint tenancy

A joint tenancy has two essential features: (a) the four unities and (b) the right of survivorship.

The four unities

The four unities are: unity of possession, time, title, and interest.

****

There cannot be a joint tenancy without the four unities

Ag Securities v Vaughan and others
[1988] 3 All E R 1058 [HL]

> [The appellants owned a four bedroom flat. Under separate contracts entered into at different times they granted the right to occupy the flat to four individuals (the 'flat sharers'). The contract entitled each occupant to use the premises in common with other people who might from time to time have a similar right. Rent payable by the occupants varied in each contract. The Court of Appeal held that the four 'flat sharers' occupied the flat as joint tenants. On further appeal to the House of Lords.]

Lord Templeman: ... The Court of Appeal ... concluded that the four respondents were jointly entitled to the exclusive occupation of the flat. I am unable to agree. If a landlord who owns a three bedroom flat enters into three separate independent tenancies with three independent tenants each of whom is entitled to one bedroom and to share the common parts, then the three tenants, if they agree, can exclude anyone else from the flat. But they do not enjoy exclusive occupation of the flat jointly under the terms of their tenancies. In the present case, if the four respondents had been jointly entitled to exclusive occupation of the flat then, on the death of one of the respondents, the remaining three would be entitled to joint and exclusive occupation. But, in fact, on the death of one respondent the remaining three would not be entitled to joint and exclusive occupation of the flat. They could not exclude a fourth person nominated by the company. I would allow the appeal.

Lord Ackner: ... [E]ach of the respondents commenced his occupation of the flat on different dates, each of their agreements covered different period and each agreement provided for different payments for that occupation. In such circumstances there could not have been a grant of a joint tenancy to all four respondents. ...

Lord Jauncey of Tullichettle: ... I should be surprised indeed if a joint lease could be created by four separate documents of different dates in favour of four independent persons each paying a different rent and also for different periods of six months. Such an arrangement would, as Sir George Waller [dissenting Judge in the Court of Appeals] pointed out be notably deficient in the four unities of interest, title, time and possession ...

****

Ag Securities v Vaughan and others
[1988] 2 All ER 173(CA)

[The following extract is from Sir George Waller's dissenting judgement in the Court of Appeal, which was approved by the House of Lords.]

Sir George Waller: ... A joint tenancy is one where the tenancy commences on the same day for all, where the term is the same for all, where the rent should not be altered without due notice to all possibly where all are jointly liable for the rent.

Fox LJ has referred to the four unities set out in Megarry and Wade *The Law of Real Property* (5th edn, 1984) pp 419-422 as the requirements for a joint tenancy and I will consider them.

Unity of interest: The extent, nature and duration of each occupant's interest is different. Each one started on a different day and as a result the extent was different because the duration was six months in each case and then monthly. Although each one became monthly after six months, there is no 'act' to create a joint tenancy, as I shall refer to under unity of title.

Unity of title: The unity of title for a joint tenancy has to be the same act or document. Megarry and Wade were repeating that which was contained in *Blackstone's Commentaries* (2 Bl Com 180):

> Joint-tenancy cannot arise by des/cent or act of law; but merely by purchase, or acquisition by the act of the party: and, unless that act be one and the same, the two tenants would have different titles. ...

Each occupant started with a different document on a different date. Can it be said that it was the same act? In my opinion a new joint tenancy could not arise each time a new person came because the new occupant had six months to run whereas every other occupant was monthly, and it could not arise at the expiration of six months because there was then no 'act' which could create a joint tenancy.

Unity of time: The interest of each must vest at the same time. If we were considering the first four occupants it would follow that their interest vested at the same time, but as each new occupant arrived the interest of the others had already vested and at the time when the notices to quit were delivered each occupant's interest had vested on different days.

Unity of possession: This must be possession of the whole. Each occupant was given the right to use the flat and so it could be said that there was unity of right to use the flat. But was that possession of the whole? In *Addiscombe Garden Estates Ltd v Crabbe* [1957] 3 All ER 563 at 568, [1958] 1 QB 513 at 524-525, a case where the 'licence' contained a clause entitling the landlord to enter the land, Jenkins LJ said:

> The importance of that is that it shows that the right to occupy the premises conferred on the grantees was intended as an exclusive right of occupation, in that it was thought necessary to give a special and express power to the grantors to enter. The exclusive character of the occupation

> granted by a document such as this has always been regarded, if not as a decisive indication, at all events as a very important indication to the effect that a tenancy, as distinct from a licence, is the real subject-matter of the document.

The indication is in the opposite direction in this case, but the plaintiff never claimed the right.

I am prepared to accept that there may be an exceptional case where there might be a special arrangement about one of these characteristics, but in my opinion there cannot be a joint tenancy where there are serious doubts about each of the four unities.

****

Right of survivorship

Upon the death of one joint tenant, his or her share in the co-owned property is extinguished and that of the remaining joint tenant(s) correspondingly enlarged. This is what is known as the right of survivorship or *jus accrescendi*. Because of this doctrine, land owned in joint tenancy cannot devolve by will or under intestate succession (*Swift d Neal v Roberts* (1764) 3 Burr.1488; 97 ER 941).

****

CREATION OF JOINT TENANCY AND TENANCY IN COMMON

Common law

At common law, a grant of land to two or more persons without words of severance creates a joint tenancy. Conversely, a grant with words of severance creates a tenancy in common. The cases below illustrate this rule.

****

Unless a contrary intention appears, a grant of land to two or more persons without words of severance creates a joint tenancy at law.

Morley v Bird
(1798) 3 Ves 629; 30 ER 1192

> [A testator devised and bequeathed real and personal property to the defendant on condition that she paid £400 to four persons named in the will. Three of the four named persons pre-deceased the testator. The plaintiff survived him. The issue was whether the legacy was given to the four as joint tenants or tenants in common. If they were joint tenants, the plaintiff as the sole survivor would be entitled to receive the whole £400. On the other hand, if they were tenants in common, the plaintiff would only be entitled to receive his share (ie £100), the remainder of the gift, having lapsed, reverting to the estate of the testator.]

Master of the Rolls [Arden]: ... I wish to give my opinion very explicitly. Great doubts have been entertained by Judges both at Law and in Equity as to words creating a joint tenancy or a tenancy in common; ... and it is clear, the ancient law was in favour of a joint tenancy; and that law still prevails: unless there are some words to sever the interest taken, it is at this moment a joint tenancy, notwithstanding the leaning of the Courts lately in favour of a tenancy in common. A legacy of a specific chattel, a grant of an estate, is a joint tenancy. It is true, the Courts seeing the inconvenience of that have been desirous, wherever they could find any intention of severance, to avail themselves of it; and their successive determinations have laid hold of any words for that purpose. 'Equally to be divided' (*Rigden v Vailler*, 2 Ves sen. 252), 'equally, among, between,' even in Law I believe, certainly in Equity, create a tenancy in common: but without those words it is a joint tenancy. ... Therefore, legacies, gifts, grants, &c., are both at Law and in Equity joint; except from the nature of the contract or from the words some intention of severance appears.

This is a legacy to four persons; and there are no words of severance; therefore it is a joint legacy; and the whole interest survives to the survivor, three being dead; and though I agree with those, who think it the least evil, that it should be a tenancy in common, this is one of those cases, in which it is more convenient, that it should remain joint.... The legacy therefore belongs to the Plaintiffs.

****

Robertson v Fraser

(1871) 6 Ch App 696

> [A testator bequeathed his estate to J and F for their absolute use and benefit. By a subsequent amendment of the will, he added the name of W so that he too 'shall and may participate in the bequest with J and F'. J died in the testator's lifetime while F and W survived him. The issue was whether the bequest to J, F and W was in joint tenancy or tenancy in common.]

Lord Hatherley L.C: ... I cannot doubt, having regard to the authorities respecting the effect of such words as 'amongst' and 'respectively', that anything which in the slightest degree indicates an intention to divide the property must be held to abrogate the idea of a joint tenancy, and to create a tenancy in common. Perhaps it would have been well if the Courts had held that in bequests, as in partnerships, every community of interest was to be considered a tenancy in common. But that has not been done. However, putting aside such words as 'alike' and 'equally' – for they may be considered more decidedly inconsistent with joint tenancy, inasmuch as the interests of joint tenants are very rarely quite equal, considering the difference that may exist in the ages of the legatees – it does not appear to me that such words as 'amongst' and 'respectively' are at all stronger than 'participate'. I have, therefore, no doubt that the word 'participate' is sufficient to indicate an intention to divide, and to create a tenancy in common.

****

Questions

1. Why did the common law tend to favour joint tenancy, over tenancy in common?
2. A testator devised his estate to his children Kato and Kakulu 'to share alike as joint tenants'. What sort of co-ownership did the testator intend to create? Do you see any contradiction in the grant?

****

Equity

In equity, as at a common law, a grant of land to two or more persons without words of severance creates a joint tenancy. However, in certain circumstances even where there are no words of severance equity, unlike the common law, presumes that the parties intended to create a tenancy in common rather than joint tenancy:

> [A]s where persons are in trade, and have joint debts due to them; the Courts say, it could not be intended to the prejudice of the family of the deceased partner; therefore not doubting, that it would be a joint-tenancy at Law, in Equity they say, it could not be the agreement. So if two people join in lending money upon a mortgage, Equity says, it could not be the intention, that the interest in that should survive. Though they take a joint security, each means to lend his own and take back his own.

But that was never extended to grants. A voluntary bond would survive, if no intention of the party to make a severance appears (per Arden MR in *Morley v Bird, supra*).

****

Property purchased with funds contributed unequally

Equity presumes a tenancy in common where the purchase price was contributed in unequal proportions

Robinson v Preston
70 ER 1192

Sir William Page Wood: ... The law is settled as to the investment of moneys in the names of two or more persons in the purchase of property. If invested in unequal shares, the purchasers remain tenants in common of the purchased property; if in equal shares, and the matter on the face of it purports to be a joint tenancy, then it is considered by this court to be a joint-tenancy, and no equity is supposed to intervene by which it can be reduced to a tenancy in common.

****

Partnership assets

Equity presumes that partners intend to hold the firm's assets in tenancy in common

Lake v Craddock
[1558-1774] All ER Rep R 419

[Five people contributed equally to purchase certain swamp land which they planned to drain and re-sell the land in smaller blocks at a profit to themselves. The land was conveyed to the five of them without words of severance. Some years later Craddock, one of the five investors, abandoned the project but the others continued and even bought more land. Upon Craddock's death, his heir claimed the deceased's share in the land. The issue was whether the five owned the land as joint tenants or tenants in common. If the former the deceased's interest was extinguished by operation of the doctrine of survivorship.]

Sir Joseph Jekyll Mr: ... [T]he survivorship should not take place, for the payment of money created a trust for the parties advancing it, and an undertaking upon the hazard of profit or loss was in the nature of merchandising, when the jus accrescendi was never allowed. Supposing that one of the partners had laid out the whole of the money, and had happened to die first, he must, according to the contrary construction, have lost all, which would have been most unjust. Wherefore it is decreed that the five purchasers were tenants in common. ...

Notes

1. Three people formed a partnership for acquiring a lease of public land. Soon after the grant one of the partners died. The survivors purported to exclude the successor of the deceased from the land. It was held that where a partnership is dissolved on the death of one of the partners, the successor to the deceased partner becomes entitled to the right that had accrued to the deceased as they held the land as tenants in common (*Kitiiza v Registrar of Titles* Misc. Appn. No 82 of 1977).
2. The rule in *Lake v Craddock* has been enacted in s. 24(1) *Partnership Act* (cap 86). For discussion of the meaning of a similar provision, see *In re Bourne, Bourne v Bourne* [1906] 2 Ch 427 at 432.

****

Other circumstances

Circumstances in which equity presumes a tenancy in common are not limited to specific categories

Malayan Credit LTD v Jack Chia-MPH Ltd
[1986] AC 549 (PC)

[The plaintiff and defendant together leased certain office premises for their separate business interests. The lease was conveyed to both of them without words of severance. At the outset, they agreed that the plaintiff should occupy approximately one third of the office space and the defendant the remainder. Payment for rent and other outgoings was apportioned in proportion to the area occupied. A dispute having arisen between the parties, the plaintiff sought a judicial order for sale of the land and equal division of the net proceeds; alternatively for equal partition of the premises. The main issue was whether the parties held the land in joint tenancy or tenancy in common. If the former, then the plaintiff was entitled to an equal share of the proceeds of sale or partition of the premises. The Court of Appeal held that the plaintiff and the defendant were joint tenants holding in equal shares. This is an appeal to the Privy Council.]

Lord Brightman:... Their Lordships will deal first with the general principles involved in the case. As the lease itself contains no words of severance, it necessarily takes effect as a grant to the lessees as joint tenants at law. As regards the beneficial interest in the lease in equity, there are three possible situations.

Situation A. The lessees at the inception of the lease hold the beneficial interest therein as joint tenants in equity. This will be the case if there are no circumstances which dictate to the contrary. On subsequent severance, the lessees would hold the beneficial interest in equal shares.

Situation B. The lessees at the inception of the lease hold the beneficial interest as tenants in common in equity in equal shares.

Situation C. The lessees at the inception of the lease hold the beneficial interest as tenants in common in equity in unequal shares.

Situation A is that which is advocated by the plaintiff. The argument is that, in the absence of an express agreement, persons who take as joint tenants at law hold as tenants in common in equity only in three classes of case: first, where they have provided the purchase money in unequal shares; in this case they hold the beneficial interest in similar shares: secondly, where the grant consists of a security for a loan and the grantees were equal or unequal contributors to the loan; again they would hold the beneficial interest in the same shares; and thirdly, where they are partners and the subject matter of the grant is partnership property. See for example, Snell's *Principles of Equity*, 28th ed. (1982), pp 37 and 38. The plaintiff contends that the instant case falls into none of these three categories. Therefore it is said that the lessees hold as joint tenants in equity as well as at law, with the result that either party was at liberty to sever the joint tenancy and thus ensure that the beneficial interest was thereafter held in equal shares. Subject to severance, which either party can secure at will, there is no difference between the end result of situation A, and situation B.

Situation C is that which is advocated by the defendant. If situation A applies to the present case, it is not in dispute that there has been a severance.

The matter came before the High Court on affidavit evidence. The trial judge held that as the premises were disproportionately divided between the parties, there was a tenancy in common in unequal shares; in other words, situation C. He said that he was fortified in this view by the fact that the stamp duty was paid in unequal shares, as also the rent. The Court of Appeal reversed the trial judge, holding that there was a joint tenancy which, on later severance, became a tenancy in common in equal shares; in other words, situation A. The Court of Appeal directed a sale.

It seems to their Lordships that where premises are held by two persons as joint tenants at law for their several business purposes, it is improbable that they would intend to hold as joint tenants in equity. Suppose that an accountant and an architect take a lease of premises containing four rooms, that the accountant uses two rooms, and that the architect uses two rooms. It is scarcely to be supposed that they intend that if, for example, the accountant dies first without having gone through the formalities of a severance, the beneficial interest in the entire premises is to survive to the architect. Their Lordships do not accept that the cases in which joint tenants at law will be presumed to hold as tenants in common in equity are as rigidly circumscribed as the plaintiff asserts. Such cases are not necessarily limited to purchasers who contribute unequally, to co-mortgagees and to partners. There are other circumstances in which equity may infer that the beneficial interest is intended to be held by the grantees as tenants in common. In the opinion of their Lordships, one such case is where the grantees hold the premises for their several individual business purposes.

Furthermore, there is no fundamental distinction to be drawn for present purposes between joint tenants who acquire a term of years on payment of a premium and at a token rent, and joint tenants who acquire a term of years on the payment of no premium but at a rack rent. If in the first case the lessees contribute unequally towards the premium, it is plain that they hold the term of years (in the absence of contra-indications) as tenants in common in equity in unequal shares. The premium is the purchase money. In the second case the rent is equivalent to the purchase money. If that is paid in unequal shares, logically the joint tenants should hold the beneficial interest in equity (in the absence of contra-indications) as tenants in common in unequal shares.

There are features in the instant case which appear to their Lordships to point unmistakably towards a tenancy in common in equity, and furthermore towards a tenancy in common in unequal shares: (1) the lease was clearly taken to serve the separate commercial interests of the defendant and the plaintiff. (2) Prior to the grant of the lease the parties had settled between themselves what space they would respectively occupy when the lease came to be granted. This was roughly 62 per cent to the defendant and 38 per cent to the plaintiff. (3) Prior to the grant of the lease, the parties had made meticulous measurements of their respected allotted areas, and divided their liability for the rent and service charge in unequal shares in accordance with the respective areas they would occupy. (4) Prior to the grant of the lease, the plaintiff was invoiced for its due share of the deposit which was to be paid to the landlord as security under the terms of the lease, the apportionment being made in unequal shares in the like manner. This deposit was a sum which was not to be refundable by the landlord until the termination of the lease. The plaintiff did not dispute the principle of this apportionment. (5) After the grant of the lease, the defendant and the plaintiff paid the stamp duty and the survey fees in the same unequal shares. (6) As from the grant of the lease, the rent and service charges were paid in the same unequal shares.

With great respect to the Court of Appeal, their Lordships feel unable to support their conclusion that the parties are beneficially entitled to equal shares. In the opinion of their Lordships, the payment of rent and service charge in unequal shares, the payment of the stamp duty and the survey fee in unequal shares, and the unequal contributions to the deposit payable under the terms of the lease which was to be outstanding for the whole period of the lease, are comparable to the payment of purchase money in unequal shares. All the circumstances point decisively to the inference that the parties took the premises in equity as tenants in common in unequal shares, those shares being (as a result of the meticulous calculations made by the parties) 3,614 shares to the defendant and 2,306 shares to the plaintiff.

****

Questions

1. Why does equity make a presumption of tenancy in common in certain situations?
2. Assume that Mr and Mrs Kalanzi contribute unequally to purchase their residential home. Two years later, Mr Kalanzi dies. In his will, he devised the house to Amina, his former girl friend. Advise Mrs Kalanzi. Has s 40 of the *Land Act* any relevance to your advice? Explain.

****

Presumption of Joint Tenancy under the *Registration of Titles Act*

Section 53 provides that:

> Two or more persons who are registered as joint proprietors of land shall be deemed to be entitled to the same as joint tenants; and in all cases where two or more persons are entitled as tenants in common to undivided shares of or in any land, such persons shall in the absence of any evidence to the contrary be presumed to hold any such land in equal shares.

The effect and meaning of a corresponding provision in the New Zealand Torrens legislation was considered in the following case.

****

In *Re: Foley (deceased), Public Trustee v Foley and other*
[1955] NZLR 702

> [The testatrix and her sister, Gertrude, were together registered as the mortgagees under a mortgage, which secured a principal sum of £4,000. Gertrude survived the testatrix for a period of slightly over two months. The Court was asked to determine whether she became solely entitled both at law and in equity to the mortgage and to the principal and other moneys thereby secured.]

Henry J: The *Land Transfer Act*, 1952, provides, in s. 61, as follows:

> ... any two or more persons named in any Crown grant or in any instrument executed under this Act as transferees, mortgagees, or proprietors of any estate or interest, shall, unless the contrary is expressed be deemed to be entitled as joint tenants with right of survivorship, and every such instrument, when registered shall take effect accordingly.

So far as the legislation is concerned, the testatrix and her sister are 'mortgagees' within the meaning of the word in s. 61; and, they were, upon registration of the said mortgage, deemed under s. 61 to be entitled as joint tenants with right of survivorship. Mr Stephenson argued that s. 61 concluded the matter, and, that the Court was bound to hold in the absence of a contrary expression in the instrument, that registration caused the instrument to have the effect of creating a joint tenancy in the mortgagees both in law and equity with right of survivorship. Mr Adams argued that s. 61 is a 'registration' section; and, that the section does not interfere with the jurisdiction of the Court in 'trust matters'.

It will be observed that s. 61 uses the expression: 'shall, unless the contrary is expressed, be deemed to be entitled as joint tenants'. Where the Legislature uses the word 'deemed' the Court is entitled and bound to ascertain for what purposes and between what persons the statutory fiction is to be resorted to. The Legislature has not enacted in s. 61 that the persons 'shall be entitled as joint tenants' but that they 'shall be deemed to be entitled as joint tenants'.

In order to ascertain the effect of s. 61 it is necessary to consider ss. 61 to 64 (inclusive), which sections are all grouped under the heading 'Registered Proprietors'. Section 62 provides that the estate of the registered proprietor shall, with certain exceptions, be paramount. Section 63 protects the registered proprietor against ejectment except in the cases appearing in paras. (a) to (e). Section 64 prevents any person from acquiring by possession or adverse user any title in derogation of the title of the registered proprietor. If s. 61 had not been enacted, anyone dealing with the survivor of the persons referred to would be faced with questions as to the exact estate which the survivor took. The section is clearly intended to define the position of a survivor so that the registered instrument may be looked at for the purpose of ascertaining who the person or persons are who are entitled to deal with the estate. ...

After considering ss. 61 to 64 (inclusive) in the light of the above, I am of the opinion that the intention of the Legislature is to make registration conclusive so far as it concerns parties who act in reliance of the registered instrument. In the case of two or more registered mortgagees appearing in a memorandum of mortgage, they may be treated by the Registrar, and by all persons dealing with them, as joint tenants with right of survivorship, and the registered estates and interests will pass accordingly. But this does not, in my view, exclude the jurisdiction of the Court in determining questions between the mortgagees themselves. The purpose of the fiction in s. 61 is to make the Register, in so far as the mortgagees are described in the instrument, paramount as between the mortgagees, on the one hand, and any person dealing with the survivor of them, on the other hand. In the result, my conclusion is that s. 61 does not preclude the Court from entering upon an inquiry as to whether or not a tenancy in common exists between registered mortgagees where the registered instrument is silent on that point. ...

(His Honour concluded on the facts of the case that the two sisters intended to hold the mortgage as tenants in common and not as joint tenants.)

****

Question

Mr and Mrs Karuhanga are registered as joint tenants of certain freehold land. Is that conclusive of the nature of their co-ownership? If not, who would bear the burden of proof that they are not joint tenants? Can you think of any circumstances where the parties are registered as joint tenants, but, in equity, are deemed to be tenants in common?

****

Rights of Co-owners amongst themselves

Co-owners enjoy certain rights and owe certain obligations towards each other. The most important right of a co-owner is the right to possession and enjoyment of the entire co-owned land irrespective of the size of his or her share. In the eyes of the law the entire land is his or hers to enjoy. For this reason, a co-owner who merely occupies or enjoys the land cannot be forced by his or her co-owners to pay them 'occupational rent' or contribute towards repair expenses or to reimburse them for costs already incurred. Nor can they hold him or her liable for trespass to land. These rules and their exceptions are illustrated in the materials bellow.

****

Occupation rent

Unity of possession entitles a co-owner to occupy any part of the co-owned land irrespective of the size of his or her share as long as he or she does not prevent the others from doing the same.

****

A co-owner is not liable to pay occupation rent to fellow co-owners

Jones (A.E.) v Jones (F.W.)
[1977] 1 WLR 438

[The defendant's father purchased a house for him. The defendant contributed one-quarter of the purchase price and understood from his father that the house was his. In his will, the defendant's father bequeathed the house to the plaintiff, the defendant's stepmother. The plaintiff brought proceedings for an order that the house be sold and an order for the defendant to make a payment in the nature of rent for the period the defendant was in sole occupation of the house. The trial judge ordered the defendant to pay the plaintiff three-quarters of a fair rent for the sole occupation of the house. On appeal by the defendant.]

Lord Denning MR: ... First the claim for rent. It is quite plain that these two people were in equity tenants in common having a three-quarter and one-quarter share respectively. One was in occupation of the house. The other was not. Now the common law said clearly that one tenant in common is not entitled to rent from another tenant in common, even though that other occupies the whole. ... Of course if one of the tenants let the premises at a rent to a stranger and received the rent, there would have to be an account, but the mere fact that one tenant was in possession and the other out of possession did not give the one that is out any claim for rent. It did not do so in the old days of legal tenants in common. Nor does it in modern times of equitable tenants in common. In *Bull v Bull* [1955] 1 Q.B. 234, 239, I said:

> ... the son, although he is the legal owner of the house, has no right to turn his mother out. She has an equitable interest which entitles her to remain in the house as tenant in common with him until the house is sold.

As between tenants in common, they are both equally entitled to occupation and one cannot claim rent from the other. Of course, if there was an ouster, that would be another matter: or if there was a letting to a stranger for rent that would be different, but there can be no claim for rent by one tenant in common against the other whether at law or in equity.

****

In some circumstances a co-owner may be held liable to pay occupation rent

Dennis v McDonald
[1981] 2 All ER 633

[The plaintiff and the defendant cohabited in a de facto relationship. Together they bought a dwelling house which they intended to be their family house. The house was conveyed to them in their joint names as tenants in common. After several years of living together, the plaintiff left the house because of the defendant's violence towards her. The plaintiff made an application for the sale of the house, alternatively for the defendant to pay her occupation rent. The defendant opposed the application and he submitted that as a co-owner he was not liable to pay occupation rent.]

Purchas J. ... Counsel for the plaintiff submitted, I think correctly, that ... the true position under the old authorities was that the Court of Chancery and Chancery Division would be always ready to inquire into the position as between co-owners being tenants in common either at law or in equity to see whether a tenant in common in occupation of the premises was doing so to the exclusion of one or more of the other tenants in common for whatever purpose or by whatever means. If this was found to be the case, then if in order to do equity between the parties an occupation rent should be paid, this would be declared and the appropriate inquiry ordered. Only in cases where the tenants in common not in occupation were in a position to enjoy their right to occupy but chose not to do so voluntarily, and were not excluded by any relevant factor, would the tenant in common in occupation be entitled to do so free of liability to pay an occupation rent.

In the instant case the plaintiff is clearly not a free agent. She was caused to leave the family home as a result of the violence or threatened violence of the defendant. In the event, whatever might have been the cause of the breakdown of the association, it would be quite unreasonable to expect the plaintiff to exercise her rights as a tenant in common to occupy the property as she had done before the breakdown of the association with the defendant. ... Therefore, the basic principle that a new tenant in common is not liable to pay an occupation rent by virtue merely of his being in sole occupation of the property does not apply in the case where an association similar to a matrimonial association has broken down and one party, for practical purposes, excluded from the family house. ...

****

A co-owner who is in possession of the land as a lessee is liable to pay rent

Uganda Thrift Co Ltd v J. M. Nnambale
(1970) ULR 66

[A group of ten people including the defendant together bought land and constructed on it several houses for renting. The co-owners incorporated the plaintiff company with the view to transfer to it title to the land. For several months before the title was transferred to the plaintiff, the defendant occupied one of the houses and paid rent to the plaintiff. When he defaulted the plaintiffs brought these proceedings for arrears and eviction.]

Wambuzi J: Learned Counsel for the defendant argued that the other tenants in common could not use the company to evict the defendant, an act they themselves were incapable of doing, and relied on *Bull v Bull* (1955) 1 All ER. 253. I am not persuaded by this authority. In that case a house was bought by two people who apparently intended to live in it. Differences arose after they had lived in the house for some time. The situation is different in the instant case. The land in question was not bought for occupation by the purchasers nor was house No. 9 Mutagwanya estate erected for the occupation of the eleven purchasers. On the contrary the house was built for commercial purposes, and could have been rented to any person other than the defendant. Apparently, the defendant went into occupation pursuant to a verbal contract for a lease between him and the Society. If he fails to pay the rent reserved, he is not immune to eviction merely because he is a tenant in common, a relationship which does not exist between him and his acknowledged landlord – the Society or in this case the Company. It appears that even if the relationship of tenants in common were relevant, if the defendant remained in occupation without complying with the terms thereof, he would enjoy the benefit of this house to the exclusion of the other tenants in common and also claim a share in the rest of estate. It is too theoretical to suggest, even without knowledge of the size of House No. 9, that the defendant would be content to be joined there by nine or ten others as they are all entitled to live there. There would otherwise be no explanation as to why in practice the defendant should be entitled to more benefits than the others....

There will be judgement for the plaintiff as prayed.

****

A co-owner has no legal obligation to pay compensation to the other co-owner for the expenses he or she incurred in improving or repairing their property

Leigh v Dickeson
(1884) 15 QBD 60

[The plaintiff and defendant were co-owners of a house. By mutual agreement the house was leased to the defendant for a certain period. The plaintiff brought this action to recover rent due from the defendant. The defendant by way of counter-claim sought to recover from the plaintiff a proportion of the money he spent towards repairs and improvements to the house in proportion to the benefit the plaintiff had received. The trial judge dismissed the counter-claim. On appeal.]

Brett MR.: ... Tenants in common are not partners, and it has been so held: one of them is not an agent for another. The cost of the repairs to the house was a voluntary payment by the defendant partly for the benefit of himself and partly for the benefit of his co-owner; but the co-owner cannot reject the benefit of the repairs, and if she is held to be liable for a proportionate share of the cost, the defendant will get the advantage of the repairs without allowing his co-owner any liberty to decide whether she will refuse or adopt them. The defendant cannot recover at common law; he cannot recover for money paid in equity, for that is a legal remedy: there is no remedy in this case for money paid. ... If the law were otherwise, a part-owner might be compelled to incur expense against his will: a house might be situate in a decaying borough, and it might be thought by one co-owner that it would be better not to repair it. The refusal of a tenant in common to bear any part of the cost of proper repair may be unreasonable: nevertheless, the law allows him to refuse and no action will lie against him.

Cotton, LJ.: ... I think that it must be assumed that the house was in a bad state of repair, and that the repairs executed by the defendant were necessary. As to the claim for improvements, it has been urged that no tenant in common is entitled to execute improvements upon the property held in common, and then to charge his co-tenant in common with the cost. This seems to me the true view, and I need not further discuss the question as to improvements. As to the question of repairs, it is to be observed that when two persons are under a common obligation, one of them can recover from the other the amount expended in discharge or fulfilment of the common obligation; but that is not the position of affairs here: one tenant in common cannot charge another with the cost of repairs without a request, and in the present case it is impossible even to imply a request. ... Therefore, no remedy exists for money expended in repairs by one tenant in common, so long as the property is enjoyed in common....

****

Question

What advice would you give to a co-owner who wishes to carry out repairs and development to the co-owned land?

****

Note

In *Leigh v Dickeson* [1881-85] All ER Rep 1099 at 1102-1103, Cotton LJ observed:

> It has been urged that one tenant in common cannot recover against another for rent, for either of them may enjoy the possession. But in the present case the defendant, although he himself was tenant in common, had possession of the whole of the house by virtue of a lease from his co-tenant in common. A correspondence ensued, as to the terms under which he should remain in occupation of the house. Under these circumstances, I think that the defendant must be considered as holding exclusive possession of the house upon the terms of the lease, and therefore, that he is liable for rent at the same rate as was reserved by the lease.

****

Power to deal with the land

A tenant in common has a distinct, though undivided, share in the land. A joint tenant on the other hand has no distinct share in the land; however, equity regards a joint tenant as having a distinct interest, which he or she may dispose of prior to his or her death.

****

A tenant in common has no right to lease the co-owned land without the authority of the other co-owners

Mutual Benefits Ltd v Patel and another
[1972] EA 496 (K)

[The respondents owned the subject land as tenants in common with J C Patel. Without knowledge of the other co-owners, J C Patel entered into a contract to lease the land to the appellant. The latter lodged a caveat against the land to protect the lease. The trial Judge ordered the caveat to be removed on the ground that J C Patel had no right to lease the land to the appellants without the consent of the other co-owners. Hence, this appeal.]

Apry AG P: ... Mr Gautama submitted that a tenant in common of land has authority to make agreements for leases binding on his co-owners. He could cite no authority for this submission and I have no hesitation in rejecting it. It is of the essence of tenancy in common that owners can deal with the title to their shares but that possession is common to them and cannot be granted by one alone. ... I would dismiss the appeal.
Mustafa JA.: I agree that the appeal be dismissed. ...The land on which the two godowns are built was held by the two respondents and two others who are dead as tenants in common in undivided equal shares. The said tenants in common were also partners in a business. Mr. Gautama for the appellant has submitted that J. C. Patel, who was a tenant in common, had express or ostensible authority to enter into agreements to lease the godowns which will be binding on the other tenants in common. No authority was cited for this proposition and in my view, it is palpably invalid . . .

LAW, Ag. VP, agreed.

****

Notes

1. Though the issue did not arise in this particular case, it is submitted that JC Patel had a right to lease (or even sell) his undivided share in the land to whomsoever he wished. In that event, for the duration of the lease the lessee would enjoy possession of any part of the land in common with the remaining co-owners. For example, in *Citanzariti v Whitehouse* (1981) 55 FLR 426, the wife left the matrimonial house, which she jointly owned with her husband. The husband leased the house to the plaintiff for a period of 12 months. Before the period expired, the wife came back to the house and interfered with the tenant's personal effects. The Federal Court of Australia held that whilst her entry onto the premises was not wrongful as against the tenant, she could not prevent the tenant from exercising the right of use and occupation. She was held liable for damages to the tenant's personal effects.
2. The statement by Spry Ag P in *Mutual Benefits Ltd,* that though a co-tenant can deal in his or her individual share he or she *cannot alone grant possession*, needs clarification. It is thought that His Honour did not intend to say that a co-owner could not alone lease his or her right to possession. Rather, he meant that a co-owner who leases his or her individual share cannot alone grant possession that is exclusive of the other co-owners who had not joined in the grant. See, for example, the Australian case referred to in note 1, above.
3. As to the ability of one co-owner to create a mortgage binding his or her own share, see *Thames Guaranty Ltd v Campbell* [1984] All E R 153. It has been held in a number of Australian cases that where a co-owner mortgages the land without consent of the other co-owners, the mortgage only binds the mortgagor's undivided share of the land, see eg *Fulton v 523 Nominees Pty Ltd* [1984] VR 200.

Questions

1. Suppose X and Y, brother and sister, own certain land in joint tenancy. X borrows money from Z. Without Y's knowledge or consent, X deposits the certificate of title with Z as security for the loan, thereby creating an equitable mortgage. Z lodges a caveat against the title to protect the mortgage. X dies before he pays off the mortgage debt. Z threatens to seek a judicial order for the land to be sold unless he is paid all the outstanding moneys. Advise Y.
2. What difference, if any, would it make in the above question if Y died before X?

****

The other co-owners may sue for trespass a person who enters into possession of the land with consent of only one of the co-owners

Katuku et al v Kalimbagiza
CS No 1823 of 1984 (unreported); [1987] HCB 75

[A and B were joint tenants of a leasehold. They invited the defendant to join them as a co-owner. They agreed that on payment of a specified amount the defendant's name would be added to the lease and registered. After paying the agreed sum, the defendant entered into possession and started using the land before his name was registered as co-owner. Meanwhile, A and B without the defendant's knowledge sold the land to the plaintiff. The plaintiff entered into possession and commenced proceedings for the eviction of the defendant. The defendant counterclaimed for damages for trespass and an order for the eviction of the plaintiff.][28]

Okello J: ...As the defendant was admitted as a joint tenant (*sic)*, his right of possession, interest, title and time over the land was the same as those of A and B. It followed that entry into the land which was in his possession by any other person without his consent amounted to trespass even if the other co-tenants permitted that entry. The defendant was entitled to damages and an eviction order.

****

Notes

1. It is suggested that the reason the plaintiff was liable for trespass was that he attempted to evict the defendant who, as a co-tenant, had a right to enjoy possession of the land. The plaintiff would not have been liable if he attempted to 'share' possession of the land with the defendant in the same way as A and B were entitled to do prior to selling their interest to him. In our view, the plaintiff purchased A and B's interest in the land and, therefore, had a right to possession previously enjoyed by them.
2. With respect, it is submitted that Okello J erred when he held that the plaintiff was 'admitted as a joint tenant' of A and B. The defendant could not be a joint tenant with A and B because there was no unity of title or time between him and the other two (see *Ag Securities v Vaughan and others* [1988] 3 All ER 1058). A and B continued to own a two-thirds share in the land in joint tenancy, whilst C held his one-third share in tenancy in common with them.

****

[28] The facts based on the edited facts of the case in the High Court Bulletins.

DETERMINATION OF JOINT TENANCY

Joint tenancy determines by operation of the doctrine of survivorship, when all but one of the joint tenants die. Apart from that, joint tenancy may be determined during the lifetime of the joint tenants by (a) partition and (b) by severance.

Partition

This is the physical division of the land amongst the co-owners. The process is completed by registration of the former co-owners as individual owners of their respective share. Partition may be voluntary or by court order.

Severance

Severance describes the process whereby joint tenancy is converted into tenancy in common. Sir William Page in his famous statement in *Williams v Hensman* (1861) 1 J & H 546; 70 ER 862, at 867, declared that there were three methods of severance of joint tenancy:

> In the first place, an act of any one of the persons interested operating upon his own share may create a severance as to that share. The right of each joint tenant is a right by survivorship only in the event of no severance having taken place of the share which is claimed under the *jus accrescendi*. Each one is at liberty to dispose of his own interest in such manner as to sever it from the joint fund – losing, of course, at the same time, his own right of survivorship. Secondly, a joint-tenancy may be severed by mutual agreement. And, in the third place, there may be a severance by any course of dealing sufficient to intimate that the interests of all were mutually treated as constituting a tenancy in common

The three methods are illustrated in the following cases.

****

Severance by unilateral action

Under the first rule in *Williams v Hensman*, *supra*, a joint tenant may unilaterally sever the joint tenancy by doing an act that operates upon his or her share. For example, he or she may sell or donate, inter vivos, his or her interest to a third party. The case which follows, *Corin v Patton*, deals with the issue of unilateral severance of joint tenancy of land registered under the Torrens System.

****

Joint tenancy of land registered under the RTA, is not severed unless the person wishing to sever has done everything that needs to be done to effect a transfer

Corin and another v Patton
(1990) 92 ALR 1(HIGH COURT OF AUSTRALIA)

> [The respondent, Mr Patton, and his late wife were registered the proprietors of certain land as joint tenants under the Real Property Act 1900 (NSW). Shortly before her death, Mrs Patton, without knowledge of her husband, sought to sever the joint tenancy with a view to benefit her children. To that end, she executed a form of transfer of her estate and interest as joint tenant in the said property to her brother, Corin, on trust to hold as tenant in common with her husband. She named herself as the beneficiary of the trust. Corin signed a deed of trust whereby he acknowledged that he held the interest as a trustee for Mrs Patton. The form of transfer and the deed of trust signed by Mrs Patton and Corin was handed over to their solicitor to do 'what was necessary' to complete the transaction. At the time, the certificate of title was kept by the Bank of NSW, which had an unregistered mortgageover the land. Mrs Patton took no action to procure the production of the certificate of title

to enable the transfer to be registered. By the time of Mrs Patton's death the transfer had not been registered and the certificate of title was still with the Bank. In her will, Mrs Patton purported to devise her interest in the land. The issue was whether the joint tenancy had been severed by Mrs Patton's unilateral action prior to her death. The lower courts held that it had not and, therefore Mr Patton was entitled to the whole property by virtue of survivorship. This is an appeal to the High Court of Australia.]

Mason CJ and McHugh J.: ... [I]t is necessary in this case for the appellants to demonstrate that Mrs Patton effectively alienated the property in equity. Although this may involve questions of whether or not Mrs Patton could have withdrawn from the transactions, the issue is primarily whether or not the property was alienated.

Mr Bennett [QC for the appellants] contended that the rules for determining whether there has been an effective transfer should be relaxed in a case, such as the present, where the purpose of asking the question is to determine whether or not a joint tenancy has been severed. But such an approach cannot be reconciled with principle and would be productive of great uncertainty. Once it is accepted that a transfer is required, it is the general rules relating to transfers of land which must be applied. This particular case involved a voluntary transaction. In this respect, we agree with Hope JA that the consent or agreement of Mr Corin to act as trustee did not constitute valuable consideration, and in any event it was not seriously suggested otherwise. Indeed, in the famous case of *Milroy v Lord* (1862) 4 De GF & J 264; 45 ER 1185, in very similar circumstances, the consent or agreement of the transferee to act as trustee was not regarded as constituting valuable consideration.

The long line of earlier authority concerning voluntary conveyances and transfers culminated in the judgements in *Milroy v Lord.* In that case ... Turner LJ stated, at 274-275 [1189-1190):

> I take the law of this court to be well settled, that, in order to render a voluntary settlement valid and effectual, the settler [*sic*] must have done everything which, according to the nature of the property comprised in the settlement, was necessary to be done in order to transfer the property and render the settlement binding upon him. He may of course do this by actually transferring the property to the persons for whom he intends to provide, and the provision will then be effectual, and it will be equally effectual if he transfers the property to a trustee for the purposes of the settlement, or declares that he himself holds it in trust for those purposes; ... but, in order to render the settlement binding, one or other of these modes must, as I understand the law of this court, be resorted to, for there is no equity in this court to perfect an imperfect gift. The cases I think go further to this extent, that if the settlement is intended to be effectuated by one of the modes to which I have referred, the court will not give effect by transfer, the court will not hold the intended transfer to operate as a declaration of trust, for then every imperfect instrument would be made effectual by being converted into a perfect trust.

Accordingly, the purported transfer could not be supported as a declaration of trust, and failed as a transfer because the powers of attorney did not suffice to permit Lord to execute a transfer in his favour without express directions from Milroy, which Milroy had not given.

Two propositions emerged from the observations of Turner LJ. First, the donor must have done everything necessary to be done, according to the nature of the property, in order to transfer the property and render the gift binding. Secondly, if the gift was intended to have been effectuated by one means, the court will not give effect to it by another means. However, as the later cases were to reveal, there was an element of uncertainty in the first proposition. Did it require that the donor must have done himself all that was necessary to be done in order to transfer the property or did he only have to do all that was necessary to be done by him in order to achieve that result?

[Their Honours reviewed several Australian cases and continued.] Accordingly, we conclude it is desirable to state that the principle is that, if an intending donor of property has done everything which it is necessary for him to have done to effect a transfer of legal title, then equity will recognise the gift. So long as the donee has been equipped to achieve the transfer of legal ownership, the gift is complete in equity. 'Necessary' used in this sense means necessary to effect a transfer. From the viewpoint of the intending donor, the question is whether what he has done is sufficient to enable the legal transfer to be effected without further action on his part....

The question is then whether Mrs Patton did all that it was necessary for her to do in order to effect a transfer. Two obstacles are suggested to completion of the gift. First, the certificate of title remained throughout with the mortgagee and Mrs Patton took no steps to arrange for its production for the purposes of registration. Secondly, it is not clear whether or not Mr Smallwood [the solicitor] held the executed transfer on Mrs Patton's instructions or those of Mr Corin.

Whether or not it is correct to say that the production of a certificate of title is 'necessary' to achieve registration on a transfer of Torrens System land, it is apparent that a gift of such land cannot be regarded as complete in equity while the donor retains possession or control of the certificate of title. ... That is because it can scarcely be said that the donor has done everything necessary to be done by him if he has retained the certificate of title, by virtue of the possession of which the gift might well be thwarted.

In the present case Mrs Patton gave no authority for the mortgagee bank to hand the certificate of title to Mr Corin for the purposes of registration. At least, if she authorised Mr Smallwood to obtain the certificate, there is no clear evidence to that effect. [Appeal dismissed.]

Brennan J.: ... In the present case, let it be assumed that Mrs Patton delivered to Mr Corin a registrable transfer with the intention of parting with it and the property in it so that Mr Corin might be registered as proprietor of an estate in fee simple as tenant in common with Mr Patton and let it be further assumed that Mr Corin was thereby enabled to require production of the relevant certificate of title to allow registration of the transfer: on those assumptions Mrs Patton had done all that was necessary on her part to make the transfer effective and the transfer was not revocable by her prior to registration. On those assumptions, the elements of an effective gift ... are fulfilled and Mr Corin would have acquired a right under, but subject to, the Real Property Act to have the transfer registered. Yet, at the time of Mrs Patton's death the transfer had not been registered and (in the absence of a certificate of title or a dispensation from production) was not then able to be registered. In those circumstances, it cannot be said that any title to the estate or interest in the land intended to be given by Mrs Patton had passed to Mr Corin. It follows that, prior to her death, Mrs Patton had not divested herself of her estate or interest in the land. She remained a joint tenant; she did not hold her estate or interest as trustee for any person. On her death, Mr Patton took by survivorship and his enlarged estate may be registered under [the Real Property Act].

Toohey J.: ... The real point is that the transfer to Mr Corin had not been registered at the time of Mrs Patton's death. There was no transaction that equity would enforce; there was a transaction that had not been consummated. There had been no divesting by Mrs Patton of her interest as joint tenant.

[Appeal dismissed.]

****

Questions

1. Is *Corin v Patton* a sound decision? Why did the Court refuse to give effect to Mrs Patton's plain intention to sever her joint tenancy? Are there any policy reasons for the decision?
2. Suppose Mrs Patton had handed Corin a signed memorandum of transfer and the certificate of title, would the joint tenancy have been severed in equity?
3. Would the joint tenancy have been severed if Mrs Patton had entered into a legally binding contract of sale of her interest to Corin, but she died before registration of the transfer?

****

Severance by mutual agreement

Severance by mutual agreement is where all the joint tenants agree to sever the joint tenancy. The case below considers what constitutes an effective agreement to sever the joint tenancy.

****

A joint tenancy may be severed by mutual agreement

Burgess v Rawnsley
[1975] 3 All ER 142

[Mrs Rawnsley, the defendant, and Mr Honick, deceased, together bought a flat each contributing half the purchase price. The flat was conveyed to them as joint tenants. The two lived independently in separate parts of the flat. There was evidence that prior to Honick's death, he entered into a verbal agreement with Mrs Rawnsley to buy out her interest, but subsequently she changed her mind. By the time Honick died, the sale had not taken place. The plaintiff, administrator of the deceased's estate, claimed that the tenancy was severed in equity by the oral agreement. The defendant denied the claim arguing that the flat was hers by right of survivorship. The trial judge held in favour of the plaintiff. The defendant appealed.]

Browne LJ: ... Counsel for Mrs Rawnsley conceded, as is clearly right, that if there had been an enforceable agreement by Mrs Rawnsley to sell her share to Mr Honick, that would produce a severance of the joint tenancy; but he says that an oral agreement, unenforceable because of s 40 of the Law of Property Act 1925, is not enough. Section 40 merely makes a contract for the disposition of an interest in land unenforceable by action in the absence of writing. It does not make it void. But here Mrs Burgess is not seeking to enforce by action the agreement by Mrs Rawnsley to sell her share to Mr Honick. She relies on it as effecting the severance in equity of the joint tenancy. An agreement to sever can be inferred from a course of dealing ... and there would in such a case ex hypothesi be no express agreement but only an inferred, tacit agreement, in respect of which there would seldom if ever be writing sufficient to satisfy s 40. It seems to me that the point is that the agreement establishes that the parties no longer intend the tenancy to operate as a joint tenancy and that automatically effects a severance. I think the reference in Megarry and Wade [*The Law of Real Property* 3rd ed., 1966, pp. 418, 419] to specifically enforceable contracts only applies where the suggestion is that the joint tenancy has been severed by an alienation by one joint tenant to a third party, and does not apply to severance by agreement between joint tenants.

The result is that I would uphold the county court judge's judgement on his second ground, namely, that the joint tenancy was severed by an agreement between Mrs Rawnsley and Mr Honick that she would sell her share to him for £750. In my view, her subsequent repudiation of that agreement makes no difference. I would dismiss the appeal on this ground.

Sir John Pennycuick: ... It is not in dispute that an agreement for severance between joint tenants effects a severance. This is the rule 2 propounded by Page Wood V-C in *Williams v Hensman* [(1861) 1 John & H 546 at 557; 70 ER 862 at 867]. The words he uses are contained in one sentence: 'Secondly, a joint tenancy may be severed by mutual agreement.' ... In the present case the judge found as a fact that Mr Honick and Mrs Rawnsley at the beginning of July 1968 agreed on the sale by her to him of her share at the price of £750 ... Once that finding of fact is accepted, the case falls squarely within rule 2 of Page Wood V-C. It is not contended that it is material that the parties by mutual consent did not proceed to carry out the agreement. Rule 2 applies equally, I think, whether the agreement between the two joint tenants is expressly to sever or is to deal with the property in a manner which involves severance. Counsel for Mrs Rawnsley contended that in order that rule 2 should apply, the agreement must be specifically enforceable. I do not see any sufficient reason for importing this qualification. The significance of an agreement is not that it binds the parties; but that it serves as an indication of a common intention to sever, something which it was indisputedly within their power to do. It will be observed that Page Wood V-C in his rule 2 makes no mention of specific enforceability ... I would dismiss the appeal.

(Lord Denning L.J, also dismissed the appeal on this ground. Alternatively he held that the appeal be dismissed on the basis of rule 3 'course of dealing'. See below.)

****

Note

In Uganda a contract for sale of land need not be in writing, see *Mayanja-Nkanji v National Insurance Corporation* [1972] 1 ULR 37.

******

Severance by course of dealing

Even in the absence of an actual agreement between the parties, a joint tenancy may be severed by any course of dealing sufficient to intimate that the interests of all were mutually treated as constituting a tenancy in common. What constitutes a 'sufficient' course of dealing? How does it differ from mutual agreement in rule 2 above? Can a course of dealing be inferred from the conduct of only one of the joint tenants? See the following excerpt from *Burgess v Rawnsley.*

****

Burgess v Rawnsley
[1975] 3 All ER 142

[The facts of this case have already been stated above.]

Lord Denning L.J: ... In ...[*Williams v Hensman*] Page Wood V-C distinguished severance 'by mutual agreement' and severance by a 'course of dealing'. That shows that a 'course of dealing' need not amount to an agreement, expressed or implied, for severance. It is sufficient if there is a course of dealing in which one party makes clear to the other that he desires that their shares should no longer be held jointly but be held in common. I emphasise that it must be made clear to the other party. That is implicit in the sentence in which Page Wood V-C says, 'it will not suffice to rely on an intention, with respect to the particular share, declared only behind the backs of the other persons interested.'

Similarly, it is sufficient if both parties enter on a course of dealing which evinces an intention by both of them that their shares shall henceforth be held in common and not jointly. ...

I come now to the question of notice. Suppose that one party gives a notice in writing to the other saying that he desires to sever the joint tenancy. Is that sufficient to effect a severance? I think it is. It was certainly the view of Sir Benjamin Cherry when he drafted s36(2) of the Law of Property Act 1925. It says in relation to real estates:

> where a legal estate (not being settled land) is vested in joint tenants beneficially, and any tenant desires to sever the joint tenancy in equity, he shall give to the other joint tenants *a notice in writing of such desire or do such other acts or things as would, in the case of personal estate, have been effectual* to sever the tenancy in equity, and thereupon under the trust for sale affecting the land the net proceeds of sale, and the net rents and profits until sale, shall be held upon the trusts which would have been requisite for giving effect to the beneficial interests if there had been an actual severance.

I have underlined italicised the important words. The word 'other' is most illuminating. It shows quite plainly that, in the case of personal estate, one of the things which is effective in equity to sever a joint tenancy is 'a notice in writing' of a desire to sever. So also in regard to real estate. ...

It remains to apply these principles to the present case. I think there was evidence that Mr Honick and Mrs Rawnsley did come to an agreement that he would buy her share for £750. That agreement was not in writing and it was not specifically enforceable. Yet it was sufficient to effect a severance. Even if there was not any firm agreement but only a course of dealing, it clearly evinced an intention by both parties that the property should henceforth be held in common and not jointly.

Sir John Pennycuick: ... Counsel for Mrs Burgess advanced an alternative argument to the effect that even if there were no agreement by Mr Honick to purchase Mrs Rawnsley's share, nevertheless the mere proposal by Mr Honick to purchase her share would operate as a severance under rule 3 in *Williams v Hensman*. ...

I do not doubt myself that where one tenant negotiates with another for some rearrangement of interest, it may be possible to infer from the particular facts a common intention to sever even though the negotiations break down. Whether such an inference can be drawn must I think depend on the particular facts. In the present case the negotiations between Mr Honick and Mrs Rawnsley, if they can be properly described as negotiations at all, fall, it seems to me, far short of warranting an inference. One could not ascribe to joint tenants an intention to sever merely because one offers to buy out the other for £X and the other makes counter-offer of £Y.

(*Browne LJ* felt it was unnecessary to express his views on the 'difficult' question of what the effect of negotiations not resulting in an agreement or of a mere declaration would have been. However, he agreed with both Lord Denning and Sir John Pennycuick, that the third rule of severance is separate from the second.)

****

Notes

Lord Denning's holding that a course of dealing sufficient to sever a joint tenancy can be inferred from the situation where one party informs the others that he or she desires severance has received severe criticism, especially in Australia. It has been argued that a course of dealing must be one in which all the joint tenants are engaged in such a way that it is possible to infer a mutual agreement to sever. Hence, a mere declaration (short of *actual* alienation of one's interest) by one joint tenant is not sufficient to constitute a course of dealing to effect severance. See Butt, *Land Law* ,2nd ed, Sydney, LBC, at 209 – 210. However, Megarry and Wade, *The Law of Real Property, supra,* at 432, argue that *Burgess* and other recent English decisions which have found course of dealing on the basis of conduct of only one of the joint tenants 'reflect a natural judicial distaste for the right of survivorship, which is generally unsuitable for beneficial interests and which ought to be confined to trustees and other non-beneficial owners. Consequently, the policy of the law is to facilitate severance'. We should reiterate that the English courts are probably influenced by s 36(2), *Law of Property Act 1925,* which expressly provides that a joint tenancy can unilaterally be severed in equity by a mere written notice to the other co-owners. In the absence of an equivalent provision under the Ugandan law, the courts might, rightly, decline to follow Lord Denning's precedent in *Burgess* on this point.

****

Determination of tenancy in common

Tenancy in common is determined by partition or by physical division of the land amongst the co-owners in accordance with their shares. Partition may be by mutual agreement of the co-owners or by court order under its inherent powers. The process is completed by registration of the former co-owners of their individual shares.

****

13

Easements and Restrictive Covenants

Easements

An easement is a right which attaches to a particular piece of land and which allows the owner of that land to use the land of another person in a particular way or restrict its use by that other person to a certain extent. A common example of an easement is a right of a landowner to walk or drive over his or her neighbour's land.

Essential features

There are four essential features of an easement:

1. there must be a dominant and a servient tenement;
2. an easement must accommodate the dominant tenement;
3. dominant and servient owners must be different persons; and
4. a right over land cannot amount to an easement unless it is capable of forming the subject-matter of a grant.

These characteristics of easements are discussed in the following famous English case.

Re: Ellenborough Park
[1955] 3 All ER 667

[Developers subdivided a large block of land into small plots, which they sold to various persons. They left out an inner portion of the block, known as Ellenborough Park, to be maintained as a pleasure ground for the enjoyment at all times by the owners of the surrounding plots in common with each other, subject to contribution of a proportionate amount to the cost of the upkeep of the park. During the Second World War the Government compulsorily occupied the park. Owners of the plots (ownership of the plots had changed hands many times so that none of the current owners was an original purchaser) claimed a share of the compensation paid by the Government, on the basis that they had an easement over the park. The trial Judge found in their favour. Appeal to the Court of Appeal.]

Evershed MR: (Read the judgement of the Court): ... The substantial question raised in this appeal is whether the respondent ... being the owners of certain houses fronting on, or, in some few cases, adjacent to, the garden or park known as Ellenborough Park. ... have any right known to the law, and now enforceable by them against the owners of the park, to the use and enjoyment of the park. ...

The substantial question in the case ... is one of considerable interest and importance ... [I]f the owners of the houses are now entitled to an enforceable right in respect of the use and enjoyment of Ellenborough Park, that right must have the character and quality of an easement as understood by, and known to, our law. It has, therefore, been necessary for us to consider carefully the qualities and characteristics of easements ...

For the purposes of the argument before us counsel were content to adopt, as correct, the four characteristics formulated in Dr Cheshire's *Modern Real Property* (7th End.), p.456 et seq. They are (i) there must be a dominant and a servient tenement; (ii) an easement must accommodate the dominant tenement; (iii) dominant and servient owners must be different persons; and (iv) a right over land cannot amount to an easement unless it is capable of forming the subject-matter of a grant.

The four characteristics stated by Dr Cheshire correspond with the qualities discussed by Gale in his second chapter, sections 2, 5, 3, and 6 and 8 respectively. Two of the four may be disregarded for present purposes, viz, the first and the third. If the garden or park is, as it is alleged to be, the servient tenement in the present case, then it is undoubtedly distinct from the alleged dominant tenements, viz, the freeholds of the several houses whose owners claim to exercise the rights. It is equally clear that if these lands respectively constitute the servient and dominant tenements, then they are owned by different persons. The argument in the case is found accordingly to turn on the meaning and application to the circumstances of the present case of the second and fourth conditions, i.e., first, whether the alleged easement can be said in truth to 'accommodate' the dominant tenement, in other words, whether there exists the required 'connection' between the one and the other; and, second, whether the right alleged is 'capable of forming the subject-matter of a grant'. The exact significance of this fourth and last condition is, at first sight perhaps, not entirely clear. As between the original parties to the 'grant' it is not in doubt that rights of this kind would be capable of taking effect by way of contract or licence. But for the purposes of the present case, as the arguments made clear, the cognate questions involved under this condition are: whether the rights purported to be given are expressed in terms of too wide and vague a character; whether, if and so far as effective, such rights would amount to rights of joint occupation or would substantially deprive the owners of the park of proprietorship or legal possession; whether, if and so far as effective, such rights constitute mere rights of recreation, possessing no quality of utility or benefit; and on such grounds cannot qualify as easements. [His Honour stated the terms of the conveyance and continued:]

... [I]t is clear from the deed from which we have quoted, and from the other deeds in like form made (as must be assumed) in respect of the remaining premises in Ellenborough Crescent, that the original common vendors were engaged on a scheme of development of this part of the White Cross Estate designed to produce a result of common experience; namely, a row of uniform houses facing inwards on a park or garden which was intended to form, and formed in fact, an essential characteristic belonging, and properly speaking 'appurtenant', to all and each of them. In substance, instead of each house being confined to its own small or moderate garden, each was to enjoy in common, but in common exclusively with the other houses in the crescent, a single large 'private' garden. In our judgement, the substance of the matter is not in this respect affected by the fact that some few houses in the immediate proximity of, but not actually fronting on, the park were also entitled to share the privilege. This extension of the privilege may no doubt be unusual and (at first sight at any rate) out of line with the conception of the square and its surrounding houses as a symmetrical unit. It has, therefore, a bearing on the question of the 'connection' between the right enjoyed and the premises of the relevant house owners; and must be discussed under the head of Dr Cheshire's first condition. In our judgement, the language of the deed of 1864 is clear to the effect that the right of enjoyment of the garden was intended to be annexed to the premises sold, rather than given as a privilege personal to their purchaser. The enjoyment was not exclusive to those premises alone; it was to be held in common with the like rights annexed to the other houses in (and in some few cases in close proximity to) the square or crescent. But it was not contemplated that like rights should be otherwise extended so as to belong in any sense to premises not forming part of (or at least closely connected with) the square or their owners. The position of the grant in the deed and its language show that, in the respects we have mentioned, the right granted was intended and treated as in pari materia with the rights of way and drainage similarly conferred. The relevant part of the deed opens with the general formula 'Together with all ways ... easements rights and appurtenances to the said plot of land ... appertaining'. The rights of way (admittedly easements properly so called) follow immediately the general formula, being linked to it by the words 'and particularly'. The next two words are 'And also', which, in turn, introduce the garden rights now in question in language which repeats the phrase used in relation to the rights of way – 'in common with the other persons to whom such easements may be granted'. In our judgement, if the construction of this part of the deed does not tend to the conclusion that the garden rights, like the rights of way, were particular examples of the general grant of easements and rights appurtenant to the plot conveyed, it is at least made clear that the garden rights were (so far of course as they properly could be) of the same character quoad the land conveyed as the rights of way and drainage. It was conceded that the rights, if effectual and enforceable, were conditional, that is, on the house owners making their appropriate contributions to the cost of upkeep. In this respect, again, they were analogous, by the terms of the deed, to the rights of way over Crescent and Walliscote Roads. As a complement to the rights of enjoyment of the garden, subject to the condition of contribution, was the covenant by the vendors against building on the park and to the effect that the park should at all times remain as an ornamental garden. Counsel for the owners of the park did not seriously challenge the contentions of counsel for the owners of the houses that in their context the words of the covenant to which we have last referred could fairly be construed as implying a negative covenant on the vendors' part against any user by them of the park otherwise than as a garden. There is clear authority that, if such be the substantial effect of the covenant, its benefit and burden will run with the land. The last consideration appreciably reinforces the view which we take of the meaning and intention of the deed to attach the garden rights in all respects like the rights of way and drainage to the land conveyed.

It remains to interpret the actual terms of the grant itself – 'the full enjoyment of the pleasure ground set out and made...' Counsel for the owners of the park fastened on the presence of the word 'full', and the absence of any indication of the way in which the pleasure ground was to be used – or of any limitations on its use – and contended that the right or privilege given was a jus spatiandi in its strict sense, that is, a right to go or wander on the park and every part of it and enjoy its amenities (and even its produce) without stint. We do not so construe the words in their context. Although we are now anticipating to some extent the question which arises under the fourth of Dr Cheshire's conditions, it seems to us, as a matter of construction, that the use contemplated and granted was the use of the park as a garden, the proprietorship of which (and of the produce of which) remained vested in the vendors and their successors. The enjoyment contemplated was the enjoyment of the vendors' ornamental garden in its physical state as such – the right, that is to say, of walking on or over those parts provided for such purpose, that is, pathways and (subject to restrictions in the ordinary course in the interest of the grass) the lawns; to rest in or on the seats or other places provided; and, if certain parts were set apart for particular recreations such as tennis or bowls, to use those parts for those purposes, subject again, in the ordinary course to the provisions made for their regulation; but not to trample at will all over the park, to cut or pluck the flowers or shrubs, or to interfere in the laying out or upkeep of the park. Such use or enjoyment is, we think, a common and clearly understood conception, analogous to the use and enjoyment conferred on members of the public, when they are open to the public, of parks or gardens. ...

We pass accordingly to a consideration of the first of Dr Cheshire's conditions – that of the accommodation of the alleged dominant tenements by the rights as we have interpreted them. For it was one of the main submissions by counsel for the owners of the park that the right of full enjoyment of the park granted to the purchaser by the conveyance of Dec 23, 1864, was insufficiently connected with the enjoyment of the property conveyed in that it did not subserve some use which was to be made of that property; and that such a right accordingly could not exist in law as an easement. In this part of his argument, counsel was invoking a principle which is, in our judgement, of unchallengeable authority, expounded, in somewhat varying language, in many judicial utterances. We think it unnecessary to review the authorities in which the principle has been applied; for the effect of the decisions is stated with accuracy in Dr Cheshire's book at p.457. After pointing out that 'one of the fundamental principles concerning easements is that they must be not only appurtenant to a dominant tenement, but also connected with the normal enjoyment of the dominant tenement', and referring to certain citations in support of that proposition the learned author proceeded:

> We may expand the statement of the principle thus: a right enjoyed by one over the land of another does not possess the status of an easement unless it accommodates and serves the dominant tenement, and is reasonably necessary for the better enjoyment of that tenement, for if it has no necessary connection therewith, although it confers an advantage upon the owner and renders his ownership of the land more valuable, it is not an easement at all, but a mere contractual right personal to and only enforceable between the two contracting parties.

Can it be said, then, of the right of full enjoyment of the park in question which was granted by the conveyance of Dec 23, 1864, and which, for reasons already given was, in our view, intended to be annexed to the property conveyed to ... [the respondent], that it accommodated and served that property? It is clear that the right did, in some degree, enhance the value of the property and this consideration cannot be dismissed as wholly irrelevant. It is, of course, a point to be noted; but we agree with the submission of counsel for the owners of the park that it is in no way decisive of the problem; it is not sufficient to show that the right increased the value of the property conveyed unless it is also shown that it was connected with the normal enjoyment of that property. It appears to us that the question whether or not this connection exists, is primarily one of fact, and depends largely on the nature of the alleged dominant tenement and the nature of the right granted. As to the former, it was in the contemplation of the parties to the conveyance of 1864 that the property conveyed should be used for residential and not commercial purposes. That appears from the conveyance itself, and the covenant by the purchaser already quoted, that the dwelling-house, etc, which he bound himself to build should not 'be occupied or used as an open or exposed shop or for any purpose of trade or commerce other than a lodging house or private school or seminary' without the vendor's written consent.

Since it is stated in para 4 of Mr Rendell's affidavit in support of the summons and has been conceded that all the conveyances of plots for building purposes fronting or near Ellenborough Park were as regards (inter alia) user substantially the same as the conveyance of 1864, the inevitable inference is that the houses which were to be built on the plots were to constitute a residential estate. As appears from the map which is exhibit 'G' to Mr Rendell's further affidavit of Oct 13, 1955, the houses which were built on the plot around and near to Ellenborough Park varied in size, some being large detached houses and others smaller and either semi-detached or in a row. We have already stated that the purchasers of all the plots which actually abutted on the park were granted the right to enjoy the use of it as were also the purchasers of some of the plots which, although not fronting on the park, were only a short distance away from it. As to the nature of the right granted, the conveyance of 1864 shows that the park was to be kept and maintained as a pleasure ground or ornamental garden, and that it was contemplated that it should at all times be kept in good order and condition and well stocked with plant and shrubs; and the vendors covenanted that they would not at any time thereafter erect or permit to be erected any dwelling-house or other building (except a grotto, bower, summer-house, flower-stand, fountain, music-stand or other ornamental erection) within or on any part of the pleasure ground. On these facts counsel for the owners of the park submitted that the requisite connection between the right to use the park and the normal enjoyment of the houses which were built around it or near it had not been established. He likened the position to a right granted to the purchaser of a house to use the zoological gardens free of charge or to attend Lord's cricket ground without payment. Such a right would undoubtedly, he said, increase the value of the property conveyed, but could not run with it at law as an easement, because there was no sufficient nexus between the enjoyment of the right and the use of the house.

It is probably true, we think, that in neither of counsel's illustrations would the supposed right constitute an easement, for it would be wholly extraneous to, and independent of, the use of a house as a house, i.e., as a place in which the householder and his family live and make their home; and it is for this reason that the analogy which counsel sought to establish between his illustrations and the present case cannot, in our opinion, be supported. A much closer analogy, as it seems to us, is the case of a man selling the freehold of part of his house and granting to the purchaser, his heirs and assigns, the right appurtenant to such part, to use the garden in common with the vendor and his assigns. In such a case the test of connection, or accommodation, would be amply satisfied; for just as the use of a garden undoubtedly enhances, and is connected with, the normal enjoyment of the house to which it belongs, so also would the right granted, in the case supposed, be closely connected with the use and enjoyment of the part of the premises sold. Such, we think, is in substance the position in the present case. The park became a communal garden for the benefit and enjoyment of those whose houses adjoined it or were in its close proximity. Its flower beds, lawns and walks were calculated to afford all the amenities which it is the purpose of the garden of a house to provide; and apart from the fact that these amenities extended to a number of householders instead of being confined to one (which on this aspect of the case is immaterial) we can see no difference in principle between Ellenborough Park and a garden in the ordinary signification of that word. It is the collective garden of the neighbouring houses to whose use it was dedicated by the owners of the estate and as such amply satisfied, in our judgement, the requirement of connection with the dominant tenements to which it is appurtenant. The result is not affected by the circumstance that the right to the park is in this case enjoyed by some few houses which are not immediately fronting on the park. The test for present purposes, no doubt, is that the park should constitute in a real and intelligible sense the garden (albeit the communal garden) of the houses to which the enjoyment is annexed. But we think that the test is satisfied as regards these few neighbouring, though not adjacent, houses. We think that the extension of the right of enjoyment to these few houses does not negative the presence of the necessary 'nexus' between the subject-matter enjoyed and the premises to which the enjoyment is expressed to belong.

Counsel for the owners of the park referred us to, and to some extent relied on, *Hill v Tupper* (10) (1863) (2 H&C 121), but in our opinion there is nothing in that case contrary to the view which we have expressed. In that case the owner of land adjoining a canal was granted the exclusive right to let boats out for hire on the canal. He did so and then sought to restrain a similar activity by a neighbouring landowner. He sought to establish that his grant constituted an easement but failed. As Pollock, CB, said in his judgement (2 H&C at p.126):

> ... it is not competent to create rights unconnected with the use and enjoyment of land, and annex them to it so as to constitute a property in the grantee.

It is clear that what the plaintiff was trying to do was to set up, under the guise of an easement, a monopoly which had no normal connection with the ordinary use of his land, but which was merely an independent business enterprise. So far from the right claimed sub-serving or accommodating the land, the land was but a convenient incident to the exercise of the right. For the reasons which we have stated we are unable to accept the contention that the right to the full enjoyment of Ellenborough Park fails in limine to qualify as a legal easement for want of the necessary connection between its enjoyment and the use of the properties comprised in the conveyance of 1864 and in the other relevant conveyances.

We turn next to Dr Cheshire's fourth condition for an easement – that the right must be capable of forming the subject-matter of a grant. As we have earlier stated, satisfaction of the condition in the present case depends on a consideration of the questions, whether the right conferred is too wide and vague, whether it is inconsistent with the proprietorship or possession of the alleged servient owners, and whether it is a mere right of recreation without utility or benefit.

To the first of these questions the interpretation which we have given to the typical deed provides, in our judgement, the answer; for we have construed the right conferred as being both well defined and commonly understood. In these essential respects the right may be said to be distinct from the indefinite and unregulated privilege which, we think, would ordinarily be understood by the Latin term '*jus spatiandi*, a privilege of wandering at will over all and every part of another's field or park, and which, though easily intelligible as the subject-matter of a personal licence, is something substantially different from the grant in question, viz, the provision for a limited number of houses in a uniform crescent of one single large but private garden. Our interpretation of the deed also provides, we think, the answer to the second question; for the right conferred no more amounts to a joint occupation of the park with its owners, no more excludes the proprietorship or possession of the latter, than a right of way granted through a passage or than the use by the public of the gardens of Lincoln's Inn Fields (to take one of our former examples) amount to joint occupation of that garden with the London County Council, or involve an inconsistency with the possession or proprietorship of the council as lessees. ....

The third of the questions embraced in Dr Cheshire's fourth condition rests primarily on a proposition stated in Theobald's *The Law of Land* (1929), at p.263, where it is said that an easement 'must be a right of utility and benefit and not one of mere recreation and amusement'. It does not appear that a proposition in similar terms is stated by Gale... In any case if the proposition be well-founded, we do not think that the right to use a garden of the character with which we are concerned in this case can be called one of mere recreation and amusement. ... No doubt a garden is a pleasure, and on high authority it is the purest of pleasures; but, in our judgement, it is not a right having no quality either of utility or benefit as those words should be understood. The right here in suit is, for reasons already given, one appurtenant to the surrounding houses as such, and constitutes a beneficial attribute of residence in a house as ordinarily understood. Its use for the purposes, not only of exercise and rest but also for such normal domestic purposes as were suggested in argument – for example, for taking out small children in perambulators or otherwise – is not fairly to be described as one of mere recreation or amusement, and is clearly beneficial to the premises to which it is attached ...

For the reasons which we have stated, Danckwerts, J, came in our judgement, to a right conclusion in this case and accordingly the appeal must be dismissed.

****

Distinction between an easement and a public right of way

Makumbi (Mrs E) and another v Puran Singh Ghana and another
[1962] EA 331 (U)

[The plaintiffs sought an injunction to restrain the defendants from obstructing a road access to their houses, which traversed the defendants' plot. The land over which the road ran was mailo land owned by the second defendant and leased to the first defendant. The defendants admitted that prior to 1958 the plaintiffs had used the subject track to obtain access to their plots, which had no road frontage. In 1958, the defendants erected a wire fence round their land, thereby obstructing the track and rendering it impossible for the plaintiffs' use. In their original plaint, the plaintiffs claimed an easement of way for foot-passengers and vehicles over the defendants' land to their respective plots. With leave of Court the plaintiffs amended the plaint to enable them to allege a public right of way over the defendants' land. The defendants denied that the track was a public footpath.]

Bennett J: In this suit the two plaintiffs seek an injunction to restrain the first defendant from obstructing a road. They also claim damages from the first defendant. . . . . In their original plaint the plaintiffs claimed, as an easement, a right of way for foot-passengers and vehicles over the first defendant's plot to their respective plots. ... The reference to 'easement' is unfortunate since an easement enjoyed by the public at large is unknown to the law. In *Rangeley v Midland Railway Co. (1) (1867), L.R. 3 Ch. App. 306 at p.311,* LORD CAIRNS, L.J., said:

> There can be no such thing according to our law, or according to the civil law, as what I may term an easement in gross. An easement must be connected with a dominant tenement. In truth, a public road or highway is not an easement; it is a dedication to the public of the occupation of the surface of the land for the purpose of passing and re-passing. ...

However effective may be the plaintiff's pleading, I am satisfied that the defendants have not been misled since the hearing was adjourned by consent on February 1962, for the express purpose of enabling the plaintiffs to plead that there was a public right of way over the track.

The evidence called on behalf of the plaintiffs tends to establish that there had been a track leading from the Kabaka's palace to what is now the road to the social centre, from the early years of the present century. The plaintiffs claim that this track was not merely a footway but that it was also a carriage-way and that it was used by the public at large.

There is no evidence that the track was ever maintained as a road either by the Public Works Department or by the Buganda Government, or that it had been declared a road reserve, so that the Roads Ordinance, Cap. 165, would not have applied to it. The Roads Ordinance, consisting as it does of seven sections and concerned, as it is, with a very limited aspect of highway law, is not, in my opinion, exhaustive of the law of highways in Uganda. Recourse must be had to s.15 of the Uganda Order-in-Council, 1902, and to the common law of England so far as circumstances admit. In *Attorney-General v. Mambule (2), [1959] E.A. 665 (C.A.),* SIR KENNETH O'CONNOR, P., expressed the opinion that there are obvious difficulties in the way of importing the doctrine of the common law making highways repairable by the inhabitants of the parish, but I can find nothing in the judgement to support the view that the common law relating to highways is generally inapplicable in Uganda.

According to English law a highway can only be created by statute, or by dedication to the public and acceptance: See 19 HALSBURY'S LAWS OF ENGLAND (3rd Ed.), para. 60. In the instant case there is no evidence of any express dedication of the land for use as a carriage-way or footpath either by the existing owners or by their predecessors in title. The question of substance to be determined in this suit is whether there is sufficient evidence from which a dedication by the predecessors in title of the present owners can be inferred.

The evidence upon which the plaintiffs rely is evidence of long user of the track by members of the public. To quote from PRATT AND MACKENZIE ON LAW OF HIGHWAYS (19th Edn.), 28:

> The use and enjoyment from which it (dedication) can be inferred must be use and enjoyment as of right known to the owner and acquiesced in by him . . .User by the public over land belonging to a non-resident owner is less cogent evidence of dedication than where the user is necessarily brought to his personal knowledge . . . The length of time during which the user must exist in order to raise the presumption varies with circumstances. In a case mentioned by LORD KENYON, C.J., a period of six years was held sufficient. Where a new street, which was neither paved nor lighted, had been used as a public road for four or five years, the court thought the jury were warranted in presuming that it was used with the full assent of the owners of the soil . . .
>
> The presumption arising from long uninterrupted user of a way by the public is so strong as to dispense with all inquiry into the actual intention of the owner of the soil, and it is not even material to inquire who the owner of the soil was.

The plaintiffs' witnesses, to whose evidence I have alluded, impressed me as being disinterested and worthy of credit, I am satisfied that there was a track leading from the palace to what is now the Old Budonian's Club, and that it crossed the land now let to the first defendant. There is, however, no sufficient evidence that it was ever used extensively by rickshaws or motor vehicles. No plans or survey maps have been produced on which the track is shown either as a road or as a footpath. It is not marked on the plan, exhibit A. It was a mere grass or earth track and had never been made up so that it cannot have been suitable for use by motor vehicles. It was so inconspicuous that the second defendant failed to notice it when he inspected his land at the time of purchasing it in 1946. In my judgement, the occasional user of the track by rickshaws and motor vehicles is insufficient evidence from which to infer a dedication of the track as a carriage-way. On a balance of probabilities, I am satisfied that successive owners of the soil had acquiesced in its use as a footpath by members of the public. The extent of the public right, as regards the mode of using the way, is a question of fact: See PRATT AND MACKENZIE AND LAW OF HIGHWAYS (19th Edn.), p.35. The plaintiffs have succeeded in establishing that the track is a public footpath, but not that it is a public carriage-way.

On behalf of the defendants, it has been contended that the obstruction of a public way amounts to a public nuisance, and that the Attorney-General should have been made a party to the proceedings having regard to sub-s (1) of s.63 of the Civil Procedure Ordinance. Sub-section (1) must be read with sub-s. (2) and my interpretation of s.63 is that it is an enabling section and that the right of individuals who are injuriously affected by a public nuisance to claim damages or other relief is unaffected.

The fact that the plaintiffs have only succeeded in establishing that the track is a public footpath must materially affect the damages to which they are entitled, since it is plain from their evidence that any pecuniary loss which they may have sustained stemmed from deprivation of the use of the track as a carriage-way. They are, however, entitled to damages for the inconvenience, which they have suffered.

****

Question

Why were the defendants not protected by the principle of indefeasibility? See s 61, *Registration of Titles Act* (discussed in materials in Chapter nine).

****

Creation of easements

At common law, an easement may be created in various ways: express grant or reservation, implied grant or reservation and by prescription.

Express grant or reservation

An easement is created by express grant where a landowner formally grants an easement to another landowner, whilst express reservation is where a landowner disposes of part of his or her land and reserves an easement over the land sold in favour of the land he or she retains.

Implied grant or reservation

Where a landowner grants part of his or her land, an easement may be implied in favour of the grantee exercisable over the land retained ('implied grant') or in favour of the grantor over the land conveyed ('implied reservation'). Courts readily imply an easement in favour of the grantee but are reluctant to imply reservation of an easement except in case of intended easement and easement of necessity. The cases below illustrate the application of the relevant principles.

****

Easements implied under the rule of Wheeldon v Burrows

Easements are created by implication in favour of a grantee of land in respect of certain benefits previously enjoyed by that land. Such easements are known as quasi-easements or easements implied under the rule of *Wheeldon v Burrows.*

Wheeldon v Burrows
[1874-80] All ER 669

[T was the owner of certain land which included a plot of vacant land and an adjoining plot on part of which was erected a workshop whose windows overlooked the vacant land. In January 1876, T sold the vacant plot to the plaintiff. The conveyance contained no reservation in express terms of any right to the grantor in respect of the land he retained. A month later, T sold the rest of the land to the defendant. Following a dispute between the plaintiff and the defendant, the plaintiff erected hoardings near the edge of her land facing the windows of the defendant's workshop, thereby obstructing the light entering through the workshop windows. The defendant knocked down the hoardings asserting a right to an easement of light in respect of the windows. The plaintiff brought an action in trespass.]

Thesiger LJ: ... This action arises from a claim on the part of the defendant to have as of right the light enter into those windows, or, to put it in another way, to prevent the plaintiff from obstructing these windows by building on her land. Upon the matter coming before the Vice-Chancellor, he held that no right in respect of the windows was reserved, either impliedly or expressly, under the conveyance of January, 1876; and consequently that the defendant, as privy in estate with the grantor of the land which was the subject of the conveyance, was entitled to no right of light through those windows. In other words, he decided that the plaintiff was entitled to build upon her land, although the result of that building might be to obstruct these lights.

I am of opinion, both upon principle and upon authority that the Vice-Chancellor decided rightly. We have had a considerable number of cases cited to us, and out of them I think that two propositions may be stated as what I may call the general rules governing cases of this kind. The first of these rules is that on the grant by the owner of a tenement of part of that tenement as it is then used and enjoyed, there will pass to the grantee all those continuous and apparent easements and quasi easements which are necessary to the reasonable enjoyment of the property granted, and have been and are at the time of the grant used by the owner of the entirety for the benefit of the part granted. The second proposition is that, if the grantor intends to reserve any right over the tenement granted, it is his duty to reserve it expressly in the grant. Those are the general rules governing cases of this kind, but the second of those rules is subject to certain exceptions. One of those exceptions is the well-known exception which attaches to cases of what are called ways of necessity; and I do not dispute for a moment that there may be, and probably are, certain other exceptions. ...

Both of the general rules which I have mentioned are founded upon a maxim which is as well established by authority as it is consonant to reason and common sense – namely, that a grantor shall not derogate from his grant. It has been argued before us that there is no distinction between what has been called an implied grant and what is attempted to be established under the name of an implied reservation; and that such a distinction between the implied grant and the implied reservation is a mere modern invention and one which runs contrary, not only to the general practice upon which land has been bought and sold for a considerable time, but also to authorities which are said to be clear and distinct upon the matter. So far, however, from that distinction being one which was laid down for the first time by, and which is to be attributed to, Lord Westbury in *Suffield v Brown* [(1874) 4 De GJ & SM 185], it appears to me that it has existed almost as far back as we can trace the law upon the subject. [His Lordship discussed several authorities and continued.]

These cases in no way support the proposition for which the defendant in this case contends; but, on the contrary, support the proposition that in the case of a grant you may imply a grant of such continuous and apparent easements or such easements as are necessary to the reasonable enjoyment of the property conveyed, and have in fact been enjoyed during the unity of ownership, but that, with the exception to which I have referred of easements of necessity, you cannot imply a similar reservation in favour of the grantor of land...

For these reasons, therefore, the appeal must be dismissed.

******

Questions

1. Why are the courts disinclined to imply reservation of an easement in favour of the grantor?
2. Why are the courts more inclined to find an easement by implied grant?
3. Do you understand Thesiger L.J., to be saying that 'continuous and apparent' on one hand, and 'reasonably necessary to the enjoyment of land' on the other, are distinct or are alternative requirements for implying that a quasi-easement was intended to pass with the land conveyed? (See Meggary and Wade, *The Law of Real Property, supra*, at 862-863).

******

Intended easements
Easements required to carry out the common intention of both parties will be implied even though not expressly granted.

Wong v Beaumont Property Trust Ltd
[1965] 1 QB 173

[The defendant's predecessor in title leased the basement of a building to the plaintiff's predecessor in title for purposes of carrying on a business of a restaurant, the lessee covenanting, inter alia, to keep the premises open as a popular restaurant, to control and eliminate all smells and odours caused by such a use of the premises and to comply with the health regulations. At the time the lease was entered into, the covenants as to ventilation could not be complied with unless a ventilation system was installed on the premises with a duct fixed to the outside back of part of the landlord's building not leased to the tenant. The plaintiff, current tenant, in order to comply with the health ventilation regulations sought to construct a ventilation system with an external duct installed on the landlord's building. But the defendant, current landlord, refused to give permission for the erection of a duct on the back of its building. The plaintiff claimed that he was entitled to put up a duct outside the building without the landlord's consent. The trial judge granted the declaration. The defendant appealed.]

Lord Denning MR: ... The question is: Has the plaintiff a right to put up this duct without the landlord's consent? If he is to have any right at all, it must be by way of easement and not merely by way of implied contract. He is not the original lessee, nor are the defendants the original lessors. Each is a successor in title. As between them, a right of this kind, if it exists at all, must be by way of an easement. In particular, an easement of necessity. The law on the matter was stated by Lord Parker of Waddington in *Pullback Colliery Co Ltd v Woodman* [1915] AC 634, where he said, [at 646] omitting immaterial words, 'The law will readily imply the grant or reservation of such easements as may be necessary to give effect to the common intention of the parties to a grant of real property, with reference to the manner or purposes in and for which the land granted ... is to be used. But it is essential for this purpose that the parties should intend that the subject of the grant ... should be used in some definite and particular manner. It is not enough that the subject of the grant ... should be intended to be used in a manner which may or may not involve this definite and particular use'. That is the principle which underlies all easements of necessity. It you go back to Rolle's Abridgment you will find it stated in this way: 'If I have a field inclosed by my own land on all sides, and I alien this close to another, he shall have a way to this close over my land, as incident to the grant; for otherwise he cannot have any benefit by the grant'.

I would apply those principles here. Here was the grant of a lease to the lessee for the very purpose of carrying on a restaurant business. It was to be a popular restaurant, and it was to be developed and extended. There was a covenant not to cause any nuisance; and to control and eliminate all smells; and to comply with the Food Hygiene Regulations. That was 'a definite and particular manner' in which the business had to be conducted. It could not be carried on in that manner at all unless a ventilation system was installed by a duct of this kind. In these circumstances it seems to me that, if the business is to be carried on at all ... if the lessee is to 'have any benefit by the grant' at all – he must of necessity be able to put a ventilation duct up the wall. It may be that in Blackaby's [the plaintiff's predecessor in title] time it would not have needed such a large duct as is now needed in the plaintiff's time. But nevertheless a duct of some kind would have had to be put up the wall. The plaintiff may need a bigger one. But that does not matter. A man who has a right to an easement can use it in any proper way so long as he does not substantially increase the burden on the servient tenement. In this case a bigger duct will not substantially increase the burden.

There is one point in which this case goes further than the earlier cases which have been cited. It is this. It was not realised by the parties, at the time of the lease, that this duct would be necessary. But it was in fact necessary from the very beginning. That seems to me sufficient to bring the principle into play. In order to use this place as a restaurant, there must be implied an easement, by the necessity of the case, to carry a duct up this wall. The county court judge so held. He granted a declaration. I agree with him...

******

Easement of necessity

An easement of way of necessity arises by operation of the law, and it binds subsequent purchasers of the servient land whether or not the easement is recorded on the certificate of title of the servient or dominant land.

Barclays Bank D.C.O. v Patel
[1970] EA 88

[In 1941, Tebbutt, proprietor of certain land in Nairobi, subdivided the land into three plots: A, B, and C. The plots were registered under the Kenya *Registration of Titles Act* (cap 281). Plot A fronted on Langata Road, a public road, but there was no means of access to plots B and C except via surrounding land with permission of the respective owners. In 1944, Tebbutt sold plots B and C to Moore. Neither the transfer nor the certificate of title issued to Moore mentioned any right of way to the two plots from Langata Road over Plot A, which Tebbutt retained. Tebbutt sold Plot A to Henning who later sold the plot to the appellant bank. Once again, there was no reference to a right of way. Indeed, the certificate of title specifically declared that Plot A was not subject to any encumbrances. Ultimately, Patel, the respondent, purchased plots B and C. Several years later the respondent brought proceedings against the appellant claiming a right of way of necessity over Plot A. The trial Judge held that the respondent was entitled to a right of way of necessity over Plot A even though the easement was not registered.]

Sir Charles NewBold P: ... From this decision, the bank has appealed and counsel for the appellant has urged the following points. First, that if the trial Judge was right in holding that the way of necessity exists then he should have limited its use to agricultural and residential purposes. Secondly, that the trial Judge was wrong in awarding damages against the bank in respect of any acts of obstruction committed by Mr Matthews. Thirdly, that Mr Patel was not entitled to the easement of a way of necessity as no reference to such easement existed either in the transfer to Mr Henning or in his certificate of title, all of which documents had been issued subsequent to the creation of the alleged way of necessity and that by reason of the provisions of the *Registration of Titles Act* (Cap. 281) no such easement existed over the Henning plot.

Dealing with the third point first, under the *Judicature Act* 1967, s.3 the common law of England on 12 August 1897 is the common law of Kenya, subject to the provisions of the Constitution and to any legislation, 'so far as the circumstances of Kenya and its inhabitants permit and subject to such qualifications as those circumstances render necessary'. Under the common law of England, where a landowner grants part of his land to a grantee and no possible way of entry to one of those parts exists, other than a way based upon the permission of a neighbouring owner or upon trespass, then a way of necessity arises by implication of the law over the other part (see *Tichmarsh v Royston Water Co.* (1899), 81 L.T. 673 and *Barry v*

Haseldine, [1952] 2 All E.R. 317). This was the position which arose in 1944 when Mr Tebbutt sold the back plots to Mr Moore. There is nothing in the circumstances of Kenya or of its inhabitants which would require any qualification in the application of such common law to Kenya. I am satisfied therefore that, subject to any change effected as a result of legislation, on such sale in 1944 under the common law of Kenya a way of necessity arose over the front plot from Langata Road to the back plots. I shall consider later the exact nature of such way of necessity.

It is [argued], however, that by reason of the provisions of the *Public Roads and Roads of Access Act* (Cap.399) the legislation of Kenya has substituted for the way of necessity which arises under the common law a statutory means of obtaining access to land. Under that Act a landowner may apply to a Board for the right to make a road of access over another's property in order to obtain reasonable access to a public road or railway station. The Act gives to the Board a discretion to grant or refuse the application and power to grant the application subject to conditions such as the payment of compensation, alignment and the maintenance of the road. The existence of a discretion is wholly alien to the common law concept of a way of necessity and the conditions which may be imposed are equally alien to the common law position under which no compensation is payable and the alignment is determined by the owner of the land over which the way runs, and by the limited nature of a way of necessity and the right of the person entitled to the way of necessity to abandon it should some other means of access be obtained. I am satisfied that this Act has not abolished the common law way of necessity but has merely provided a means whereby, under wider and different circumstances a landowner may acquire and make a road of access over another's land.

It is next [argued] that, even if a way of necessity arose in 1944 under the common law on the sale by Mr Tebbutt to Mr Moore of the back plots, this way of necessity was an easement and as it was not registered under the *Registration of Titles Act* (Cap.281) (hereinafter referred to as the Act), which applied both to the back and to the front plots, and as the back plots were sold in 1965 by Mr Moore to Mr Patel without any mention of this easement and the front plot by Mr Tebbutt to Mr Henning in 1945 equally without being made subject to the easement, this easement of a way of necessity no longer exists. Section 2 of the Act defines land as including 'all paths, . . . ways, . . . easements . . . thereon or thereunder lying or being' and s.20 provides that 'all land . . . shall not be capable of being transferred ... or otherwise dealt with except in accordance with the provisions of this Act and every attempt to transfer ... or otherwise deal with the same except as aforesaid shall be null and void and of no effect'. Section 34 provides that 'when land ... or any right of way or other easement is intended to be created or transferred, the registered proprietor shall execute ... a transfer which transfer shall ... contain an accurate statement of the land and easement ... intended to be transferred or created, and a memorandum of all ... charges and other encumbrances to which the same may be subject, and of all rights of way, easements ... intended to be conveyed' and ss.35 and 36 provide for the registration of the transfer of the easement and the issue of a certificate of title. Finally, s.23 (1) provides that ' the certificate of title issued by the Registrar to any purchaser of land upon a transfer ... shall be taken by all courts as conclusive evidence that the person named therein as proprietor of the land is the absolute and indefeasible owner thereof subject to the encumbrances, easements ... endorsed thereon, and the title of such proprietor shall not be subject to challenge...' It is urged that as the easement of the way of necessity does not appear on the certificate of title of either the back plots or the front plots and as s 23 states that the certificate of title is to be conclusive evidence that the registered proprietor is the absolute and indefeasible owner of the land mentioned therein subject to the easements endorsed thereon, the right of the way of necessity in the proprietor of the back plots has ceased to exist and the owner of the front plot, now the Henning plot, is no longer subject to this easement.

In many countries in the Commonwealth in which there exists legislation relating to the registration of title to land based on the Torrens System – and the Act is so based –the interpretation of the section similar to s. 23 providing for the conclusiveness of the register has given rise to difficulty. Not all such legislation requires, as the Kenya Act does, the easements should be registered, a fact which shows that under the Torrens System there may exist interests in land which are not registrable or need [not] appear on the register and yet nevertheless may be enforceable despite the provision that the register shall be conclusive evidence. It is also to be noted that such Commonwealth legislation differs as to what the register is conclusive evidence of; in Kenya it is conclusive evidence that the person named in the certificate of title as the proprietor of the land is the absolute and indefeasible owner thereof subject to the encumbrances endorsed thereon, which appears to be a very wide and all embracing provision. Nevertheless the Act itself provides, without, be it noted, any reservation in s. 23 for an interest in land which may validly exist without registration, as s.41 provides that a lease for a term not exceeding 12 months shall be valid without registration. Thus it is clear that the words of s.23 are to be read subject to certain limitations and that the absence from the certificate of title of certain interests in land is not conclusive that those interests do not exist (see *Farrar v Adamji* (1934), 16 K.L.R. 40). On the one hand, it is obvious that unless the whole object of the legislation is to be undermined what has been described as the sanctity of the register should be maintained (see *Govindji v Nathu*, [1962] E.A. 372; I (1923), 9 K.L.R. 167; and *Byramjee v. Attorney-General*, [1966] E.A. 198). On the other hand, it is clear that despite s 1(2) of the Act, which provides that no legislation inconsistent with the provisions of the Act shall apply to registered land, rights over land acquired by virtue of the provisions of other statutes, such as rights acquired by prescription, have effect even though they are not entered on the register (see *Gathure v. Beverley*, [1965] E.A 514 and *Tayebali v. Abdulhusein* (1938), 5 E.A.C.A/1). Similarly, it seems hardly open to doubt that where legislation charges certain sums, such as rates, on land, the fact that the charge does not appear on the certificate of title or on the register does not make the charge ineffective. Equally, it seems clear that registered land is liable to satisfy the debts of the registered owner in execution proceedings and that in the event of debts of bankruptcy such land will vest in the trustee in bankruptcy although nothing to that effect appears either on the certificate of title or on the register. Also, there can be no doubt that rights which are by law inherent to the ownership of land, such as the right to support of the land itself and the right to receive water flowing in a defined channel from adjoining lands, exist and may be enforced notwithstanding that no memorandum of such rights appears on the register or on the certificate of title either of the land itself or of the land which has the burden of providing the support or of permitting the flow of water. Analysing the nature of the rights and liabilities which are effective even though not entered on the register, it appears that s.23 of the Act should have full effect in respect of rights or liabilities expressly created by the owner thereof on or over the land, other than rights or liabilities such as leases for under 12 months which by the Act itself do not have to be registered, but that the section is not to be construed as making ineffective those rights or liabilities on or over land which come into existence by reason of the operation of law, even though such rights or liabilities do not appear on the register and are not referred to in the certificate of title. Thus, if the owner of land expressly creates an easement over it in favour of adjoining land, then unless the existence of such easement appears on the register and the certificate of title it will have no effect, at any rate as regards the subsequent owners. If, however, the easement arises by operation of the law, even though the operation of law comes into existence by reason of express acts of the owner of the land, then the easement will exist over the land and have effect notwithstanding the fact that it does not appear on the certificate of title. In this case, as I have already stated, the easement of a way of necessity arose by operation of the law on the division of the original farm into the back plots and the front plot. This easement never appeared on the register or on the certificate of title of any of these plots, but so long as the easement of a way of necessity exists by operation of the law thus long will the easement continue to have effect over the front plot, now the Henning plot, even if it is not entered on the register or on the certificate of title.

I now turn to consider the first of the points made by counsel for the appellant and in doing so I shall consider the nature of the way of necessity and the circumstances in which it will continue to exist. The title of this easement – a way of necessity – aptly describes the nature of the easement. It arises by operation of law in favour of a landowner on the division of land because it is a matter of necessity and vital to the effective ownership of one part of the land that the owner thereof should have access to it. Were this not the position the law would not confer on a landowner a benefit which he has not himself seen fit to acquire expressly. Thus, it will not arise if the owner has any other right of access to the land which is physically practicable; but a means of access based upon permission which may be withdrawn or upon trespass will not prevent the easement from arising. As it is a way of necessity, the nature of the way is related to the user of the land at the time the easement came into operation as it is only in relation to such user that it is necessary for the law to bring into operation the easement. Moreover, it will continue in existence only so long as the necessity exists. Thus the easement will cease if the owner acquires a right of access to the land by any other means. The owner of the land over which the way of necessity runs is not entitled to any compensation, since the necessity for the way must have been envisaged by him at the time he entered into the transaction which brought into operation the easement, but as it results in partial sterilisation of part of his land is entitled to determine the alignment of the way and to ensure that it is no greater than the necessity requires. As the way is for the benefit of a landowner, the cost of making and maintaining the way of necessity falls upon the owner of the land for whose benefit it exists. In order to enable that owner to make and maintain the way of necessity, he, together with his servants and agents, is entitled on reasonable notice to enter upon the land and carry out all such works as are necessary for those purposes. The right to a way of necessity may be extinguished not only by the acquisition of a different right of access to the land but also by abandonment. It must, however, be clear that the easement has been abandoned; and while non-user for a long period will be some evidence of abandonment, it must be clear indeed that such non-user was due to the abandonment of the easement.

Applying these principles to the facts of this case, since the back plots at the time they came into existence could only be used for agricultural and personal residential purposes, it is clear that Mr Moore could not be entitled to a way of necessity for any other purpose. Nor could Mr Moore enlarge the nature of the way of necessity by any enlargement of the user of the back plots. The width of the way and its alignment was a matter for the determination of Mr. Tebbutt, who continued to be the owner of the front plot on which the way ran. ...While there is little or no evidence of user between 1948 and 1965, there is no evidence of the existence of any other way of entry enjoyed by Mr Moore as of right, and I do not consider that the lack of evidence of user points conclusively to abandonment. I am satisfied therefore that in 1944 Mr Moore acquired by operation of law the easement of way of necessity 20 ft. wide running along the eastern boundary of the front plot from the Langata Road to the back plots and that he continued to own this easement until 1965, notwithstanding that it was not entered on the register and did not appear on his certificate of title and notwithstanding that the front plot was subsequently sold to Mr Henning whose certificate of title did not show that the land was subject to the easement. When in 1965 Mr Moore sold the back plot to Mr Patel this easement which was attached by operation of the law to the back plots continued to be so attached after the transfer, notwithstanding that it was not referred .to in the transfer or placed on the register, as the necessity that brought the easement into existence continued to exist. Mr Patel therefore is entitled to such a way of necessity limited to agricultural and his residential user of the back plots. For such purpose Mr Patel is entitled on reasonable notice to enter with his servants and agents upon the Henning plot and to construct and maintain at his cost such a way of necessity. As part of such way has already been constructed, Mr Patel is not liable to contribute to the cost of such construction but he is liable to contribute his proper proportion of the cost of the future maintenance of that part....

[DUFFUS VP: Concurred].

Law JA: ...The point which has caused me most concern is the one described by counsel for the appellant as being the substantial point in the appeal, and that is that the benefit of an easement of way of necessity, if such an easement ever came into existence, could not pass on the transfer of the servient tenement unless it was registered against the title under the *Registration of Titles Act*. By s 23 of that Act, the certificate of title is conclusive evidence that the proprietor of the land is the absolute owner thereof subject to the encumbrances, easements, etc, endorsed thereon. The respondent's alleged right to a way of necessity does not appear on his certificate of title or on the certificate of title of the servient tenement. In these circumstances, counsel for the respondent submitted, the easement has ceased to exist, and to give effect to the respondent's claim it would be necessary to find that his right is not an easement, or that it is a special type of easement which for some reason is excepted from the requirement of registration. In my view that is the position in this case. A way of necessity differs from most easements in that it is not created whether by grant or otherwise; it arises by implication of law when part of a piece of land is alienated, and the owner of that part has no way of entry to his land except through the other part. True, the respondent in this case has access to his land, but such means of access are permissive and not legally enjoyable, so that this does not affect his right to a way of necessity over the appellant's land. Sections 34, 35 and 36 of the Act refer to the creation and transfer and registration of easements, from which I infer that the easements which must be registered, so as to ensure their continued existence on the transfer of land affected thereby, are easements which have been 'created' and not easements which arise by implication of law such as a way of necessity. Although a way of necessity is generally referred to as an easement, it is in my view more correctly to be described as a right inherent in the right of property, comparable to a right of support or the right of light. Such rights are not 'created' but owe their existence to the very nature of things and do not, in my view, require to be registered. [His Honour concurred with the order proposed by the learned President.]

****

Question

Yiga subdivided his land into two parcels. He sold one parcel to Amooti and retained the other. At the time of sale the land sold to Amooti had access to a public road. However, following recent heavy rains the public road was permanently closed. There is another public road but it can only be reached from Amooti's land via Yiga's land. The latter refuses to let Amooti access the alternative public road via his land. Advise Amooti of her possible remedies. (See *Midland Railway Company v Miles* (1886) 33 Ch D 632. You should also refer to the *Access to Road Act*, cap 346).

Easement by prescription

At common law, a claim for acquisition of an easement by prescription is established upon proof that the right has been enjoyed since time immemorial or by proof of continuous uninterrupted use for at least twenty years under the doctrine of lost modern grant. The doctrine of lost modern grant was a fiction developed by the courts to avoid the difficulties involved in seeking to establish rights by prescription at common law. The classical case for the doctrine of lost modern grant is *Dalton v Henry Angus & Co* (1881) 6 App Cas 740.

Under s. 61 of the *Registration of Titles Act* (cap 205), title of a registered proprietor is indefeasible except, inter alia, as against 'any public rights of way and to any easement acquired by enjoyment or user or *subsisting* over or upon or affecting such land' (emphasis added). In the following Australian case, the court considers whether an easement could be acquired by prescription or lost modern grant over land registered under the Torrens System, and, if so, whether it binds a subsequent purchaser of the servient land even though the easement is not endorsed on the register.

****

Di Masi v Piromalli
[1980] WAR 57

[The plaintiffs and defendant owned adjoining plots of land. For over twenty years the plaintiffs' predecessor in title used a driveway over the defendant's land (before and after the defendant purchased the land) to gain access to the rear of their premises. When the defendant threatened to close the driveway the plaintiffs commenced these proceedings for a declaration that he had an easement of way acquired by prescription under the doctrine of lost modern grant. The defendant claimed that an easement by prescription constitutes an exception to indefeasibility, if the easement was created before the land was registered under the *Transfer of Land Act* (Western Australia), but not if the purported easement was created after the land was registered under the Act.]

Jones J:... Do the provisions of the Transfer of Land Act have the effect of positively preventing the creation of such an easement of way as appurtenant to any land *which is already under the Act*? This 'vexed question', as Wolff J called it in *Stevens & Evan v Allan & Armanasco* (1955) 58 WALR 1 at 13, is not easy to answer. [Counsel for the defendant] argued ... that the answer is 'yes'. In support of that proposition he analysed many sections of the Act, including ss 3, 4, 63, 63A, 64, 65, 67, 68, 69 and 230. The nub of his submission was that on a collocation of all those sections it appears that 'land' for the purposes of the Act can only be read as including easements appurtenant to it if either (a) such an easement is already so appurtenant when the land is brought under the Act, or (b) it has been created by grant, evidenced by a document. But in my opinion such a conclusion does not follow, in whatever way the various sections may be interpreted. Indeed, in some sections the contrary may appear, for instance:

> 'S.4 ... 'Land' includes messuages, tenements and hereditaments, corporeal or incorporeal; and in every certificate of title transfer and lease issued or made under this Act such word also includes all easements and appurtenances appertaining to the land therein described or reputed to be part thereof appurtenant thereto,' and

> 'S. 68 ... Provided always that the land which shall be included in any certificate of title or registered instrument shall be deemed to be subject to ... any right subsisting under any adverse possession of such land and to any public right of way and to any such easements acquired by enjoyment or user or subsisting over or upon or affecting such land ... '

But the truth is that the provisions of the Act are inconclusive on the subject, and therefore, in my opinion, cannot be said to *exclude* the creation of an easement of way by prescription and the inclusion of such an easement upon or is appurtenant to the relevant certificate of title. In my opinion the statement of Francis in *Torrens Title in Australasia*, vol 1 p 533, is correct: 'Because of the absence from the [Western Australia] Act of any specific provision of a means of creating an easement, it is submitted that there is also nothing in the WA Act which is inconsistent with the creation of easements by prescription, in which event the common law presumption is not excluded by WA s. 3, and that prescriptive rights to casements affecting lands under the WA Act may be acquired as well after as before those lands are brought under the Act.'

For these reasons in my opinion the plaintiffs action succeeds, and they are entitled to the declaration claimed in para 3 of the statement of claim as amended – namely, 'a declaration that the plaintiffs have acquired an easement of way 3 metres in width along the northern boundary of the land of the defendants'. The plaintiffs also claimed damages, and an injunction. But those claims were in respect not of an actual but of a *threatened* obstruction of the plaintiffs' right of way, ...and in fact no actual obstruction was alleged or proved, and obviously the plaintiffs have suffered no damage. If the defendants should, in the future, obstruct the right of way, the plaintiffs then could claim and doubtless obtain an injunction; at the present time they do not need one. The declaration as to their right is sufficient.

****

Notes

1. Section 62 of the *Registration of Titles Act*, requires the Registrar to endorse on the servient title as an encumbrance any existing easement that appears to have been granted by deed or in writing. There is no requirement to endorse an easement acquired by other means.
2. Some of the sections of the *Transfer of Land Act* 1893 (WA) mentioned in the judgement: 3, 4, 63, 65, 67, 68, and 69, correspond, respectively, with the following sections of the *Registration of Titles Act*: 3, 2, 56, 57, 58, 60, 61, and 62.

****

RESTRICTIVE COVENANTS

A restrictive covenant is a covenant, which restricts the use of the covenantor's land (servient land) for the benefit of the covenantee's land (dominant land). There are three essential requirements for the creation of restrictive covenants. These are:

1. the covenant must be negative both in nature and substance (see *Haywood v The Brunswick Permanent Benefit Building Society* (1881) 8 QBD 403);
2. the covenant must be for the benefit of land retained by the covenantee (*London City Council v Allen and another* [1914-15] All ER 1008)[29]; and
3. the original parties must have intended the benefit and burden to run with the dominant and servient land, respectively (*Federated Homes Ltd v Mill Lodge Properties Ltd* [1980] 1 WLR 594).

The classical illustration of restrictive covenants is the case of *Tulk v Moxhay*, extracted below.

Tulk v Moxhay
[1843-60] 3 ALL ER REP 9

[Tulk owned a block of vacant land in the middle of Leicester Square, London, as well as several houses adjoining the square. He sold the vacant block to E who entered into a covenant with Tulk that he would keep the square as a garden and not build on it. Ownership of the land changed several times until it was subsequently sold to Moxhay. The latter did not make any express undertaking not to build on the square, but he had notice of his predecessors' undertakings. Moxhay was preparing to construct buildings on the subject land when Tulk sought an injunction to stop him. The Court of Appeal granted the injunction. Moxhay appealed to the House of Lords.]

Lord Cottenham, LC: That this court has jurisdiction to enforce a contract between the owner of land and his neighbour purchasing a part of it that the purchaser shall either use or abstain from using the land purchased in a particular way is what I never knew disputed. Here there is no question about the contract. The owner of certain houses in the square sells the land adjoining, with a covenant from the purchaser not to use it for any other purpose than as a square garden. It is now contended, not that the vendee could violate that contract, but that he might sell the piece of land, and that the purchaser from him may violate it without this court having any power to interfere. If that were so, it would be impossible for an owner of land to sell part of it without incurring the risk of rendering what he retains worthless. It is said that, the covenant being one which does not run with the land, this court cannot enforce it, but the question is not whether the covenant runs with the land, but whether a party shall be permitted to use the land in a manner inconsistent with the contract entered into by his vendor, with notice of which he purchased. Of course, the price would be affected by the covenant, and nothing could be more inequitable than

---

[29] This requirement is dispensed with where there is a building scheme or scheme of development, see *Dolphin's Conveyance* [1070] 1 Ch 654.

that the original purchaser should be able to sell the property the next day for a greater price, in consideration of the assignee being allowed to escape from the liability which he had himself undertaken.

That the question does not depend upon whether the covenant runs with the land is evident from this, that, if there was a mere agreement and no covenant, this court would enforce it against a party purchasing with notice of it, for if an equity is attached to property by the owner, no one purchasing with notice of that equity can stand in a different situation from that of the party from whom he purchased. ...

****

Note

There in no provision for the registration of restrictive covenants in the *Registration of Titles Act*. This is probably because restrictive covenants are only enforceable in equity and the Torrens System generally discourages registration of equitable interests. It should also be noted that under s 61 of the *RTA*, restrictive covenants, unlike easements, do not constitute an exception to indefeasibility. Accordingly, it is submitted that, in the absence of fraud, restrictive covenants do not bind subsequent purchasers of the servient land even if they had notice of them.

****

Index

www.ingramcontent.com/pod-product-compliance
Lightning Source LLC
LaVergne TN
LVHW080026210926
848481LV00011B/3113